Beautiful Madness

Christiaan Bastiaans, *States of Mind: Those Who Go*, 2008, giclée print with Venetian glass, paper tape, cotton, metal wire and watercolour on 310 g/m^2 Hahnemühle paper, 176 × 251 cm. Photo: Cary Markerink.

Mark Kremer

vis-à-vis

Valiz

Beautiful Madness

Art Writing as Art Curating

Contents

The Birth of Art Writing out of Art Curating

Art curating and art writing are relatively open-ended and even experimental practices. Both construct a serious narrative about artefacts and artists, both interact with a public of viewers-readers, and both offer a setting in which art can unfold its potential. An exhibition or a text forms a constellation that brings different works and ideas together. In this setting, art and thinking ignite each other: sparks fly in both directions. What essentially defines curating and writing as two sides of the same coin is the act of making space for the experience of art.

Curators and writers tap into their source: the living artist, their work or 'world'. The proximity to the maker allows them to delve into artistic processes, observe things in a state of becoming. An essential tool for curators and writers is the dialogue with artists. Directly informing their daily practice, this exchange sharpens their understanding of the way in which art mobilizes things: demonstration (providing information; art's critical perspective or 'self-awareness' in relation to society) and evocation (art's suggestive power: 'projection'). Exhibitions and texts are enhanced through concrete

9

dialogues with artists, and through dialogic imagination: that process in which a curator or writer imagines the dialogue.

All the same, curating and writing are also distinct disciplines. Each of them is characterized by its own, proper formulation/approach to a problem, modus operandi, and type of output.

Below, I will first discuss curating and art writing separately; then I will look at the relationship between the two from a variety of angles. My focus is on art writing as a technique (curating as a technique is addressed in the preambles to the book chapters through fragments and reminiscences of exhibitions that I organized). Next, I will situate my texts on art in their own epoch, in relation to two art epistemes. Then, I will look at the book's structure, general contents, and a major motif in my 'artist studies': the dialogue or encounter with the artist. Last but not least, I will explain the book's title, *Beautiful Madness*, its background in historical art (the words are derived from a Japanese Nō play) and what I intend to say with it about contemporary art.

Definitions (Chessboards/the Blue Sky)

A crucial aspect of curating is care (Latin: *cura*, 'to take care'). Taking care of the artist, their needs when making or exhibiting work, of art objects, and of the ideas that are inherent to the artist's world, or that can be brought into relation with it from the outside, is the curator's work. Caring for all these things is pertinent; curating is evidently an act of love.

There are many types of art curating. Taking care of a museum collection, producing a new work for a Kunsthalle exhibition, being involved in the commission of a new work for a public square in the city, making an exhibition with the works from a collection, developing a solo show with one art-ist, curating the collection of books and posters in a library, and working with an artist who curates an exhibition with the work of colleagues are just some examples.

Here, my focus is on the thematic exhibition, authored by one curator, and developed in close cooperation with the participating artists. 'Live in Your Head' (1969), the ground-breaking show curated by Harald Szeemann at Kunsthalle Bern, charted the new artistic sensibilities of the 1960s by works many of which were made in situ and thus contesting the traditional limits of sculpture and painting. That show remains a formidable beacon in the genre of the thematic exhibition—today it is mostly known under its original sub-title 'When Attitudes Become Form'. At the time, in one of the Kunsthalle's galleries, the visitor was suddenly confronted with a black telephone placed on the ground, suggesting a live connection with the artist Walter De Maria, with his mind-in-action! By presenting (the possibility of) this direct link, De Maria's work was a strong and intriguing response to the exhibition concept/title.[1] It illustrates the attraction of a thematic exhibition, organized by one curator, for this artist. His work embodies the idea of an open platform, and it refers to an atmosphere of trust (between curator and artist) in which everything is possible.

II

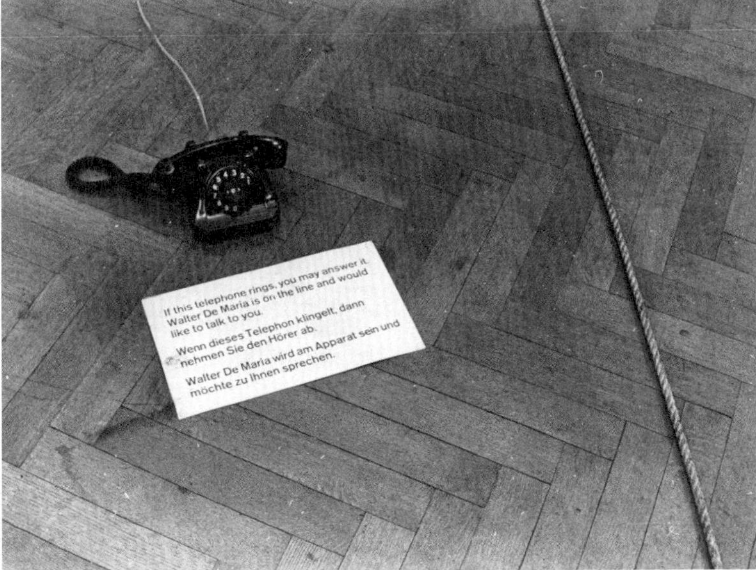

1 Walter De Maria, *Art By Telephone*, 1969, installation, 'When Attitudes Become Form', Kunsthalle Bern, 1969.

2 Wikipedia, www.
en.wikipedia.org/wiki/
Category:Art_writers, accessed
10 December 2023.

Art curating is a creative and selective process, starting with the development of the curatorial concept and the first invitations to artists to build a dialogue, through the entire production phase, to the final stage in which the exhibition takes form in a specific set-up of works and is opened to the public. While preparing such a show, the curator is in constant contact with co-workers and artists, taking responsibility for all aspects of the production: organization, administration, budgeting, public relations and press material, transport, installing the works, and so on. All the instances of contact—human and material—along a trajectory have an influence on a show. In other words: a curator's thinking about art is informed by practical as well as philosophical aspects.

The experience of curating an exhibition with living artists is inspiring in a special way. The curatorial process depends on words (for its transmission) but it is a journey to the other side of language, arriving in a realm of visual experience. During the working process, the curator is taking part in an expedition, getting all kinds of glimpses of what lies beyond the looking glass.

Art writing takes on many forms as well. The genre is rather diffuse: it includes essays written for artist's catalogues or for a group show publication, texts in art magazines, and online reviews. My mind goes to a genre from the 1980s where writers-curators sought to describe their experience of 'the artist's world': a sphere that is both fiction and reality, a realm within reach that yet also eludes us, a domain where different things aggregate, and art and life commingle.

The term 'art writing' possibly derives from 'art writers'. Under that header, Wikipedia lists several authors who, specializing in contemporary art, practice art writing and art criticism in a worldwide context.[2] The generic term 'art writing' also includes a genre that came up in the 1980s, but then was cast aside again, because its relation to art became idiosyncratic and arbitrary. Here I mean the 'parallel text'. Using literary techniques and philosophical inquiry, the genre was for a while popular among artists who, recognizing writers and philosophers as masters of thinking and writing, saw them as colleagues absorbed in similar creative searches.

Art criticism is related to art writing but there are also substantial differences. Essential for art criticism is the making of a general argument (often on art & society) whereas art writing revolves around the evocation of a specific experience (of a particular artist's oeuvre). Of course, the art writer can't do his work without a critical, discerning mind. Art writers can learn from the aim that art critics set themselves: to create an objective discourse, as they ponder the relation of art and reality in historical perspective, and the way in which contemporary art can critically reflect socio-political issues. Jerry Zaslove: '[art] criticism is institutionalized cultural literacy which constructs an object [a train of thoughts, MK] for collective understanding.'[3] In comparison, the approach of art writers to their subject could seem more open, despite the fact that they have a specific critical task as well: doing justice to the artist's singular work, for example, by drawing relevant lines that connect it to reality. Underlining existing connections, creating new ones, is one aspect of their work. Writing a text about art is always also a new beginning. In this, art writing should be a transparent act. Here I think of an Italian writer-curator, who did this in a compelling way.

Pier Luigi Tazzi published several fine texts in the European and American magazines of the 1980s. His approach of art writing is intelligent and susceptible. I think especially of Tazzi's text on Reinhard Mucha's temporary installations, made with devices and materials at hand in art institutions, such as 'Das Figur-Grund Problem in der

3 Jerry Zaslove, 'Faking Nature and Reading History: The Mindfulness Toward Reality in the Dialogical World of Jeff Wall's Pictures', *Jeff Wall*, Vancouver Art Gallery, 1990, p. 70.

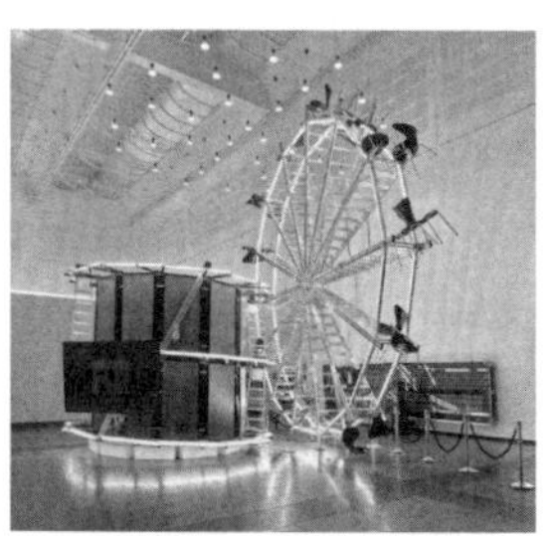

4 Reinhard Mucha, *Das Figur-Grund Problem in der Architektur des Barock (für dich allein ist nur das Grab),* ('The Figure-Ground Problem in Baroque Architecture (for you alone is only the grave')), 1985/2022, installation.

Architektur des Barock (für dich allein ist nur das Grab)' 1985/2022 ('The Figure-Ground Problem in Baroque Architecture (for you alone is only the grave')).[4] Tazzi wove his personal experience as a young, aspiring actor (for a while he performed with Magazzini Criminali, an Italian experimental theatre company)—his waiting in the wings of a theatre in between the scenes of a performance, and during the daytime for the entire performance to finally start—around the experience of waiting (for something to happen, or not) which Mucha's in-situ sculptures do evoke. It resulted in a wonderful, existential text.

Specific for Tazzi's writing approach, is the talent/skill to tune in to the frequency, the artist's actual subject, and hitting the crux of the matter: in Mucha's case a melancholy state of mind.

In everyday practice curating and writing can seem far apart. In short: when one is curating, there's no time to write. An intriguing paradox! Thinking about curating versus writing, the two images that come to my mind are almost polar opposites. Of course, curators and writers tap from a common source: the living artist, their work and world. Proximity to the maker allows them to delve straight into artistic processes, consider things in a state of becoming. Through their dialogue with the artist, they bring the spectator or reader very close to the work. However, in reality, the curator and writer have rather different jobs. The curator preparing an exhibit is always busy in a physical sense, in ongoing contact with co-workers, eyes fixed on practicalities: no time to lose! Whereas the writer composing a text is working in relative solitude, sitting in front of an empty page or screen, absorbed in an internal process. Their job is to create an open course that will carry them along and—by enlarging space and time—beget an original texture.

An image that could capture the curator's frantic activity is that of someone playing on several chessboards simultaneously. Whereas the image for the writer's process is a very different one: I see a person walking in a park, marvelling at the blue sky, letting the thoughts come to him.

What links my exhibitions with my writings is the prominence given to the artist's stance, the nature of the work, and the ideas that inhabit an oeuvre or infuse it from outside. This third element is essential: it is through the ideas that we articulate art's connection to reality, to the changes in our societies, to a global world in flux. This element has larger ramifications: over the last decades, in the museum world we observe a tendency of progressive museums who are building a new basis for exhibition programmes and acquisitions, by giving more importance to artist's ideas—trumping the museum's traditional focus on objects—in relation to a changing world. L'Internationale, a recent confederation of European art museums, research centres and think tanks, is an inspiring example of this new approach to art. Here, ultimately, the ideas of artists amplify today's social-political questions, such as how we can live together as humans.

Getting back to my work: I believe that exhibitions and art texts can bridge the divide between the artist and the viewer-reader by bringing out a 'third figure'. The encounter with a work in an exhibition or text can be such a revelation. This essence—partaking in a communal spirit—was the subject of an act by Duchamp, when the proto-conceptual artist had this text printed on candy wrappers for the opening of an exhibition of his friend, the painter William Copley: 'A Guest + A Host = A Ghost'.[5]

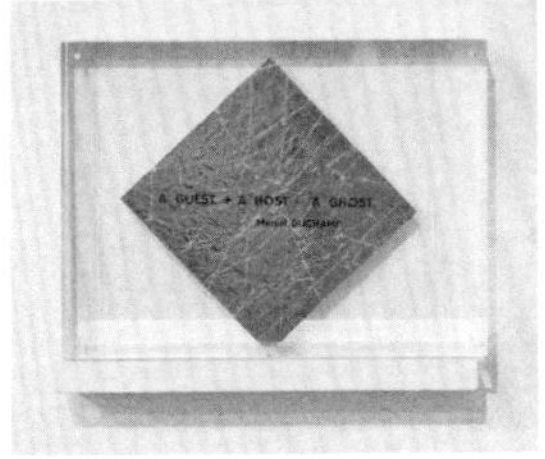

5 Marcel Duchamp, *A Guest + A Host = A Ghost*, 1953, offset print on tinfoil wrappers.

Art Writing as a Technique

6 Adam Szymczyck, in public discussion of Alexandra Bachzetsis' artist book *SHOW TIME BOOK / BOOK TIME SHOW*, San Seriffe, Amsterdam, 8 December 2023.

'Writing has to mobilize something.'
—Adam Szymczyck[6]

Art takes part in a collective sphere: it is part of a larger whole, the way a tree connects underground with other root systems and vegetation. Over the years, I've become susceptible to the role of other voices in the artist's work (works by other artists, poems, the state of mind of other makers). Such voices resonate with the individual artist's voice, like sympathetic strings on a sitar, but they may also go against it, in contrapuntal movement. This observation sheds another light on the artist's plight: it relativizes the individual position, taking away something of the importance attached to ego, instead emphasizing the collective connection/embedding.

This idea matters in a time that acknowledges the importance of collectives. Many initiatives shape new ways of being together and alert the world about alarming issues, through art and activism (in 2022, 'documenta fifteen' brought practices from all over the world together in Kassel). Here, people of different professional backgrounds discuss the problems and work on finding solutions together. Today it seems as if the art field is looking to collectives for new élan and courses of action. The view developed in my texts—many of the discussed oeuvres are open to and involve works, ideas and experiences of others—suggests a strong connection to these recent developments. I argue that the individual artist's position is in reality a porous Gestalt.

What is my approach to art writing? Is there an underlying method: if so, can it be passed on? My writings represent the art experience through argument and evocation. Analysis of topics is important but also rendering art's free flow (or resistance). I work from inductive reasoning, where a general principle is derived from a body of observations. Across a generic template—the current developments of art and reality—my texts explore 'the artist's world'. This notion refers to a sphere where life and art commingle. 'The artist's world' is a chronotope (fabric of time and space); a material field where fact meets fiction, and a concrete and fantastic terrain.

The notion 'the artist's world' of course also refers to artistic perspective per se: the world/life as seen by artists. 'The artist's world' is connected to reality, ever so lightly perhaps, but still attached to life at all four corners, like a spider's web (Virginia Woolf). I want to puncture 'the artist's world'; the dialogue with the artist (directly or indirectly) is my way in. Useful here is a chameleonic method, identification with the artist's outlook. For example, my essay on Jeff Wall departs from the artist's theoretical observations on his photographic works, while looking for the subcutaneous aspect. It made sense for me to follow this course: I thought that his works would reveal their existential-poetic element in this way. After all, through art history, there runs a long line of compelling pictures revealing the fabric of life, and perspectives on life.

Today my writing process is rather intuitive. I have acquired experience by doing, trying out many different things. When I began to publish, at the apex of post-modernism, the 'parallel text' was in vogue, in which literary figures would stand next to (photos of) the artist's work. I see this development in my writing: 1990–2000 explorations of the terrain; 2000–2010 getting the facts straight; 2010–today contemplation and an eye for meaningful connections. I find it hard to transpose all this into a formula for writing—it concerns my singular experience, plus it is so essential for other writers to find their own voice—but I can give some considerations:

NINE RULES OF THUMB FOR WRITING

1   Acknowledge your artistic/intellectual material: the artist's work, process, attitude.

2   Identify what you don't know yet; define the pertinent questions.

3   Develop your sensitivity to connections:
art ⟷ thought; work ⟷ word; form ⟷ affect/idea.

4   Become empty, 'the great receiver', work with the aspects that come spontaneously to you.

5   Contact the artist in a direct way, or not. If you choose the second approach, try to get as close as possible, imagine that you are next to the person of the artist, their work, their ideas.

6   Read random stuff and specific texts alongside each other, listen to music, see what pops up and use this.

7   Come up with a strong beginning; think of your text's title during the whole process; what's your message?

8   Alternate macroscopic viewpoint with the microscopic perspective: details count.

9   Develop your own language, trust in yourself, and always mind the rhythm of the sentence.

Two Epistemes: Autonomy Versus Engagement

How do my writings relate to the art world's shift of epistemes? Today, in 2024, art discourse is driven by a political purpose. Artistic agendas are set on social change, with topics such as decolonialization, the climate crisis, recognition of gender fluidity, and economic equality. Many artists pursue these changes, through art and protest. It fills me with respect: art is a weapon to pierce reality and unveil deception;

art has the power to develop a counter-narrative, set things in motion for a way of life better than that of today.

Around 1990, when I began to write, the art episteme changed in a fundamental way. The 1980s was the decade of post-modernism and artistic autonomy. Everything was possible, there were no obstacles: think of neo art styles, such as neo-expressionist painting, object art that celebrated and questioned consumerism, or curatorial notions such as 'Unexpressionism'.[7]

The AIDS crisis in America ended this situation; artists began to make work that reflected on the pain, state of exposure and vulnerability of the body, announcing a whole new chapter of artistic engagement. 1989 saw the fall of the Berlin Wall and a series of events leading to the destruction of the Iron Curtain, the fall of communist regimes in Central and Eastern Europe, and the gradual establishment of a new global, neo-liberal and capitalist world order. Artists responded to that with work that looks at the direct environment (e.g., Allan Sekula, *Fish Story*).[8]

In art history or theory, the autonomous position versus social engagement are epistemes with their own antecedents/narratives. But in practice, the positions are closer to one another than the terms would suggest. The artistic ideas on autonomy and engagement are not separated by fences or iron bars. Historically, the two epistemes coalesced in the mindset of the Romantic artists, poets, and philosophers. This sensibility was versatile or ambivalent: on one hand, the Romantics embraced the nascent revolutions in Europe wholeheartedly. On the other hand, the Jena group of (wo)men took an extreme interest in the study of inner life: in their poems or critiques it flows in all directions. When Friedrich Schlegel arrived in Berlin in 1797, at the dawn of the historical period that we call Romanticism, he wanted to

7 'Unexpressionism' was the title of an exhibition on current art tendencies curated by Germano Celant in 1988.

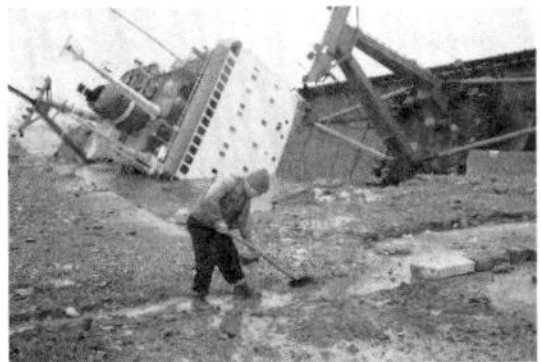

8 Allan Sekula, *Fish Story*, 1988–1995, photograph.

9 Andrea Wulf, *Magnificent Rebels: The First Romantics and the Invention of the Self*, London, John Murray, 2022, p. 157.

change the world, with words rather than swords. Sometime later he wrote: 'The letter is the true magic wand.'[9]

Schlegel's words have a contemporary, activist ring. Whereas Hölderlin's introverted poems express otherworldly enchantment and elation. They evoke an image of this poet sensing a last splinter of divine presence on earth. Hölderlin was deeply affected by Pietism (the religion); in his modern-mystical attitude one still senses his need for a living connection to heartfelt faith.

Autonomy and engagement come together in today's art too. In 1987, I attended Jeff Wall's lecture at De Appel in Amsterdam. In an erudite presentation, he explained the art historical references of his photographic works, and their political nature—his works contain encrypted allusions to social inequality, and make the viewer sense the frustration and the lack of autonomy felt by people living in precarious conditions. But he also made it clear that this 'social-critical content' was not his objective: there are limits to our pursuit of knowledge. Through his art, he was rather looking for, and opening himself up to, something else: call this beauty, freedom, poetry.

The Book's Structure: Five Thoughts

The material in this book is arranged along five thought-axes. Essays and short reflections on, and some interviews with artists—twenty-eight 'artist studies' from the period 1993–2023—appear here in a new coherence. There are five sections. Every section opens with a preamble, in which I elaborate a thought in connection to a topic that encircles an important property of art, and functions as an interesting gateway to the oeuvres that I discuss in the texts that come next. I examine the following five topics: Trace, Gesture, Rudiment, Polyphony, and Steadfastness.

While considering many alternative options, I chose these topics because they strongly reflect the different dimensions through which art speaks to us, or artworks hook into us. Trace thus refers to art's intellectual aspect; Gesture to its physical dimension and the visceral component that rather escapes the verbal; Rudiment opens up the field of connections of form with what went on in art before; Polyphony addresses the voice or voices speaking through a work that do not necessarily coincide with an all-knowing author; and Steadfastness most importantly pertains to the artist's work as a long-term project—their determination to change course every so many years, making an about-face, totally changing the work's outlook, would paradoxically be one illustration of a steadfast compass.

Each section features texts on various artists: Dutch and international, known, not very known. The arrangement of texts was inspired by curatorial logic/sensibility. The reason for bringing different artists together (on these successive pages) is: 1. synergy: the notion that their positions reinforce each other, and 2. the law of stimulating contrasts: differences between oeuvres may mask underlying affinities. The everyday expression 'opposites attract' makes sense in the art field as well: the dialectic coherence of differing works is one stimulating reason why thematic group shows are made. For example, 'The Third Mind', curated by artist Ugo Rondinone at the Palais de Tokyo (Paris, 2007)[10] featured a string of contrasting positions, most often by the arrangement of the work of two artists in twelve rooms, together illustrating the dialectic power of the pair.

My texts reflect my developing perspective on various current art forms. They have a special connection with my

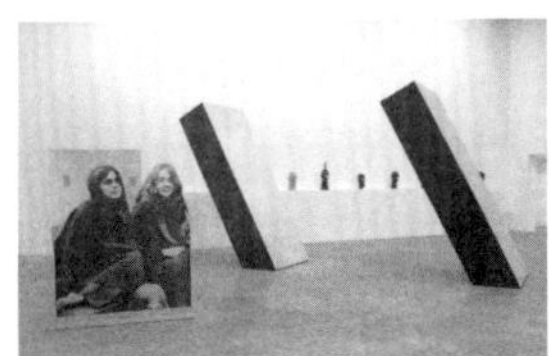

10 Exhibition view of 'The Third Mind', Palais de Tokyo, 2007, with work by Cady Noland, Ronald Bladen and Nancy Grossman.

11 Mikhail Bakhtin, *Problems of Dostoevsky's Poetics*, Minneapolis/London, University of Minnesota Press, 1984, p. 6–7.

exhibitions. I could hang this motto above them: *The Birth of Writing out of Art Curating.* With half of the artists discussed here, I've curated exhibitions, holding their work in my hand. My practice as a tutor is another inspiration: many talks with young curators and art students have influenced my thinking on art's multiple origins and long-term development.

One major motive in the texts is the dialogue, and the encounter (with art and artists). The aforementioned expression 'standing next to the artist', where you look at the exhibition and talk about the works together, symbolizes this kind of creative interaction.

Scholars have proposed that a dialogic principle is active in art. In this process, the artist and writer-curator play complementary roles: they are links in a chain of communication. In daily practice, a work of art, oeuvre or exhibition asks for interlocution. This corresponds with the idea of the artist as a medium, channel or conduit through which energies flow, to the viewer. Mikhail Bakhtin, the philosopher and literary theorist, has written on the role of dialogue in the development of common language, on the fact that words evoke their very counterparts, and on the way in which writers and poets of old have used dialogic forms in their literary works. Bakhtin's *The Dialogic Imagination: Four Essays* (1975), a collection of works published at the end of his life, can be seen as a hopeful testimony of how people can live side by side in peace. Bakhtin wrote about dialogue in Dostoevsky's novels, arguing that his novels are characterized by 'a plurality of independent and unmerged voices and consciousnesses, a genuine polyphony of fully valid voices'.[11] His emphasis on acknowledging both our differences and similarities as human beings, and of the role of the open exchange of thoughts, can still inspire us today. His life in Soviet Russia was difficult; Bakhtin was greatly affected by oppressive acts of subsequent communist regimes that mistrusted his humanist stance. All the more remarkable that he, in his elated spirit, argued for dialogue as the innate, sacrosanct element of literature, read: art.

The notion of the dialogue or encounter (with the artist, as both a professional and a human being) has an anthropological-humanist ring to it. I found this in the 'travel writing' of Bruce Chatwin, Ryszard Kapuściński and Colin Thubron. These authors were interested in the life and opinions of the people who they met on their journeys. What their books transmit is the modesty of the writer, his interest in the place, his awareness that the other knows more.

Beautiful Madness

'Beautiful Madness' is a motive in *Sumida-gawa*, a Nō play composed by playwright Motomasa Kanze (my essay on Christiaan Bastiaans explores this motive in detail, see page 95. Kanze's play features a so-called madwoman roaming the countryside of Japan where she is desperately searching for her only son, who was kidnapped by human traffickers. In order to make a living, she gives public performances about her grief. The very fabric of her inner life is a unique artistic currency!

I find Kanze's conflation of art and life intriguing; it reminds me of the Romantic artists, their aim was to bring art and life together. I chose the book's title for a reason: two words refer to the artist's project per se—in my opinion, the work of artists is often based on a combination of folly (madness, fantasy) and studious dedication. *Beautiful Madness* versus artistic research? In order to penetrate art, the irrational aspect (folly) should be addressed.

12 J.M.G. Le Clézio, *Désert*, Paris, Gallimard, Le Chemin, 1980.

When I write about an artist, I am looking for true connections. Each time I imagine that, I make a new beginning. For more than thirty years now, I have been a wanderer in the artist's world. Today, I feel like a guardian, an animator standing at the threshold, inviting others in. An open mind, sensitivity to impressions is what artists desire to transfer: wake up both the mind and the body, so that we experience the world as an eternal initiation. This makes me think of Lalla, the protagonist in Le Clézio's novel *Desert*. To hold the reader's attention, while preserving the unique sensation of being in the desert, the author begins with the narrative of a young girl. She's the guardian of the experience.[12]

Trace

Works of art relay INFORMATION. The means that constitute a work—visual language (lights, colours, shapes), symbolic signs (words, numbers), or other means—can be read by the experienced viewer as ever so many potential traces. These indexes/references lead to the next thing: outside reality, an inner state of mind, or back to the making process itself. Advice for the curator/art writer: follow the traces indicated by the work, treat these traces as promising clues, like a detective would do, and see where this brings you.

Roland Barthes was an avid reader of traces, for instance in his 1970 essay 'Le troisième sense. Notes de recherche sur quelques photogrammes de S.M. Eisenstein' ('The Third Meaning: Notes on Some of Eisenstein's Stills'), an investigation of how Eisenstein articulates meaning in his film *Ivan the*

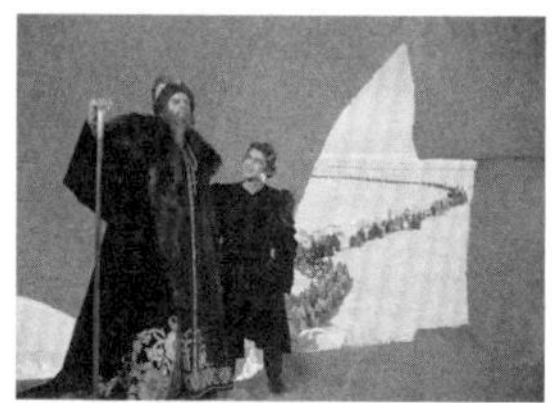

1 Sergej Eisenstein, *Ivan the Terrible (Part 1)*, 1945, film still, b/w film, 90'.

2 'When Elephants Come Marching In: Sixties' Echoes in Today's Art', exhibition at De Appel arts centre, Amsterdam, 27 September 2014–11 January 2015. Artists: Melanie Bonajo, Boyle Family, Hugo Canoilas, Walter De Maria (USA, 1935–2013), Chiara Fumai, gerlach en koop, Taf Hassam, CM von Hauswolff, Yutaka Matsuzawa (Japan, 1922–2006), Hidenori Mitsue, Emilio Moreno, Jan van de Pavert, Roland Schimmel, and Mu Xue.

3 Mark Kremer, 'Psychedelia and Conceptualism Are Reconciled', 2015, unpublished essay.

Terrible I,[1] and in books such as *L'Empire des Signes* (*Empire of Signs*, 1970; about his experience of Japan) and *Fragments d'un discours amoureux* (*A Lover's Discourse:* Fragments, 1977). His explorations of high and low cultural forms relate to the field of semiotics—the systematic study of sign processes (*semiosis*) and meaning-making—but Barthes' approach is scholarly *and* poetic. He invites the reader to follow him on his course of looking into traces.

In preparation of my exhibition 'When Elephants Come Marching In: Sixties' Echoes in Today's Art',[2] I began by pondering the art and ideas of the 1960s, drawing a line to the present. I was interested in the (potential) connections between two art-historical movements that the art canon tends to treat as opposites: 'Precisely the two artistic complexes that we today practically identify with the 1960s, played with the senses and the mind: Psychedelia and Conceptualism. The vestiges of two complexes are still traceable in art today.'[3]

My project was inspired by two observations:
1. Artworks from the 1960s give little occasion to think that there was such a strict opposition of Psychedelia and Conceptualism. Rather, there were many artists who were combining the mind-expanding elements of Conceptualism with Psychedelia's sensory enchantment. Among them were individuals

as diverse as Walter De Maria, Alighiero e Boetti, James Lee Byars, Mark Boyle and Yutaka Matsu-zawa. Their work is permeated with psychedelic and conceptual elements, while formally it refuses to conform to medium-specific painting/sculpture.

2.   When speaking to artists of today, I felt that many were very interested in Psychedelia as art, possibly also since this form is lingering on the periphery of the art field, as opposed to the field of today's experimental music where it is a central force.

To share my search with the public, giving them an idea of the historical traces informing my exhibition, I wrote a statement that begins like this:

> Art connects to the 'here and now' but it also creates its own time. A fine work will erase the barriers of space and time, inviting us to roam through historical time-space. For instance, in a fraction of a second, one single line—'between thought and expression lies a lifetime'—from a song written and sung by Lou Reed in 1968, and released by The Velvet Underground in 1969 on their third album, today carries us back to the 1960s atmosphere, or even to the 1950s and the exciting and perplexing sense of rootlessness that the American beat poets expressed so wonder-fully—for that sense of life comes through in the

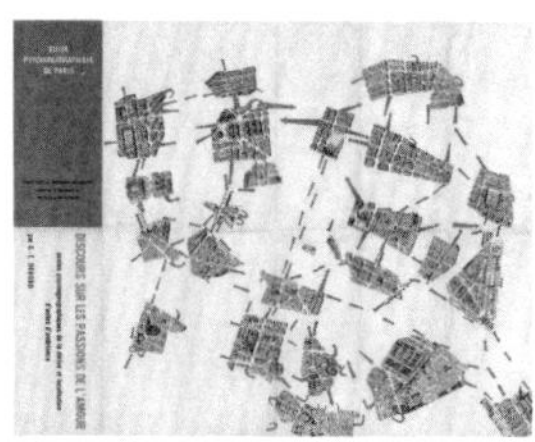

5 The Situationists
International, *Psychogeographic
Guidebook of Paris*, 1956.

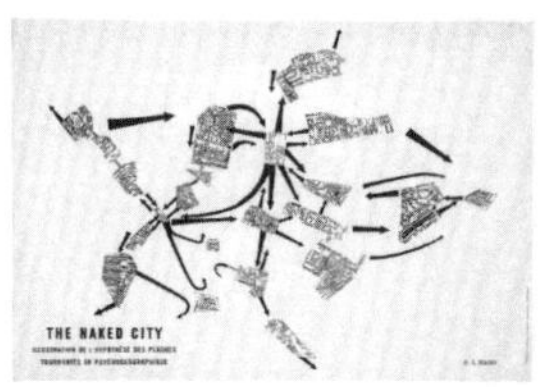

6 The Situationists
International, *The Naked City*,
1957.

song *Some Kinda Love*. Thus, the Velvets'
music approached a sentiment that found a radical voice in Europe in this period (the post-w w 2
Reconstruction) in the manifestos and critical
procedures (e.g., *détournement*: the hijacking of
artistic material or the turning around of social
situations) of the poets/artists of the *Situationist
International* in Paris. The Situationists wanted
to shake things up; they revolted against a society that saw capitalism and materialism as its ful-
filment, and instead searched for personal freedom. A Situationist archetype is that of
comrades who wander the streets of the city in
the dead of night, smoking, talking, drinking.
Of course, that image symbolizes our own search
for the essence of life. But it is also an artwork
that opens a window, an event in the spirit of
Fluxus: a gay, wandering company draws 'free
figures' in the night.[4]

The thought above resembles a fictitious artwork.
The Situationists encouraged such follies. Guy
Debord and Asger Jorn depicted paths of opportunity in their 1956 *Psychogeographic Map of Paris*,[5]
and 1957 *The Naked City*.[6] Today we can still follow
the patterns of traces creating imaginary situations
suggested by the maps.

Traces, as art draw our attention to different things. Christian Boltanski integrated personal objects such as photographs or garbs from inventories of dead (or vanished) people in his installations. The objects are potent traces of human presence and absence. Other artists use traces matter-of-factly. Jan van de Pavert acknowledges their relevancy for his art: in his works traces should speak up, inviting the viewer to identify them.[7] Again other artists play with traces, leading the viewer into unknown territory. Consider this work by Yutaka Matsuzawa, from the series *My Own Death (Paintings Existing Only in Time)*[8]: a text with the zest of an intriguing Zen koan:

> Now I hand over my future death to you who is passing by. At that very instant, in a cavern on a plateau in Middle-Japan, I pull out both your hearts from your breast and let 'em fly into the milk white mist that often appears there.[9]

Without further ado, I will introduce five 'artist studies'. This section consists of an interview with Mike Kelley and texts on Rirkrit Tiravanija, Wineke Gartz, Jan van de Pavert, and Aernout Mik. In their work, traces light up that refer to the world. As the readers follows them, they encounter social realities and fantasies on today's world, its beauty, vulnerability and strangeness. But mind you: the trace walks a

7 Mark Kremer, 'The Illuminator', *Jan van de Pavert: Collected Works*, Prinsenbeek, Jap Sam Books, 2023, p. 334.

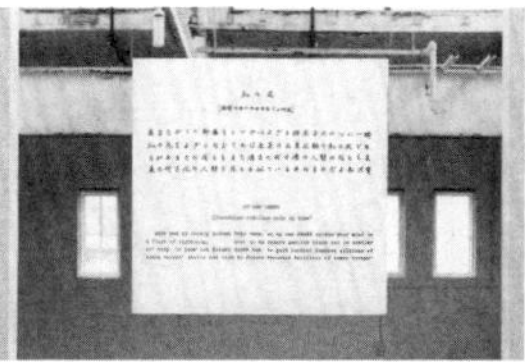

8 Yakuta Matsuzawa, *My Own Death*, 1970, installation view.

9 Matzusawa's work was exhibited at the 'Japan Art Festival' in 1971 at the Guggenheim Museum. See Adriaan van Ravesteijn, 'Over yutaka matsuzawa en de tentoonstelling *nirvana*', *Museumjournaal*, Vol. 15, No. 5, Nov. 1970, pp. 256–60.

fine line, given this open definition: 'a trace is a mark, object, or other indication of the *existence or passing* of something'.[10]

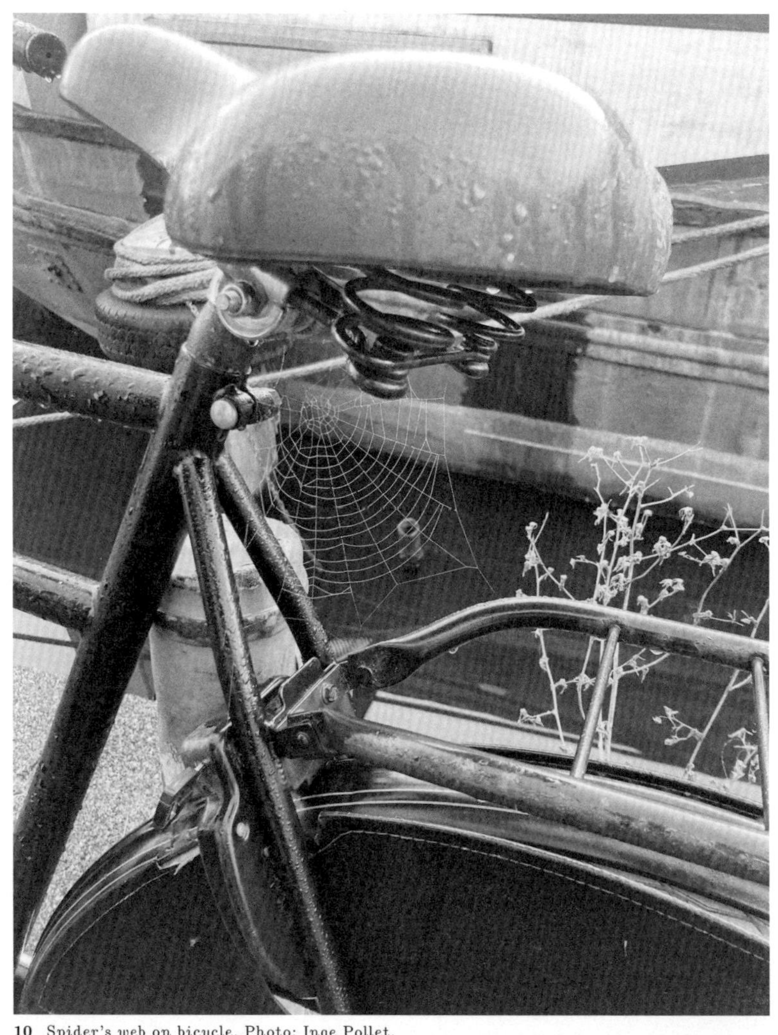

10 Spider's web on bicycle. Photo: Inge Pollet.

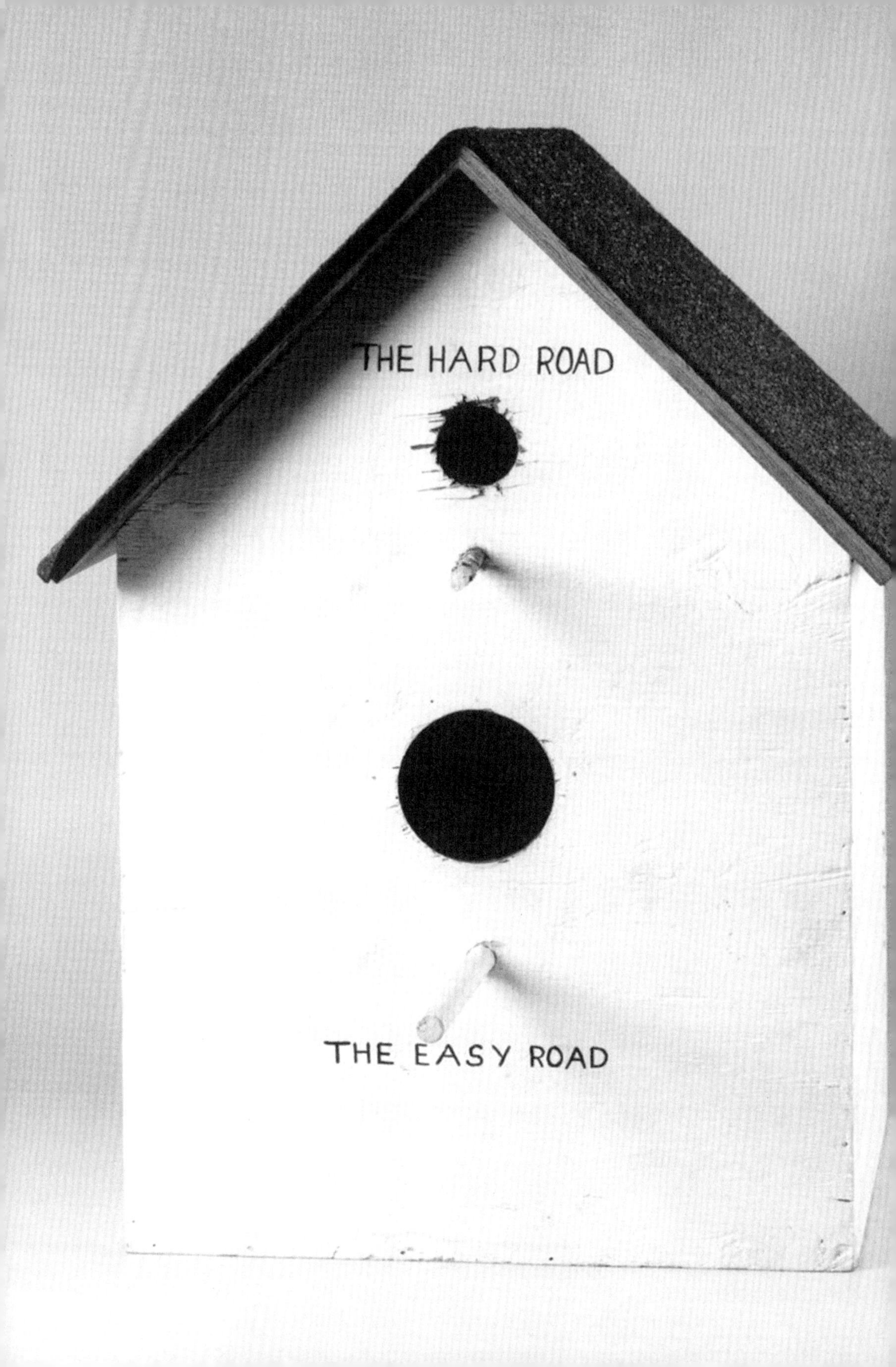

THE HARD ROAD
THE EASY ROAD

A Fucked-Up Mirror of Dominant Image-Making

The interview with Mike Kelley took place on the eve of
'The Uncanny' (Municipal Museum of Arnhem, 5 May–
26 September 1993), an exhibition curated by the artist that
brought together works of art, objects used in medical practice, film props, and different photographs: all representations
of the human figure. Working from an anthropological-
artistic perspective, Mike Kelley wanted to raise the question
how close to or far from our own body such images are.

Mark Kremer (MK)   Your contribution to 'Sonsbeek 93'
consists of curating an exhibition at the Municipal Museum
of Arnhem entitled 'The Uncanny'. What is the concept of
this show?

Mike Kelley (MK)   I will tell you about its genesis. I did a
collaborative work with Paul McCarthy in Galerie Krinzinger
in Vienna based on Joanna Spyri's novel *Heidi*. We decided
we wanted to make a videotape that employed sculptural figures as stand-ins for actors and to treat ourselves in a similar
way. In film, the use of props for stand-ins for actors is always

hidden, but we wanted to make it overt by presenting a set that would actually be the main body of the work. You would see the tape someplace else: its narrative was fractured and it revealed the parts that were used for its construction.

In working on that project, I started compiling pictures of figurative sculptures. I was interested in the quality of Gerry Anderson's television shows (*Thunderbirds*): the figures are moving but the spectator knows they're being moved. I made a pinboard with pictures of things from a wide cultural range that had this creepy feel. I was reminded of Freud's essay on the uncanny where he discusses its aesthetic. The uncanny is a confusion about whether something's alive or dead. Freud gives examples like automata, wax figures, puppets and funeral sculpture. But then he makes the definition of the uncanny narrower by saying that it's differentiated from things that are just fearful or horrific by being also an aesthetic of that which is familiar. And then I realized that a lot of the things that I found uncanny were very familiar things, like the television shows that I mentioned. So, I decided that would be the theme of the show.

MK   How do you see the figurative sculpture that is included in 'The Uncanny'?[1]

36

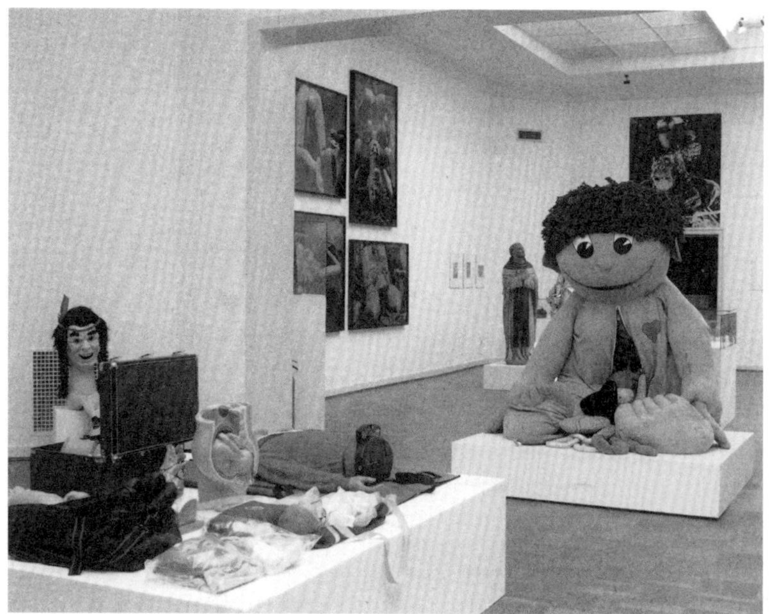

1 Mike Kelley, 'The Uncanny', Municipal Museum of Arnhem, 'Sonsbeek 93', 1993, exhibition view. Photo: Pieter Boersma.

1960s Counterculture

MK   At the moment there is a revival of figurative sculpture.
In America it's mostly talked about in terms of censorship
issues and the AIDS crisis, which is somewhat of a smoke
screen. I think we are witnessing an attempt to resuscitate
figurative sculpture that is similar to what has already happened in painting. Because of the general culture climate
right now, the focus is on issues of the body. I'm interested in
this issue, but not from such a simpleminded political angle.
I think its politics are more complicated. If you look through
the history of modernism, there's hardly any polychrome
figurative sculpture. Monochrome was a sign for being outside of time and so any reference to the deathlike nature of
sculpture or the carnal nature of the body is repressed in
modernist art works. Now people are interested in these
repressed aspects; it's most apparent in works that are themselves repressed in their aesthetics, like academic works.

The Whitney Biennial

MK   Your show consists of an accumulation of cultural arti-
facts from various historical periods,[2] many of which refer to

37

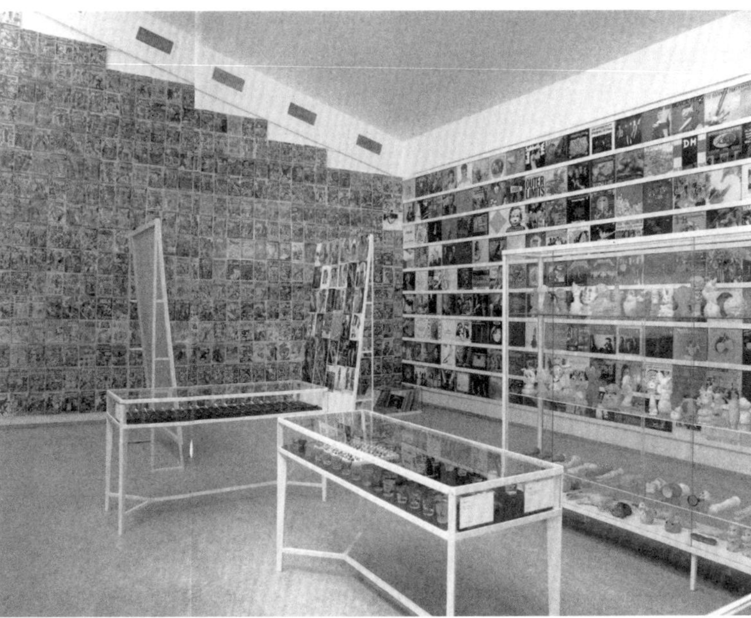

2   Mike Kelley, 'The Uncanny', Municipal Museum of Arnhem, 'Sonsbeek 93', 1993, exhibition view. Photo: Pieter Boersma.

the body. Is this a reaction against the way art criticism approaches this issue? Is it meant as an attempt to define more precisely?

MK   Yes, definitely. Even terms like body art or mannequin art, which are the general terms used now, are unspecific. Work that's diverse and about a specific aesthetic understanding of visual material is homogenized by talking about it generically. I think this is a critical problem. Whenever things in the art world go into some examination of cultural use, the critical discussion of them becomes homogenized. It's an art world's strategy to prevent any serious discussion of the social use of art.

Take the recent Whitney Biennial. Maybe this was not such a good show, but the critics aren't doing anything to help you understand what the problem is. They go, "We're sick of this," instead of discussing each artist and trying to explain what the different connotations are of the visual language. They don't treat it as art. If that was a show of abstract painting, they would go through it and they'd categorize it and they'd talk about how it functions, because there's a history of allowance to do that. But there isn't in this other way. I think that's a real problem because it promotes a division between certain kinds of visual languages. There is this prejudice about the transparency of popular idioms, the idea that you can look right through them, and that there aren't even any visual codes there.

MK   But there is a history of artists whose work is embedded in popular culture.

MK   I think there's a history of practice, but not so much a history of criticism. You can buy an anthology of Greenbergian history or an anthology of deconstructive history, but you can't buy an anthology of class-oriented visual history.

MK   What are your roots? Where did you encounter the material for your work?

MK   I come from a blue-collar, working-class, industrial city in the Midwest. My family didn't have any connection with art. My introduction to avant-garde art was through the 1960s' counterculture. Though now that's being dismissed as a form of popular culture, at the time it was a form of avant-garde culture. And I realized, here's people using certain popular forms and deconstructing them to have a different meaning than normal. Like in an underground comic, they adopted a popular form and then they warped it to reverse the values of the dominant culture, the same with psychedelic posters. That's what got me into art. Then after a while I became bored with the anti-intellectualism and the kind of ghettoization of that and I became more interested in the history of avant-garde fine art.

MK   And what happened?

MK   I found out that there was an incredible bias against dealing with class issues or popular culture, especially during the period in which I went to graduate school, which was the period of high conceptualism. There was a real backlash at that period against Pop Art, because Pop Art was understood as being a kind of formalism in disguise, which I agree with. Instead, most Conceptual Art dealt with the deconstruction of academic language codes. As a student, I was interested in low culture and in subcultures. My generation of artists, the post-conceptual, so-called Pictures generation, had a fixation with the gloss of dominant culture. My interests were just the opposite. I was interested in the politics of degradation, failure, the lowest things. I investigated the culture that operated in between advertising, movies, and television, and how that was misinterpreted by the people at home. When they tried to ape it and make it themselves, they couldn't do it and they would end up with this fucked-up mirror of dominant image making. These are the most invisible things, and I was always very interested in that.

MK   The generation that you mention wanted to produce perfect objects, sort of mirroring the images to which they referred. You once stated, 'I want to make artefacts with their failures built in'. This remark seems to oppose that object-oriented approach.

MK   That was just what it said. Objects and images are heavily coded, complicated constructions. It reveals more when they're done wrong, than when they're done right. If something's done wrong, you can see how it's composed. If something's done right, you don't see that. So, if I make something that doesn't work, you can see what it's supposed to do and you become more conscious of what its perfect state is.

Beyond the Media Cliché
━ ● ━ ● ━ ● ━ ● ━ ● ━ ● ━ ● ━ ● ━ ● ━ ● ━

MK   Your works with dolls have been related to the breakdown of the nuclear family.

MK   I've always had problems with that reading. A lot of people said that the dolls looked like abused children because they're crooked and damaged. I've always thought the work had more to do with the power relation between parents and children. The parents are the ones who design these objects and they design them to represent the child in their perfect state, which is clean and neutered and basically not like children at all. So dolls, I've always maintained, are statues of perfect children for adults, not for children. They are given to children but they are really designed for the adult's psychological pleasure.

MK   European critics labelled your work as a project to expose the dark side of American WASP (White Anglo-Saxon Protestant) ideology.

MK   It's easy to kick WASPS, especially now when multiculturalism is in vogue in America. There's this funny thing about thinking that all white people are the same. My work has always been about totally the opposite. It's always been about all these subgroups in American culture. The notion of the subculture isn't just a caricature of a black home boy and an uptight WASP in a suit. That's a media cliché. So, I'm not interested in the work being seen that simply. On a very broad level, there is some kind of cultural criticism going on but it's always within terms of art, in terms of specific visual languages and how they operate.

A Construction, Not a Given

MK   You once said that if, seeing your work, there is a moral point to make, it's within the responsibility of the viewer.
MK   Of course, I have my own morals and I think often my morals are fairly implicit in the work. On the other hand, I

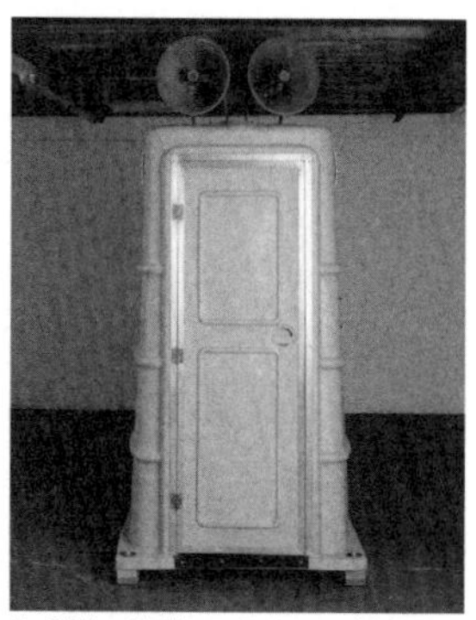

3 Mike Kelley, *Private Address System*, 1992, speakers, microphones, electronics, portable toilet, 254 × 116.84 × 120.65 cm.

think if somebody knows what issues are addressed in the work, but if they're not quite sure what the thing is saying about that, then people's ideologies become very clear to themselves. Like, this is what I think![3]

MK   You use the art world as a kind of free zone, to make people react that way.

MK   That's what the art world is for. I think the art world is a kind of discussion arena about visual language and how visual language operates. You have to be given a situation where you can experience visual language as a construct, not as a given.

MK   You once made critical remarks about Dada and I think also Surrealism. That surprised me, as these movements could be explained in terms of a counterculture.

MK   I have a more favourable view of Surrealism. Those movements could be defined in terms of a counterculture, but that's not how they're taught in art schools. Pictorial Surrealism is always presented as a kind of extension of pre-modernist painting, which isn't true at all. A lot of Surrealist work is like action painting in that the focus wasn't on the art object; the focus was on the psychological reading of the object after the fact. The art objects were produced unconsciously and then you would talk about them and decode them.

MK   Duchamp referred to the idea of counterculture—he called it the nonconformist spirit of every century—when talking about Dada, Alfred Jarry, but also of Rabelais.

MK   Jarry plus a lot of popular figures were obviously the main inspirations for much work of that period. Those figures have become acceptable now. In every generation there are two or three low figures that are elevated to the status of high art. As time progresses, more and more have slipped in. The class and cultural differences are so strong that it's difficult. I noticed in the New York 'High and Low' show, Robert Crumb was the figure who was all of a sudden integrated in art history. He was all of a sudden made O.K. Just like in the 1930s George Herriman and in the 1960s Saul Steinberg. They are promoted to being fine-artists.

MK   Duchamp always tried to destabilize conventions. His work is hard to integrate within the collection of a museum, especially when the collection mainly consists of paintings.

MK   I think Duchamp is best talked about in the painting discourse. That's where he's most ungainly, even perverse. The reason for that is that his paintings are so poor, like *Pharmacie*. It's an amazing painting because it's a pre-printed picture and he just puts two dots on it. That is really a radical painting gesture. It's very intelligent and it's very poetic, but it doesn't relate to any of the painting issues of the period. I think that *Tu m'* and *Pharmacie*, those are really interesting paintings.

MK   Duchamp was striving after a sort of visual indifference. With this he wanted to sidestep the problem of taste. What is your view on taste?

MK   I think all art that's about status quo is about perfection or wholeness, no matter whether it's in the art world or whether it's in folk art. There are these ideas about what constitutes a good version and there's a strong attempt at keeping those rules operating.

In terms of my own background, I have a clear notion of middle-American aesthetics. But when I go to New York, I meet people who have lived there their whole life, surrounded by art and culture, and they don't understand anything west of New Jersey, not even New Jersey, the river… it's amazing. Sometimes in Europe I run across that, because here people are raised on culture, but they don't understand that the culture of the next class down is just the same; it's only a different set of conventions. It could be Bavarian kitsch, but it's just as strongly codified. I don't see any difference.

The Style of Wittgenstein

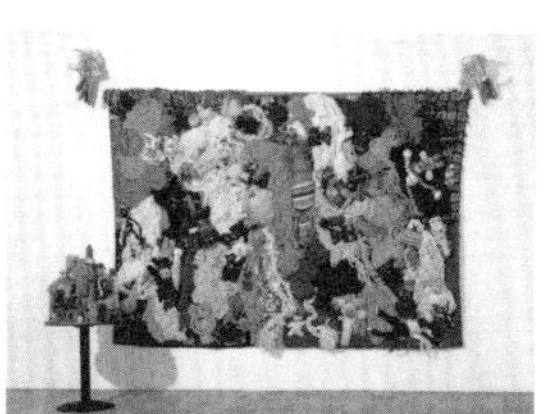

4 Mike Kelley, *More Love Hours than Can Ever Be Repaid and the Wages of Sin*, 1987.

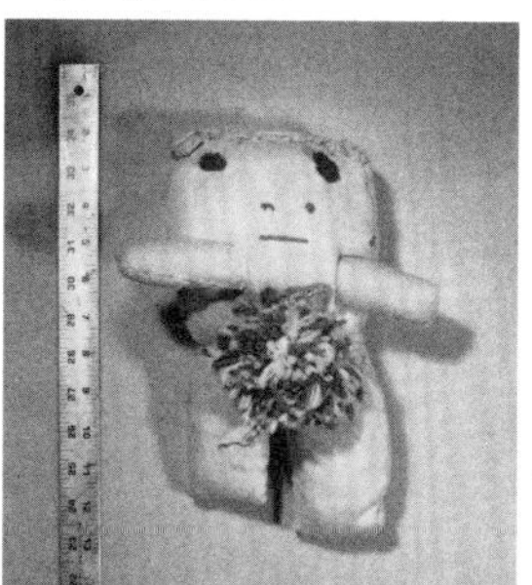

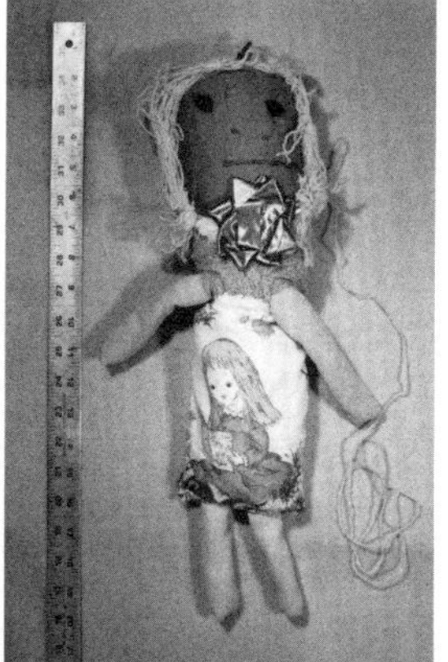

5 Mike Kelley, *Craft Morphology Flow Chart*, 1991.

MK   When talking about macrame, folk art, you once said: 'Dead things are art'.[4]

MK   Anything when it goes out of fashion is art. Science, once it's not true anymore, is art. Once you don't believe Greek ideas on the nature of the universe, it becomes poetry. You respect it for the complexity and the poetics of the ideas. I'm using 'dead' in a broad way. Dead things, by not operating in the world in a full manner, have a certain remove that allows you to look at them critically.

MK   I want to talk about *Craft Morphology Flow Chart*. Last year I saw the work in London at the ICA. As opposed to your other works with stuffed puppets, that installation seemed to be an attempt to objectify the dolls, or sort of freeze them. What was your intention with that work?[5]

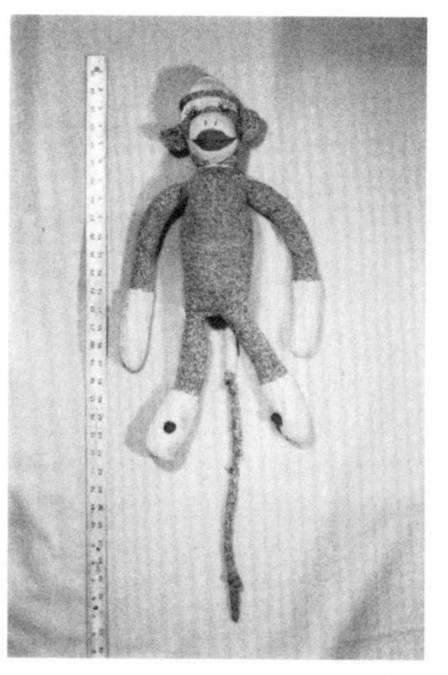

44

MK   I was sick of everybody psychologizing these stuffed
animals. No matter what I did and no matter how many cues
I gave, instead of looking at them critically, everybody just
sank to the level of baby talk. And I said to myself: 'Well, I'll
drown you in them with no aesthetic at all'. Then I realized I
just couldn't work with them anymore. You can visually point
out something over and over again and people just forget it. It
shows how strong the objects are. And that was the last piece
I did with them. 'The Uncanny' is a similar exercise. But
instead of dealing with the non-art-world version of the doll,
I'm dealing with the art-world version of the doll.

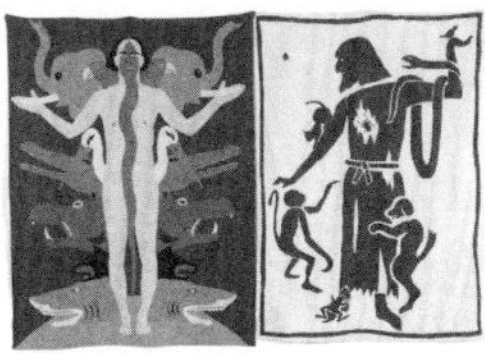

6 Mike Kelley, *Animal Self and
Friend of the Animals*, 1987.

MK   Your early works, in which objects are strongly connected to language, sometimes seem embedded in a kind of
shamanistic ritual.[6]

MK   I don't like that word, because in America it is often
used to refer to a certain kind of neo-primitive art. In my
early sculpture I would manipulate objects and as the language shifted, the meaning of the objects shifted. There was a
one-to-one relationship between the shifting physical use of
the object and the shifting metaphoric use of the language.
The cut felt banners were interesting because there's a certain
kind of language that's always on them, a clipped way of
speaking, and I had to limit myself to working with that kind
of cadence or poetic form.

MK   In the cut felt banners you worked with destabilized
clichés. In the works with dolls this interest in language
seems absent.

MK   I did a set of works with stuffed animals that was
shown in Cologne.[7] The animals talked and everything had

to be written out and recorded. I elaborated a lot of ideas about how dolls are experienced into dialogues; the way classical philosophy is written. There were about eight different ones. Two white ones recited simultaneously two sections of nineteenth-century literature that was specifically about white. It was a kind of cacophony. There were two other ones called *Ambiguity and Amorphousness* where the two shapes were just two kind of blob forms. There was a dialogue about differences between the definitions of ambiguity and amorphousness, but you couldn't hear it because the sound tape was played backwards. There was also a dialogue that was very poetic. That was all about pink and it was written in the style of Wittgenstein.

There was also a dialogue that was like a conversation in a restaurant, like people talking at a dinner table. And that one was pretty abstract. It was about presentness and non-presentness. These dolls were talking about philosophy and how it is a real problem that when you saw the philosopher you didn't believe him as much as if you just read it. So, the dolls talked about how they shouldn't be seen so they could philosophize without someone projecting into them.

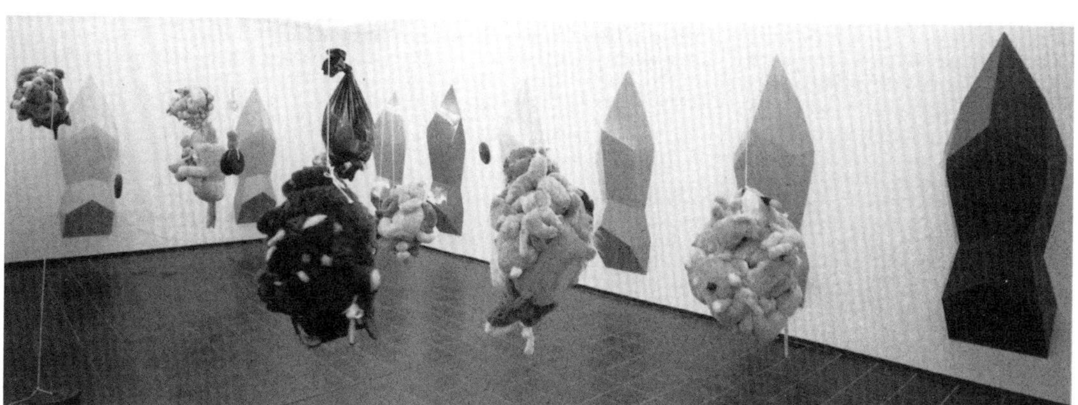

7 Mike Kelley, exhibition view, Jablonka Gallery, 1991–92.

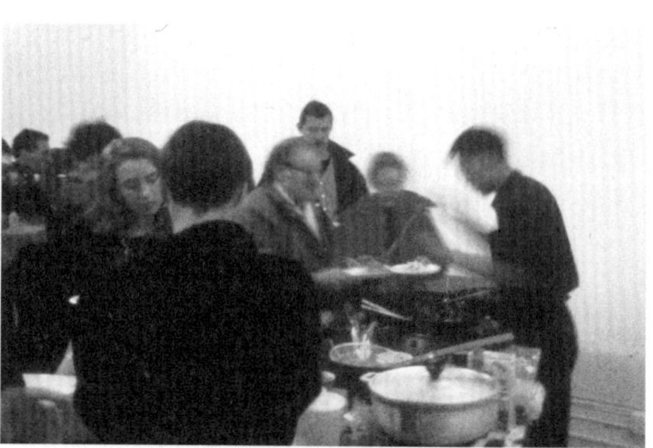

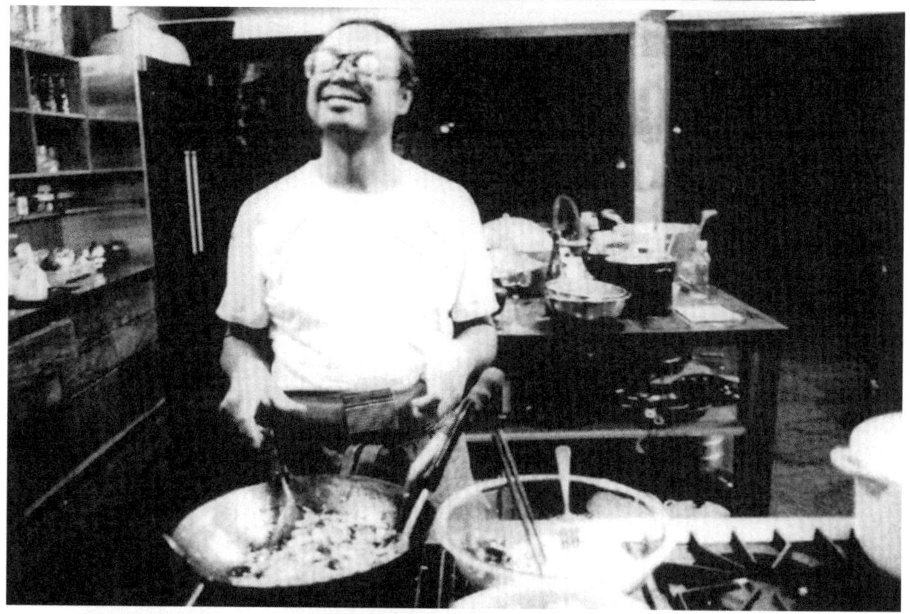

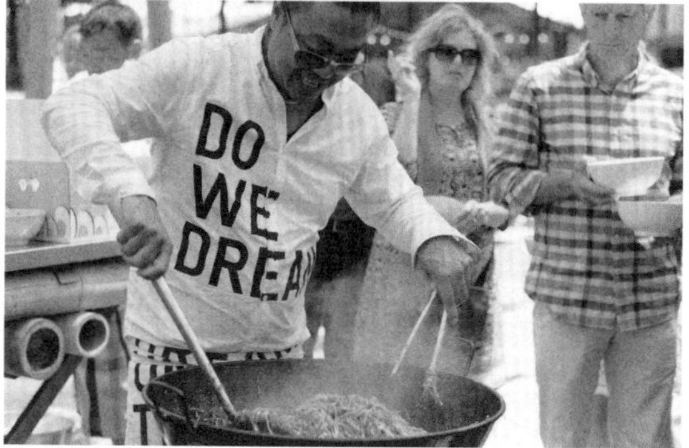
DO
WE
DREA

Communitas
Rirkrit Tiravanija

Can art take the form of generosity? Between December 2004 and February 2005, Museum Boijmans Van Beuningen in Rotterdam presented a solo exhibition of Rirkrit Tiravanija's work.[1] This show looked back at the work of an artist whose life and art almost come together in a special way. Tiravanija's oeuvre reflects a philosophy of life. Residing in New York, Berlin and Bangkok alternatively, he is a cultural nomad, and used to life on the road. Since 1990, Tiravanija has been traveling from one exhibition to the next, mostly making his work on the spot. The work does not consist of objects that can be viewed in silent contemplation. Instead, the artist constructs social situations.

His exhibitions take the form of occasions for people to meet and talk, share time, and do things together. The artist orchestrates these events by creating a subdued setting where people feel free to reach out. Through these events, Tiravanija wants to release a positive energy. This energy is already embedded in society, as a residue and potential. But all too often, this energy is not released, since our society clings to formal and business-like structures, groups that divide

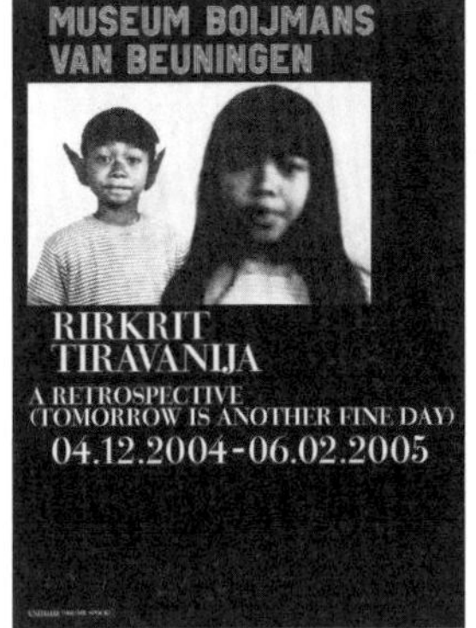

1 Rirkrit Tiravanija, 'A Retrospective (tomorrow is another fine day)', Museum Boijmans Van Beuningen, Rotterdam, 2004–05.

49

people, and masks that we wear to play our role. Tiravanija creates occasions for new encounters; in his first exhibitions he prepared a simple rice-curry meal and served it to the visitors.

He always carries basic necessities—cooking stove, eating utensils, foodstuff, manpower, his good spirits—with him. He shares a meal with visitors of his shows but also with those who have almost no connection with contemporary art. In 1994, for instance, in Spain, he went on a walk from the airport to the museum where they were already expecting him. He used his bicycle to transport the stove, but it had no saddle or pedals. So, every few kilometres he had to stop, and prepared food, talking to people who were curious about his cooking kit. He filmed these encounters with his video camera, integrated them into his exhibition, and called his work *Untitled (Baragas to Paracuellos de Garama to Torrejon de Ardaz to San Fernando to Coslada to Reina Sofia)*.

In addition to his self-cooked meals, the artist uses other means to bring people together. For the group show 'Shift' in De Appel (1995), he bought 14 bicycles on the street in Amsterdam for the artists participating in the exhibition— that idea goes back to the Dutch White Bicycle Plan, initiated in Amsterdam in 1965 by Luud Schimmelpennink, the Provo. Tiravanija also designed scenarios for activities that could be executed during 'Shift'. For 'Skulptur Projekte Münster' (1997) he developed a work to retrieve a part of Münster's forgotten collective history. He had a covered stage built on the site of the former zoo, where high school pupils performed a marionette play. It was based on the carnival happenings of the 'Abendgesellschaft Zoologischer Garten', the proceeds of which were used to build that old zoo.

Tiravanija's artistic practice has two antecedents: Buddhism
and conceptual art. Tiravanija was born in Buenos Aires in
1961 as a diplomat's son. He spent his youth in Ethiopia,
other countries, and with his family in Thailand. That last
experience was crucial. The philosophical tradition of
Buddhism, to which his family adheres, is a strong inspiration for his work. The image of the man carrying a stove on
the bicycle, who accepts life as it comes, sharing his few
possessions with those he meets on the road, evokes the
image of the Japanese wandering monk. Those Buddhist
monks carry cooking utensils inside their high hat and they
walk on, staff in hand.

In the Buddhist philosophy, it is paramount to respect
all life forms and one's fellow humans in particular. That attitude transpires in the way Tiravanija makes contact with people. He is generous and kind, through his work; he likes to
listen and does not place himself above others. But his oeuvre
also has Western references. When he was nineteen, he
moved to Canada with his father, where he studied at two
universities and a bit later, he attended the Whitney
Programme in New York. During these studies, he became
impressed by conceptual art. It can be seen in one of his early
works, created for the group show 'Real Time' (ICA, London,
1993) with the artists Gabriel Orozco, Andrea Zittel and
Lincoln Tobier. The catalogue features black-and-white
photographs of Tiravanija buying edibles at a Thai shop in
London and unloading the food at the ICA. The photos are
disarming, showing the artist doing what he does, simple and
without pretence. The catalogue featured an artist statement
in two parts: a recipe for rice and Thai Vegetable Curry, and
an explanation of the title of his work, *Untitled (View)*: 'false

wall peeled away from existing obscured gallery windows to reveal view of St. James Park'. By taking away the wall, contact with the world was restored. With his contributions to 'Real Time'—a meal prepared for the public and an architecture intervention—Tiravanija aspired to remove the decorum of the art institution and shift the focus to that which is close by. These actions resonate strongly with certain interventions of conceptual artists. Michael Asher removed a wall in a gallery, exposing the office and connecting it to the showroom; Lawrence Weiner scratched the stucco off a gallery wall, revealing the bricks of the bare construction, and onto yet another gallery wall Blinky Palermo painted the contours of the banister in the adjacent stairwell around the corner.

Here material transformation and critical thought some together. Through these conceptual works, the exhibition space itself is being exhibited, but also the larger framework within which art acquires artistic meaning and commercial value. But there is also a basic quality to these works: they created an experience of the here and now, momentum. Their works pointed out facts to the viewer: this is the space, it looks like that, but this is not the whole story: here is the history of the space, this here is the connection to the world, et cetera.

Being Together

When he installs a stove and prepares a meal for other people, Tiravanija highlights the value of the here and now. The experience of the place, topic of the conceptual artists, does not interest him so much; he is interested in the experience of being. Critics often argue that Tiravanija's work almost coincides with reality. But is that true? Can art and reality really merge? Does for example reality TV, when it is broadcast, concur with what is or was being filmed? And does art not always involve a measure of projection?

In my view Tiravanija creates, as befits an artist, his own world. He does it by doubling reality. He chooses parts or extracts from the world that which he loves, in order to reveal the positive elements within it. Due to his commitment to reality, his work reflects a way of life. What the artist has, he willingly shares. In 1996, he had a replica made of his apartment in New York, which was then placed in an exhibition at the Kölnischer Kunstverein (Cologne). The show was open 24 hours a day, food being prepared and eaten, mattresses present for those who wanted to stay. Everyone was welcome, and many people stayed overnight in the show.

With his socially engaged oeuvre, Tiravanija is seen as one of the most important artists of the 1990s. His work was a big inspiration in these years. In its wake there followed a radical change in the direction that art would take, coined by the curatorial term *Relational Aesthetics* (Nicolas Bourriaud) for the new artistic practices. The reversal from old to new meant, in short, that the notion of art as an object—think of Jeff Koons' splendid sculptures produced and widely exhibited in the 1980s—was replaced by its opposite notion: art as a process. There was a real paradigm shift. The idea that art was first of all a visual metaphor became obsolete. Human presence became art's motto. Artists wanted to make the experience of life, in particular our social relations, palpable.

Tiravanija's exhibitions from the 1990s showed this approach. After the opening, his presentations often showed the remnants of a meal, which at the start of his career aroused discussion. Critics saw the exhibitions as parties that were over. This was, I think, the artist's wilful intention. As though he wanted to point out that a work of art leads its own

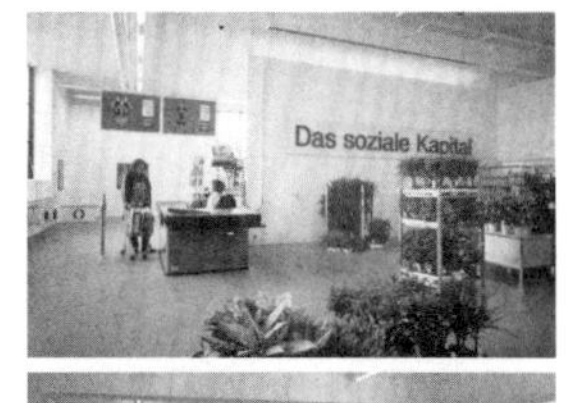
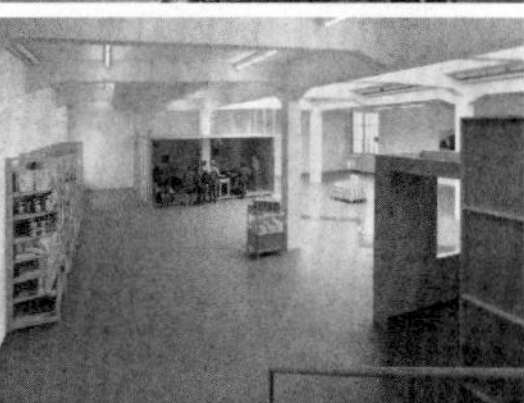
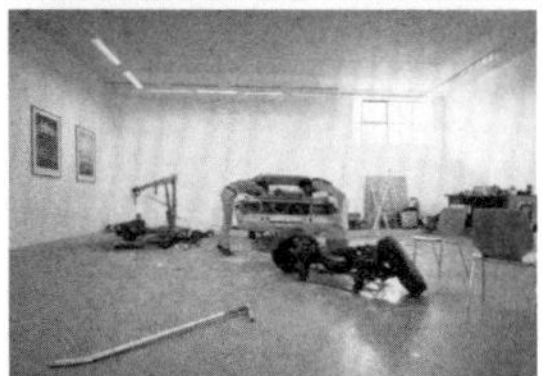
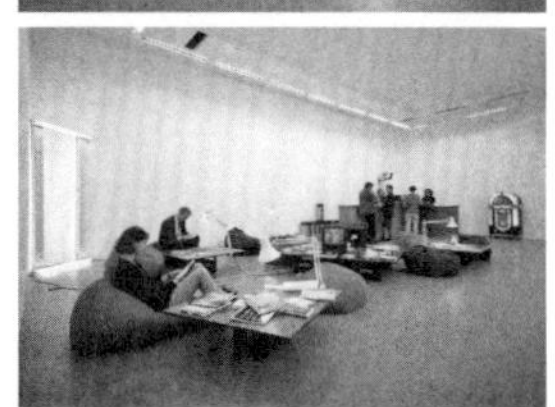
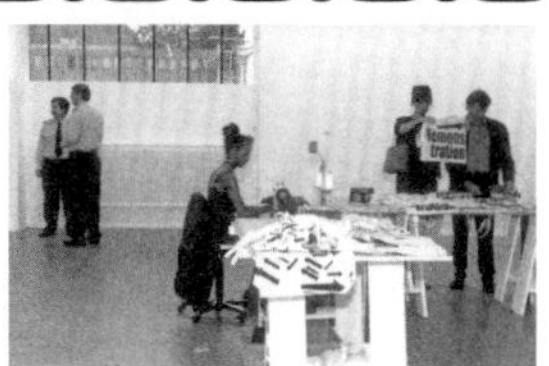

2 Rirkrit Tiravanija, 'Das soziale Kapital' ('Social Capital'), Migros Museum für Gegenwartskunst, Zürich, 1998.

life: it is born, then it lives and finally it dies.

In 1998, Tiravanija organized an exhibition in the Migros Museum in Zürich that departed from a fantasy about the ideal society. Called 'Das soziale Kapital' ('Social Capital') the show hosted several live economic and social activities: the activities occurred side by side, one thing flowing into the other.[2] The museum space was divided into units: there was a studio for bands, an auto shop, a kitchen, a bar, a seamstress' atelier, and a branch of Migros—the supermarket chain and museum financer—where visitors could do their daily shopping. The only place where you had to pay for your wares or the work that was done for you was—oh irony—the supermarket! At the time, *ArtForum* featured a lovely story about the lively opening, where people came and drank beer and discussed all these different activities happening around them. For a moment, a harmonious micro-society was a fact.

Utopia

The description above alludes to a short-lived ideal, the temporary construction of a utopia. That image brings us to the core, the drive of Tiravanija's artistic practice. It was his preoccupation from the start. In 1995, when he participated in a group show about new utopias in Malmö, he spoke of the pursuit of a better world. He argued that the old utopias, the absolute ideals of modernist artists like Mondrian, have not worked: there was no room for failure. Yet failure is so human. According to him, a new utopia would recognize that failure offers an opening to something new, in contrast to the Western thought that failure closes something off. For his show in Sweden, a historical house for a family, designed in

54

the 1940s by a socialist architect, was rebuilt on half-scale and placed in the hall of the art institute. Toddlers decorated the inside of the house with drawings and paintings. The work was a modest proposal for a new utopia.

Tiravanija, however, does not only use his own art exhibitions to raise awareness for his ideals. He collaborates with other artists and curates projects. He is one of the founders of the art initiative *The Land*, an area of several square kilometres on the Thai countryside. This rice field was released in 1998 for alternative development. The farmers no longer wanted to cultivate the land; it yielded too little due to the unfavourable climate. *The Land* reflects the ideal of a small utopic community. The idea of ownership does not exist here, and those who choose to live here do so on the basis of a sustainable and environment-friendly economy. Over the years, various artist houses have been built; others are in the making. Artists from different countries have already contributed: SUPERFLEX, Tobias Rehberger and Alicia Framis, among others.

Tiravanija is also, with Hans Ulrich Obrist and Molly Nesbit, one of the curators of 'Utopia Station', the exhibition-in-progress that began in Summer 2003 at the Venice Biennale and then went on to other places, such as the Haus der Kunst in Munich. Humanity's quest for happiness is the project's topic, in which more than sixty artists, architects, writers or performers have participated. Tiravanija, together with the English artist Liam Gillick, designed the layout of the entire project. Central to it is a platform—partly dance floor, stage and (in Venice) quay—with circular benches arranged around it. A wall with many doors gave access to individual presentations of artists and others.

His energetic approach to art, and the ambition to convince (young) people that art can touch us and has things to say about the world, typifies the generation of artists of which Tiravanija is part. As an exhibition, 'Utopia Station' branched out into other productions. One of its outcomes was an initiative by Anri Sala, an artist living in Paris who, in collaboration with Eli Rama, the mayor of Tirana, conceived a plan for the city where Sala was born, to paint the houses of the Albanian capital in a colourful floral pattern. The catalogue text 'Utopia Station', co-signed by Tiravanija, clarified what inspired this project, namely a statement by George Bush from 2002. In a speech to graduating West Point Academy cadets, Bush said: 'America has no empire to extend or utopia to establish'. The refusal to acknowledge that people are capable of creating harmony, that they can live in peace with each other, that collective effort could create a better world, demanded a response. Would a utopia lived in art be the answer?

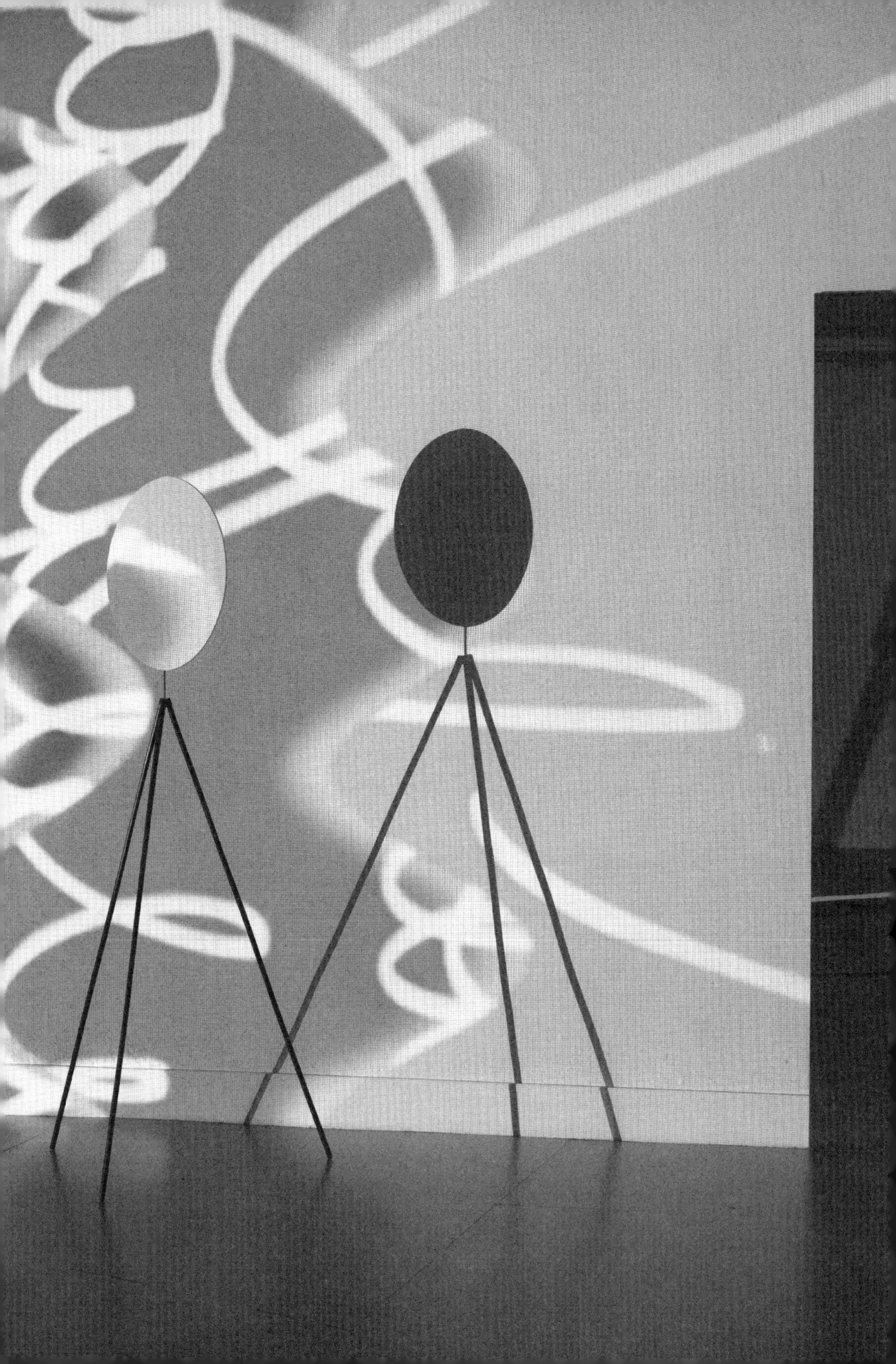

Bodies Soar By

Wineke Gartz

I travel to Breda to drink from the source. Making my way from the Central Station to Club Solo, I pass the Boterhal, watched over by a devout, sword-bearing Judith. The peace memorial dates back to 1952, but the style looks more medieval-martial. 'What an old city Breda is', I find myself thinking. Piety and combativeness make a curious pair. Pierre Michon writes about Columbkill, a roughneck who, when he's not waging war or plundering treasure, visits monasteries where he reads the most marvellous objects known today as 'books': 'This wolf is also a monk, as they were in that age, but which is hardly conceivable today.'[1]

A tall, skinny man is standing in the middle of the street. No way around him. The gentle giant accosts me for a talk about Jesus, his neck swaying like a flower stem in the wind.

Wineke Gartz creates liminal worlds where bodies and spectres linger, or pass by, sometimes in full flight. She refers to the multimedia installations that she builds, on-site, as 'landscapes to wander around in'.[2] When she spends time in a place, and sees the work grow before her eyes—this is a long and meticulous process—she is the first wanderer, or

1 Pierre Michon, *Vuur van Brigid en andere wintermythen*, trans. Rokus Hofstede, Amsterdam, Van Oorschot, 2002, p. 14.

2 Artist quotations in conversation with the author, 3 August, 9 September & 16 September 2022.

Wineke Gartz, *Mother Song*, site-specific installation, 2022. Photo: Peter Cox.

3 Yukio Mishima, *Vijf moderne noh-spelen*, trans. Jef Last, Amsterdam, De Bezige Bij, 1966, p. 7.

4 Gartz was struck by film stills in a publication about Dan Graham's video documentary *Rock My Religion* (1983–84). She looks into the theme of this sacred dance through a number of works.

5 Papa Tarahumara, *The Bush of Ghosts I*, Amsterdam, Het Muziektheater, 1995.

vagrant. Her 'landscape' is foremost a physical environment: at once wondrous and familiar, replete with heterogeneous images and 'fixed building blocks' that overlap or coalesce in the rays of light (the projections): nature and its rhythm is a recurring motif. But this is just as much a space for inner life, from love to suffering.

The term 'liminal world' refers to the twilight where light and dark meet and forms lose their colours and contours as they transform into enigmatic shadow images, or to reverie where the mind's eye wanders through Delphic places. It also evokes the Nō play—perhaps Nō is derived from *Sarugaku*, the art of the monkey dance, originally belonging to a Shinto temple, a dance that belonged to the deity worshipped there[3]—which so often is set in the shadowy world between life and death, where tortured spirits seek to exact sweet revenge for or find acceptance of the painful events in their earthly life. Gartz mentions an old film of a memorial for the three hundred Lakota who died in the *Wounded Knee* massacre (1890) where the Lakota perform a ghost dance to be united with the spirits of the dead and to resurrect them, so that they might drive out the white men together.[4] In a different context, she refers to the ancient Japanese practice of *tsuji-ura*, divination at a crossroads in the twilight: 'Our ancestors freed their minds at this time of day, opening them up to the whispered words of passing silhouettes'.[5]

Gartz occupies an interesting position in the art world. Her work is related to that of the Pictures Generation: from the mid-1970s, American artists like Barbara Kruger, Richard Prince and Dara Birnbaum lifted imagery from the mass media to challenge assumptions such as gender clichés. This Pictures Generation is mostly associated with New York (John Baldessari, who was active in Los Angeles, is an important forerunner). But the movement also had strong

European counterparts, like Rob Scholte, and the art manifestation 'Talking Back to the Media' (Amsterdam, 1986).

Like them, Gartz lifts her images from the torrent.[6] The
work GOLD HURTS III (1999) is a product of her love for
martial arts movies, focusing on the pain of the warrior. A
video projection is combined with two slide projections to
form an angle, but small mirrors placed in the room create
boundless reflections, and the site is seized by what looks like
one kaleidoscopic picture (sequence). Footage of Bruce Lee
in *Enter the Dragon* (1973), filmed from the TV screen, is jux-
taposed with images of Gartz herself wistfully admiring Lee
as he kills his foe—evil-incarnate. Am I wrong, or is this
remarkable constellation another liminal realm? Here restless
images return as phantoms! Gartz compares the mood evoked
by GOLD HURTS III to a medieval altarpiece. Soothing
music completes her piece.

The artist prefers to work with footage that she's shot
herself. Her archive of still and moving pictures is a treasure
trove. She favours the ordinary things: sunsets, city outskirts,
activities at a building site, cyclists waiting at the red light,
orange street decorations for the football world cup.

61

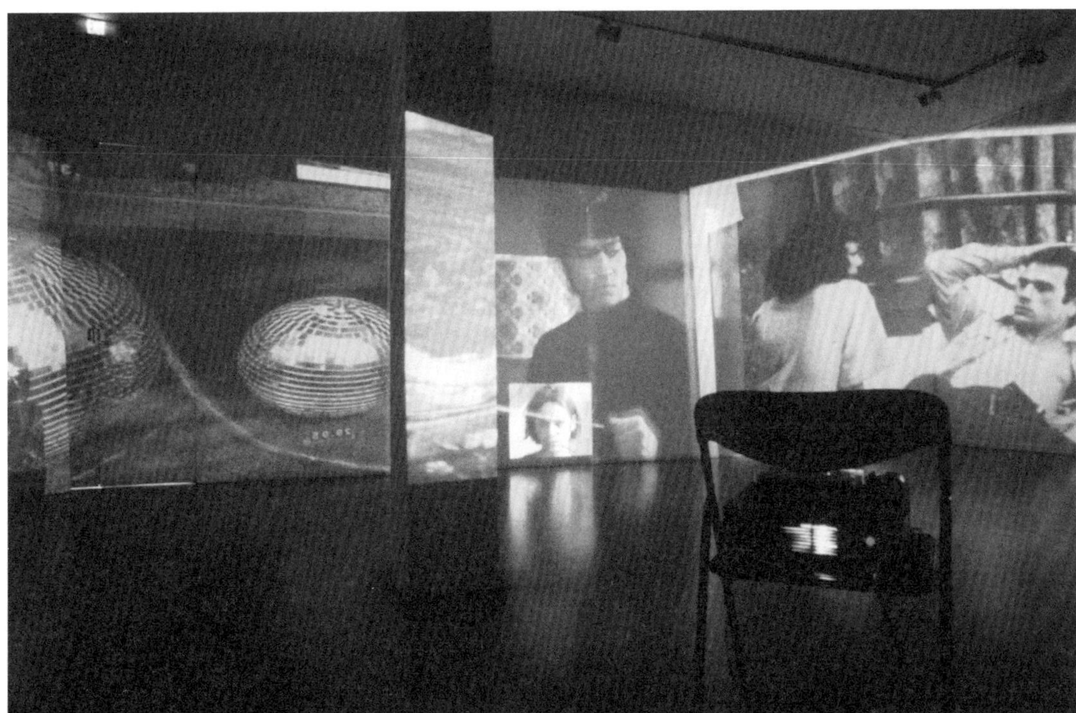

6 Wineke Gartz, *GOLD HURTS III*, site-specific installation, 1999.

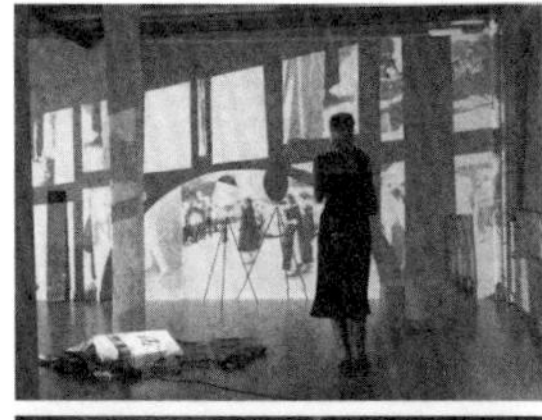
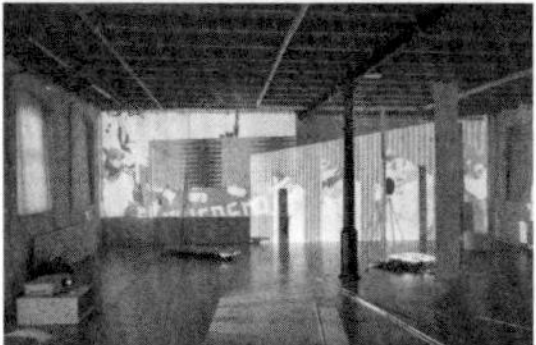
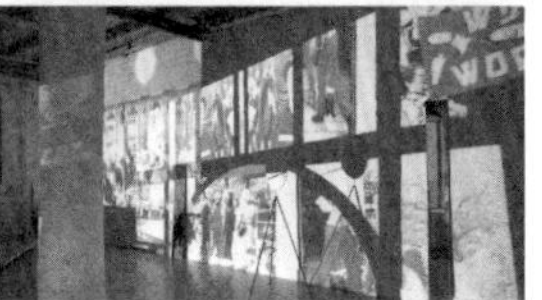

7 Wineke Gartz, *Mother Song*, site-specific installation, 2022. First photo: Dorith de Bie; other photos: Peter Cox.

Her Club Solo exhibition comprises two video installations. For all their differences, they are nonetheless intricately connected. Gartz herself leaves no room for misunderstanding: 'These works are about the "war within" and the "war without"'. The main hall is transformed into a limbo where a woman resists inner torment. It makes one feel stasis, a leaden atmosphere; at the same time, everything points to a deeply human potential. With these pictures (sequences), charging each other like batteries, we get the ominous sensation that change is around the corner.

The first-floor room shows a fairylike scene. Light abounds as soft colours float whirlingly by. This is about Brave Women and the strength of the collective. We see footage of a playful demonstration by the women's rights organization Vrouwen voor Vrede (Women for Peace) carrying a paper cruise missile to its grave in 1986.[7, 8]

The missile conceals a cornucopia of delicious foods, which shoot out in a joyous explosion at the climax in a reference to the earth's ability to feed all people. In her installation, the artist uses vj techniques evocative of pre-cinema (and the magic lantern). She turns the room into a zoetrope, with the walls playing the role of the rotating cylinder.

62

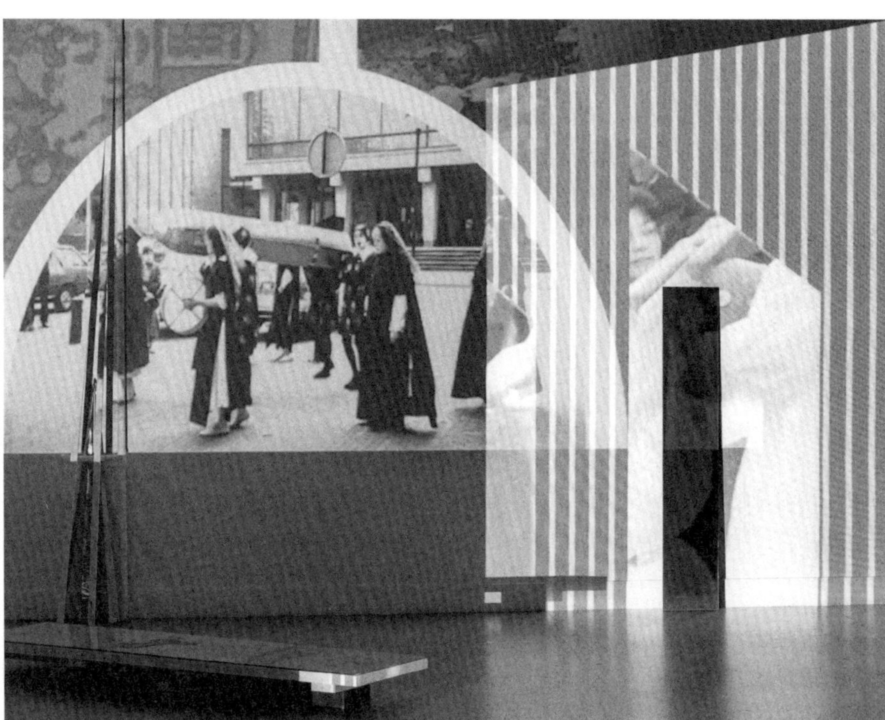

8 Wineke Gartz, *Mother Song*, site-specific installation, 2022. Photo: Peter Cox.

Gartz was happy to be invited by Club Solo. She was given carte blanche to develop an exhibition about topics she deeply cared about. She comments: 'When I'm commissioned to create a work intended for a specific place, every aspect of that place comes into play. At the same time, I've always had the desire to bring my own soul to light.' Inspirational! I do love romantic artists, but I'd add a critical observation. Stanley Kauffmann points out the main pitfall: 'Since the romantic artist's life and internal experience become more and more circumscribedly his subject matter, he is led to early burnout and repetitiveness, a quick depletion of resources.'[9]

I return to Breda for another look. The main hall at Club Solo has been changed into a dark bunker through minimal means. The work on show, *The Way Home II* (2022), is a retake of an installation with the same name from 2008, built in a former nuclear bunker.[10] A woman's face lights up, she stares into the distance, deep in meditation. The artist has filmed herself. The mind-in-action gives a performance! A second projection is directly linked to the face: a display window full of fans blows cool air towards her; or a cable car leisurely makes its way down. The third projection on the opposing wall serves as a side scene: a façade with golden light pouring out from the windows appears in the night. Powerful music resounds intermittently. A poem by the artist about loss hangs at the entrance to the 'bunker'. Close to the floor, in another dark spot, there's a large panel with inkjets: the visual and verbal fragments refer to amputation. Made in 2008, this work, called *Open Water*, helped the artist process her father's unfortunate death in 2005 and the impact it had on her life.[11]

In the first-floor room, *Mother Song* (2022) is on display. The installation is an ode to Gartz' mother. We see her walk in the Vrouwen voor Vrede protest march; elsewhere, she's

9 Seymour Chatman, *Antonioni, or, The Surface of the World*, Berkeley, University of California Press, 1985, p. 166.

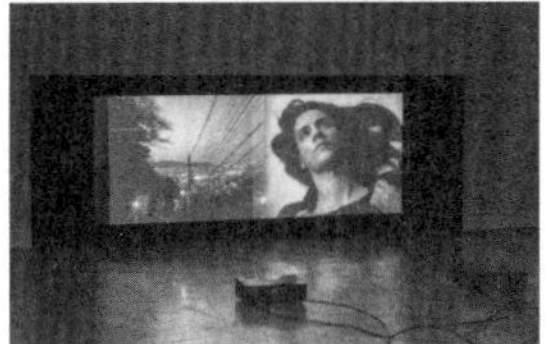

10 Wineke Gartz, *The Way Home II*, site-specific installation, 2022. Photo: Peter Cox.

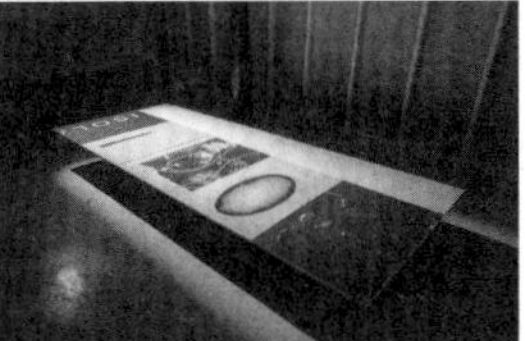

11 Wineke Gartz, *Open Water*, installation, 2008.

performing a *Sacred Dance* in the town of Son en Breugel. The whole work seems to be modelled after that dance, as the visuals frolic around. Gartz describes the installation as a big rhythmic spatial collage. Colours and objects like mirages evoke works of Matisse and Magritte. Attributes dwell in the room; banners hanging from the ceiling and small oval reflectors mounted on tripods give off a mesmerizing effect; sets of rods lean against the wall like swords and spears on tarot cards. The projections take on a lamella form: a sunset is shown in the scissoring shapes. A clever mould functions as a conveyor belt: photos from her mother's album are inserted in the arrow-shaped openings: protesting and dancing people enter and exit. The shape of the mould is reminiscent of a sieve or strainer: the super structure that all this historic material is pumped through. Does it refer to a prevalent force—time, social reality, petrified power structures? A small showcase in the walkway has drawings for posters: with their abstract, arabesque-like elements they extol the notion of activism and the need for change. *Mother Song* is a charismatic, tremendously rousing whole. But the work also has a hint of melancholy. All that effort, and what's the result? 'We are furious! We are furious! We are furious!' cry the protesters. The women express their anger about wars, hunger, the global refugee crisis. Gartz says: 'I still intend to incorporate this protest song into the installation.' The soundtrack's already there, a Dirk Bruinsma composition for percussion and shaman drum, adding a new layer to the visuals, in the form of an underground, driving, activating energy. The sound of this singing hurts, according to the artist, 'and I applaud that'. Meanwhile, bodies soar by and get scattered in space and time.

First impressions matter. In Club Solo, I'm immediately struck by the openness (exposure) of the figure in *The Way Home II*. Extreme and physical: this is 'naked life'. But one floor up, everything is different. Openness, that state that can be so awkward, is transformed into susceptibility. *Mother Song* enables us to experience an awareness around which everyone and everything lives. The artist has become a very perceptive receiver of sensations: she seeks the eye of the storm.

This brings me back to Romanticism. The story goes that a 64-year-old Turner had himself tied to the mast of a steam ship for four long hours in the dead of winter, to experience a snow storm. Long prior to this, Sor Juana de la Cruz, the Mexican poet, wrote the fantastical poem *First Dream* (1685/1692)[12], a grand, baroque edifice of 975 stanzas in the form of the *silva* with lines of eleven or seven syllables. It has a distinctly expressive style, peppered with epithets and a continuous convoluting pulse—recalling the caterpillar and the butterfly. Revolving around a character and her inner journey, the poem begins as follows:

> Pyramidal
> death-born shadow of earth
> aimed at Heaven
> a proud point of vain obelisks
> pretending to scale the Stars;
> but these lovely lights
> —free always, always shining—
> so easily evaded
> the obscure war,
> (whose black breath announced
> the dreadful, unfettered shade)
> the darkened brow

12 Octavio Paz, *Sor Juana, or, The Traps of Faith*, Cambridge (MA), Harvard University Press, 1988, p. 357 ff.

13 Translation by John Campion.

could not even reach the convex Orb
of the thrice-blessed Goddess
who shows three shining faces,
but remained
in profound imperial silence,
mistress only of the air
sullied with the dense breath
it exhaled
—admitting only
submissive cries of nocturnal birds,
so deep and plangeant,
the silence was not broken.[13]

Near the end, the protagonist shows up. She examines the universe, takes in the silence, discovers that her knowledge is surpassed by her ignorance, and is overcome by the feeling that she is utterly alone… But what a poem! It exudes motion and well-aimed movement-edification—from the very first line, the mind spreads and stretches out so as to better register the world around her, along with her own experience of it.

I want to compare the poetic-political conscience of Sor Juana with that of Wineke Gartz. She aims to understand and change the world: she shows interactions in her works, the way things inter-affect, the way one person can touch another. And all this makes me sense a drive and a joy borne by more than just the artist alone.

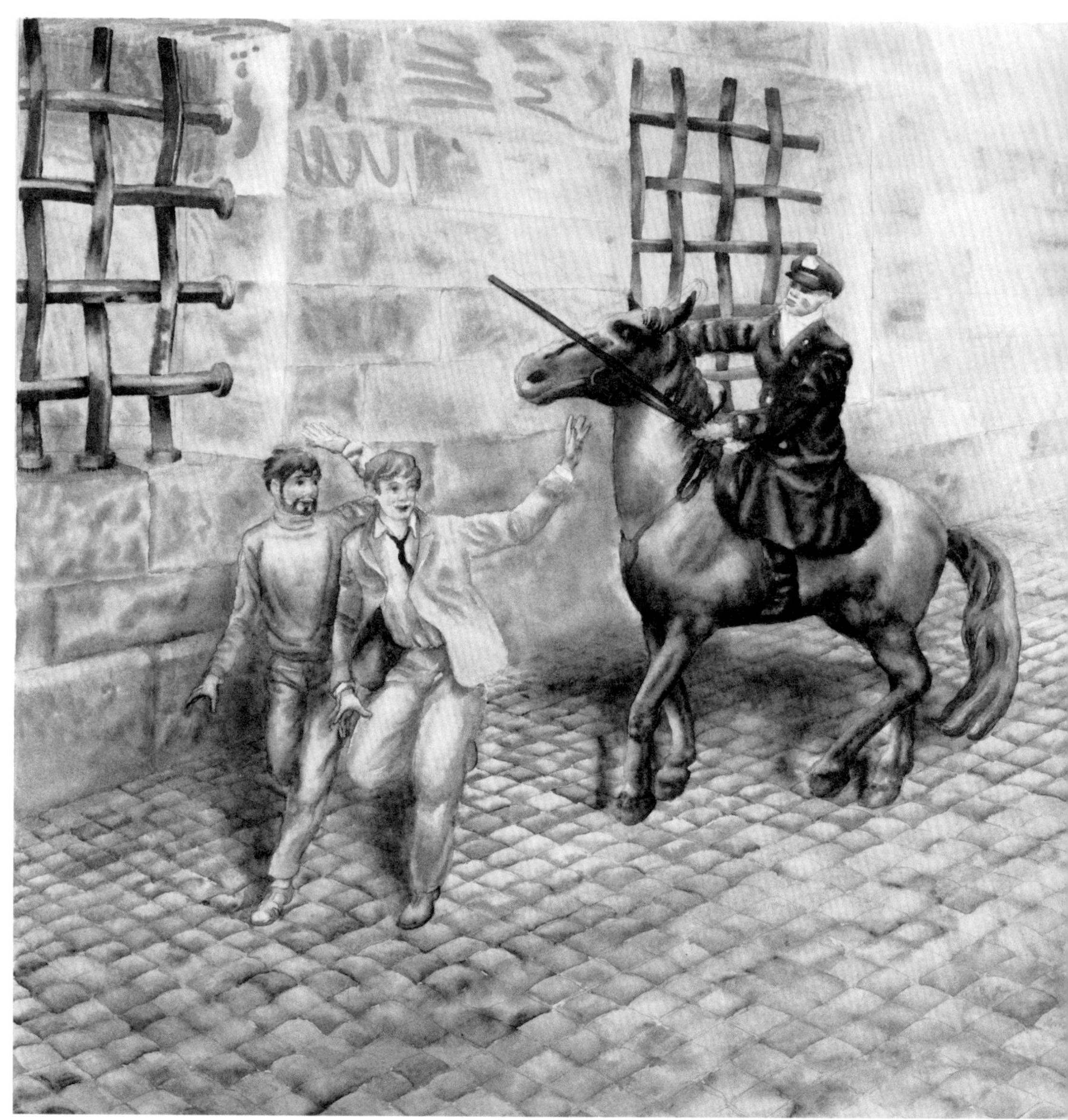

The Dream of the Avant-Gardist

Jan van de Pavert

In his body of work, Jan van de Pavert builds on the projections of the twentieth-century avant-garde. Within a context of idealistic art that suggest the outlines of a new social order, he creates images of constructed environments. This can range from a simple concrete house, or a subway with figurative wall paintings, to a lounge in a futuristic complex. These fictitious environments, which take shape in all sorts of media and materials, are emphatically modern. The straight line prevails; there is a suggestion of the functional; and they have that emptiness, so characteristic of modernity, which gives rise to tingling expectations as to what is about to happen in that place.[1, 2]

With some frequency, Jan van de Pavert explains his work in writings. He also writes and publishes essays on the critical role of art. Evidently this artist has a lifelong project that is centred on the idea of giving shape to something. How does this project fit into the present day? According to Roger M. Buergel, one of the makers of 'documenta 12', modernity may already be regarded as the antiquity of our time, thus as an age which is definitely over and which can only be

1 In the work of Jan van de Pavert animations have constituted a core around which his artistic production is organized. His other work, such as *Huisje* (Small House, 1993), a concrete sculpture at a busy roundabout in Arnhem, *Diego Rivera in de Sovjet-Unie* (Diego Rivera in the Soviet Union, 1998), a painting in a bus shelter in Zeewolde, and *Matras* (Matrass, 2005), an inflatable sculpture with a print of young sleepers, can often be seen as crystallizations of the films.

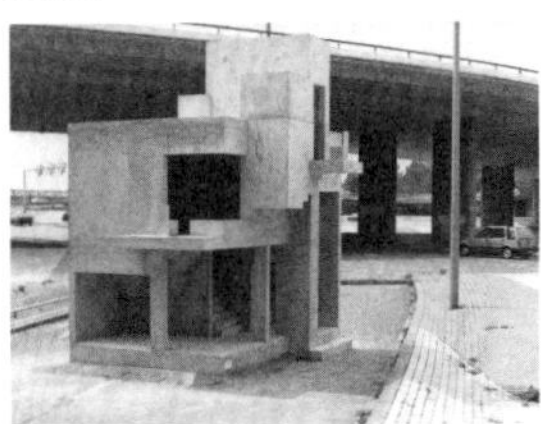

2 Jan van de Pavert, *Small House*, 'Sonsbeek 93', Roermondsplein Arnhem, 1993, concrete, 280 × 310 × 480.

Jan van de Pavert, *Two Provos and Mounted Police*, 2006, watercolour and pencil, 57.2 × 57.2 cm. This watercolour was made for the unfinished film *Lounge II*, 2006–2007

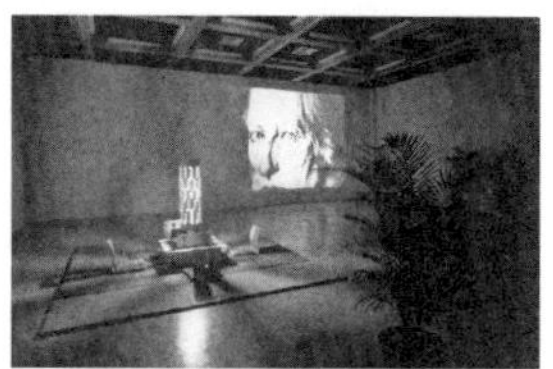

3   Cerith Wyn Evans, *Dream Machine*, 1998, installation.

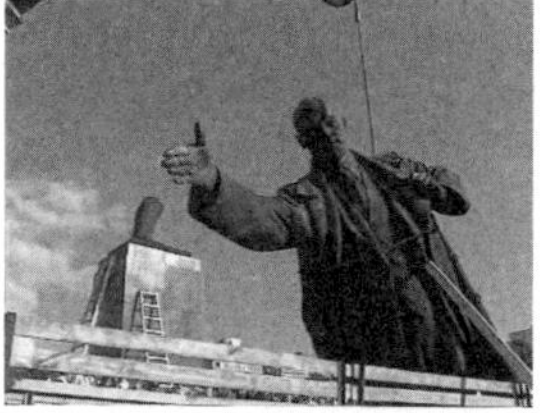

4   Deimantas Narkevicius, *Once in the XX Century*, 2004, 16mm film.

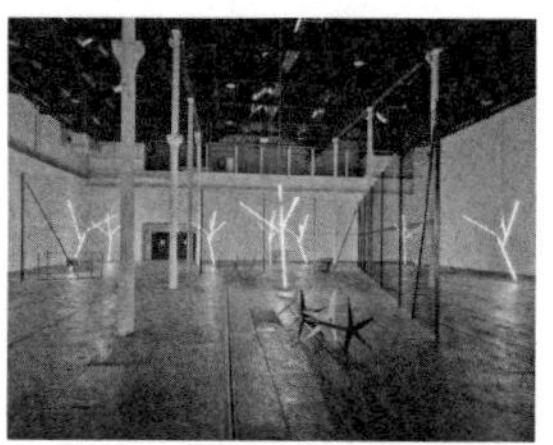

5   Martin Boyce, *Our Love is Like the Flowers, the Rain, the Sea and the Hours*, 2003, installation.

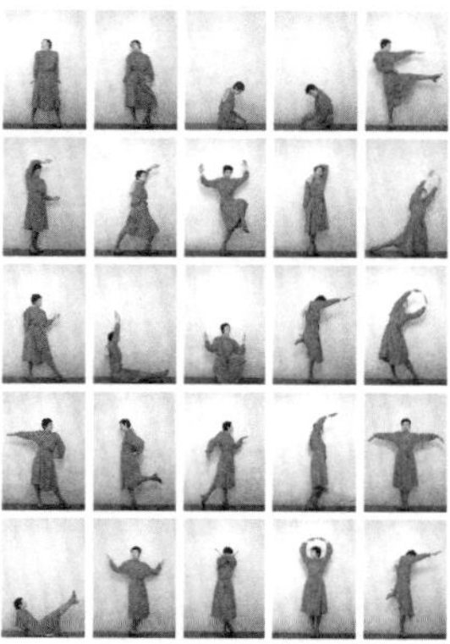

6   Paulina Olowska, *Alphabet*, 2005/2012, live performance.

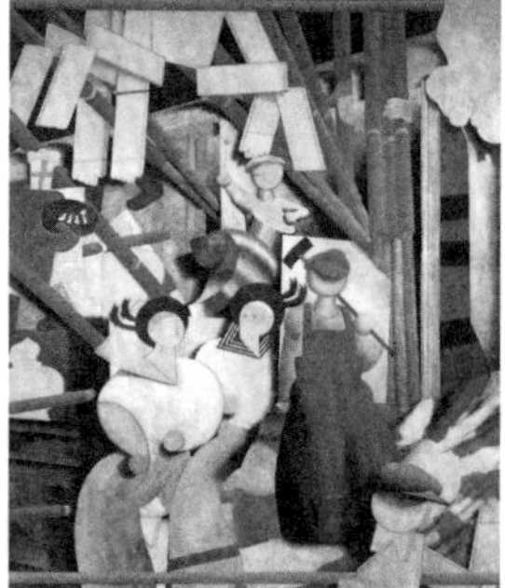

7   Jan van de Pavert, *Agitprop Train*, 1998, silicate paint on plaster on panel, 205 × 170 cm.

remembered.

In the 2000s, we see a large-scale remembrance offensive, in which modernity is once again being examined by artists and theorists. There is concern for the traces that it has left behind; where it has done well and gone wrong. Modernism is no longer a sacred domain. Academic discourse, for example, has exposed it as a tool by which the colonial powers imposed their will on other countries. In the work of the most interesting artists, modernity is unmasked. Here, within the European sphere, a striking division can be discerned: artists from Western Europe, such as Cerith Wyn Evans[3], show—in a dandyish style—that modernity was fascinated with itself, that its crystalline hallucinations did obstruct its view of reality. Artists from Eastern Europe, such as Deimantas Narkevicius[4], reveal—in a matter-of-fact way but also with compassion—the disillusionment of the communist utopia, the realization of the dream that was thus destroyed at the same time.

And between those two extremes, from critical tribute to bittersweet exposure, there are also the bodies of work where typical elements of modernity take shape once again. Think of the sculptural installations of Martin Boyce[5]: severe and, due to their 'corporate style', imbued with faceless danger. Think, also, of the playful performance-related projects of Paulina Olowska[6]: her Salons and Bauhaus Yoga resume the avant-garde's experiment of reconciling art and life.

The work of Jan van de Pavert[7] should be placed in the above-mentioned artistic context. My stance is that his work shows the radiant vision of a modernity that never existed. Perhaps it mainly aims to recollect an extraordinary dream. Because the hallucinatory quality of his work, the enchantment of a bright, forward-looking mind that continues to build on the ideals of the avant-garde, does conceal

70

melancholy. In his case the melancholy is lucid, due to an understanding of the impossibility of the utopia, which indeed can be conceived but, because of human shortcomings, cannot be brought about. Take this passage from an artist's text:

> I think that man should be invented all over again. But not as an ideological subject, not for instance as the centre of a philosophical construction and not as an individual, but as a group of people.[8]

Artist's House

About ten years ago Jan van de Pavert produced a design for a modern residence in the form of an animation. The basis for this consists of monochrome-like watercolours in grey, green and brown, which were first painted and drawn in a time-consuming process and then digitally processed. The house does not need to be built; the point is the idea and the experience of that idea.[9]

The short video film *Een huis* (A House, 1993–1995)[10] takes us on a walk through a house with many rooms. Some of these contain work by the artist. The whole of it resembles a labyrinth, because walls have been erected everywhere, even around the garden for instance. First, we see a façade with protruding geometric elements; then we go inside, enter a corridor, pass through rooms, climb stairs, enter yet another corridor, cross the landing, pass beneath a void, above a cellar, down a ladder, upward, outside, and again there is the façade, since we're back we on the street. A new house is being inspected; it is not yet inhabited. Could there be any finer image for the artist as an avant-gardist, someone who is

8 Jan van de Pavert, 'A Proposal for Arnhem', *Catalogue Sonsbeek 93*, Ghent, Snoeck Ducaju, 1993, p. 275.

9 *Huisje* was made for the 'Sonsbeek 93' exhibition and is based partly on the film. This small building has two different scales, 1:1 and 1:2. A sleeping bag was placed in the upper part of it, and this could be used during the exhibition. The work was later purchased by the city of Leeuwarden and has been located in Camminghaburen since 1994.

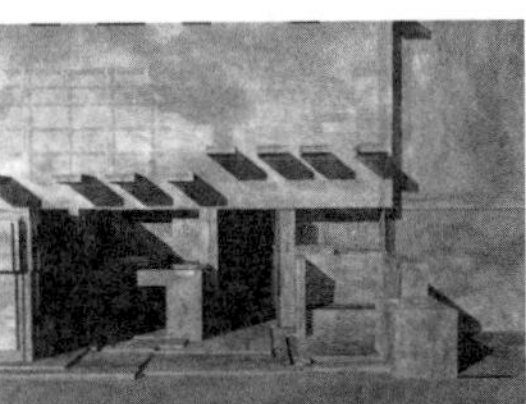

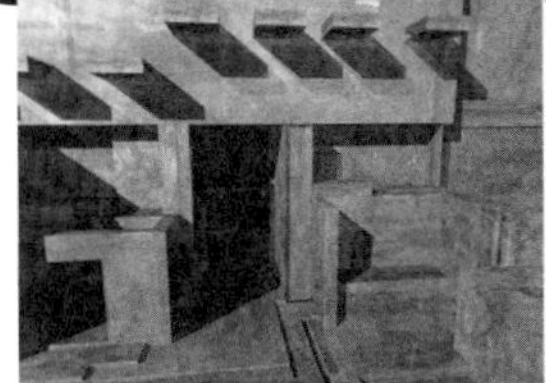

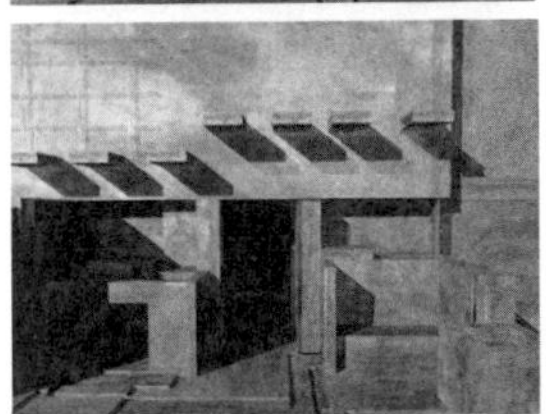

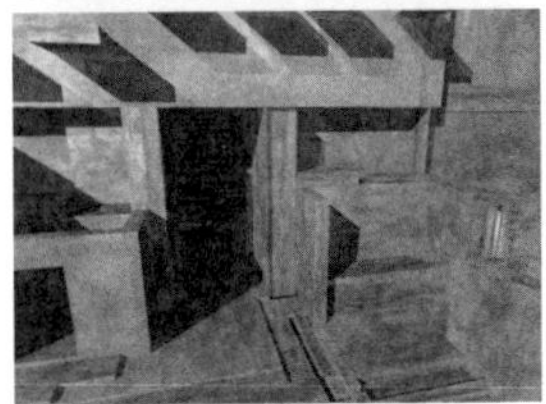

10 Jan van de Pavert, *A House*, 1993–1995, 4 stills from computer animation, 3'36".

11 Dominic van den Boogerd, 'A New House. The Typology of Jan van de Pavert', *Jan van de Pavert: HUIS*, exhibition catalogue, Utrecht, Centraal Museum, 1994, pp. 10–30.

12 Jan van de Pavert, 'A Short Account', *Jan van de Pavert: Tapehousewall*, exhibition catalogue, Utrecht, Centraal Museum, 1998, p. 74.

aware of being on the threshold of a new age, a new world, and attempting to fathom this in a creative way?

Yet the film does evoke a certain degree of sadness. Grey hues predominate in the fairly dark house; it seems to be one of those autumn days when we have to do without sunshine—and then there is the sound of steps by an imaginary person walking through the house. Whose steps are these? Is the artist looking at his home? Is it someone else? The walker's stride is disciplined, deliberate as well; this is probably a man, and his shoes are rather smart; the heels do make a nice sound on the concrete.

Converging in this work are aspects of painting, sculpture and architecture that were previously more distinct from each other in Jan van de Pavert's work. During the 1980s, he produced, for instance, floor plans for imaginary buildings, drawings of mirrored baroque spaces and paraffin sculptures in which the parts of a house (door, threshold, windows) are doubled. And in a work that has a more explicitly spatial component, such as *Kamer voor een flaneur, het rustpunt na zijn flaneren* (Room for a Saunterer, the Resting Place after his Sauntering, 1988), the concern is not so much the physical environment but the suggestion of a mental zone, this one being marked off by three elegant wooden walls. Due to this artistic interest in the idea and experience of space, Jan van de Pavert's work has been said to revolve around 'a typology of architecture'.[11]

With the video film *Een huis* (A House) Jan van de Pavert created his first 'work as environment'.[12] This was a logical step within his whole of his work. But there was also a practical reason for it. At a certain point the artist was struck by the notion that it would be ideal if he could attend his next exhibition with a videotape in his pocket. No more hauling of heavy sculptures; just order the projector by phone and then,

at the opening, shove the tape in the player and let it run. A
work which is its own environment is less dependent on art
institutions and on the way in which group exhibitions function. It makes the artist more autonomous. But for this to
happen, it was necessary to retreat: the film cultivates an artist's world, because its maker wonders whether the business-
minded art world offers, in fact, any room for that.

Due to the rise of the culture industry during the
1980s—think of the ever-increasing size of exhibitions—art
gradually came to be seen and used as amusement for the
masses. Both physically and mentally, the space where art can
exist as a critical entity therefore shrank. Within the Dutch
context, Jan van de Pavert experienced that development per-
sonally, and he tried to resist it. During the early 1990s, he
conceived the plan for a figurative sculpture based on city
statues that Hildo Krop produced within the socialist environment of the Amsterdam School.

Twee meisjes op tafel (Two Girls on the Table, 1994)[13] is
a sculpture made of black modelling wax, which could possibly, as a bronze statue, be erected in a city or village. An
earlier working title, *Monument van de wanhoop* (Monument
to Despair), expresses how dismal the artist became when he
did his best to envisage how such a sculpture could hold its
own in the city today. In other words: in an environment
where billboards, illuminated advertising and other signs
scream for attention. The political climate during the early
1990s, the lack of constructive ideas for urban development
and the decline of public space caused him to despair. This
feeling is exemplified by the precarious situation of the girls
in his sculpture: vulnerable, being naked and served up on a
dish, they hold each other in a fervent embrace.[14]

I suspect that Jan van de Pavert wanted to safeguard his
own body of work at the start of the 1990s. His 'work as

73

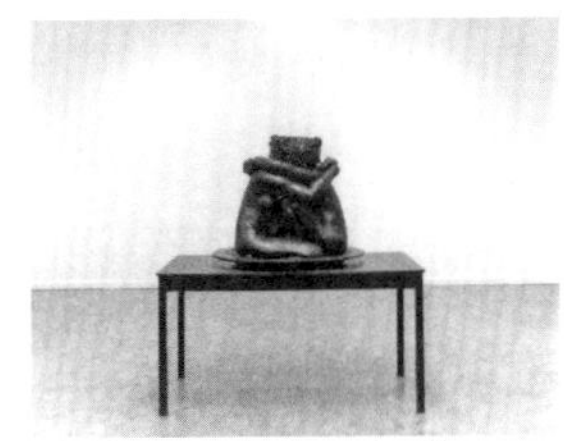

13 Jan van de Pavert, *Two
Girls on the Table*, 1994, wax,
wood, 150 × 173.5 × 240 cm.

14 The work is placed in the
context of the discussion on art
and public space in: Mark
Kremer, 'Art and Suburbia: A
Small Test for the Planners',
Archis, No. 5, 2001, p. 8.

environment' is also an environment for his work. In the film of the house we see, in one of the rooms, *Het straatje* (The Little Street), a sculpture consisting of four connecting façades. This is a form taken from Dutch public housing: houses that have such façades, built during the 1970s, can still be found in every town in the Netherlands. The sculpture is about the pureness of a scene, the pristine moment just before life begins to take shape behind those walls. Here, of course, is a link with Vermeer's painting of the same title, a tribute to cleanliness. But a crucial aspect is that this work—a sculpture, which, in the real world, is part of a private collection— has now been stowed away in a fictitious space. As though the artwork and all the ideals that it brings to mind need to be protected from the big world.

This artistic manoeuvre is reminiscent of the way in which the over-sensitive dandy Des Esseintes, the main character in J.K. Huysmans' novel À *Rebours,* furnishes his new house outside Paris. But the nineteenth-century dandy goes a step further, since he confronts his neuroses, acquired in actual experiences of the world's depravity and of himself, and embraces them. In one of the rooms, he reconstructs the interior of a ship, a saloon where the porthole looks out at nature, which announces the inescapable catastrophe of an imminent hurricane. In order to undergo the physical shock of this sublime danger, he needs only to take one step; just as easily, he can step back.

Marionette Theatre

The house protects the daydreamer, writes Gaston Bachelard in *Poétique de l'Espace* (The Poetics of Space), and so it comes as no surprise that Jan van de Pavert situates his second animation again in an interior space. This time we find ourselves in a modern building which, in a curious way, stands in the midst of society. The building has been integrated into the surroundings of a subway under construction; we see this from the vantage point of an empty space. Deep in the earth lie no tracks yet, but it won't be long. As viewers we are taken on a walk through several spaces in the building, apparently rooms that are part of a more extensive complex. A striking aspect here is the very bright light: artificial lighting shines constantly.

It took some time for Jan van de Pavert to finish this animation. In *Diego Rivera in de Sovjet-Unie* (Diego Rivera in the Soviet Union, 1998–2002)[15] we see, across many walls in the building, a painting that would have an actual width of fifty metres. The end of the painting connects with its starting point; it begins at a height of two metres and rises to six metres, just beneath the ceiling.[16] Here we are struck by a whirling figuration, which stands in contrast to the distilled abstract imagery of the earlier work. The artist is introducing a new subject: a cross-section of society. The painting depicts a continuous scene including all kinds of characters who are doing something; among the locations is a railway yard where Agitpropist figures, known from the art of the early Soviet Union, appear on the railway cars; in this context, however, the figures also enter three-dimensional space. Actually, this is one huge, amazing workplace containing figures that build, dance and climb; among them, one encounters a painter, who is doing a portrait of a group of figures which happens to include himself; butchers are about to slaughter a boar;

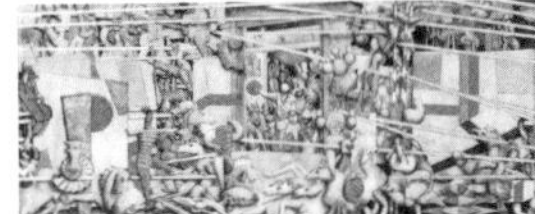

15b Jan van de Pavert, *Diego Rivera in the Soviet Union*, watercolour and pencil, 40 × 96.5 cm (4 sheets total).

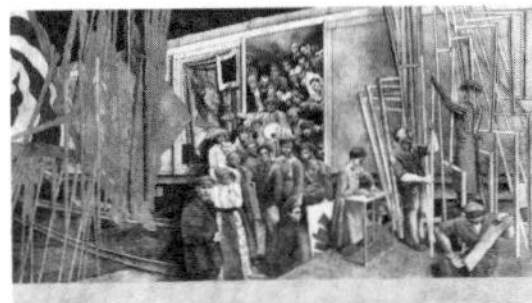

15c Jan van de Pavert, *The Emplacement*, watercolour and pencil, 50.3 × 96.5 cm (5 sheets total).

75

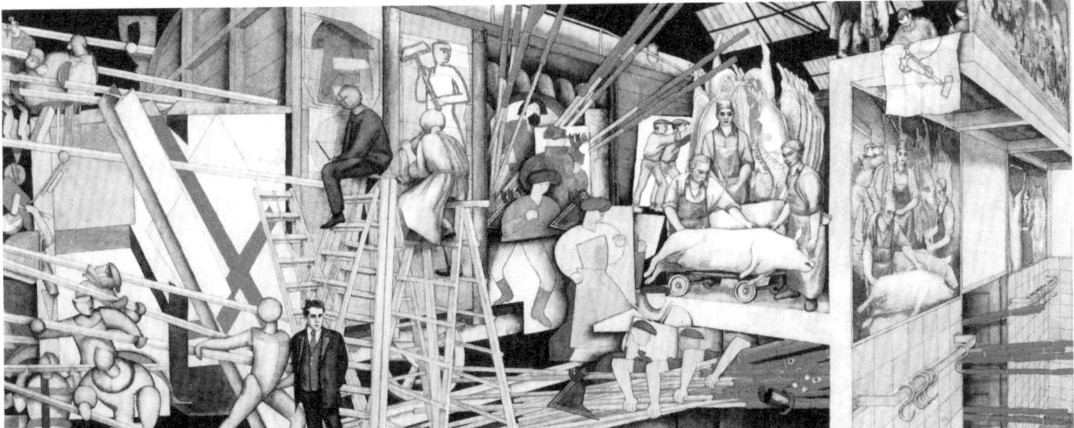

15a Jan van de Pavert, *Diego Rivera in the Soviet Union*, watercolour and pencil, 40 × 96.5 cm (4 sheets total).

17 Idem, pp. 76–77.

further on is a wall painting involving the same burly men. And standing in the foreground are well-known avant-gardists, naturally the Mexican artist Diego Rivera, who visited the Soviet Union during the 1930s and acquired a following in the Ukraine, then the poet Mayakovski, architect Mart Stam and so on.

The painting combines tradition and modernity. Jan van de Pavert mentions Charlot and Schlemmer as sources of inspirations.[17] Charlot was a French-Mexican artist who extended the animism in Mayan art to his narrative (wall) paintings. Schlemmer, the Bauhaus artist, made abstract ballet drawings based on principles of movement. The puppet-like figures in his theatre, conceived by him with vaudeville in mind, symbolically echo the lightness of life in the modern age, which holds such potential for leaving the past behind and embracing the future. Tradition and modernity are usually seen as being contradictory. In Jan van de Pavert's fictitious paintings the two are linked with each other, the result being an astonishing scene that, in its treatment of space, brings to mind the foldout architecture of paintings from the Baroque, but also the cardboard movie sets of Hollywood.

In this film, too, there is the sound of someone walking ahead. Whereto does this journey take us? We walk through one space, arrive in another, and with that we've seen the entire painting. But then it goes on, around the corner, and in the next space the painting begins all over again! A Piranesi-like experience… Is this an image of modernity, doomed to produce its own dream over and over?

There is yet another incongruity. The cheerfulness of the painting obstructs our view of an essential contrast: that between masters and slaves. What are we to think of the discrepancy between the faces of the avant-gardists, so full of character, mainly contemplating quietly and taking time to smoke a cigar, and all of those expressionless, cartoonish workers, so diligently occupied? Are these labourers projections of the artists? Are they being brought to heel here? Or is the depiction about the shaping of matter by the mind, about animation as such? Here dead figures—not just lifeless dolls but ideas, too, that lie buried—come to life one more time.

In the next film, *Undergrondse* (Subway, 2002–2003)[18], the subterranean surroundings of the same building are shown. We are standing in the middle of a construction site, actually a wasteland, deep in the earth. There is no longer someone walking ahead of us. What business does anyone have down here? Colourful hoists, attached to large chains, seem to charge themselves for a fight with rocks on the ground beneath them. The stones need to be crushed, ground evened out. The hoists are sinking ominously. Chains are grinding. Above us looms, once again, once again, the colourful wall painting with the diligent workers, a painted marionette theatre that has nothing to do with this harsh reality.

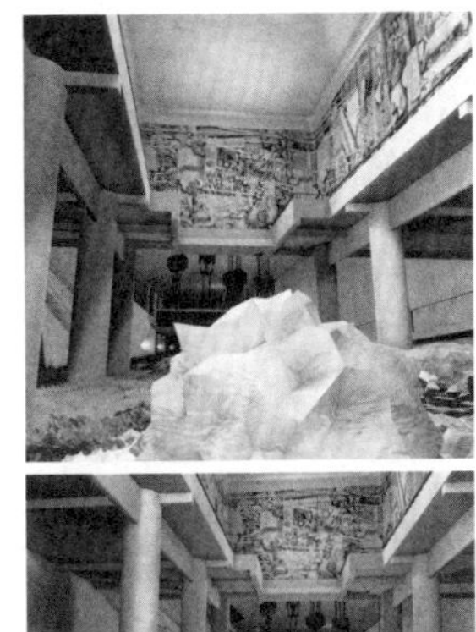

18 Jan van de Pavert, *Subway*, 2002–2003, stills from computer animation, 3'31".

Paradise

From a world below to a world above, from hell to paradise: in earlier days, with medieval writers for example, this was only a small step. In the animation *Lounge I* (2003–06), we enter a futuristic environment, whose architecture has a jelly-like aspect that would not have been out of place in Stanley Kubrick's *2001: A Space Odyssey*. There is no indication of this environment's location; it could be a free-floating constellation in space, like those drawn by the nineteenth-century caricaturist Grandville in *Un nouveau monde*. The interior shows a typically modernist language of forms, in which the nineteenth-century European domestic interior is

19 Mario Praz, *An Illustrated History of Interior Decoration: From Pompeii to Art Nouveau*, London, Thames & Hudson, 1982, p. 66.

thoroughly stripped down. Mario Praz has written beautifully on the nineteenth-century interior that aims to preserve the memory of the past. He suggests that, to a greater extent than we assume, there is a link between the traditional interior and the modern interior. 'That tightened phase of Art Nouveau, the Dutch phase, known as De Stijl, contained the first indication of the modern preference for the essential nakedness of lines, of pure, powerfully expressed mathematical forms.'[19]

With Jan van de Pavert's *Lounge I* we arrive, after a short trip through several spaces (divided by transparent walls) in which electronic music can be heard, in a modern salon which is in fact quite traditional.[20] Here we are reminded, above all, of an ideal of the future based on a recent past. The most striking aspect of the space is its vaulted structure. Applied to this structure's ribs, which are evidently also transparent, are figurative paintings reminiscent of a social cosmology. This takes its inspiration from Diego Rivera's *Water, Origin of Life*, a mural that, by means of optical effects in a rectangular space, presents a mirage-like panoramic scene. In Jan van de Pavert's painting we see imams on sneakers with orange laces and icons from the 1960s, such as Heintje (a popular singer of Dutch sentimental songs), Johan Cruijff and the pop group Shocking Blue with a sultry Mariska Veres. There is a boxer, and there are slender youngsters, girls and boys who are resting, and even sleepers, many sleepers, some of whom are nude. The entire work exudes the contemplative life of an era: flower power. The

78

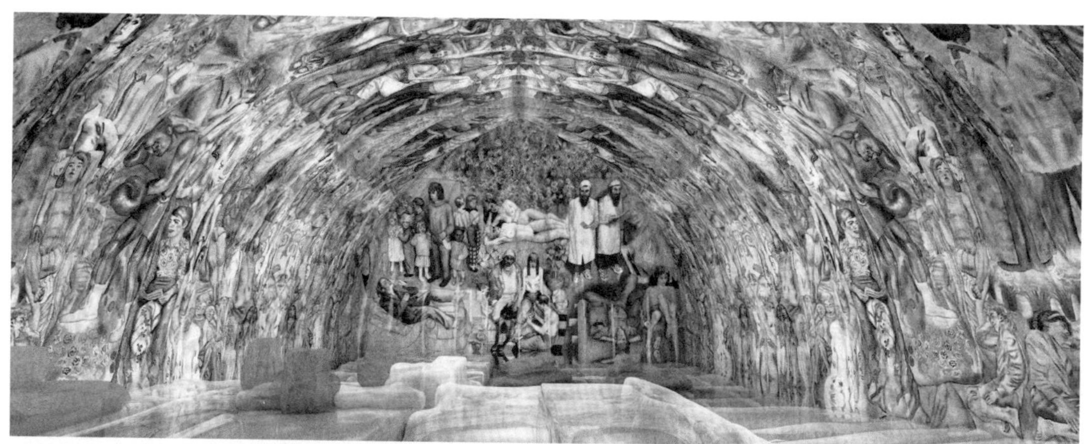

20 Jan van de Pavert, *Lounge I*, 2003–2006, rendering from computer animation, 7'10".

ribs bring to mind the architectonic skeleton of the *wharenui,* the sacred place where the Māori honour the spirits of the ancestors: a supportive structure in the form of human bones.

With this painting as well, one can speak of animism; spirits from the modern past, their hearts pledged to 'love & peace', are invoked. The figuration is in duplicate: the depicted figures from the one side appear again, as a mirror image, on the opposite side. The doubling of the delicate shapes emphasizes the fact that it is an illusion. Because of the transparency of the ribs, one might think that the figures are stored inside them. Now that their spark is simply gone, they are 'undead' and continue to exist as creatures who are no longer living yet not dead. One detail is especially amazing: the scene involving the mullahs, who have arrived in the past, from today as it were. One is looking at us, and the other has a book in his hand. Here, they seem not to be in the right place at all, and yet somehow, they do. As though they are holding up a mirror, about the situation in paradise. Harmony abounds, but isn't this also an image of *modern gloom?* The film, of which this painting is a part, shows the quest of an artist who wants to position himself with respect to modernity and who sees that, in order to hold onto that dream, it might be necessary to become a zombie himself.

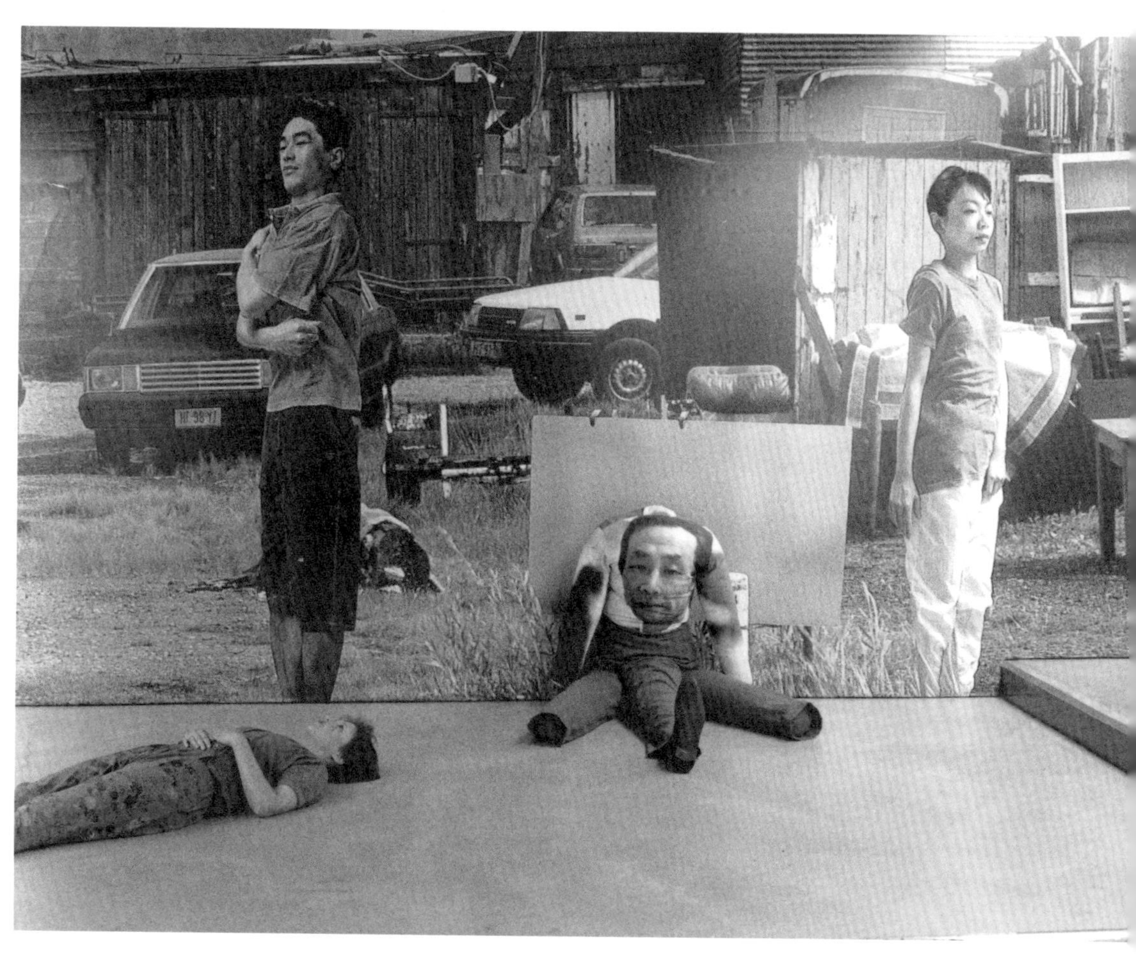

A Cheerful Nihilist Drinks Orange Juice and Eats a Brownie

Aernout Mik

From the early 1990s, Aernout Mik caused quite a stir in the Netherlands, Belgium and Germany with exhibitions of spatial works in which living creatures—human figures, dogs and hamsters—semi-automatons, furniture and other household goods appeared in dramatic settings. Sometimes these scenes seemed to have been frozen in mid-action. The art lover could reconstruct the story on the spot from images created with the aid of photos, manipulated objects and things that looked like refuse. In other works, Mik presented a *tableau vivant* in which people with an indeterminate identity carried out an act or gesture, or were lost in thought. Some of the activities were endlessly repeated, so that the whole work seemed like an invocation of the tyranny that controls our life unnoticed: the long list of rules and regulations which, to a greater degree than we realize, channel our individual behaviour within the social order into fixed courses.

These spatial works have the effect of surreal paintings in which we see reflected the relation between people and objects, or people and their surroundings, albeit exaggerated and distorted as in a hall of mirrors. That is why it would be

81

Aernout Mik, *Für Nichts und Wieder Nichts*, digital photograph, 305 × 1370 cm. Photo of detail of the work, including live extra.

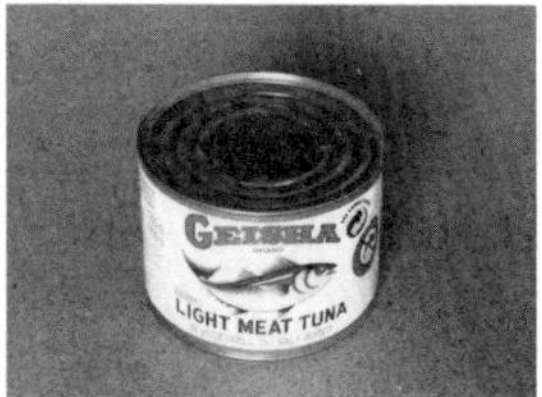
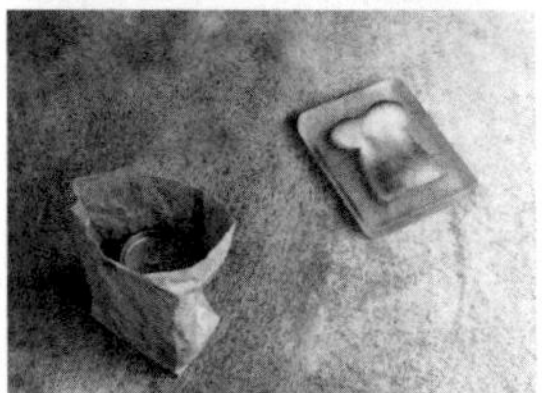
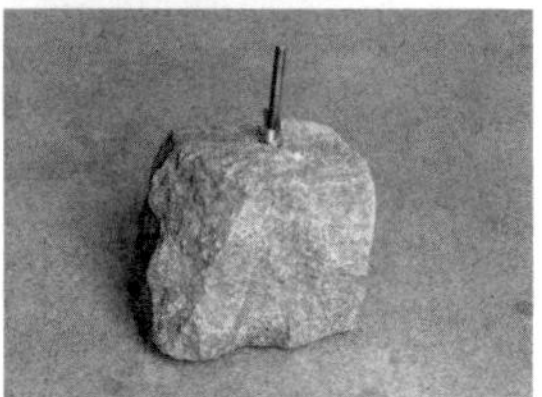
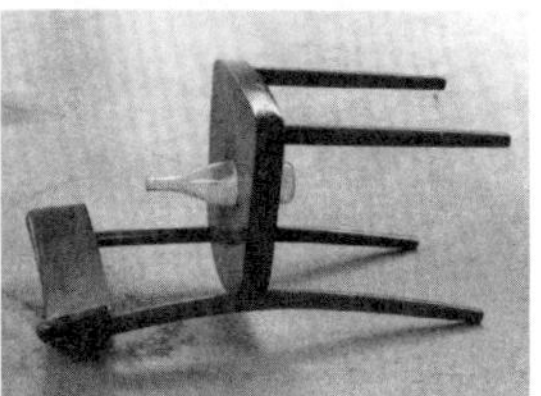
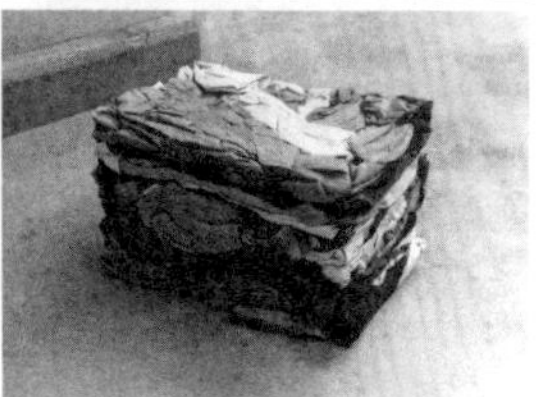
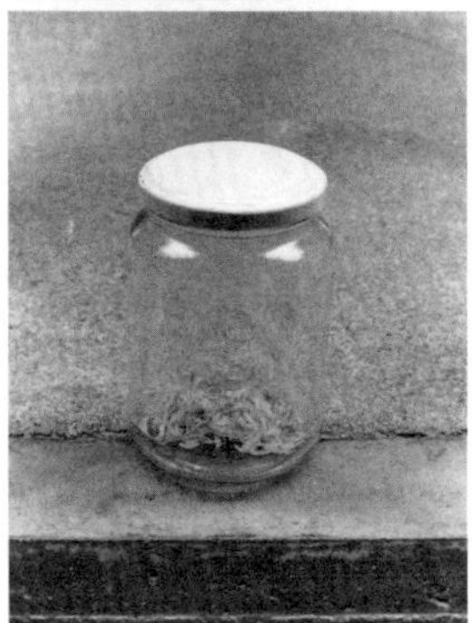

1 Aernout Mik, *Voorwerpen, achter te laten in treinen* (Objects, to be left behind in trains), 1992.

incorrect to speak of installations; that term in no way covers their magic power. Mik's works can best be defined as phantasmagorias in which the dream breaks into everyday reality. Sometimes they are very amusing. But there is also something disturbing about them, because they give a sense of all kinds of dark forces lying beneath the surface. You realize that the reality in Mik's images is not straightforward, even though you can see the things[1] concretely in front of you, and even though you are sometimes very close to these people. This makes you muse on existential questions. Are humans the product of a history written without their knowledge? Can they truly make contact with their surroundings, or have things turned away from them? To what extent do they need connections to hold their ground out there in the heart-rending reality?

The stories of Central European and Slavic authors such as Franz Kafka, Witold Gombrowicz and Vladimir Nabokov have a similar existential charge. A grotesque world is depicted that dominates us and puts a heavy burden on the individual consciousness—so that we are in fact left with little recourse but to take refuge in an inner world. These writers describe so accurately how people give substance to their earthly existence that the incongruities, conflicts and absurdities beneath the surface of the visible world are exposed. Something similar takes place in the work of Aernout Mik. His images are fragile: what appears to be an entity disintegrates before the eyes of the viewer. Mik's early photographic works have been compared with Jeff Wall's picturesque images, but the difference is that Jeff Wall is making a sort of last attempt to hold things together. If you look at Mik's large, digitally produced photographic work *Für Nichts und wieder Nichts* (For Nothing at All, 1992) you become aware of a huge gulf between the rugged, once-rural setting, filled with the most banal junk of our age, and the young Asians who stand stock-still on that spot, staring into space and appearing to transcend above the earth's surface.

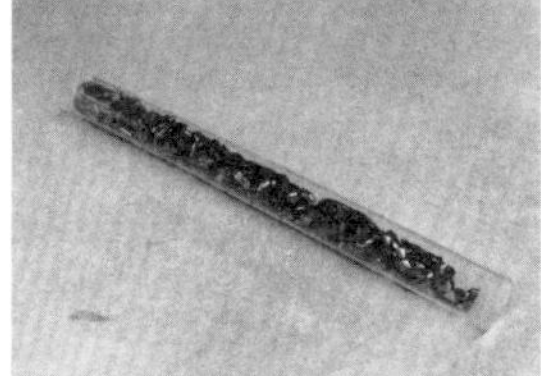

In the work of Aernout Mik serious subjects are always viewed with a certain light-heartedness. The exhibition 'Mommy, I am Sorry' (De Vleeshal, Middelburg, 1995), which he created together with the New York architect Adam Kalkin, was an ode to *homo ludens*. It is problematic and perhaps indeed tragic that as a member of bourgeois society the individual is under pressure to give up their desires, imagination and spontaneity in order to achieve various prosaic goals, and fit in. In 'Mommy, I am Sorry' saying goodbye to childhood was postponed; the title refers to the decision to put aside the carefully practiced good manners for a while, in a carnival of crazy events. What actually happened in this exhibition cannot be summarized in a single sentence. In a house built in the entrance to the Vleeshal, with tar and discarded library books among other things, various playful events took place according to a particular scenario for four weeks: two girls, one of whom dressed as a wasp, made conversation about perfume; a Dutch chess master played simultaneous games against local players; visitors were presented with biscuits; a soaking wet policeman supposedly sought shelter from the storm…

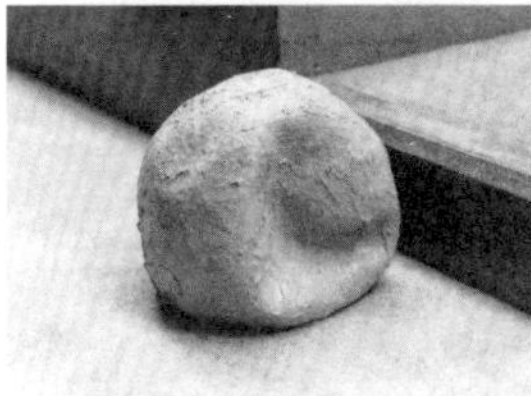

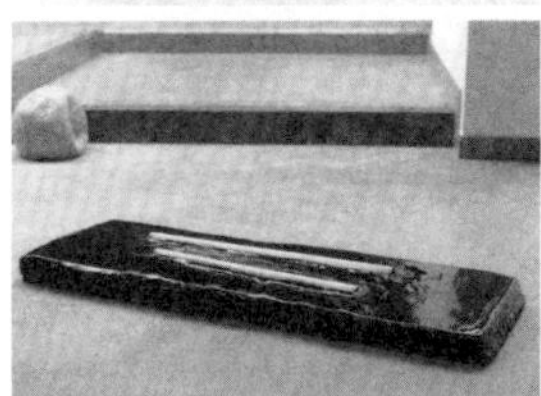

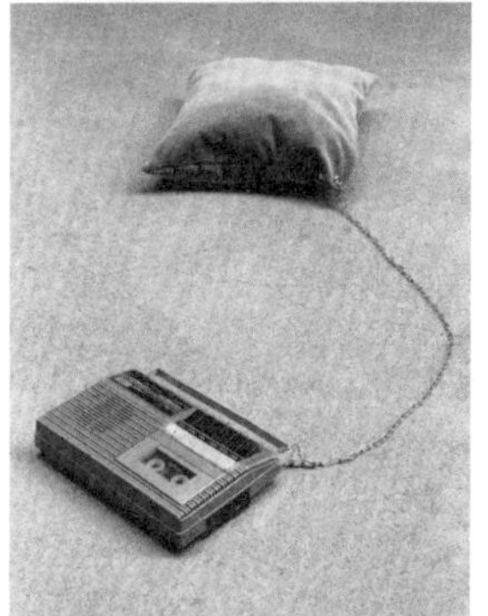

The solution Aernout Mik found for the problem of how to keep the memory of this kind of exhibition alive is characteristic of his view on how art is treated in our culture. Instead of a catalogue he devised a kind of music box. This *Mommy Box,* which was produced in a limited edition, plays a tune when you turn a mechanism by hand; you can put one of ten exhibition slides provided on a lit glass plate; there's a booklet with a short story, and inside, the box smells of camphor. Of course, the story told by the *Mommy Box* is

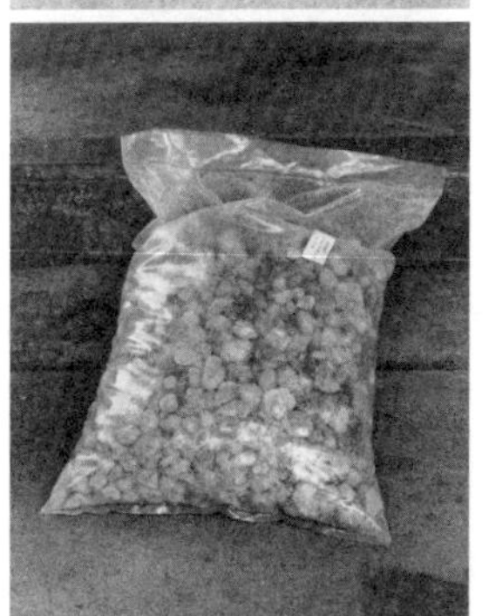

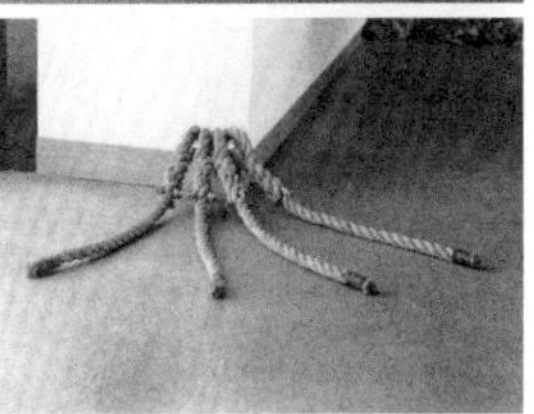

83

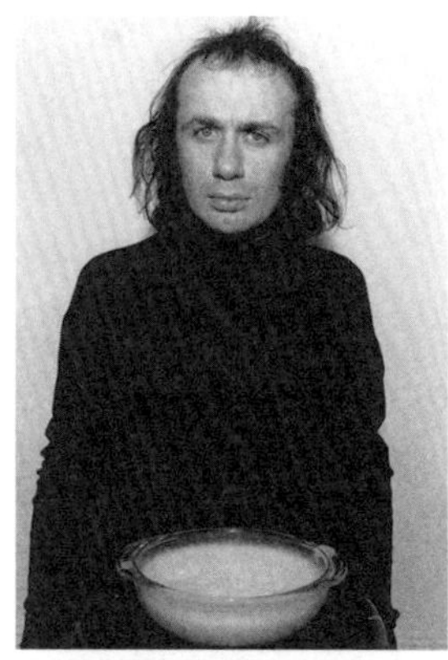
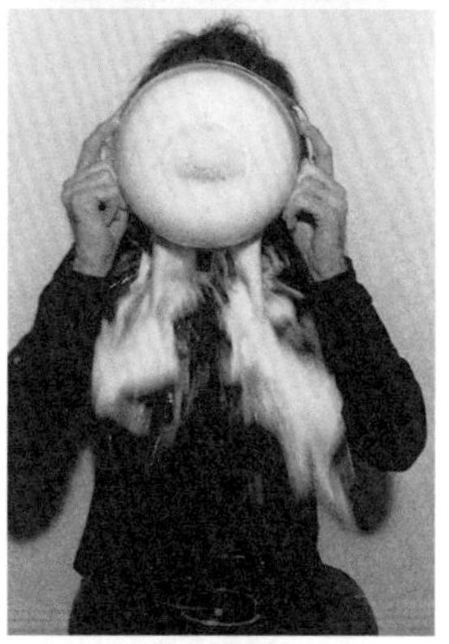
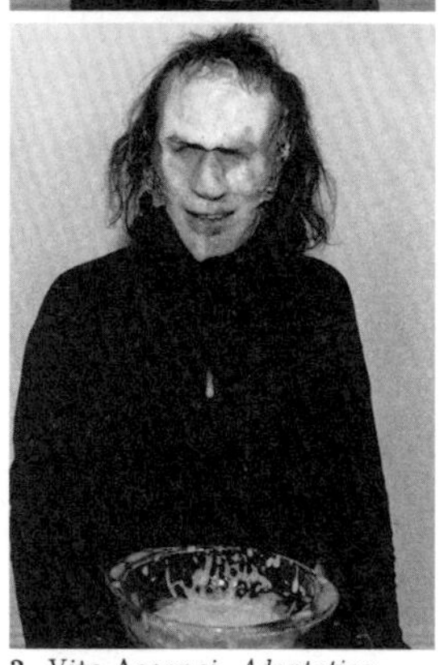

2 Vito Acconci, *Adaptation Study (Soap and Eyes)*, 1970.

different from that told by the exhibition and that is exactly the point. What matters is the recurring question of how to say goodbye to the past in the right way. The essential thing is to construct a memory that is meaningful in the present. From this point of view the accumulation of artefacts in museums, which seems to continue automatically, is problematic, because all too often, the imagination required to revive the objects with something of the life they once reflected is missing.

Although Aernout Mik occupies a position of his own, his work shows certain elements that can be understood on the basis of art's development. (His work is also inspired by 1970s body art: there is a connection to Vito Acconci,[2] whose performances exposed the area between private urges and public thresholds; the critic Donald Kuspit once described Acconci as the prototypical 'Man of the Crowd'.) The 1980s were characterized by aesthetic detachment, a specific fetishism, and the seemingly universally accepted diktat of perfect form. In the 1990s, a generation of young artists rebelled against this. The result was a veritable explosion of the object. From 1990 on we saw how the artwork as Gestalt was pushed aside by site-sensitive interventions, 'trash art' and exhibitions in which the emphasis was on processes of change, 'Sonsbeek 93' (Arnhem, 1993), 'Project Unité' (Firminy, 1993) and 'This is the Show, and the Show Is Many Things' (SMAK, Ghent, 1994) are examples. What they presented was volatile work. These developments are noteworthy. Nonetheless, it has important realize that there's a big difference between the scrutiny of Paul Valéry's maxim 'what is finished, has not been made'—with which he meant to say that a work should entertain its openness to the idea from which it originally sprang during the whole creative process—and the aforementioned practices, in which

84

misapprehensions about process prevail. This is painfully evident in exhibitions where in a primitive gesture the complete interior of the artist's study is displayed in public.

Mik certainly is interested in the potential of the process in art. But the variations in his works with live extras (the *tableaux vivants*) are always ruled by a precise score, so that each snapshot of a phased action is clearly shown. In a sense the moment in its inexplicability matters more to Mik than the narrative suggestion implicit in action that takes place time in time and space. Unlike in literature, theatre or film, here each moment contains an entire drama; all the signs are there of a story that refers to past and future. We see this when we look closely at the world around us. The question is what do you do with that insight? I have a young friend, Eleonora, who visits me from time to time. She is always hungry. In less than two hours she devours Italian biscuits, cheese sandwiches, slices of apple, fruit juice, liquorice of all sorts, et cetera. In the meantime, she plays chess, looks at picture books and draws fierce pictures. A regular feature of her repertoire consists of working the *Mommy Box*; without that ritual her visit is not complete. For Eleonora, I imagine, the music is the promise of something special awaiting her. Whereas it reminds me of something that will never return.[3]

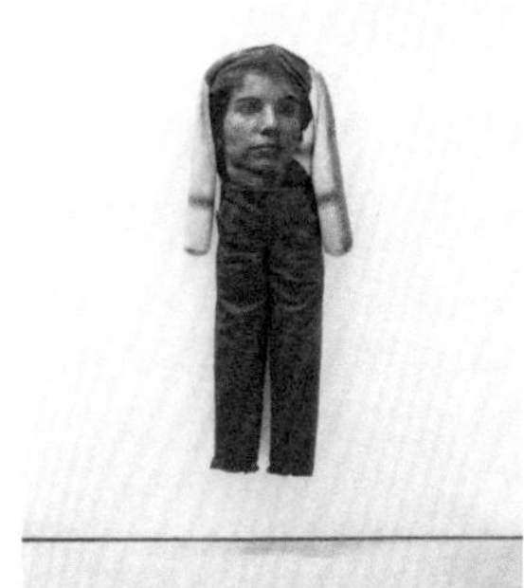

3 Aernout Mik, *Assistant*, 1992, photographic print on fabric, 170 × 67 × 25 cm.

Part 2

Gesture

Bodily gestures, as living materials in art, transfer ENERGY. The language of the human gesture is old, going back to 'pagan' times and covering diverse areas, from events in daily life to the staging of sacred rituals. As a non-verbal means, the gesture is a powerful tool in communication processes.

I particularly associate the gesture in visual art with performance, but it is crucial in all time-based arts featuring the body in relation to movement. Throughout history, art has had a reservoir of significant gestures as depicted in paintings or sculptures. In the main scene of the *Isenheim Altarpiece* (1512–1516), Grünewald has depicted John the Baptist on the left side of a crucified Jesus. Christ's body is covered with deep wounds that recall his tortures. But what draws our attention is John's stretched-out finger and emphatic gesture pointing at Christ: 'Behold this man, see his suffering!' The *Pathosformel* (passionate gesture language to express feeling/conviction) wielded by Grünewald here is typical of the earnest, Gothic religious style in late medieval Central-European art, that Grünewald continued in the new upcoming Renaissance.

Historical works easily connect to the definition of the gesture as 'a movement of part of the body, especially the hand or the head, to express an idea or meaning'. But the part played by the gesture in contemporary art is more open. I know many works that, by articulating a gesture, seem to be looking for an idea or for meaning. Here, the writer-curator can make their move! Performance—an artform embodying defiance, protest and resistance—is an area where artists work with ambiguous gestures. The spirit of performance art surrounds the artists whose work I discuss in this section. At an early stage in my studies, 1970s performance art caught my attention. The body art of Chris Burden and Gina Pane epitomized social protest and a search for individual freedom. Their works relate to the 1970s socio-cultural developments, but they also address universal existential questions.

Thomas McEvilley and Antje von Graevenitz posed that performance art has deep roots; McEvilley argues that performance art should be seen in a large cultural context, in relation to old religious and philosophical practices: Dionysian rites in Greece, Siberian shamanic ceremonies, the ascetic trainings of Zen monks.[1] Von Graevenitz has compared 1970s body art with initiation rituals (*rites de passage*) in indigenous societies. She proposes that performance artists wanted to make the viewer aware of mental conditioning, ingrained patterns and reflexes, attempting to break these open and create new perspectives.

1970s body art is imbued with modern and archaic forces. Marina Abramović and Ulay's *Relation in Time* (Studio G7, Bologna, 1977) was a fearless portrayal of what happens to two lovers in the course of time: tied to, leaning toward, and growing on one another, they wear each other out. The work's title winks to the 1960–1970s sensitivity training and therapeutic practices using non-verbal self-exploration. Thomas McEvilley pointed out the work's archaic aspect:

> In *Relation in Time*, [Marina and Ulay] sat motionless back-to-back for sixteen hours, tied together by their hair. ('Hair is a kind of antenna, like air roots of trees', Ulay says.) The public was admitted to watch the seventeenth, final hour of motionlessness. What was being exhibited in these […] pieces was not a waxwork; these were mute and unmoving monuments, but seething

1 Thomas McEvilley, 'Art in the Dark', *ArtForum*, Summer 1983.

2 Thomas McEvilley, 'Marina Abramović/Ulay, Ulay/Marina Abramović', *ArtForum*, September 1983.

3 www.youtube.com/ watch?v=bUu0m9Uizyk, accessed 7 November 2023.

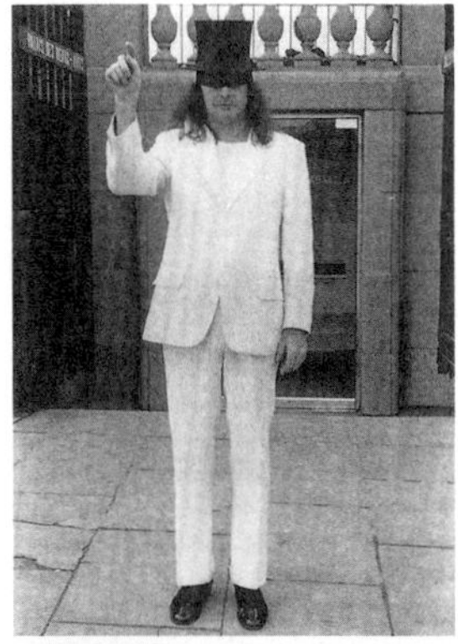

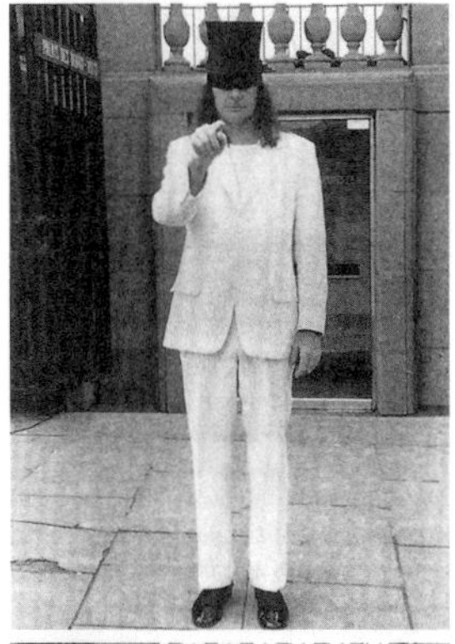

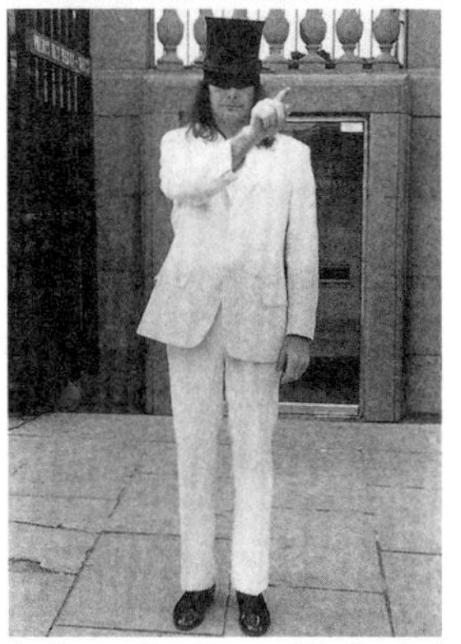

4 James Lee Byars, *The Perfect Love Letter*, 1974, performance.

with inner life and sentience, will and activity. It was that inner life transpiring invisibly within the immobile body that was the object exhibited.[2]

Gesture in performance may symbolize the desire to make contact, as in the oeuvre of artist James Lee Byars. His works are beatific gestures and unconditional gifts to the world. *The Perfect Love Letter* (1974), a performance that Byars gave in a number of European cities, was inspired by 1960s ideas of love and bliss for humankind. In 2016, the performance was re-enacted at Oslo's Nasjonalmuseet. After opening the monumental doors of the museum and stepping outside, a blindfolded mime artist penned 'I LOVE YOU' in mirror writing in the air with calm and elegant hand gestures. Byars: 'The Perfect Love Letter Is I Love You Backwards'.[3, 4]

Byars' art musters inner focus. His experience of Japan, the country he visited in his twenties, left a strong imprint. In Japanese daily life, beauty and simplicity are close. Shinto rituals are grounded in animistic views of natural life—mountains, rivers, lakes and animals—permeated by energy. Byars cultivated a mystical persona resembling that of a sage, shaman or magician. During his life he sent many hand-written letters on gold or pink paper to his many art friends and colleagues. Among the gestures or acts in his performances are the whisper, the perfect kiss, and the spoken word 'perfect'.

In 1975 Byars was a guest of De Appel in Amsterdam. Here, he realized a series of performances, *The Perfect Epitaph*, *The 25 Philosophers of Amsterdam Live* and *The Wand*. There was a film screening, where Byars appeared as a tiny particle in a black image, floating in a cosmic void. Every day he received visitors in De Appel between 2pm and 5pm for discussions on 'nothingness'. *The Wand* was a performance that compensated for—Byars' words—the Dutch excess of horizontality. Byars walked through Amsterdam with a large wand, raising the pole to a vertical stand at several locations. *The Perfect Epitaph* was another live work, for public space. While walking in the canal streets close to De Appel, Byars could be seen pushing a large cement sphere in front of him, like a latter-day Sisyphus.

Performance art in its variety of gestures is a powerful presence in today's art spectrum. The genre influences other art forms, for instance in notions of painting and sculpture as 'material performer'. Many young artists pursue performance art; other artists combine it with other forms, such as in multi-media installations. In the following texts I reflect upon the performative gestures in a variety of oeuvres, embodied in visual poetry (Job Koelewijn), a futurist-archaic *mythopoeia* (Almagul Menlibayeva), acts of 'being together' (Rirkrit Tiravanija) and 'watching over you' (Alicia Framis), and a dance/song of solace (Christiaan Bastiaans). The gestures are the artists' gifts to our world.

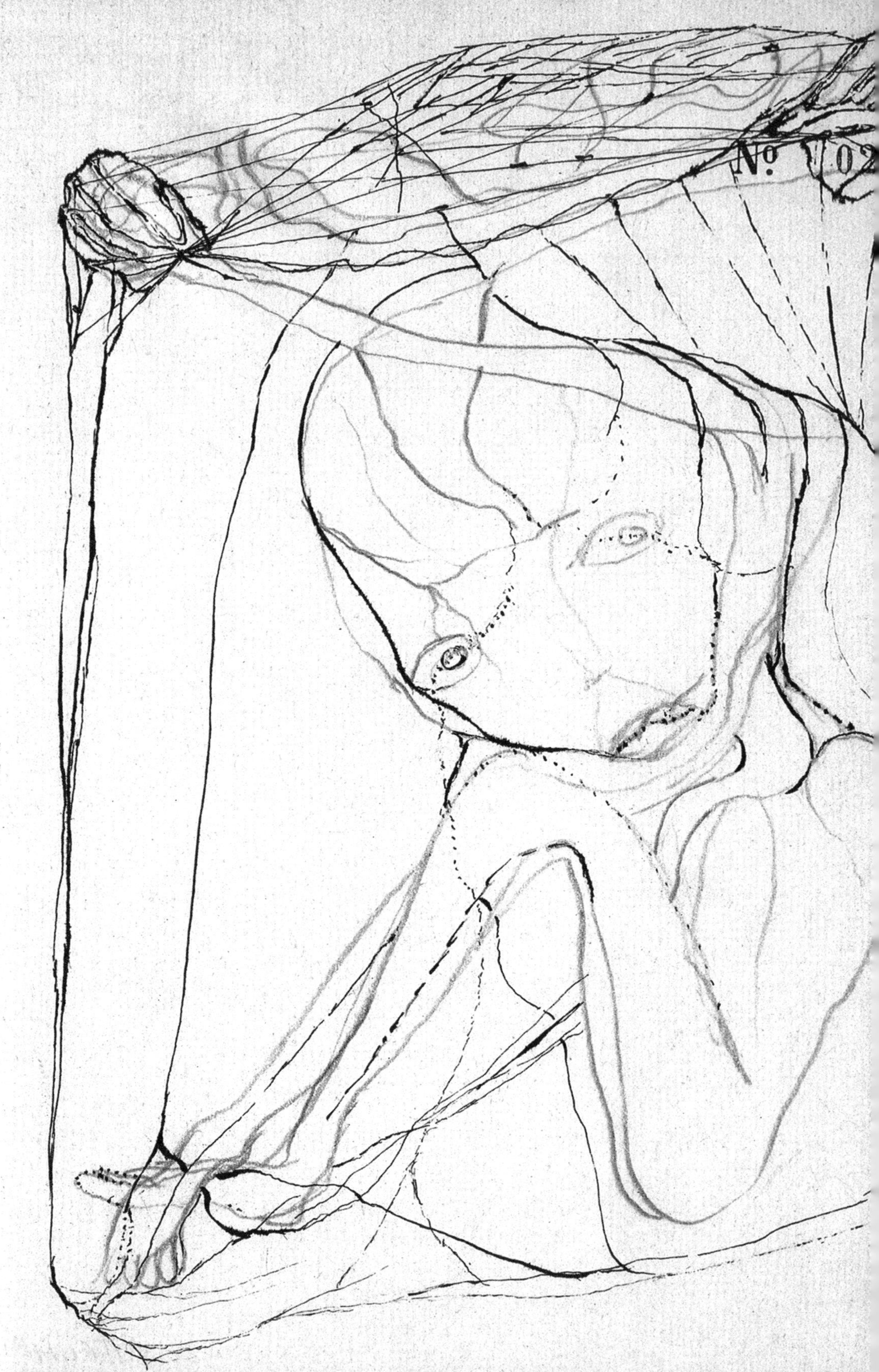
Nº 702

'Show Me Your Beautiful Madness!'

Christiaan Bastiaans

'But where there is danger,
What saves grows too.'
—Hölderlin, 'Patmos' (1803)

A mother wanders through the war-torn lands, searching for her only son who was taken by slave traders and spirited away. Grief is written all over her face, people know her as a madwoman. One spring day at dusk she arrives at Sumida River. The boatman orders her to give him a performance of her madness, in payment for the transfer. In response she recites an ancient, melancholy poem in which the ferryman pays respect to a highborn wayfarer, at exactly this crossing point. And she continues to defy his request in a solemn and dignified way. It totally changes his perspective; he tells her to hurry on board, exclaiming that he never saw such an admirable madwoman.[1]

Sumida-gawa is the name of a Nō dance-drama composed by Motomasa Kanze at the start of the fifteenth century. I want to juxtapose this Nō play with Christiaan Bastiaans' experimental film installation *Laboratories*

1 Royall Tyler, *Japanese Nō Dramas*, London, Penguin, 1992, pp. 251–263.

95

of Empire (under development). Kanze's magnification
of precarious life in feudal Japan resonates with Bastiaans'
depiction of a dystopian reality. The semblance between
Kanze's madwoman and Bastiaans' *Hurt Models* is
striking: both are symbols (archetypes) of vulnerability and
resilience.

Bastiaans' *Laboratories of Empire* project, that will
extend to a personal live performance planned for 2025,
is a fantastic reflection on global capitalism and post-
colonial reality. Biographical elements play a role in
Laboratories of Empire but indirectly, in a subcutaneous
way. Bastiaans:

> I want to implant/weave my personal family history—
> with regard to war, migration, et cetera—into worldly
> events that relate to episodes of extra-territorial violence
> but also to enlightened moments in history and routes
> of migration.
>
> My personal family history goes back to the Dutch
> East India Company flagship *Batavia,* built in 1628
> but wrecked 1629 off the coast of Western Australia
> (pastor Gijsbert Bastiaensz; mutiny, murder, survival).
> To the Aceh War: my great grand-father Elmonde
> Savinien—from my father's mother's family branch—a
> Catholic Frenchman born in Rouen and (officer) in
> the army of Napoleon III. He fought among others
> against the Prussians, possibly also during the Siege of
> Paris in 1870–1871. Recruited in the Netherlands, he
> signed up as a mercenary for the Netherlands East
> Indies Army and left for the Dutch East Indies, where
> he eventually fell in action in Aceh.
>
> To my father as a Secret Operations Executive
> (SOE) in the Second World War, and to my mother's

brothers, who as fighters for Indonesian independence stood opposite him. This history also concerns my ethnic origins: my parents are Indo-Europeans. My mother is partly Armenian, partly Sumatran; father Javanese, Dayak, French and Zealandian. My mother's stories from my childhood are part of it: about life in the former colony of the Dutch East Indies, family tales that occurred in times of peace and war, about friendship and mysterious spirits.[2]

The madwoman's life is the topic of a special Nō genre: *kyōjomono*. The genre reflects a historical reality: in feudal Japan, which at the time was not a nation but a patchwork of lands divided by clan disputes and suffering from poverty, there were many such wandering women. They were searching for family members who had vanished on the battlefield, or been captured by human traffickers to be sold off elsewhere (also in payment for a debt). To earn their living, many of these women were known to give public performances of their grief.

Bastiaans' *Hurt Models* carry mystery within them.[3] The artist has been developing this body of work since 1998, changing the outward form over time. The first works are ethereal sculptures composed of delicate fabrics, exquisite materials and elements such as amulets, newspaper cuttings, objects found in conflict areas, and waste materials.[4] These 'apparitions', as he calls them, are partly inspired by his encounters with rebels and (child) soldiers in Sierra Leone, Uganda, DR Congo, Chad and Sudan during his travels in Africa (1998–2010).[5] The bizarre, self-crafted attires that they wore, as a way to impress the enemy and protect themselves, made an impression on Bastiaans. His first *Hurt Models* resemble exhausted figures; their heads often point

2 Artist quotations taken from e-mail conversations with the author, Summer 2020.

3 The *Hurt Models'* connection to the artist's personal story is enigmatic, but these works have an early precursor: an installation made for the exhibition 'Heart of Darkness' (Kröller-Müller Museum, Otterlo, 1994–1995, curator Marianne Brouwer). Bastiaans' *Day 7* (1994, disassembled) was a reticent and yet emotional work. This installation was the outcome of two artist journeys in the 1990s, to Irian Jaya (today: West Papua), in the footsteps of his father. In the Second World War, Bastiaans' father was a Special Operations Executive (SOE) for the Netherlands Forces Intelligence Service (NEFIS), in the Dutch East Indies. He went on secret intelligence operations in Japanese occupied territory. The work *Day 7* resembled a protective capsule. A sea container enclosed a smaller 'container' made of thin transparent plastic, resembling a dangerous *Hot Zone*. In this sealed off area hung a silhouette figure of mosquito mesh netting. It was surrounded by clothes smelling of damp and mould. There is a biblical ring to the title *Day 7*. Genesis tells us that God rested on the seventh day, when he blessed and sanctified his work. That sense of peacefulness is the missing element in the father's story.

4 Based on Evert van Straaten, 'Club Mama Gemütlich Introduction', *Club Mama Gemütlich*, exhibition catalogue, Bielefeld, Kerber Verlag, 2009, p. 12.

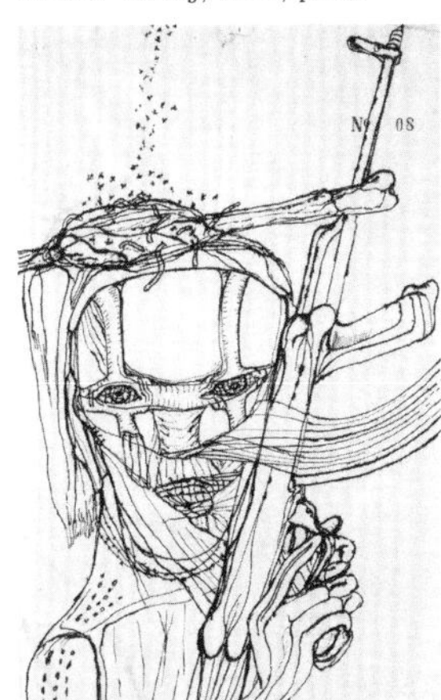

5 Christiaan Bastiaans, *Rebel Fighter at Border Crossing*, 22 February 2004, South Sudan—North Uganda, watercolour and collage on paper, 21 × 12,5 cm.

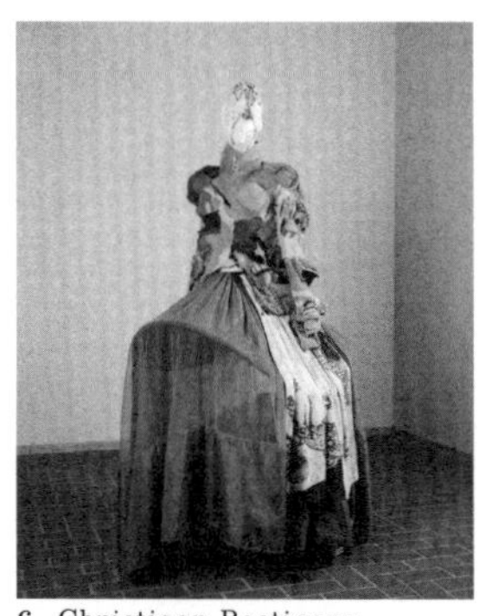

6 Christiaan Bastiaans, *MADONNA OF HUMILITY (FOR TRENCH WARFARE INFANTRY)*, 1999–2002, pigmented inkjet print and embroidery on mosquito netting, wool and various materials, ca. 192 × 115 × 80 cm. Photo: Cary Markerink.

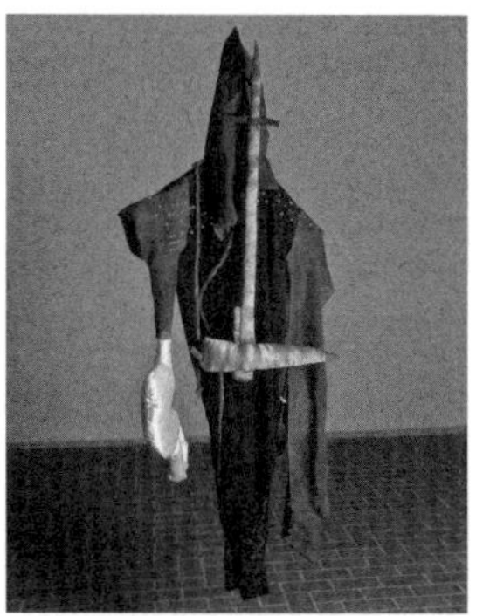

7 Christiaan Bastiaans, *ERSATZ BODY (REPLACEMENT ITEM FOR AUTOPSY BODIES IN THE LEAR ZONE)*, 2003, Japan, Japanese silk, Japanese linen (asa), satin, cotton with gold and silver lurex, thread, rope, leather, nylon thread, metal, text in braille: *I have no way and therefore want no eyes I stumbled when I saw*, 227 × 82 × 32 cm.

8 From Christiaan Bastiaans' *Script Studies Laboratories of Empire*, 2020.

downwards. But something is happening under the surface. Hidden resources seem to linger in them.[6, 7]

Apparitions—figures in a state of becoming—are central to Nō plays. Out of the darkness (symbol of a liminal setting, an in-between realm), ghosts and human beings step into the light, to tell their stories of life and death. Nō is an art of contrasts: the (male) actors, dressed in robust masks and exquisite costumes, move on a small stage in slow and stylized ways; the tiniest gesture may indicate a huge shift in time. The chorus complements the actors' speech and chant; a small band of musicians accompanies the drama with invigorating music. Nō is spectacle, in every sense of the word. But the art form fathoms deep feelings.

In Bastiaans' *Laboratories of Empire*, the *Hurt Models* are the living characters. His live performance departs from this premise: the world has been destroyed by an unnamed disaster and is literally on fire, only a few liveable areas are left. The neo-colonial *Imperial Revivalist Company*, led by *Chaplain*, wants to conquer the world to gain control over the natural resources. In the *Unaffiliated Commune*, headed by former nightclub singer *La Vivre*, *Hurt Models* have found refuge. The *Insurgents*, a group of resistance fighters headed by *Navigator*, oppose the *Imperial Revivalists'* aggression; among its latest members is *Uta*, a young political activist with a crucial role in future events. This work depicts a complex social web in which various characters cross paths: *La Vivre* a good spirit, powerful figures-in-function such as *General* and *Chaplain*, and vulnerable characters: *Hurt Models* and the *Elderly*.[8]

Laboratories of Empire begins *in media res*: we do not know what occurred before or how it came to this. Personages that signify hard forces—aggression, greed, will to power—confront characters radiating soft power. The latter feel close to us, in their longing for tenderness and shelter, in their capacity to love and protect others. That element, and the redemption brought by it, is emphasized in this live performance. Is soft power Bastiaans' actual theme? When I visit him in his study (summer 2020), his notebooks on *Laboratories of Empire* lie open on the table. Layers of texts and images beckon me. These palimpsests suggest a grim world. But my eye falls on a sentence: '*Escargot Sympathique* finds shelter in the *Hot Zone*'. Instantly I feel drawn to this figure—in fact, it is Uta—and I think: 'Miss Snail smoothly blazes her philosophical trail!'

Bastiaans helps me out of my dream. He hasn't made any drawings yet, but his script explains the character as follows: '*Escargot Sympathique*: a message dispatcher for the *Insurgents*. She carries secret, minuscule messages on microfilm in hollowed buttons. She travels through the *Hot Zone* to deliver these messages, last words from dead *Insurgents* to their loved ones at home. *Navigator* realizes that he can use such a valiant woman! Escargot is sent on secret mission. She has to go into the *Hot Zone* and track down a mysterious *Blind Man* who knows about a precious substance called *Valuable Cargo*.' Is *Valuable Cargo* the wisdom of experience? Bastiaans calls it *Secret Miracles* of the World.[9, 10]

I ask Bastiaans if *Laboratories of Empire* is an orchestration of hard versus soft forces? He says: 'Yes, that's right. In

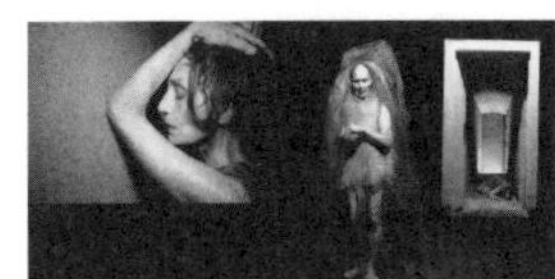

9 Christiaan Bastiaans, *Valuable Cargo*, 2019, live performance, Takamatsu Theater, film still.

99

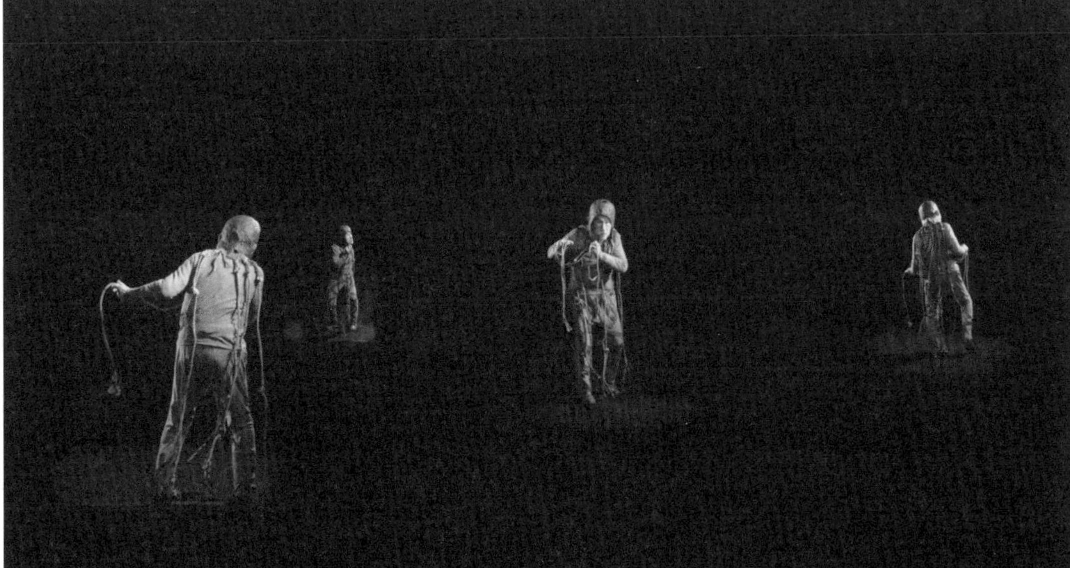

10 Christiaan Bastiaans, *Valuable Cargo*, 2019, live performance, Takamatsu Theater, film still.

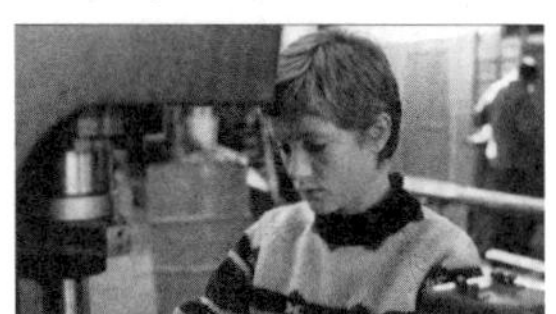

12 Jean-Luc Godard, *Passion*,
1982, film, 88′, film still.

addition: Yin (passive, feminine) and Yang (masculine,
active) are naturally opposite forces that do, however, comple-
ment each other. One can't exist without the other; they
depend upon one another.' Dynamism in Balance and
Stillness in Movement are exercise forms in Taikiken, the
discipline of Great Ki Boxing. 'Small movement better than
big movement; no movement better than small movement.'
Bastiaans took up his Budo training again—in his twenties
he practiced on daily basis. He is taught by Jan Kallenbach
Kyoshi Master Teacher in Taikiken (1943–2021). 'It was in
the late 1960s or early 1970s that I saw a photograph in *Times
Magazine* of Yukio Mishima as Kendoist with the caption:
"Ashes from Mt. Fuji —the Temple of Dawn." Shortly afterwards I bought Miyamoto Musashi's *A Book of Five Rings*
(*Go Rin No Sho*). Back then, still dormant, these nebulous
figures announced themselves: Shuji Terayama, Yoshi Oida
& Co and of course Jan Kallenbach.'[11]

Bastiaans wants to integrate his Budo into his work.
What does it mean? *Laboratories of Empire* proposes a narrative that makes me think of medieval allegory: the depiction
of the conflict between vices and virtues as a battle of opposing souls (Psychomachia). *Laboratories of Empire* stages such
a conflict. The opera's final act is a standoff between militia
members of the *Imperial Revivalists* and members of the
Unaffiliated Commune: only an act of grace can save them
and their world. The *Hurt Models* give a performance to sof-
ten the soldiers' deadly stance. What will their gestures look
like? What song will they sing? In Godard's *Passion* (1982),
soft power wins at the end. A filmmaker has to abandon his
film, but in return receives the love of a Marxist factory
worker. Isabelle compares the gestures of work to the gestures
of love, proposing they are rather alike.[12]

The combative element (war fever) needs spiritual

counterpoise. Pondering grace and serenity, I see Bastiaans' *Hurt Models* before me: *Scarlet*'s dance of vulnerability, the *Blind Man*'s walk as he listens to his stones tapped together: echoes tell him if objects are nearby.[13] Grace also finds an original expression in his large testimonial photograph *Körper zur Beobachtungs Station IX, April is the Cruellest Month (Cairo, 9 April 2011)*.[14] Taken on Tahrir Square by the artist, almost three months after the Egyptian Revolution (25 January 2011), it captures the moment after an army officer's blood has been spilled; he had joined the anti-government protests of the common people. His badges must have been cut off; they lie on the ground in pliers. Two hands hold up the bullet shells: his blood has soaked the soil. Unwound barbed wire invokes a biblical image: the crown of thorns. The work's title is telling: Körper zur Beobachtungs Station translates as 'body (or bodies) to observation station'. This reads like code: start the operation; take this body to that place, as swiftly as possible! But we can also read it differently: be patient, stay here, behold this ghost!

Kanze's *Sumida-gawa* ends with redemption. When the ferryman peddles his boat across the river, he tells the woman about a long-awaited Buddhist invocation on the other side. It is dedicated to a young boy, Umewakamura, who was left here by a slave trader. People tried to save him but it was too late. From his deathbed, the boy asked them to bury him at this spot, and remember him in a year's time. Thus, the woman can finally say goodbye to her son. As his restless spirit leaves the tomb mount for a second, to manifest himself invisibly at his ceremony in front of the people, she soothes the ghost.

Laboratories of Empire ends in a similar way. The *Hurt Models* perform a Dance of Grace and sing a Song of Solace, as gifts to the world. The healing powers of their art conjure

13 *Scarlet* appears as a living character in the video installation *Pharmacy Deux Milles* (2015); *Blind Man* is a character in the video installation *Valuable Cargo* (2019).

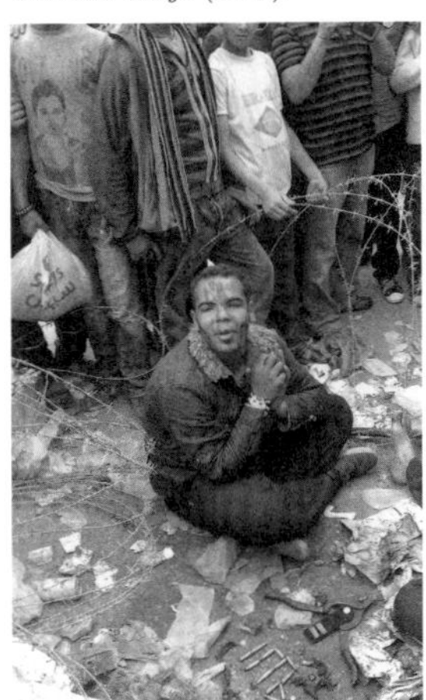

14 Christiaan Bastiaans, *Körper zur Beobachtungs Station IX, April is the Cruellest Month (Cairo, 9 April 2011)*, 2011, photograph.

15 Samuel Beckett, *Molloy, Malone Dies, The Unnamable*, London, Calder, 1955, p. 27.

inner peace. In the modern Western tradition, such magical thinking is looked upon with scepticism. Samuel Beckett kept the question, as to the might of the spell, open. His character Molloy says:

> Yes, the whole thing is to know what saint to implore, any fool can implore him. [...] It's for the whole that there seems to be no spell. Perhaps there is no whole, before you're dead. An opiate for the life of the dead, that should be easy. What am I waiting for then, [the spell] to exorcize mine? It's coming, it's coming. I hear from here the howl resolving all, even if it is not mine.[15]

In his stories and plays, Beckett integrated his experience of the Second World War and Reconstruction era's poverty. To him, incantation was like news from a far planet. Today, filmmaker Alejandro Jodorowsky continues the practice. In his latest films—*The Dance of Reality* (2013) and *Endless Poetry* (2016) tell the tales of his dominant father, and of himself as a young poet—a comely opera star does it: the Mother sings her lines: 'Oh, Alejandro'. Where Jodorowsky is an Artist of the Sun, Bastiaans is One of the Moon.

> Experimenting...
> I hung the moon
> On various
> Branches of the pine
> —Tachibana Hokushi

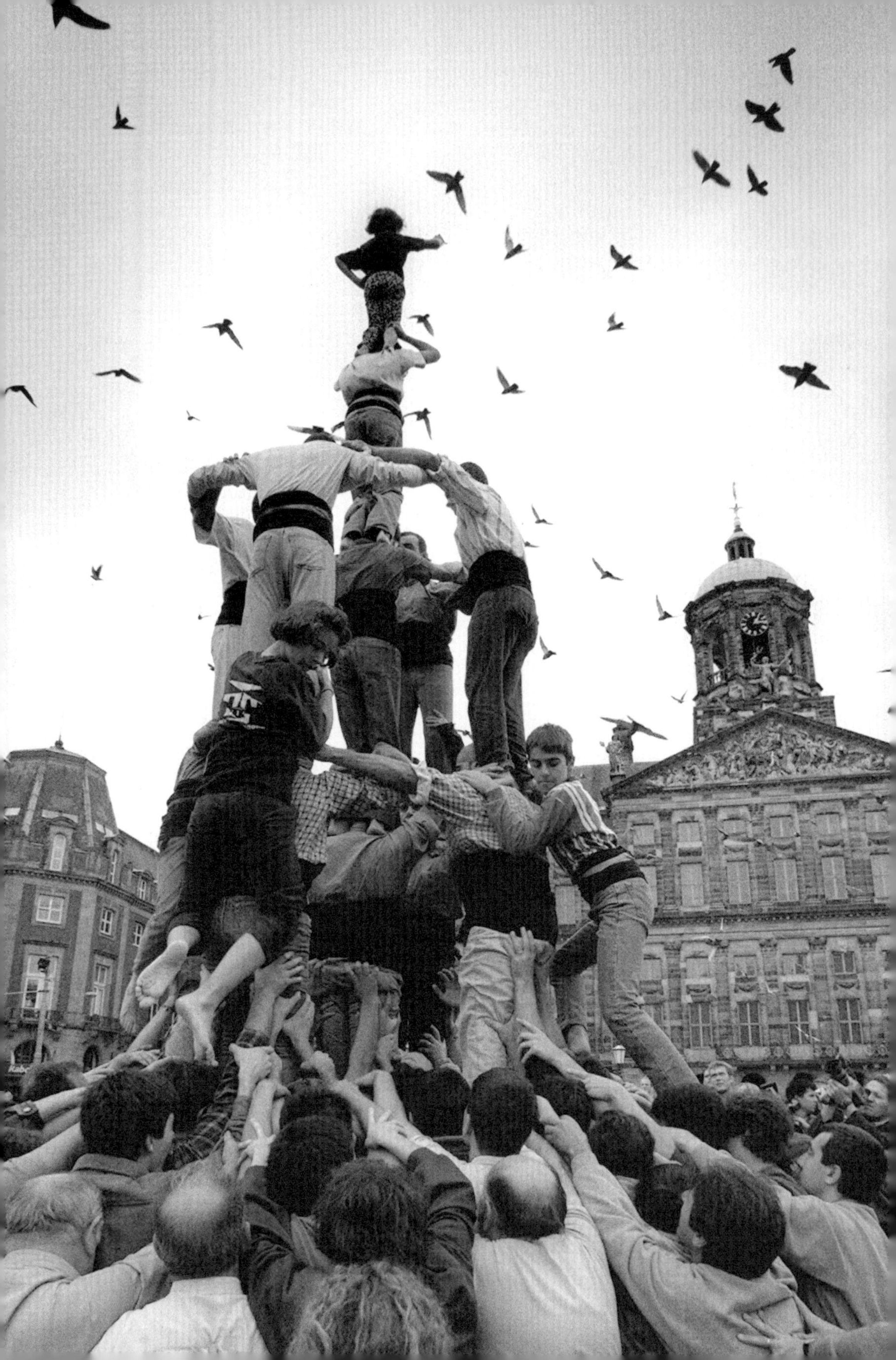

Trust and Terror

Alicia Framis

The interview with Alicia Framis took place in the summer of 1998 when she participated in 'Manifesta 2' in Luxembourg. In her performance *Dreamkeepers* (1998) she would go to a stranger's house and, equipped with a protective garment-as-bed, keep watch over that person in the night. Our email conversation is followed by a text written by Alicia Framis on her contribution to 'Pictures for the Blue Room', an exhibition that I curated in the Vigeland Museum, Oslo, for the Nordic Institute for Contemporary Art, in that year.

1 Alicia Framis, *The Dreamkeepers*, 1998, performance.

Conversation with Alicia Framis

MARK KREMER   Let's start with *Dreamkeepers*, the performance you did in Amsterdam and New York this year, and which you are currently doing in Luxembourg as part of 'Manifesta 2'. You wear a special nightdress when you are at people's homes, and you interact with them.[1] What is your motive for wanting to do this piece?

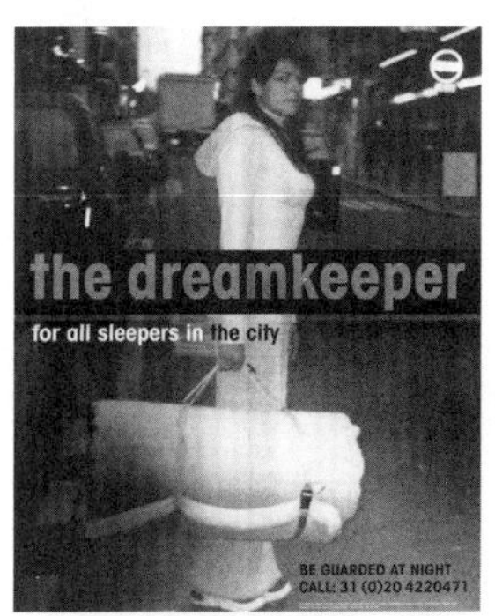

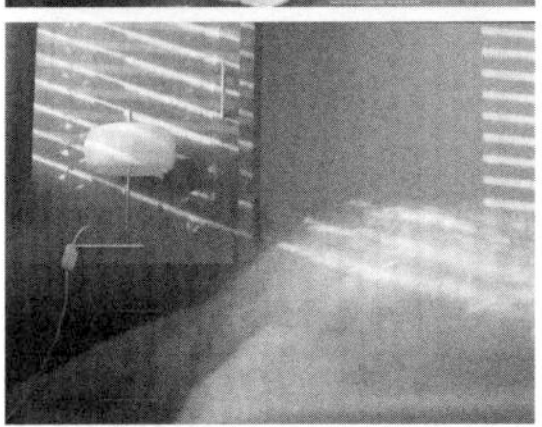

105

Alicia Framis, *Walking Monument*, 1997, Dam Square, Amsterdam, performance involving 300 people as a living monument for 2.5 minutes.

ALICIA FRAMIS   I wanted to watch over the dreams of people who live alone. I go to a stranger's home, and I'm so afraid of them it always brings a sweat out in me. There is no system for relating to strangers, so I concentrate on acting as a mirror for the other person. Each time I go through someone's door and into their bedroom, the situation becomes completely unpredictable and different from what I was expecting. Obviously, it's a piece about loneliness, which is such a phenomenon of our time. Cities make people in the industrialized countries lonely and unhappy, particularly in the North. There's always an energy that's generated by my encounters, and it can sometimes be quite impressive. Who was it who said that the revolution begins in the kitchen?

MK   You told me about your interest in Situationism. Do you see a relation between the performance and with the ideas of the Situationist movement?

AF   With *Dreamkeepers*, I want to dismantle the difference between the spectator and the artist, and break down the Greek theatre situation, where there's an audience and the actors determine what they're allowed to see. I'm not interested in that kind of power game; I want to create a situation of real equality. When I go to people's homes, there's no predetermined relationship of any kind, except for the inevitable fear of the unknown. We're both involved in the same play of forces; they could surprise me, hurt me, kill me even, but then they're also vulnerable themselves and I'm on their territory, so there's an equality. I think it's time to change our systems of power and put more emphasis on the two-person nucleus; there's a great deal of potential in the encounter between two people.

MK   Did this desire to erase the difference between the spectator and the artist also play a part in *Walking Monument*, the piece you created in Amsterdam?[2]

AF   Yes. I wanted to create a monument where the spectators, the pedestal and the sculpture formed a single unit, even if it was only for two minutes. It was very much an attempt to bridge the gap between people. For example, the Situationists believed in the possibility of creating a society, which is not really the case with me. I believe more in experiencing life through encounters with other people; I'm more interested in the person who sells me my cigarettes every day, the Portuguese guy I buy my cheese from, the façades of banks, the fact that no one smiles in the street. Sex is not the purpose of these encounters between people, though there is a certain eroticism involved; there's an attraction in finding out about the other person. And it works both ways. I'm thinking of that phrase: when I'm with another person, I love them for who I am.

MK   What experience has made the biggest impression on you in doing *Dreamkeepers*?

AF   When I sleep with a stranger, when I set up my bed beside theirs, there's a feeling of both trust and terror. I wait in the darkness for them to fall asleep, and I can hear them breathing and the sheets rustling when they turn over, and then comes a point when it's as though they're no longer there, and then there's a feeling of loss which I imagine is very close to that of death. I feel alone, I wander round the house, I make things, I write and sew in their absence while I wait for them to wake up.

107

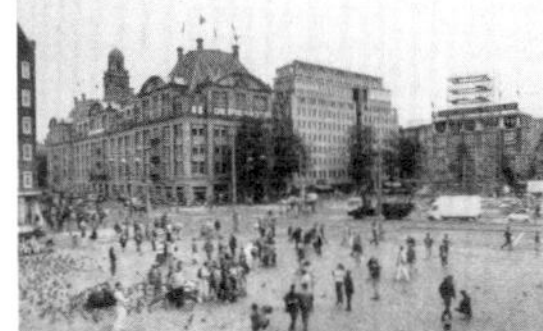
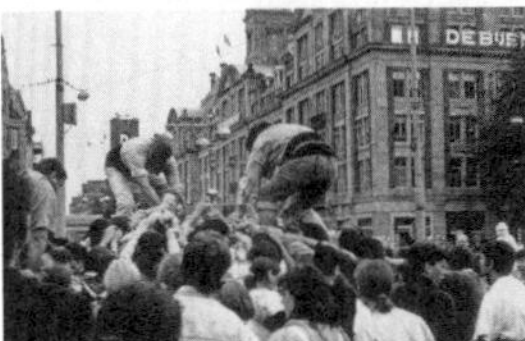
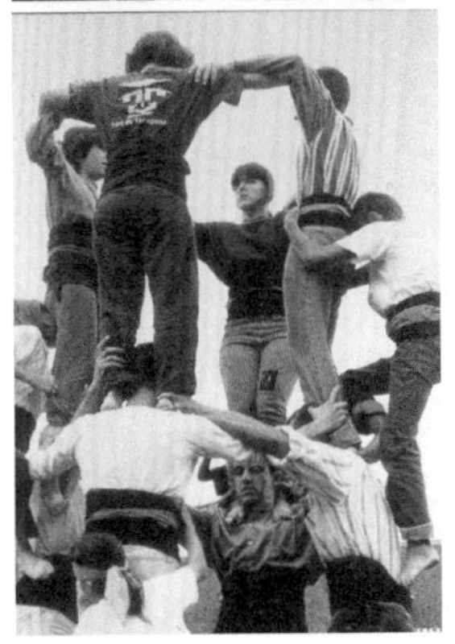
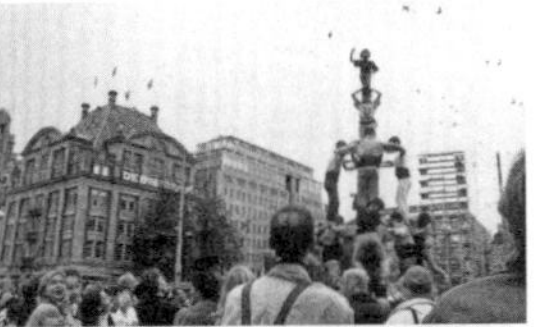
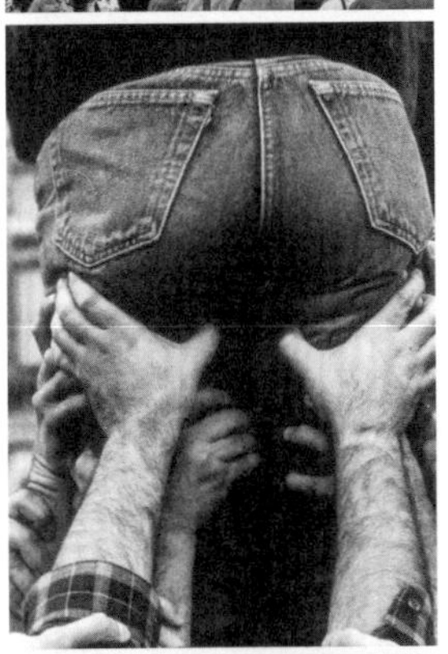
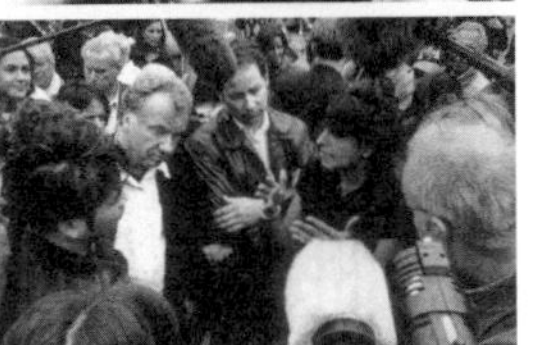

2   Alicia Framis, *Walking Monument*, 1997, performance.

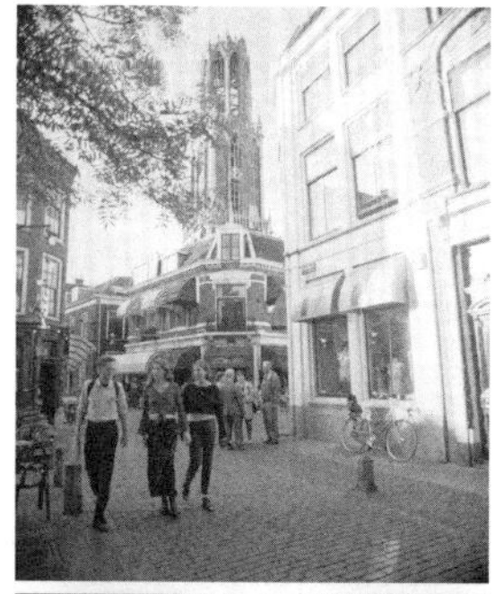

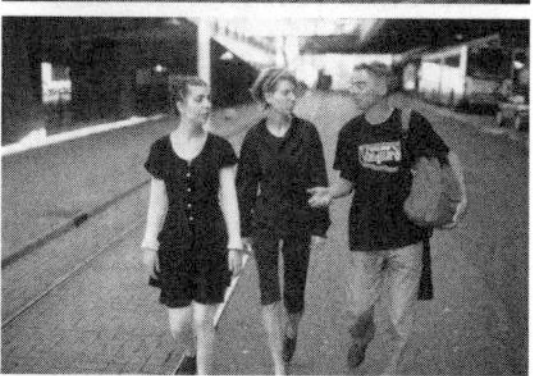

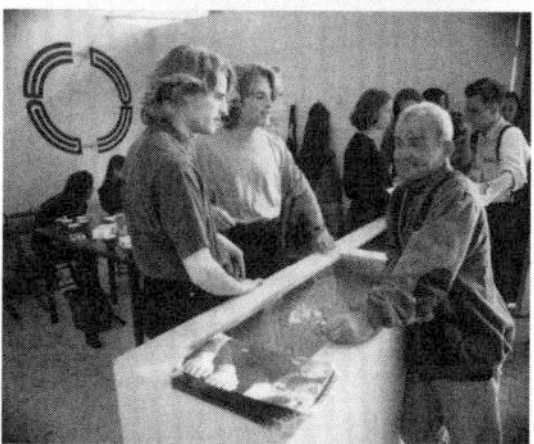

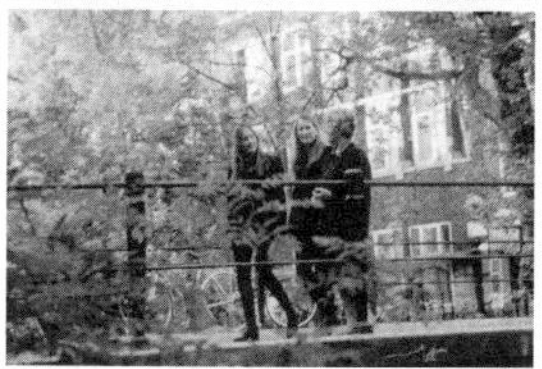

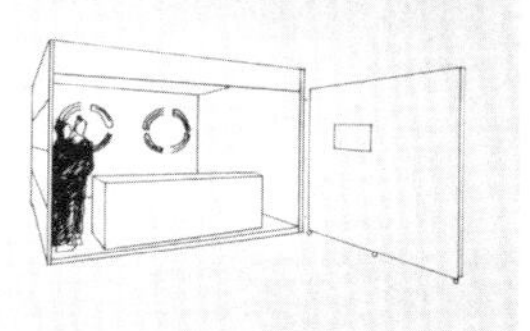

3 Alicia Framis, *Compagnie de Compagnie*, 1996.

There's one other thing that makes me sad, and that's women who are dependent on food, women who starve due to lack of affection and deal with loneliness by raiding the fridge, using food as consolation for their emotional dramas. Men are different: they hide their shame by drinking themselves into a stupor.

MK   You say loneliness is a serious problem at the moment. You have done other pieces that depict or offer a counterweight to loneliness, such as *Compagnie de Compagnie* (1996), *Cinema Solo* (1997) and *Hijas sin Hijas* (Girls without Girls, 1997). What's the link between these pieces?

AF   What they have in common is loneliness in relation to other people because of their presence or absence. For example, in the case of *Compagnie de Compagnie* you could borrow a pair of twins to go for a walk in the street with you, or to come to your home, or just go wandering.[3] The experience meant that you had to confront your loneliness because of the oneness that existed between the twins. In the video *Cinema Solo* my own solitude is emphasized by someone's absence—perhaps they are already dead—and I used a window-dresser's dummy to embody this. In *Hijas sin Hijas*, I show a hundred women who've chosen to live alone talking about their situation: what will they leave behind when they die? This decision not to have children, the absence of self-reproduction, means that women question the meaning of life in a different way.

MK   How has your confrontation with loneliness developed?

A F   In *Compagnie de Compagnie*, I wanted to highlight an architectural problem of the 1980s, which was the habit of turning shops into interiors; it's still the case in the Nordic countries. So, if you're on your way to the station, for example, you have to absorb all the products in the shop windows, but then at six o'clock when the shops close, the junkies and the homeless go and live in the doorways to keep warm. You get this real feeling of a poverty-stricken urban desert; it's a kind of loneliness in situ. But now, three years after I did that piece, I prefer to go and stay with people because there's no way out; you're inside someone's mind. It's as though they're naked, and so am I; there's nothing more extreme than sharing a house with a stranger for eight hours.

M K   To what extent does loneliness result in the creation of your work?

A F   My point of departure is the impossibility of reaching out to other people, but my work allows me to depict the distance between me and the other person. I spend days or even months exploring this distance. I imagine work as having a social effect because I'm doing something in the world, I'm intervening, but it's always based on this impossibility of coming close to anyone and this terrible fear of loss; it's a reaction to the architecture I inhabit and cohabit.

M K   Do you think that in the entertainment society, art has lost some of its intimacy—for example, the intimacy you feel in old paintings like interiors and portraits? Are you withdrawing from the realm of spectacle with *Dreamkeepers*?

A F   Yes. Entertainment is aimed at the mass of people, not the individual; it's someone else's dream that they've

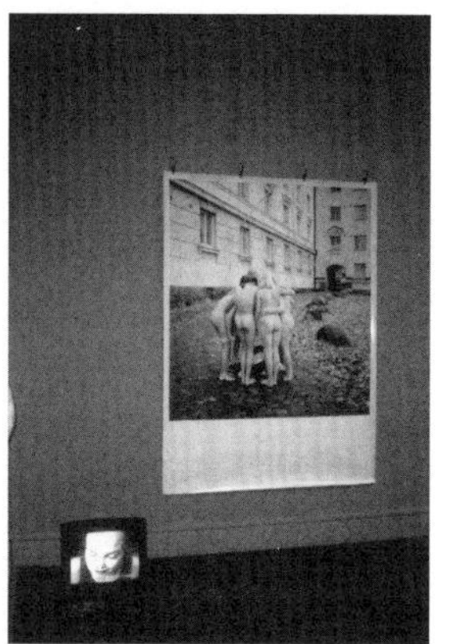

4 Alicia Framis, *Before Your Name*, 1998, photograph and video.

constructed for you. With entertainment, you sacrifice your own personality and submit yourself to a myth that's handed to you on a plate. The one place where you can really dream freely, away from all the alienation created by the entertainment society, is in people's homes. But this is not a happy story per se. Architect Adolf Loos said that in the home, everyone is an actor on their own stage. Everyone has their own tragedy. Every object tells you something about the person, their memories and desires; they're a means of constructing the self. In entertainment, you always want to identify with the myth, but you can never go beyond it. For example, that's the problem with women and advertising: they can come close to the ideal feminine image, but they can never improve on it, and I think this alienation is dangerous. Whereas when I go to strangers' homes, there's no way they can identify with me.

MK   You're now preparing a project for the exhibition 'Pictures for the Blue Room' in Oslo, in which you'll be photographing a group of naked young girls, posing side by side with their backs to the camera. It is an image that that appears in a sculpture by Gustav Vigeland, who was fascinated by nudity and created a body of work that could be described as a monumental representation of intimacy. Can you tell us about your new work?

AF   I want to recreate the sculpture, which shows a group of five naked girls in the street.[4] They'll be thirteen years old. Nudity in sculpture has always been a form of representation where everything is perfectly modelled and a travesty of real life. In Vigeland's sculpture, for once, the nude body is not treated as a representation of a fantasy. The girls are themselves; they have no pretences, and the strength they project transforms the stone into a glorious monument. They have their backs to the spectator, and I imagine them sharing some sort of secret in the space between their bodies. At the same time, it's the only way you can look at naked children of that age without robbing them of their dignity. We're always hearing about girls disappearing and being raped or killed, but seeing them in the street naked, just with each other and with this very ordinary softness, they'll be fragile, stripped to their essentials. I'm trying to confront the more powerful reality of the personal reverie and the secret.

MK   I think art is a way of keeping secrets, and at the same time telling them to other people.

AF   I like that definition. It certainly applies to me, particularly with *Murmur*, a piece I recently did for the civic centre at Serre di Rapolano in Italy. I made five hundred holes in the wall of a room, and got visitors to write down a private wish or desire in invisible ink on a piece of paper and then put it in one of the holes.

Eventually, the wall will be covered over again and become simply the wall of an exhibition hall, but it'll be hiding people's secrets. To me, secrecy is about intimacy. Being confronted by a blank wall and putting in a piece of paper with nothing visible on it is an act without purpose, but it's totally personal, unique and invisible. I wanted *Murmur* to give people a chance to sit down and think about what they really wanted. In that sense, it's a very positive work; it's up to you what you put into the wall of the museum. The wall becomes a mirror of your own imagination. It reminds you that in your own personal imagination, it's you who is the star.

III

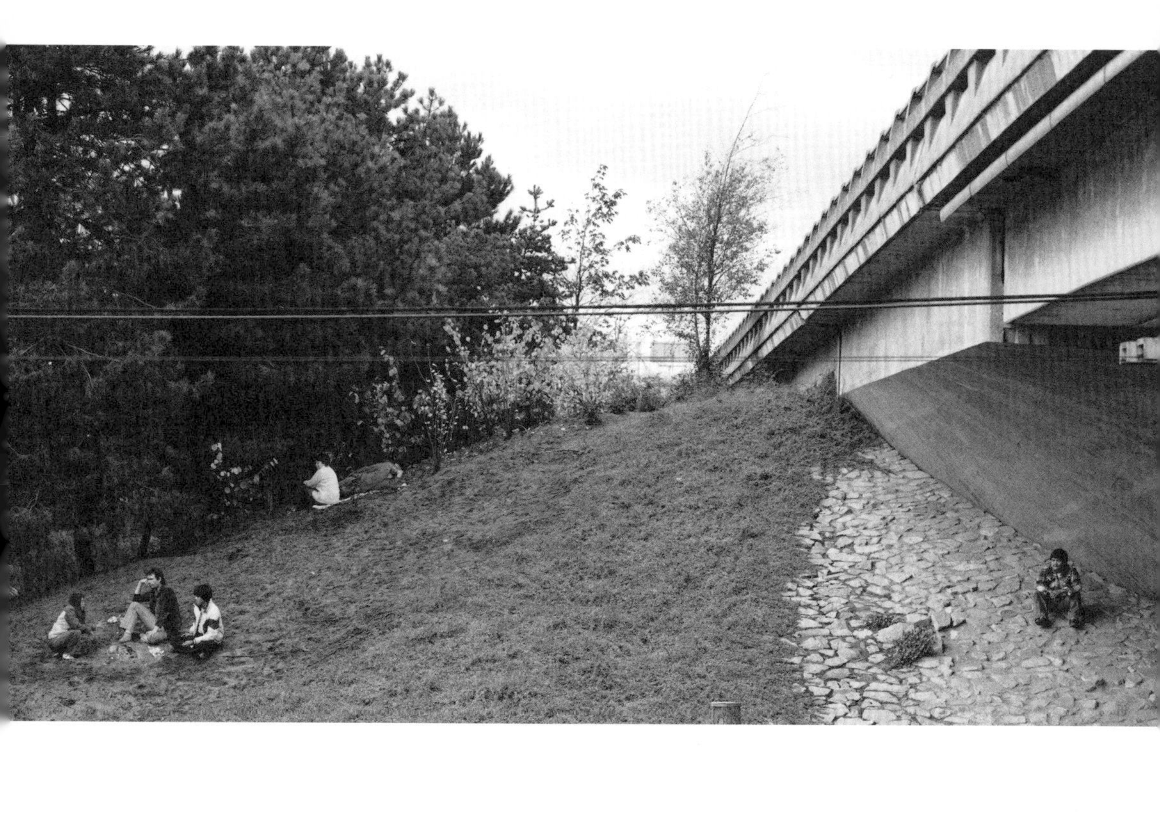

In Search of Ghost Notes

Jeff Wall

1 Peter Sloterdijk, *Critique of Cynical Reason*, trans. Michael Eldred, Minneapolis, University of Minnesota Press, 1987 [1983], p. xxxvi.

Adorno dedicated a well-known essay to Heinrich Heine, *Die Wunde Heine* ('The Sore, Heine'). Out of the self-healing of deep sores come critiques that serve epochs as rallying points for self-knowledge. Every critique is pioneering work on the pain of the times ('Zeitschmerz') and a piece of exemplary healing.
—Peter Sloterdijk, *Critique of Cynical Reason*[1]

I

I wish to discuss some recent works by the Canadian artist Jeff Wall (Vancouver, 1946) such as *Dead Troops Talk (A Vision after an Ambush of a Red Army Patrol near Moqor, Afghanistan, Winter 1986)* (1991–1992), *Adrian Walker, artist, drawing from a specimen in a laboratory in the Dept. of Anatomy at the University of British Columbia, Vancouver* (1992), and *Restoration* (1993). I will discuss the changing relation between Wall's work and his engagement with art history. Current literature mostly emphasizes Wall's use of highly advanced digital techniques, to make his photographic

Jeff Wall, *The Storyteller*, 1986, transparency in lightbox, 229 × 437 cm.

2 'Wall Pieces: Jeff Wall interviewed by Patricia Bickers', *Art Monthly*, No. 9, 1994, p. 3.

3 'Representation, Suspicions and Critical Transparency: An Interview with Jeff Wall by T.J. Clark, Serge Guilbaut and Anne Wagner', *Parachute*, No. 59, 1990, p. 8.

4 'I am not necessarily interested in different subject matter, but rather in different types of pictures: Jeff Wall interviewed by Martin Schwander', *Jeff Wall: Restauration*, Basel, 1994, p. 22. Reprinted in: Thierry de Duve et al, *Jeff Wall*, London, Phaidon, 1996, pp. 126–139.

works, and the continuous inspiration that he finds in nineteenth-century painting. But these explanations do not suffice to really clarify Wall's recent change of course and new choice of subject matter.

Wall is a visual artist and erudite art historian. He has been teaching art history at art academies and university faculties since 1974. In his view, art history is above all an instrument to augment our knowledge. He has often discussed historical paintings—predominantly nineteenth-century French ones—that served as reference points for his works, but he has also said that the experience of art works, and making that experience productive in the present, is something that happens on a primary level. In his words: 'I feel that my experience of a work, which may be centuries old, still takes place here and now. And so to that extent that work is contemporary art'.[2]

Wall is fascinated by visual typology. In 1990 he observed:

> I think the process of experience of a work is controlled, above all, by genre, by the generic character of the picture-types and types of subjects. Bakhtin said that genre was the collective, accumulated meaning of things that has come through time and the mutations of social orders. It is the foundation of the guarantee of objectivity, the basis of the 'truth content' of representations.[3]

Later he expanded this notion:

> The curious thing about the phenomenon of genre is that it operates whether the artist is very much conscious of it or not. That is what Bakhtin was referring to when he spoke about it as an aspect of what he called 'collective memory'.[4]

Taking these observations as a starting point, what can we say about the three works that were mentioned above: a landscape where a strange war scene unfolds, a portrait of a draftsman at work, and an interior of a huge museum space showing repair works on a historical painting?

Wall's interest in the typology of images, in what genre representations achieve, extends beyond an art historical preoccupation. It can be understood in tandem with his statement on the liberty that artists (should) take in their view of the past and the way they bring that experience into the present. Wall chooses to make graphical, demonstratively realistic pictures, because of their built-in function: the capacity to preserve tradition and lore.[5] That is the actual subject of these works. Through them, Wall asks a topical question: how can we maintain our cultural heritage and keep this alive?

Restoration shows the repair works on the Bourbaki Panorama in Lucerne.[6] This painting was made by Edouard Castres, an artist who, as Wall suggests, had one major experience in his life: military service under general Charles-Denis Bourbaki in the French army. Towards the end of the Franco-Prussian War (1870–71), the French Armée de l'Est had to retreat to Switzerland, where they were offered asylum. Castres painted a white, mountainous winter landscape; scattered troops are awaiting transport to new destinations, a train of wagons is stand-by. Wall's photograph focuses on the panorama's recent restoration; although the repair works have been in place since 1977, he staged his scene. Three restorers linger in a vast space. One woman observes the work from a distance on the ground; she has a folder in her hand. A second woman gazes into space, absent-mindedly. Only the third woman is doing manual work on a minuscule surface to which sheets of white paper are attached. The picture's greys

5 Michael Newman, 'The True Appearance of Jeff Wall's Pictures', *Jeff Wall*, Tilburg, De Pont Stichting, 1994.

115

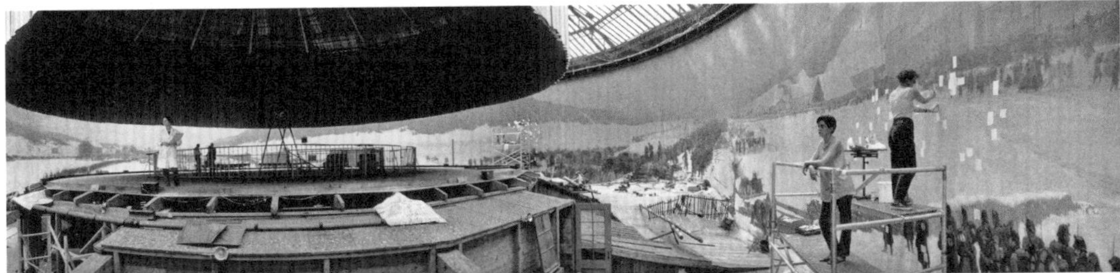

6 Jeff Wall, *Restoration*, 1993, transparency in lightbox, 119 × 490 cm

and blues create a melancholy air. In 1993, Wall addressed the work's symbolism as follows:

> I was interested in the massiveness of the task the figures are undertaking. That for me was an important part of the theme. There might be associations of that massiveness with the futility of ever bringing the past into the 'now'.[7]

The restorers seem detached from their surroundings. Their aloofness and especially their self-absorption invite other symbolical readings. Today I associate it with the silent contemplation of the hesychast navel gazers, the ascetic monks of Mount Athos. Reverie is an important theme in Wall's oeuvre, the figure of the dreamer/thinker a recurring personage. The work that illustrates that in a clear and wondrous way is *The Thinker* (1986), where a pondering figure sits at the edge of urban scenery, his pose reflecting that of Rodin's *Thinker*. Rodin's sculpture, called *The Poet*, was originally part of a commission, which he completed in 1880, for the doorway surround *The Gates of Hell*. In Wall's work, the thinker has lost his ground, he sits on a slab of concrete stacked on the road side, a sabre protruding from his back. Wall borrowed this saliant element from Dürer's *Peasant's Column* (1525), the proposal for a monument that would recall the German Peasants' War. Wall's dreamer/thinker, plunged in thought at the edge of town, suggests that we should uphold this figure, place him on a pedestal—are thinking and dreaming not vital for how we shape our reality?

Dead Troops Talk, Adrian Walker… and *Restoration* defy the typical demarcations between genres. The works depict a landscape, a portrait and an interior. But in each of them are elements of the 'nature morte' (still life)! *Dead Troops Talk* is a fictional scene with thirteen Soviet soldiers

116

who, having been slain by the Afghan mujahideen, rise up from the dead.[8] This scene has a Goyaesque excess. In the first instance you think it is a documentary, deadpan picture of the fallout of war. But that reading is immediately invalidated by lavish details: in particular the startled expressions on the soldiers' faces, accentuated by whitish makeup. The composition recalls baroque paintings where the image has exploded and colourful figures enter space. Here these figures are grey and morose, dead yet living, alive but in a dead way. The soldiers' grimaces indicate an overwhelming disorientation. *Adrian Walker…* is, in contrast to *Dead Troops Talk*, a picture that conveys an enormous stillness. We see a crafts-man-artist engrossed in his work.[9] The master's hand draws the dead hand lying before him. The scene is harmonious but also uncanny, which has everything to do with this artist's ambition.

Wall is interested in radical specificity. He wants to sharpen the function of genres so that they can be used as vehicles for cultural criticism. This aim supersedes the social critique articulated by Wall in the 1980s, which would typically transpire in works conceived as social situations, where a shady man would stand out in a splendid setting, on the brink of doing mischief, or caught in the act (e.g., *Doorpusher*, 1984). Wall's later works are meditations on how images work. His goal much broader: raising awareness about the state of our civilization. In our era, where the abundancy of information has hacked everyday imagination, the theme of our cultural legacy is urgent. Where a society faces amnesia (there is too much to know) and the lessons from the past are no longer heard, freedom wanes. People lose the capacity to connect with the present. Where Wall, in the 1980s, depicted individuals suffering from a lack of freedom, later works show a dark side that threatens the collective. *Restauration* and

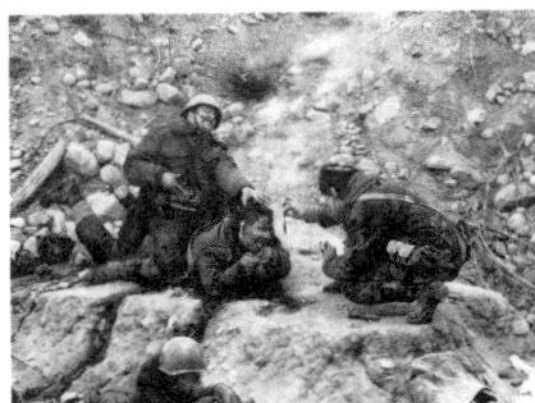

8 Jeff Wall, *Dead Troops Talk (A Vision after an Ambush of a Red Army Patrol near Moqor, Afghanistan, Winter 1986)*, 1991–1992, transparency in lightbox, detail, 219 × 417 cm.

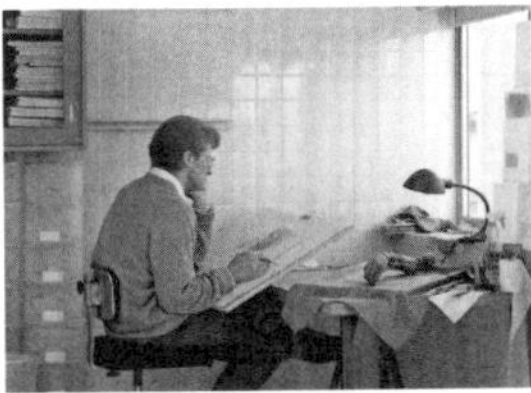

9 Jeff Wall, *Adrian Walker, artist, drawing from a specimen in a laboratory in the Dept. of Anatomy at the University of British Columbia, Vancouver*, 1992, transparency in lightbox, 119 × 164 cm.

10 'Typology, Luminiscence, Freedom: Excerpts from a Conversation between Els Barents and Jeff Wall', *Jeff Wall: Transparencies*, München, Schirmer/Mosel, 1986, p. 102.

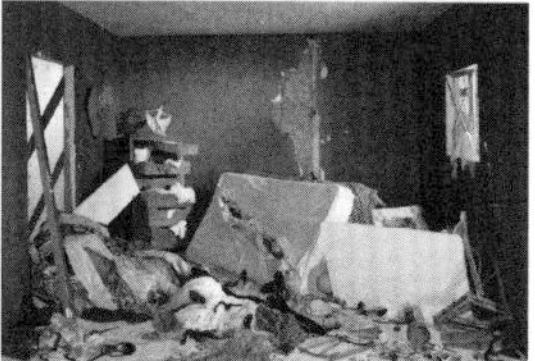

11 Jeff Wall, *The Destroyed Room*, 1978, transparency in lightbox, 159 × 234 cm.

Adrian Walker... could be considered incantations of cultural amnesia.

For a better understanding of these two works, and of *Dead Troops Talk*, I wish to return to the start of Jeff Wall's career. The official chronicle states that he exhibited for the first time in group shows in 1969–73, followed by a four-year retreat, in which he taught at art schools and studied art history at the Courtauld Institute in London. In 1978, Wall exhibited the 'first' work in his signature technique.

In my opinion, Wall is currently confronting the rigidity of his oeuvre. He distances himself from the ideological severity that is the basis of certain works from the 1980s. Consider for example the poignant picture *Milk* (1984), where a dairy carton bursts open in the hand of a man sitting on the sidewalk, his posture an expression of both passivity and aggression. The work shows a frozen dialectic. A contradiction comes to light that, as Wall has observed, raises the problem of freedom and the lack thereof.[10] A human desire to break the isolation is literally embodied in an exploding object.

2

The Destroyed Room: that is the title of the light box produced by Jeff Wall in 1978 with a Cibachrome transparent depicting a scene staged and subsequently photographed in his studio. This work is the first in a series of meticulously composed and photographed pictures in which Wall draws attention to the wounds of Western culture in the era of late capitalism, and alludes to their potential healing.[11]

Wall's image of a ravaged and partially destroyed room, which must belong to a young woman, is an allegory of an assault. In 1978, Wall exhibited *The Destroyed Room* for the first time in the window of an art gallery in Vancouver. Without entering the space, from the street, passers-by could see the image of a bedroom marked by traces of violence. Day and night, the tableau of silent destruction lit up the city. In the middle of shop windows, traffic signs and neon advertising, suddenly there was a brightly coloured image of an intimate space, the red wallpaper of which is slashed in two places and ripped away at a third spot, where a chest of drawers has been opened with brute force, furniture is lying around in disarray, personal items lie on the floor. But the scene's most striking aspect is the upturned bed with the ripped mattress resting on it. At the centre of the picture, a pink gash jumps out.

This opening invites various readings. We are looking at the female sex, an icon of desire, and at a wound, symbol for the damage inflicted on a person and moreover on the social tissue—in part, that must have been the reason why Wall presented his work to the city, open and naked. But the gash is also a place of promise. Female lust, possibly the object of the outburst of violence, is inextricably bound with the life-giving organ of the womb, a healing principle.

The work's pictorial organization is very severe. But *The Destroyed Room* refers to loss of control: the moment when a tantrum, an act of revenge, or perhaps even a whim determined the actions of an invisible perpetrator. Paradoxically, control determined the work's entire pre-production; attention to the tiniest details led to exquisite stylization. The missing factor thus decides its surface structure.

Control is also crucial in the presentation. The light box encloses a Cibachrome transparent print like a permeable membrane protecting the scene, illuminating it from the inside. The work's destination, the gallery window, functions

12 Dan Graham, 'The Destroyed Room of Jeff Wall', *Real Life Magazine*, No. 3, 1980, p. 5.

13 Camiel van Winkel, 'Blind Figures', *Archis*, No. 12, 1994, p. 65.

like a shop window. Dan Graham, in his essay on Wall's *The Destroyed Room,* writes that works of art and commercial wares displayed in showcases resemble each other, in the way they produce and control lust.[12] Both object types extend the capitalist apparatus that regulates human behaviour through (invisible) systems of representation.

In his first work, Wall uses every opportunity to point out that we are facing an apparatus that uses and replicates similar systems of representation. First, he exposes the construction of his picture. The image of the bedroom is interrupted by several openings. On the left, behind a doorframe, a white studio wall is revealed. There are two support beams here, a third one has entered the set. To the right, as part of the set, there is a barred window and behind it a glimpse of the sky. Second, Wall employs a material construction to present his scene. Doing so, he somehow imitates the modus operandi of the (invisible) capitalist apparatus. The control-mechanism for the light box is hidden from view.[13] Third, Wall has placed his light box in a second container, the art gallery. His use of the window resonates with the commanding perspective system of the Renaissance artists.

The historical reference point of *The Destroyed Room* is Eugène Delacroix's *The Death of Sardanapalus* (1827). This Romanticist painting shows the last king of Assyria lying in a languid pose on a large bed draped with red fabric; he awaits his death while the women of his seraglio are raped and murdered before his very eyes. The dominating colour in the work is an intense red which gives the depicted space a sensual, jewel-like ambiance. Wall saw the colour on reproductions of Pompeii's *Villa of the Mysteries*. This same red was adopted by neoclassicism as a colour denoting restrained passion.

Wall's image of sublime destruction has, in my view, a pendant in *The Polar Sea* (1824) by Caspar David Friedrich, a work from Northern Romanticism, on which the bow of a ship that has been blocked in its watery course sticks out like a toy between gigantic piles of pack ice. The calmness with which Friedrich imagines the polar disaster might be even closer to the mood suggested in *The Destroyed Room*. Wall's work actually seems to create distance to his historical source. This outcome, 'the productivity of creative misreadings' as it was called by the great literary critic Harold Bloom, deserves more attention in the reception of Wall's art.

The Destroyed Room is an academic exercise. The organization of its elements has been taken to the extreme. Because of a surplus of meaningful moments, the comparison with an infernal machine that may explode at a moment only known to its maker, presents itself. Blissful oblivion would then set in. Now we are looking at a stifled and in a certain sense lifeless picture: a 'tableau mort'.

Exaggerated structuring is a typical characteristic of allegory. In an important essay from the 1980s, the American critic Craig Owens proposed that this historical trope was revivified through works of artists such as Sherrie Levine, Robert Longo, and Cindy Sherman.[14] Owens perceives allegory as a redemptive trope: it can save things that threaten to disappear in the vacuum of history. In times of transition, allegory can highlight objects, energies and dispositions—ways of thinking and being in the world—that may seem obsolete but actually help us understand what's happening around us. In visual art, allegory speaks as soon as one image is doubled: it is a supplement. Sherrie Levine's painted watercolours, made after faded colour reproductions of Mondrian's paintings, are an example.

14 Craig Owens, 'The Allegorical Impulse: Toward a Theory of Postmodernism', *October*, No. 12, 1980, pp. 67–86. Reprinted in: Craig Owens, *Beyond Recognition. Representation, Power, and Culture*, Berkeley, University of California Press, 1992, pp. 52–69.

Owens describes how allegory was suppressed in the nineteenth century at a certain point, and artists got a penchant for realism: art had to portray modern life. 'Il faut être de son temps' (You have to be up to date) was Baudelaire's advice to artists: art shouldn't concern itself with the dead past. Therefore, Courbet's project to preserve allegory in his realistic works was a stubborn move, going against the Zeitgeist. Courbet's ambition was thorny indeed. The past is both the project and the problem of allegory. But he recognized the peril of the past becoming a burden. His famous work *The Painter's Studio: A Real Allegory Summing Up Seven Years of my Artistic and Moral Life* (1854–1855) shows a naked woman who seems to have come from an earlier era: the proverbial, passive, artist's model. Here she is all attention and activity! Having joined the painter behind his easel, she watches him at work in the lavish studio space. In the tenebrous background a vague figure announces himself. Arms raised; he almost peters out in a pose of suffering. Courbet makes us feel his desire to awaken these figures, giving them a new purpose, commemorating them but by juxtaposing them with contemporary life.

In Wall's photographs, the fragments of the past are disguised. *The Destroyed Room* is a fine example. On the chest of drawers stands a white figurine echoing the Nike of Samothrace. The statue is untouched, in the bedroom it seems to be the only object that is still in its original place, as if archaic powers have protected it during the calamity. The dancer's grace is the sole unambiguous life sign in the tableau. Here, allegory gives way and the picture opens itself. Beauty has averted the complete disaster and a new hope is dawning.

I attach great importance to Wall's first opus, its ominous lure attracts me to this day, and I am not alone in the sensation.[15] Combining dense visual texture with a compelling narrative, the work set an impressive standard, which becomes visible in Wall's future productions. His masterpiece prompts classical questions. Can we say that an artist essentially makes the same work over and over? Is form subject to change while content basically stays the same? To what extent should artists shake off the weight of a firstling?

In his later works, Wall returns to *The Destroyed Room*, a serrated portrayal of the ancient energy of a destructive impulse as well as its counterpart: vitality. This dialectic is hidden under the picture's polished surface. Contrasts are camouflaged by a photography that shows all visual elements in an equally clear light. In my reading of the work, I have attempted to traverse its surface structure and illustrate its ambiguity: a sore *is* a life source (compare Parsival's wound); a streamlined device *is* an infernal machine, a frozen allegory *is* a sanguine picture. The opposites feed on each other, as in a natural symbiosis. With his firstling, Wall has tried to create a 'total' work of art. *The Destroyed Room* that takes its own structure and problematics as subject matter. The work is narcissistic through and through. In other words, this work is its own source.

A similar introspective tendency also typifies the works that I discussed above. *Dead Troops Talk* is a picture of a daytime nightmare: revenants scattered in an inhospitable landscape. The work mocks any pretence of conveying horrors in realistic images (the politics of newspapers and TV). Here, a war situation is portrayed as a dark opera. The visual language of the war scene is treated with hostility: the work

15 Sonic Youth, the experimental rock band from New York, adorned the cover of an album with Wall's photograph (*The Destroyed Room: B-Sides and Rarities*, Santa Monica, Geffen Records, 2006).

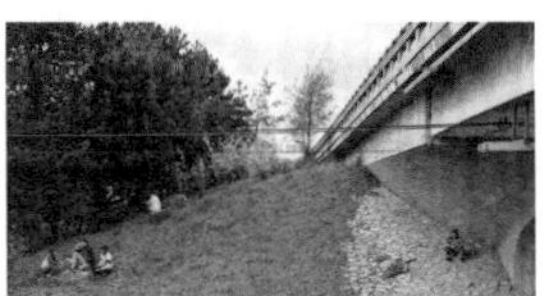
16 Jeff Wall, *The Storyteller*, 1986, transparency in lightbox, 229 × 437 cm.

embodies a petrified view on the genre. *Adrian Walker...* is a real allegory. The title almost redundantly describes what is depicted. In the composition the circular movement catches the eye, as a result of which the drawing hand is connected to the dead hand. This image shows the cycle of life. And it shows the project of art. Bringing the past into the present as a *specimen* means: keeping the memory alive. *Adrian Walker...* is a programmatic picture. That characterization also applies to *Restauration*, a meditation on (the structure and the importance of looking after) an image that passes on tradition in our time.

Now I wish to revisit a remarkable work from Wall's middle period, *The Storyteller* (1986), on which a bespectacled Indigenous woman, dressed in jeans and rain coat, addresses a small company at the edge of a forest across from a monumental overpass.[16] The woman is squatting and she supports her account with intense gestures. Two figures observe her from a distance, a third one is hiding under the overpass. In this work, there are various meaningful elements that take us on a trip. We watch a storyteller in action.

A palpable dialectic emerges here. The image splits, as it were, into two parts, both of which depict one culture. On the left is a strip of trees, peripheral nature, probably plotted by humans. On the right is the impressive overpass. Above the heads of the small human figures, a cable runs across the scenery, cutting the picture once more into two areas, adding a second division, and amplifying the sense of fragmentation and uprootedness. The role of the Indigenous woman is ambiguous. With her face turned towards the overpass, she's the link between an old culture that perhaps still retains its connection with nature and history, and the modern culture that is entirely focused on the future.

Throughout his career as a cultural critic, Walter Benjamin has investigated the connection between the archaic and modernity. Taking as his study object the fragments, vestiges and ruins of the nineteenth century—Benjamin called this the historically exfoliated material world (*Dingwelt*)—his intent was to ascertain how the archaic is embodied in modern phenomena. Benjamin had a special perspective on the physiognomy of an era. Concerning the nineteenth century, he was fascinated by the new urban figures: the flâneur, roulette player and sandwichman (someone who is walking around wearing cardboard advertising on the chest and back of his body). In a recent article Jürgen Habermas observes that Benjamin had given himself the task to decode two elements within modernity's archaic features: the destructive repetition of the old catastrophe, and a primal force aimed against modernity that could avert this destruction.[17] With that idea in mind, if we review *The Storyteller* once more, the storytelling woman could be casting a spell upon the reality to which she herself—despite her clothes, her glasses and the modern sneakers on her feet—does not want to belong: the encroaching modernity.

Wall's later works address the reality of life in a more nuanced and surprised way. Having left behind his conspicuous dialectic, these photographs point out contradictions and dilemmas lingering under the surface. Wall's view on the coherence between the old and the new—what Benjamin called the archaic element and modernity—has become more refined. As if he sees before him how the archaic has sunk into the deep layers of modernity. Aiming the gaze is what matters today. Then things will reveal their potential, hidden features will emerge, and the work will illuminate the world.

17 Jürgen Habermas, 'Das Falsche im Eigenen', *Die Zeit*, 23 September 1994, p. 77.

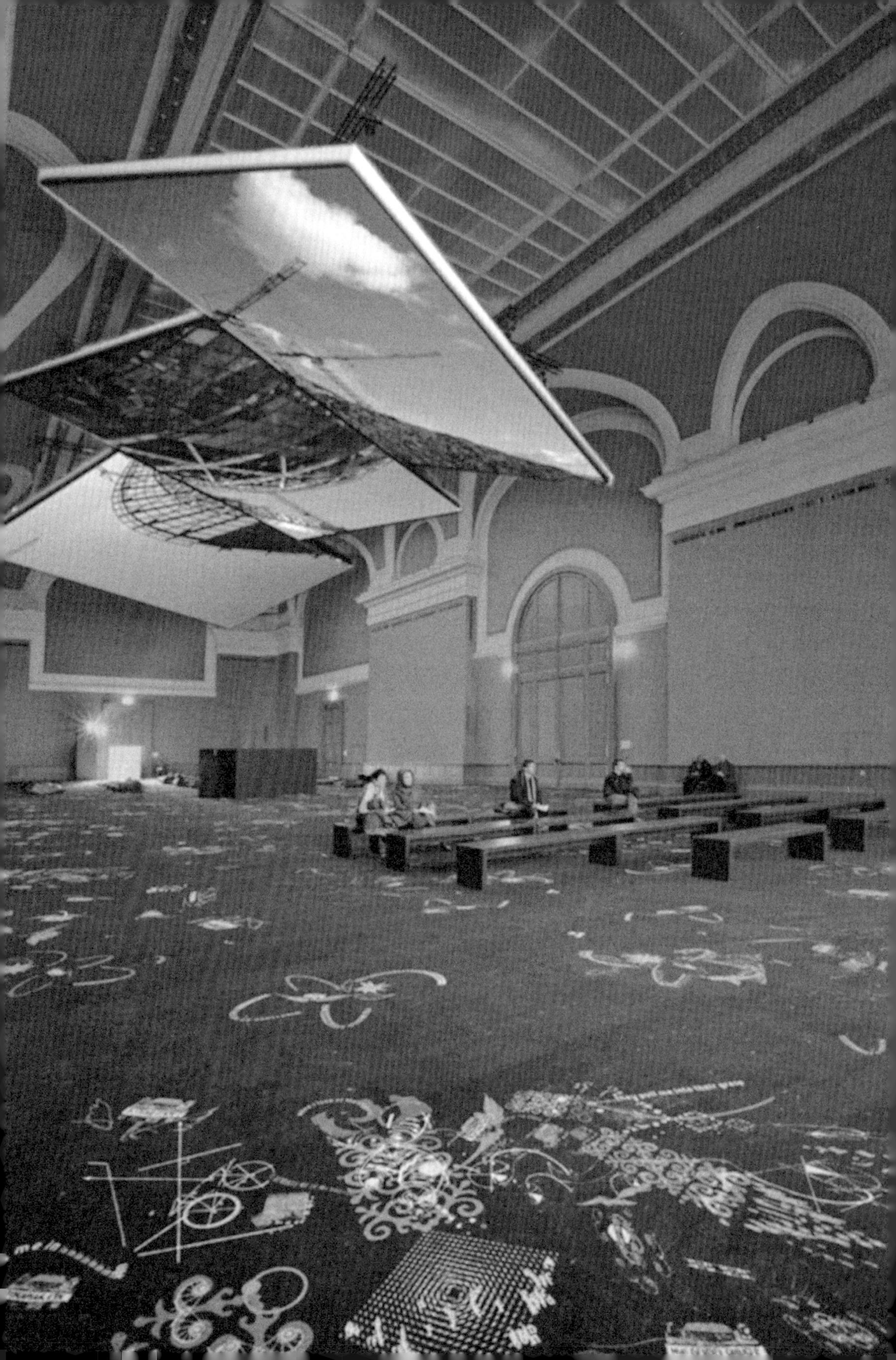

Real Phantasmagoria
Almagul Menlibayeva

Transformation is the title of the exhibition that Almagul Menlibayeva made for the honorary hall of the Grand Palais in Paris.[1] Her show addresses the material metamorphosis that Kazakhstan is currently undergoing. Indirectly it exposes a deeper desire—for spiritual change? Three video installations reach out in the monumental space with its seventeen-metre-high ceilings (two installations are shown in tandem, one work running after the other) thus unleashing streams of powerful and enchanting images. The works tell stories—although some narratives are fractured—about places in Kazakhstan, people and their dreams. These 'portraits' are completed by a floor carpet designed by the artist, featuring a spiral-motif with a recurring phrase on the experience of watching the boundless Kazakh landscape: 'When I look at the steppe…'.

The hall has been blacked out, resulting in an immersive environment of moving and still images, music and noise, and spoken words.[2] Of elemental importance are the soundscapes that accompany the images. These are the compositions of OMFO, the sound artist German Popov, who has been

127

1 The exhibition took place in Paris from 17 December 2016–2 January 2017.

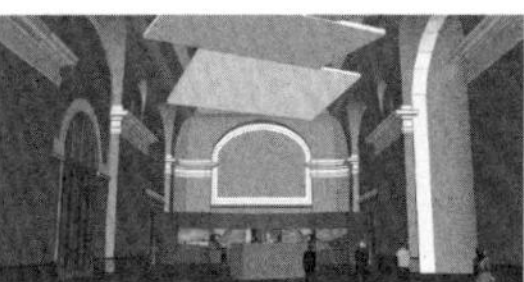

2 Almagul Menlibayeva, design for 'Transformation', Paris, 2016–2017.

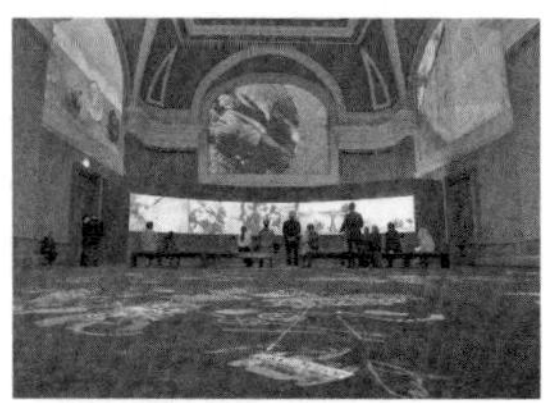

3 Almagul Menlibayeva,
'Transformation', Paris,
2016–2017.

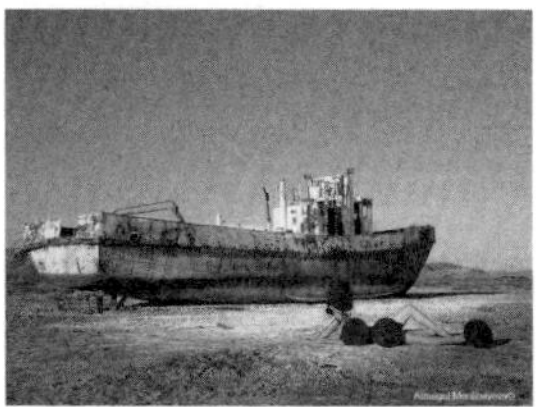

4 Almagul Menlibayeva,
Transoxiana Dreams, 2011,
single channel video, 23'.

collaborating with Menlibayeva since the beginning (2002). His sonic textures describe ethereal spheres—imagine tingling sounds that invigorate celestial dwellers… For the video installation *Kurchatov 22* (2012), OMFO made a soundtrack resembling a tapestry of delicate and abstract sounds. *Tokamak* (2016) is accompanied by an electronic symphony that begins as a darkwave opera. And for the work *Astana* (2016), he composed an electronic symphony inspired by 1960s–1970s Soviet music for cinema.[3]

Menlibayeva's video installations have a cinematic allure. Their reach in space recalls CinemaScope and other widescreen formats used for screening epic films (westerns, historical dramas). But the comparison with cinema goes deeper. Perhaps this metaphor can explain it. At the heart of Menlibayeva's art I sense the existence of an imaginary film that wants to tell a simple story about life and love, but whose footage has been lost along the way. Menlibayeva's oeuvre makes one feel grief about Kazakhstan's suppressed past, but also expectation about the future. She makes images about a fantastic present, 'counter-images' of sorts.

Her ravishing photographs and video works often revolve around social and ecological issues in Central Asia. *Milk for Lambs* (2010), *Transoxiana Dreams* (2011)[4] and *Fire Talk to Me* (2015) are titles of major works or exhibitions. Her art has been associated with the notion of Ethno-Futurism. It features dazzling female figures dressed in magnificent garments, colourful archetypical human personages, and magical hybrid creatures: centaurs and sorceresses who can mend the heartaches of the past and steer the present in the right direction—with the help of natural forces, and their own power.

Trauma and Reverie

The material for Menlibayeva's video installations comes from the artist's field research conducted in her original homeland over the years. Recent investigations led her to Astana, the country's new capital since 1997–1998, where she observed the gargantuan building works underway. And she returned to Kurchatov—the forgotten industrial city and its troubled past features in her earlier work *Kurchatov 22*—to film the new nuclear reactor and present a tale about it. The material and psychological contrasts between Astana and Kurchatov are immense, almost schizophrenic. The gap between these two cities symbolizes the distance between Kazakhstan's present and past. Traditionally, the tribes living on the vast expanse that we call Kazakhstan today were nomads. This way of life was oppressed and virtually erased in the era of Soviet domination. The authorities forced people to adopt a sedentary life, moving them to cities where they were allocated housing. Menlibayeva's recent works depict the urban-oriented Kazakhstan and the new material world that is being built. In her earlier works she depicted a mythologized past, paying tribute to the nomads, their life, their wisdom and organic connection to nature.

The recent video installations propose that in our modern age the past, the present, and future of a place are connected in mysterious ways. *Kurchatov 22* focuses on the psychological trauma and physical damage incurred in the past by the people living in a place called *22*; *Tokamak* invites the viewer on a trip—a tour for tourists?—of the nuclear plant recently built here, and *Astana* introduces the hallucinatory environs of the new capital where we observe some humans in the far distance, walking around as small particles.[5]

5 Menlibayeva's exhibition was to have a second iteration in Astana, at the World Expo of 2017, but that did not happen.

6 Colin Thubron, *The Lost Heart of Asia*, London, Heinemann, 1994, p. 337.

7 Artist in email to the author, 19 December 2016.

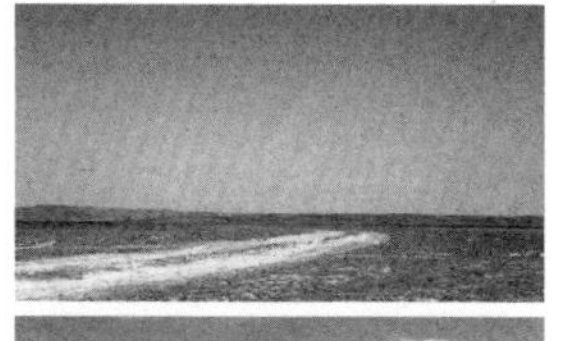

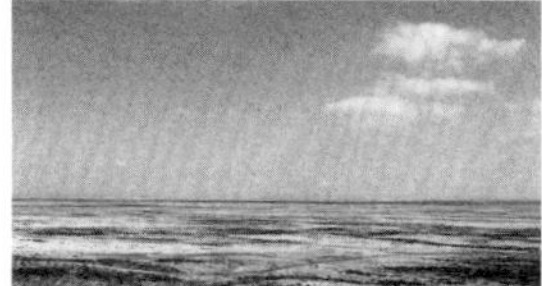

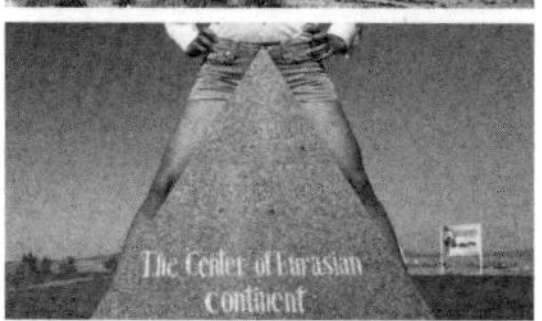

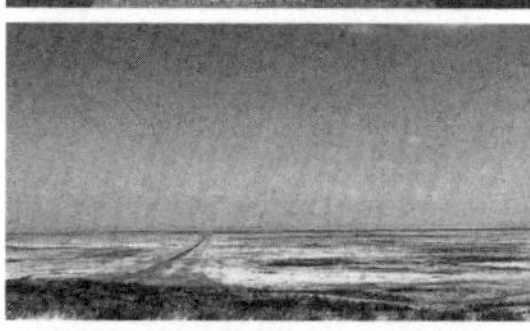

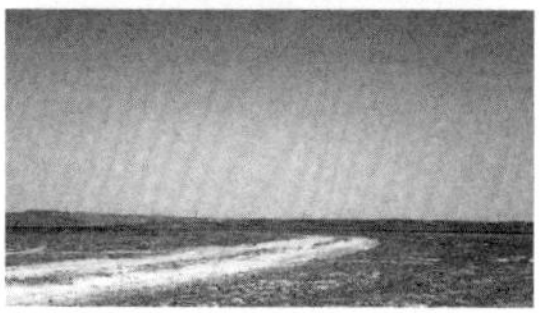

8 Almagul Menlibayeva, *Kurchatov 22*, 2013, 5–8-channel video installation, 30′, surround soundscape by OMFO.

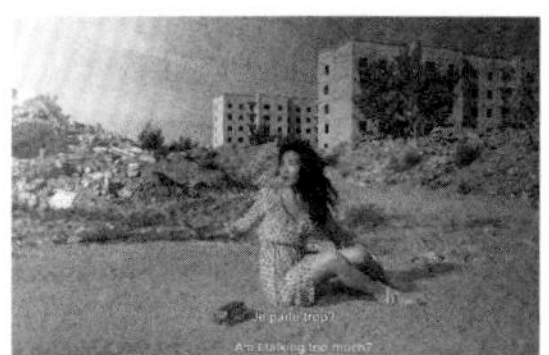

9 Almagul Menlibayeva, *Kurchatov 22*, 2013, 5–8-channel video installation, 30′, surround soundscape by OMFO.

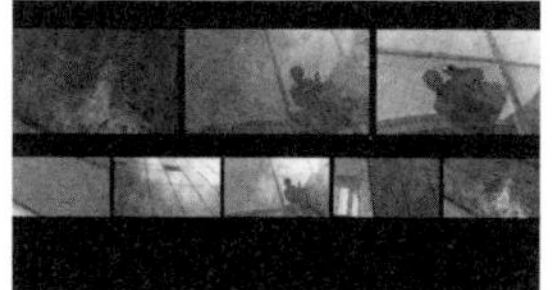

10 Almagul Menlibayeva, *Tokamak*, 2016, 8-channel video installation, 34′45″, surround soundscape by OMFO.

In *Kurchatov 22* (2012) we travel to north-eastern Kazakhstan, where there was a town and an area with nuclear test fields from 1949 to 1991, in the period when Kazakhstan was part of the Soviet Union, and called the Kazakh Soviet Socialist Republic. The place is steeped in tragedy, military tests have left half a million people sick with radioactive sickness, some of them were exposed on purpose in Stalin's time as test subjects, guinea-pigs.[6] At the time of the Soviet Union, the town with its nuclear test fields did not have a proper name, but only a number: 22. As this was a highly secret place, it was absent on maps.[7] And so the video work starts by renaming the place: on a stone shaped like a small pyramid a new name has been written: *Centre of Eurasia*.[8] For an instant, a beautiful, young Kazakh woman is sitting on the stone, as a living symbol of the present.[9] Then we travel back in time: fatal explosions occur, nuclear rain is falling—suddenly the images have turned black and white. Old folks recount the experience that shook their very lives, and we start to get a sense of the depth of their sorrow, how it lives on and reverberates today. Many people died because of the radioactive fallout, mothers birthed deformed children, and many are still dying today as an effect of the nuclear scientific experiments. In one sequence a medical doctor talks about his job, he examined persons who had been exposed to the radiation. Following a fixed scenario prearranged by the authorities, he posted findings to the central bureau, where his reports were stored away; nothing was done with the results. Today he is a patient himself; his health prospects are unclear.

In *Tokamak* (2016) we return to the place Kurchatov. Now a different tune is being played. The topic is a state-of-the-art nuclear reactor that was recently built here.[10] The tokamak was not designed to start a war; it generates energy.

130

The brand-new reactor shines in the sunlight, it looks spick and span, somehow innocuous. Was this pristine machine designed to wipe out the memories of the past? A troupe of actors clean the reactor. Their choreographed performance resembles a dance. The otherworldly beauty of the Kazakhs is arresting. These young men and women seem untouchable. For a moment I experience them as human projections, beamed to earth from a distant planet and a far future. They are smitten with the reactor; they see it as a miracle. Their suave gestures are appealing and uncanny at the same time. Do they offer us a glimpse of life, and love, in the future? In the finale a couple rests on the green grass. The man and woman feel bliss. Softly, they whisper the syllables of the nuclear formula, as if it is their mantra.

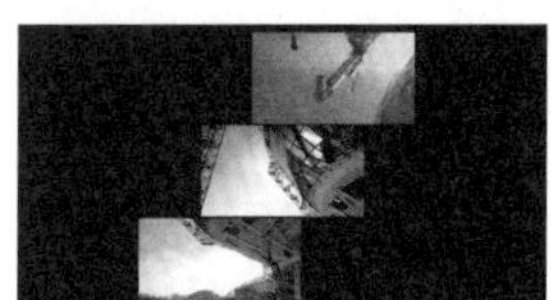

11 Almagul Menlibayeva, *Astana*, 2016, 3-channel video installation, 15′, surround soundscape by OMFO.

Astana (2016) transports us to Kazakhstan's capital.[11] That has been a place in the making since 1997–1998, but especially at the time of writing, when Astana approaches 2017, when it hosts the World Expo. The installation shows gargantuan building projects in action. What we see defies our imagination. Images of the urban scenery are projected onto the ceiling. Visitors lie down on beanbags and watch the video sequences. This work invites contemplation; its atmospheric images show castles being built in the sky. I see frenetic movements of stalwart machines, far away. The new city is a quiet entourage that harbours almost no humans, but a lady is playing the viola at a public celebration. Yet there is nature in Astana as well—suddenly we notice the blue sky, wind can be heard and seen, the sun shines abundantly. This is a picture of Urban Arcadia.

Glittering Mosaic

The beauty of natural landscapes and urban settings, indigenous people and fantasy figures seems to be a topic in its own right. But underneath the allure of these images, the artist's concern for the environment and for its people can be felt. Menlibayeva films places and individuals up-front. Her people tell terrible and frightening stories, but there is dignity in their comportment. The artist seems on a quest to uncover human self-esteem in the midst (or aftermath) of dramatic events. Her images make me feel her curiosity and surprise about her own past, the reality that she once lived, and her desire to recreate that experience.

The artist uses various film styles to encircle her themes. *Kurchatov 22* has documentary interviews but also fantastic images, 'visions'. *Tokamak* uses a gaudy-sinister style, think of science fiction *noir* in cinema, such as Godard's film *Alphaville*. *Astana* has images that resemble impressionist art, giving the work a serene and refined, introspective outlook. Altogether these images present Kazakhstan as a glittering and trippy mosaic.

The somewhat hallucinatory viewing sensation leads me back to the artist's editing process. In the studio she deconstructed the original video material that she had shot, separating the images and ordering them anew, recombining them into strings of sequences. In her exhibition the projections make up intriguing spatial formations; they deserve a special discussion. The projections of *Kurchatov 22* and *Tokamak* take on a formation resembling a newsroom. Five sequences run, one next to the other, on five video screens at the rear wall. Above this line, higher on the wall, there is a second line consisting of three monumental images. In *Tokamak* the images stand still or alternatively they slowly morph into something else. At times they even multiply themselves: then three identical images appear at the rear wall and the two side-walls. This monumental line-up of images resembles a triptych, like paintings of saints in a church chapel, and it invites contemplation. In *Kurchatov 22* a sepia colour is added to these large images, giving the 'paintings' a sacred aura—the artist calls them 'sculptures'. *Astana* is projected onto the ceiling on three rectangular slabs in a playful formation (it resembles a kite). Here we see the images of urban scenery in the making. These motile projections resemble a mirage, a contemporary version of the Hanging Gardens.

The newsroom, the chapel, and the fantasy garden are typologies that can be found in modern, historical and archaic times, and tropes related to journalism, religion, myth. Images have a powerful role in all these fields; they play their part in fact-finding and truth-seeking. They are essential in philosophy, belief systems, and fantasy/fiction.

Menlibayeva's projections raise pertinent questions. *Kurchatov 22* captures the hardship of Kazakhstan's past— the evil that went on in this place and the 'madness' of the human effort to process this tragedy—in the sequence of a young man who, filled with joy, drives his electric wheelchair out on the desert plain: an image of hope against all odds. *Tokamak* also reveals contrariness. This work is more than just a tale on a flashy nuclear reactor. The monumental triptych has a mercurial sequence of metal in a state of eternal disintegration (played as a loop); this refers to the bewildering bodily/psychological experience of people.

People's Art

12 Artist in Skype conversation with the author, 21 December 2016.

13 Artist in Skype conversation with the author, 30 December 2016.

14 See also: MuHKA Ensembles, Sergej Maslov (1952–2002), www.ensembles.mhka.be/actors/sergey-maslov?locale=en.

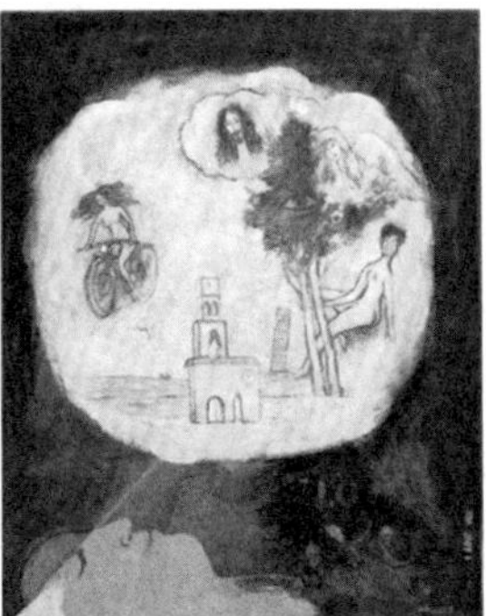

15 Sergei Maslov, *Declaration of Love* (from the *Dream series*), 1982–2000, 1 painting from 12 total.

Through her work, the artist confronts a cultural lacuna. She observes a lack of relevant images about today's Kazakhstan. In a recent conversation she said: 'There is a problem in how Kazakhstan presents itself to the world, in how it sees and understands itself. Many of the images that are circulating now and are said to represent Kazakh culture, in fact reflect the beliefs of the past when a constructed identity was imposed on people. It seems to me as if our imagination is stuck. When the Soviet Union was in charge, it tried to repress or even oust the traditional, nomadic lifestyle. But that Soviet Union is no more, it fell apart at the end of 1991. I confront the culture and its amnesia in my work—and not only Kazakhstan suffers from that. But our nomadic traditions are relevant. Take only the fact that many of the leading contemporary artists of these days, willy-nilly as it sometimes may feel to us, are cultural nomads.'[12]

The show in Paris makes us feel the artist's social-cultural engagement. 'How will the future of our planet be shaped, what role will art play in making people aware of the human impact and responsibility for the natural surroundings?' That question was on her mind at the time when the video works were installed. In another exchange she talked about her education in Almaty in the era of the Soviet Union.[13] She recalls a formative experience, just before entering the academic milieu with tutors who upheld a blend of socialist realism and utopic futurism. Any art student or future professional in the Soviet Union and its satellite countries had to fall right in line with it. The experience occurred when she, as a fifteen-year-old girl, met the outsider and myth-maker Sergei Maslow.[14, 15] Upon seeing her drawings and paintings, he related them to Surrealism and the idea of mythology. Maslow stimulated her to explore her world; and he subsequently became her private teacher.

The idea of an art for the people is relevant to Menlibayeva. Her show reminds me of Diego Rivera's social cosmologies and impressive murals. His art combined archaic/fantastic and realistic/documentary elements and used immersive experience. That is comparable to how Menlibayeva operates. Perhaps her most important trope is the empowered woman and the new world that she invokes. Traditionally, the powerful woman recurs in myths and legends, storytelling and popular folklore. The artist does not shy away from the cliché. She builds on it, gives it a kick, transforming it into a vehement agent.

Baroque Structures

Her work is propelled by another force as well. The artist has a passion for the moving image. Cinematic images move in time-space, but they also orchestrate human affect, we say that images move us! I would argue that Menlibayeva's video installations, with their interacting images and plastic multiplications, leap into space. I think her art has an affinity with a style that began in south-eastern Europe in the seventeenth century.

The art of the baroque ventures into real space. It prefers dynamic forms; upon its structures we project emotion, think of baroque music. Baroque art creates a parallel world, it prefers artifice to realism. In his study of the life and poetry of Juana de la Cruz, who lived in the seventeenth century in Mexico City, New Spain, Octavio Paz has written extensively about the baroque. In one passage, he explains the baroque through its dialectical relation with Romanticism:

16 Octavio Paz, *Sor Juana, or, The Traps of Faith*, Cambridge (MA), Harvard University Press, 1988, p. 53–54.

17 www.almagulmenlibayeva. com/artist-statement.html. The website only mentions 'the Soviet avant-garde school of Futurism' as a background. But the artist confirmed that she was also educated in the Soviet realist style. Artist in Skype conversation with the author, 30 December 2016.

Each, reacting against classicism, proclaimed an aesthetic of the abnormal and the unique; each presented itself as a transgression of norms. But while the romantic transgression centres on the subject, the baroque transgression focuses on the object. Romanticism liberates the subject; the baroque is the art of the metamorphosis of the object.

And Paz continues:

Romanticism is passionate and passive; the baroque is intellectual and active. Romantic transgression culminates in the apotheosis of the subject or its fall; baroque transgressions lead to the appearance of an unheard-of object.[16]

Menlibayeva's video installations resemble baroque structures. These sophisticated narratives release a tremendous energy. Their dynamic pictures, always in mercurial interaction, sit close to what Paz calls 'the unheard-of object'. Paz also writes about the transplantation of the European Baroque, exported to New Spain from seventeenth-century Spain and Portugal, and the change and exaggeration the style underwent once it arrived at the new place. A similar story could be told about the art styles that were exported from Moscow to Kazakhstan, when the area was part of the Soviet Union, named the Kazakh Soviet Socialist Republic. At that time, at the centre of the Soviet Union, Moscow, a new artificial Kazakh identity was constructed. Two art styles that were initially avant-garde were brought to a tribal society steeped in animistic and shamanistic beliefs (Tengrism): socialist realism and utopic futurism. The artist recalls her education at the art academy in Almaty in these two styles.[17] Her work still rests on those two pillars; it can be seen and felt in her images of places and people of power.

Real Phantasmagoria

Menlibayeva wants to liberate the stifled tropes. Her critique of clichés but also her way of working with them recalls Gustave Courbet's battles with the art movements of his time as he painted *The Artist's Studio: A Real Allegory Summing Up Seven Years of my Artistic and Moral Life* (1855). He offered it to the Paris World Fair in 1855, only to see it refused. That decision led him to build his own pavilion, a forerunner of the Salon des Refusés, next to the exposition's locale. Here he exhibited *The Artist's Studio*. The painting shows a group of individuals from various milieus gathered in the artist's atelier. The painter takes centre stage, he sits in front of his landscape in the making; a boy, dog and a naked woman—the prototypical model—follow his efforts. He stands in the light and also his painting is bright with sunshine. In the shadowy background guests are deep in thought. In the midst are remnants, ghosts from the past; a naked man raises his arms in a forlorn gesture. Is that figure the real allegory? But our painter prefers the here and now. He is ready to kick old forms out.

In Menlibayeva's work I detect a similar interest in, and a resistance to the art forms with which she was brought up. She is no realist artist the way Courbet aspired to be. She is fascinated by phantasmagoria; the type of imagery that was used in the political context where she grew up, and that initially was part of the popular funfair. Her show in Paris is a testimony of delusion: we can be blinded by the future, baffled by the past, intoxicated by the present.

137

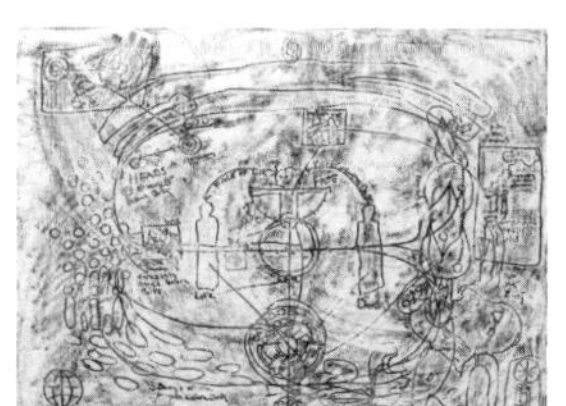

18 Matt Mullican, *Untitled (Cosmology)*, 1996, acrylic and oil stick on canvas, 154 × 204 cm.

Where can we situate the artist in today's critical discourse? We can relate Menlibayeva's work to that of Eija-Liisa Ahtila. Her video installation *Anne, Aki and God* (1998) shows a fractured narrative exploring the topic of the disintegrating subject: a man falls apart, becomes psychotic as he falls in love with the woman who is a creature that he himself invented—a figment of his imagination. Kader Attia is another artist who comes to mind. His work is concerned with trauma, individual/collective wounds, and the possibility of healing through repair; this theme is explored, for example, in his film installation *Phantom Limb*.

Menlibayeva's exhibition also suggests a wondrous balance. Through the video works, the artist seems to mould a parallel reality where a benevolent *genius loci*—the protective spirit of the place—may find a new home. Her approach reflects Eastern metaphysical ideas on equilibrium, knowledge on how to foster the natural balance. In the practice of shamanism, the topic of how to maintain the natural balance is central. I propose to relate Menlibayeva's art to that philosophy. (My suggestion is also meant to enlarge the common perspective on Western art; Matt Mullican's work, for example: his cosmology has animistic features.)[18]

Through her art, Menlibayeva embraces a reality that is changing with the speed of light; in Kazakhstan, any idea of a humane balance was given up a long time ago. With a little imagination, her exhibition can be perceived as a kaleidoscope. It is as if her images unceasingly act upon and change one another, thus redefining their properties and heightening their potential. The multiplication of her video images is born out of necessity. It is her countermeasure to bring some order to this world.

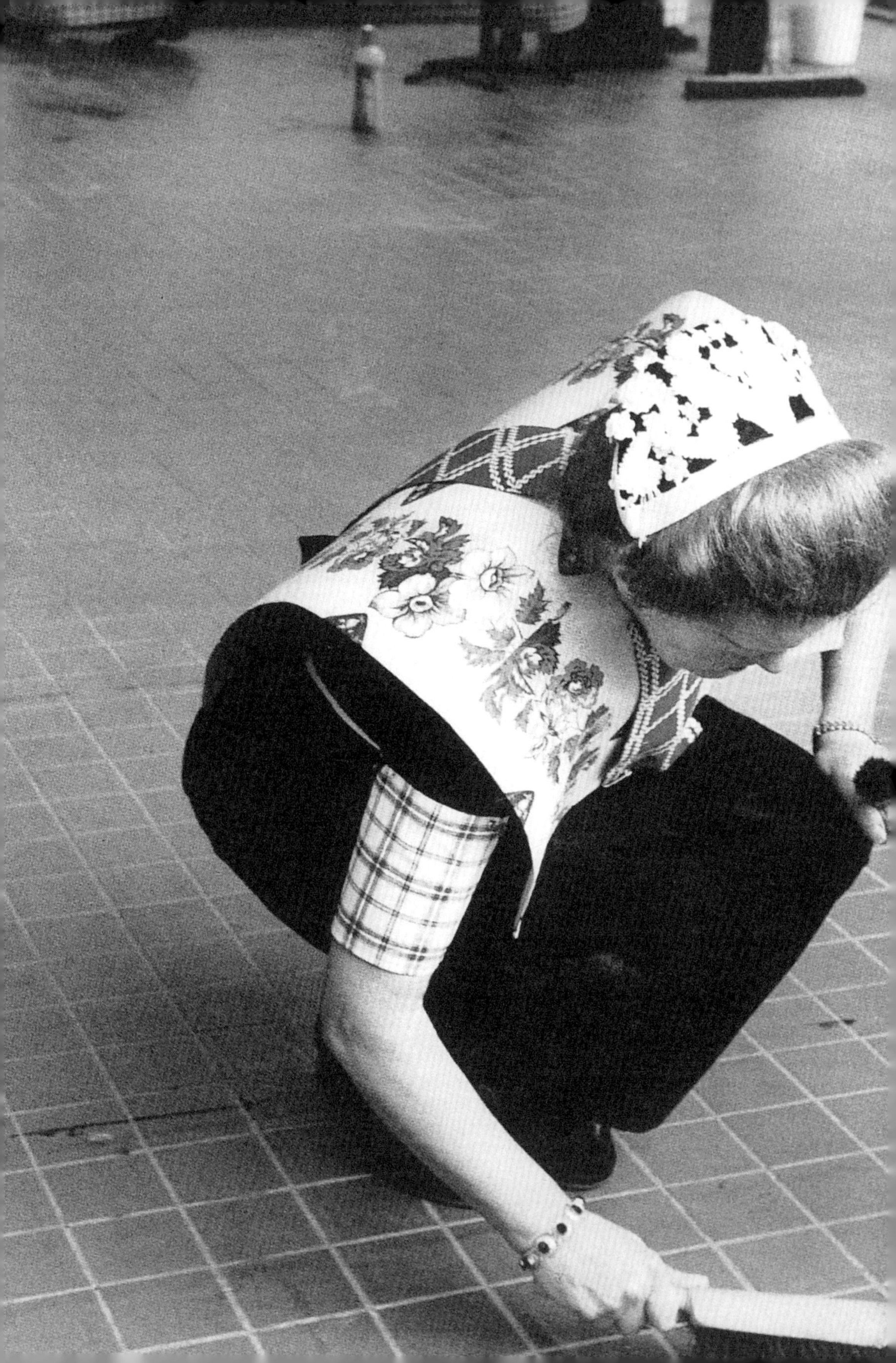

Hard Acts &
Soft Gestures

Job Koelewijn

Right between the bed and door stands Fischerle, nailed down to his place, lashing his hump. Like whip-handles his arms go up by turns and bring the five double-knotted cords from his fingers over his shoulders on to his hump. It does not flinch. As an immovable mountain it towers above the low hilltops of his shoulders, proud in its rock-like hardness. There is not a cry of: 'Enough! Stop!...' It is silent.[1]

Self-chastisement and other actions directed against the body in the 1970s formed part of a type of art production has become known as performance.[2]

In North America, Western and Eastern Europe, artists laid themselves open to tests of an extreme kind. Of legendary fame is the performance *Shoot* (1971), by the American Chris Burden (b. 1946, living in Venice, CA), in which one of the artist's friends at a pre-arranged moment fired a gun at Burden's upper left arm. The silent film on which the event was recorded shows a man looking quietly at the camera; then, suddenly, as if a stung by an insect, he grabs his left arm at the spot where the bullet hit him.

1 Elias Canetti, *Die Blendung*, Vienna, Herbert Reichner Verlag, 1935. Translated as *Auto-da-fé* by C.V. Wedgewood, London, Jonathan Cape, 1946.

2 'Performance = work, deed, game, spectacle, theatrical entertainment', *Wolters English/Dutch Dictionary*, Groningen, 1981.

Job Koelewijn, *The Cleaning of the Rietveldpaviljoen*, 1992.

3 Chris Burden & Jan Butterfield, 'Through the Night Softly', *The Art of Performance. A Critical Anthology*, eds. Gregory Battcock and Robert Nickas, New York, E.P. Dutton, 1984, pp. 222–239.

Burden is also the direct object in other performances.[3] In *Five-Day Locker Piece* (1971) he had himself locked up, after five days of fasting, in a metal box of 60 × 60 × 60 cm. He quenched his thirst with water from he got from the box above him. He urinated in an empty bottle in the box beneath him. On the fifth day he was let out. With a little help from his friends, he crawled out of his tiny cell.

Five-Day Locker Piece was realized by Burden as a work for his final exams at the University of California, Irvine. Burden said of the performance that the mental strain, including the preparation, was in a certain sense more important than the physical deed. At times when his time in the box became difficult to bear, he forced himself to think that he was the person who had set the task for himself. He himself was responsible for what he had to endure. The idea came to him more forcefully at night when there was no longer anyone left in the locked university building. Burden knew moreover that there would eventually be an end to his trials. The fear that can overcome someone in a situation with no end in sight never could therefore not get the better of him. If necessary, Burden fantasized, he could always kick the metal door to pieces.

The mythical features of Burden's final-exam piece spring to mind. Here is a man who willingly allows himself to be put to a test of endurance. His adventure reminds one of a work crowned with success as described in stories from Greek mythology. Nor will the Catholic symbolism of death—the metal box as a casket—and resurrection escape anyone's attention. Such religious motifs come back in later works. Two years after *Five-Day Locker Piece*, Burden laid out his own Via Dolorosa. In *Through the Night Softly* he crawled at night, dressed only in his underwear and with his hands behind his back, through twenty metres of broken glass strewn about Main Street in Los Angeles. Only some passers-by observed the scene. In *Trans-Fixed* (1974), one of his last performances, he had himself crucified. In the garage of a small petrol-station, Burden went leaned backwards against the rear of a Volkswagen. Assistants then drove a nail through each of his hands into the roof of the car. Then, the garage doors were opened and the car was driven half-way out. The noise of the engine, which was being revved up to the maximum, was like a long-drawn-out scream.

For four years Burden gave performances in which he faced pain and other physical hardship. In the majority of these Burden acted as a soloist whose actions were recorded on film or photographs. In other performances he made the public a participant in situations that were experienced as oppressive or dangerous. It must have been an enormous strain for Burden to keep control of the powers that were released by his actions. Looking back on it, it is not surprising that he abandoned his artistic course in 1975. With a videotape he released that year—*Documentation of Selected Works, 1971–1974*—he bade farewell to a period in which he subjected himself to trials that could also be considered as deliberate, self-redacted interventions in his biography. The radical way in which Burden initially set about his practice, brings stories to mind about the artist as a young man; tales of ambition and sacrifice. To put his life in the service of a passion, thought Burden, it was necessary to leave his individual history behind. For this reason, he conceived his final-exam piece as a rite of passage. The young Burden wanted to be like the phoenix that rises again out of its own ashes. But he realized in time that one should not defy the power of the Form.

Around 1990 the early work of artists like Vito Acconci, Bruce Nauman, Bas Jan Ader, Rebecca Horn, Marina

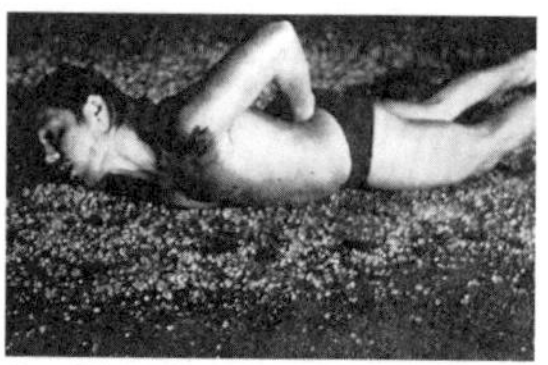

4a Chris Burden, *Through the Night Softly*, 1973.

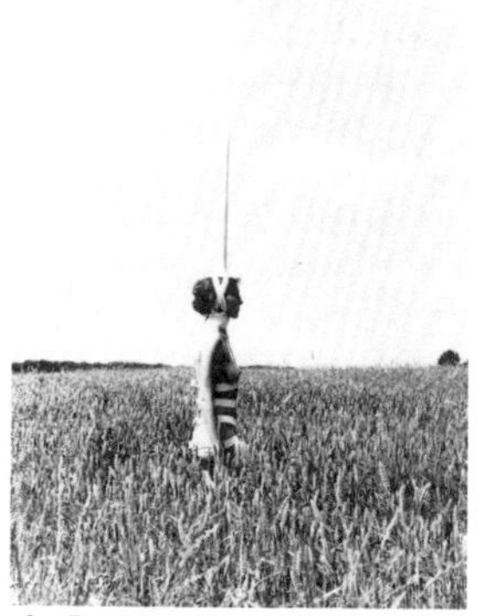

4b Rebecca Horn, *Einhorn*, 1970.

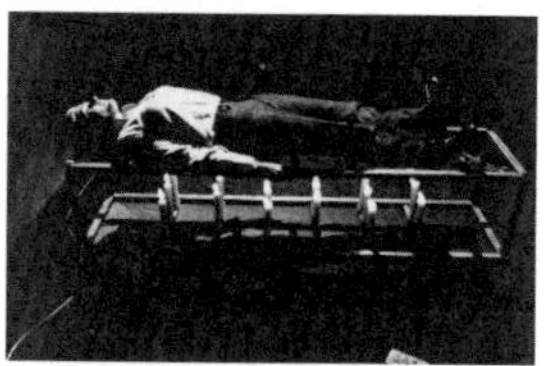

4c Gina Pane, *The Conditioning*, 1973.

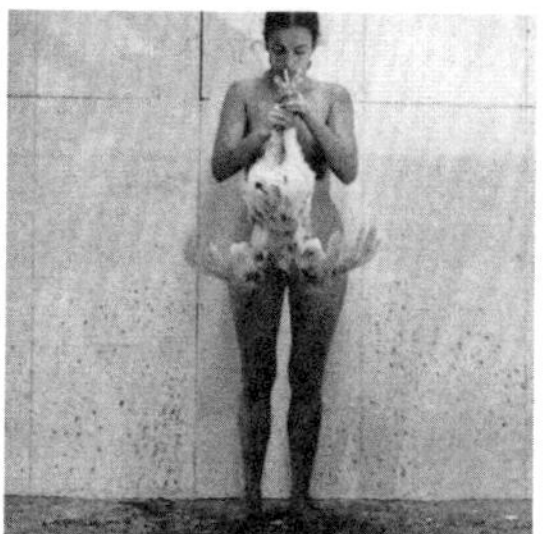

4d Ana Mendieta, *Untitled (Death of a Chicken)*, 1972.

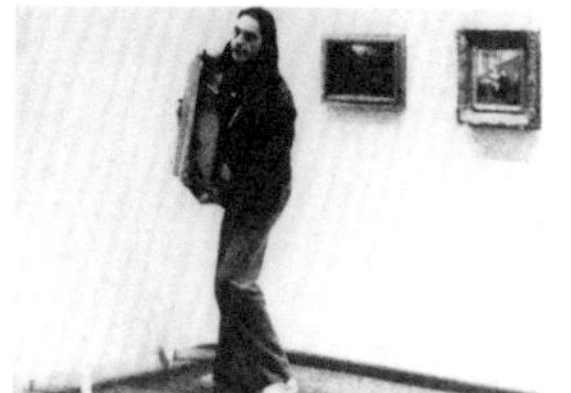

4e Ulay, *Da ist eine kriminelle Berührung in der Kunst (There is a Criminal Touch to Art)*, 1976.

Abramović & Ulay and Chris Burden was rediscovered. The public got (re-)acquainted with their performances at exhibitions in Europe particularly.[4] These artists have three things in common with each other:

1   They were born between 1940 and 1946.
2   In the 1970s they undertook performances and related actions in their studios, in semi-public places (in towns, on the land, on sea), and in art rooms, whether or not in the presence of an audience.
3   These pieces were recorded through photos, films and videotapes: secondary documents that since that time have decided our current image about performance and have even taken its place.[5]

The first performers were soloists. Vito Acconci followed a man in the street for three hours, noting down his activities like a detective, until he disappeared into a house. In *Seedbed* (1972) he masturbated during the opening hours of his exhibition under the partly raised floor of the gallery. Bruce Nauman carried out behaviourist experiments in his studio, such as walking up and down the length of a narrow corridor while imitating the contrapposto of classical sculpture. The Dutchman Bas Jan Ader drowned in 1975 during his last solo action, entitled *In Search of the Miraculous*. He wanted to cross the Atlantic in a small yacht. He met his end on the way between Cape Cod to Amsterdam. Rebecca Horn walked through green pastures with extensions fixed to her limbs. She looked like some fabled animal or mechanical construction come to life. Exhibition-maker Harald Szeemann advised her to film herself while she was dressing herself up with her *Körperobjekte* and testing how they worked. So now we know how the objects took over and extended Horn's bodily functions.

144

Marina Abramović & Ulay on the other hand gave the majority of their performances in the presence of observers. Their *Relation Works* (1976–1988), in which they put each other's physical and psychological limits to the test, were typically public affairs.[6] But these artists too had a history as soloists, up to the moment their collaborations began. This applies particularly to Ulay. For Marina Abramović the public confrontation had long been important. In 1975 she realized one of her first performances at De Appel, the Amsterdam art foundation, which from 1975 to about 1980 was the important international centre for performance. In this action her body served as raw material. In full view of the public, she carved out a five-pointed star on her abdomen with a razor blade. Photos of this aggressive act show both a mutilation and a creation.

Ulay realized his last action as a soloist in the winter of 1976. His deed had the resolve of a declaration of principles.[7] During daytime he went to the Berlin Nationalgalerie, where he took down a painting by the nineteenth-century genre painter Karl Spitzweg. It was *Der arme Poet* (The Poor Poet), a portrait of a poet in an attic who is burning the latest fruits of his pen in the stove to avoid freezing in the winter cold. Before the attendants could grab him, Ulay had carried the painting outside. He was able to escape his pursuers, got into his car and took the painting to a Turkish family in Kreuzberg, where he hung it on the wall. A few hours later he telephoned the director of the museum. Ulay told him where the painting was to be found, and asked him to go and look at it.

Over the years critics have often made the connection between the precarious body that artists investigated in their work in the 1990s, and the role of the body in performances from the 1970s. The motivation of the above-mentioned actions seems however to be of a completely different order.

6 'Performance = public activity of an artist, accompanied by showmanship', *Van Dale, Groot Woordenboek van de Nederlandse Taal*, Utrecht/Antwerpen, 1984.

7 Ulay & Thomas McEvilley, *Der Erste Akt/The First Act*, ed. Uwe Laysiepen, Ostfildern, Cantz Verlag, 1994.

The first performers strove for radicalness. As recalcitrant investigators of the world, they were not concerned with established art institutions—which did not notice them anyway. Their autonomy, independence of thought and deed is, I believe, the deeper reason why the art world in general, and a young generation of artists particularly, is so now attracted to their ideas and work. This can clearly be seen in the practices of young artists. Performance has been enjoying a renaissance over the last few years. This art form is being experimented with a great deal in the art academies—and, just as in the 1970s, artists aim high by staging an existential moment. However—and this is the difference—it seems as if these artists are no longer drawn to radicality. Strong forms have given way to fragility.

I would like to illustrate my point with three examples:

1   On 16 March 1992, the Rietveld Pavilion in Amsterdam, a small glass building for exhibitions of young artists studying at the Rietveld Academie, was being cleaned by four women in traditional dress from Spakenburg. The event was orchestrated by Job Koelewijn. Various observers on that day saw how the sober architecture of Gerrit Rietveld was cleaned inside and out. The Spakenburg women, relatives of Koelewijn, applied themselves with gusto to their task. From nine o'clock in the morning until five in the afternoon, they scrubbed the floor, polished the woodwork and cleaned the windows. Every now and then, they got together to decide on a strategy for the cleaning. In this performance, characteristic images from the Dutch cultural heritage were brought together, visual forms that are strictly separated in daily reality. For a full eight hours a link was realized between Spakenburg morality and its values such as cleanliness and

industry, and the art-ethic of Gerrit Rietveld in which sobriety and functionality were of central importance. Koelewijn, with this cleaning act, put an end to his period of studies at the Academy. At the same time, he was presenting a demonstration for the future. His piece of work evinced his high expectations of art and the ambition to give it a place among the everyday. Hence his request to relatives from his hometown to assist him.[8]

2   On 3 June 1993, the Frenchman Jean-Baptiste Bruant went off to a polder outside Arnhem. There, in view of art critics who had been taken round the exhibition 'Sonsbeek 93', he gave a performance with ritual overtones. Bruant dug a hole in the ground with his bare hands, stuck his head in the opening, gave a loud scream and then whipped his head out fast so he could close the hole, as it were, to bury his scream—an expression of *male anxiety*—for good. I was standing there observing the spectacle and was surprised about the naivety of Bruant's enterprise. I asked myself to what extent he knew about performances from the 1970s. I thought that he had appropriated a sort of historical fury for his action, which we can recognize from, for example, the works of Marina Abramović and Ulay. What it was exactly that Bruant was so angry about was not clear to me. I found it very significant that his performance was accompanied by the croaking of frogs, thus creating a pastoral setting that neutralized every possible angle of this action. But this assessment is, with hindsight, not really fair. Bruant did in fact give a series of performances, sketches of a kind, which together formed a tale with mythical features.[9]

3   On 4 June 1994, the final evening of the ninth 'Festival a/d Werf' in Utrecht, Arthur Elsenaar gave a playful

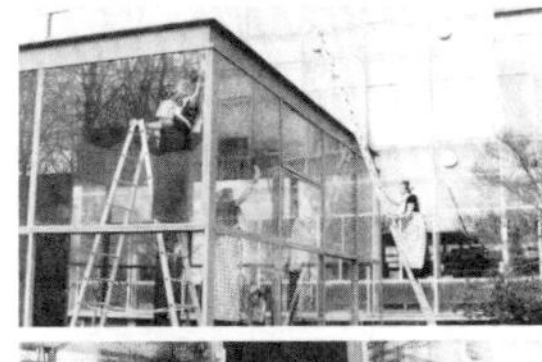
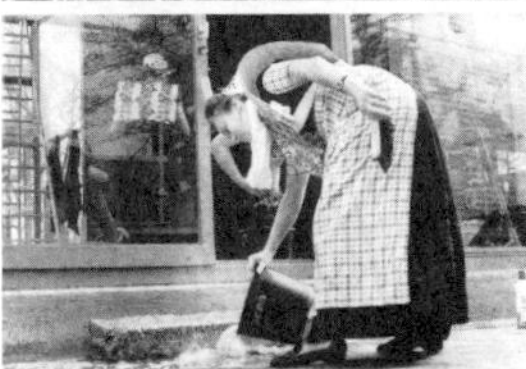
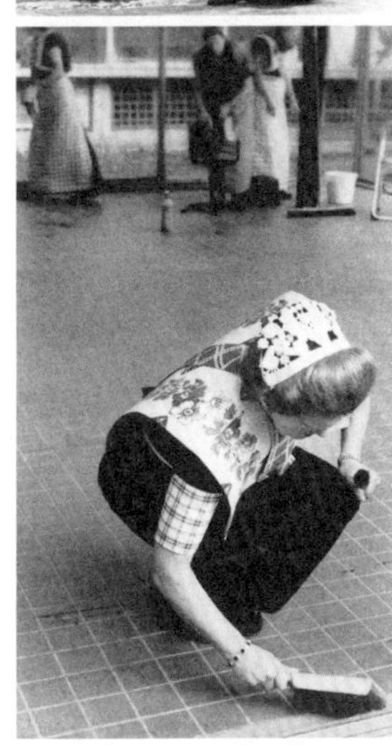

8 Job Koelewijn, *The Cleaning of the Rietveldpaviljoen*, 1992.

9 Catalogue *Sonsbeek 93*, eds. Valerie Smith, J. Brand, C. de Muynck, Gent, Snoeck-Ducaju & Zoon, 1993, p. 62–64.

performance in the open-air pavilion at Neude Square in the middle of festival-goers who were having a good time. It was a relaxed show with five characters playing the main role, whose bodies were mechanized. They reacted to the sounds around them. They automatically made a particular movement when they were spoken to by a member of the public. The volume of the sound activated an electrode fixed to their bodies which sent out pulsations to one or more muscles. These movements could be read as signs of pregnant emotions. One lady coquettishly cocked her head again and again. Another lady kept throwing her head back in an expression of haughtiness. And there was a jolly young man who was constantly raising his arm, a jovial gesture that was automatically backed up with a big wink. Elsenaar brought exaggerated qualities to the table at a place where in the evenings an exuberant atmosphere reigned. On the last night of the festival the actors came together as a group (on each of the previous nights, only one of them had appeared at a time). Now the)-: *The HumaTiCks of the Present [ ]* were complete. The image was typified by Elsenaar as an amusing portrait of society as a whole. The performance began on a small stage just behind the pavilion where the artist, not without irony, presented his troupe to the public.

In these recent performances hesitation was a crucial motif. The artists carefully deliberated about the extent to which their activities were going to encroach on the environment. A choice was made, for example, for a relaxed presentation with a similar interchange between action and environment as a result. That effect can also be described as a productive confusion between the work of art and its frame. Distinctive about Arthur Elsenaar's performance was that the onlookers, in the literal sense of the word, were able to make or break the work. The environment within which it was put on show, meant that in a certain sense it was invisible. However, a little effort from the viewer sufficed to make it visible. Jean-Baptiste Bruant's performance had timidity as its most striking feature. It was as if the artist was placing his own action between quotation marks. But, though it had much in common with slapstick, his spectacle made a mythical connection with things visible. Burying the scream seemed like an exorcism of grief or anger. Job Koelewijn's performance had a cool, subdued character. The rigorous cleaning served a practical end. The action symbolized a purification ritual, directed towards the inner man. In a booklet published afterwards with photos of the Spakenburg women who set to work on the Rietveld Pavilion, the artist quoted the mystic Theresa of Ávila: 'A woman will not lose her senses doing the cleaning'. In other words: there might well be an ideal underlying people's day-to-day activities. We must have a keen eye to see it.

It is easy to link the fragility of the illusion in those performances to the general transitoriness of life. But what is such an observation worth, when we realize that the underlying idea—performance as an art form in which the dividing line between what people call art and life dissolves—must be dubbed a misconception? The terms 'art' and 'life' are not interchangeable: they deserve further precision in any context. Just as with other art forms, performance is based on the quality of illusion. In performances from the 1970s, aspects of life, such as certain emotions, were compressed or expanded. In a metaphor borrowed from sculpture: pieces of life were chopped out, worked on and placed on a pedestal so they could be studied. Artists used, in other words, artificial processes to manipulate life. Chris Burden's early work is exemplary. Burden thought it important that his performances had a clear form. He wanted people to be able to read them at a

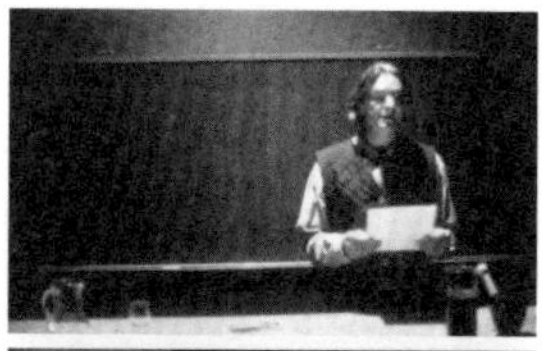

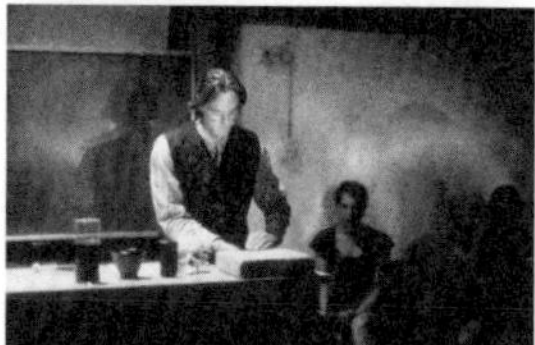

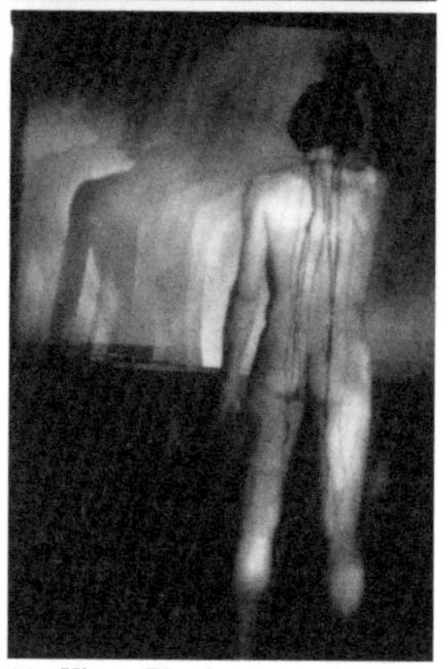

11 Ulay, *The Animator*, 1995.

glance. He typified the form to be realized as 'crisp'. He strove for the hardness of illusion: through its clarity the action was, as it were, dissociated from the surrounding space and time. The here-and-now character of the performance was elevated to a sublime moment.

In one of his writings, Ulay posed a question about performance which seems more important to me than speculations about the points of contact of the art form with life. The question contains a play of words. To begin with, Ulay breaks the word up into syllables: 'Per-for-mance'. He continues: 'The word mostly makes me think of perforation.—But what is being perforated?'[10, 11]

The works of performers in the 1970s stir the imagination so much because behind the action performed there is another reality—namely, that of the rite, myth in action. I typified the final exam-piece of Chris Burden as a rite of passage. I called it a deliberate intervention by himself in his biography. With this artist one is tempted to wonder about the existential effect of performances on its maker. It is as if the young Burden gave birth to a *persona* for whom life is equivalent to carrying out heroic deeds. Everything is in the service of developing the *persona*. Between 1971 and 1974, this determined the direction of Burden's life. The moment he stopped doing performances, he abandoned it like a shell. It was the source of the myth formation around his artisthood. Now he could follow a new artistic course. After having been the prisoner of his own mind for four years, Burden was given the same reward as the one he got in 1971 at his final exam, when he was let out of the metal box by friends. A new freedom was his.

Twenty years later Job Koelewijn shows the potential of a poetic vision on the dialectic of imprisonment and freedom.

150

He asks himself what factors are the deciding ones in his life
and how he can counteract them. The cleaning of the
Rietveld Pavilion in 1992 resembles an exorcism of his own
personal history. Depressing forces of the past are subjugated
and put into a project where optimism over the future reigns.
The Spakenburg moral is set free. In 1993 Koelewijn created
a sculpture with the motif of imprisonment chosen of his own
free will.[12] He made a wooden box with five sides of 25 × 25
cm, and covered these with mirrors to reflect the surroundings. He put the headgear on his head to mark the dividing
line with what was outside of him. The impulses of the world
would bounce off the cap. Thus, he could practice visual fasting, and withdraw into his mind. Later in 1993 he visited his
primary school. He handed out little hats to the children in
the playground, folded from thoughts on paper.[13] Drawings,
verses and stories from earlier years were given a new destination in Spakenburg. These performances had a ritual character. Old thoughts coming to life again in a new form. The
past appears to be a reference-point for the here and now,
provided it is destroyed.

The first works of Job Koelewijn are acts of renunciation.
He continually bids farewell—to his past, his surroundings,
his own thoughts. This way he creates space to produce. The
heroics of the small gesture show themselves freely in his later
works. At the end of 1993 he made a painting in his studio
with green liquid soap. On four walls he painted a continuous
washing line with a couple of items of clothing. Strips of
white paper lay on the floor. A velum filtered the light coming
through the dormer roof. In the beginning the fresh smell of
green soap hung in the air at the studio. The painting dried
after a time, grey silhouettes of a washing line with drying
clothes remained.[14] In this period, he also began preparations
of for another work, a large one this time: *De Mondiale*

151

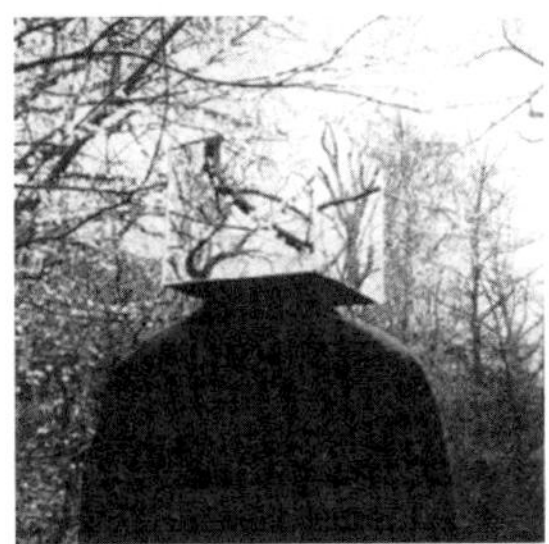

12 Job Koelewijn, *Bonnet*, 1993.

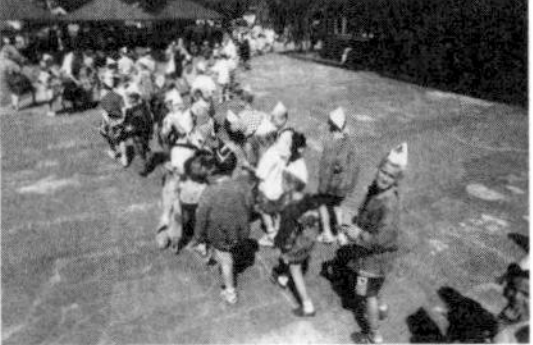

13 Job Koelewijn, *Kids Walk Away With My Thoughts*, 1993.

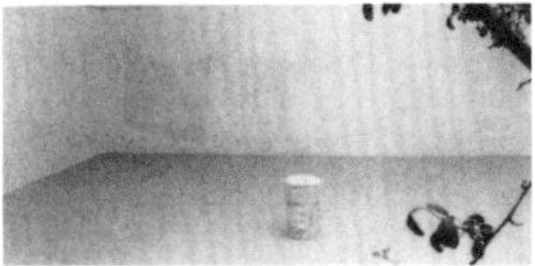

14 Job Koelewijn, *Goodbye Spakenburg*, 1994. Exhibition view Galerie Fons Welters, Amsterdam.

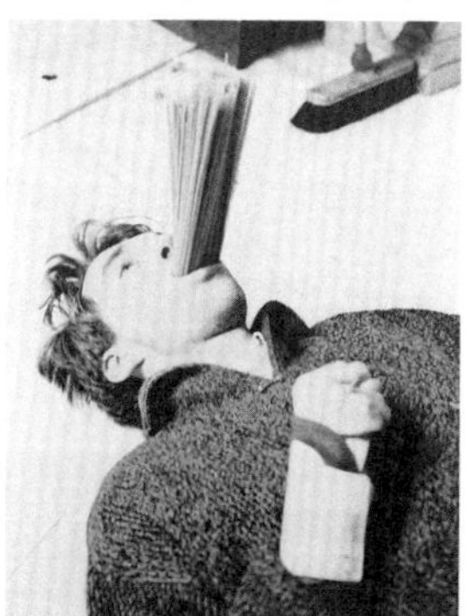

17   Job Koelewijn, *Zonder titel (Spaghetti)*, 1995.

Kleurwedstrijd (The World Colour Competition). He made studies for a drawing of a woman in traditional Spakenburg costume embroidering a map of the world on her lap. In 1994 he sent black-and-white copies of the drawing to junior schools in all parts of the world. He asked children at the schools to help him finish the work. They were invited to colour in the drawing any way they liked.

Receptiveness is the term I would use to typify the nature of these works. They are extremely sensitive to impulses from outside. The effect of humidity on a wall painting,[15] and the effect of the efforts of children from all over the world on the state of a drawing are examples of a comparable order. The works spring from transparent forms into which powers from the surroundings penetrate. Here we come up against a fundamental difference with the severe performances of the 1970s. The first performers made the environment subservient to their actions. It functioned as a framework or material to be processed. Sometimes it was brutally incised. Job Koelewijn may be representative of a generation of artists active in the 1990s. This generation is interested in the gesture by which some kind of balance with the environment is brought about. It seems that the words of the Dutch poet Lucebert are being taken to heart after all:

> en ik en ik ik ben ik jaag niet naar de letter
> luister ik jaag niet naar de letter maar ik luister...

> (and I and I I am I do not chase the letter
> listen I do not chase the letter but I listen...)[16, 17]

152

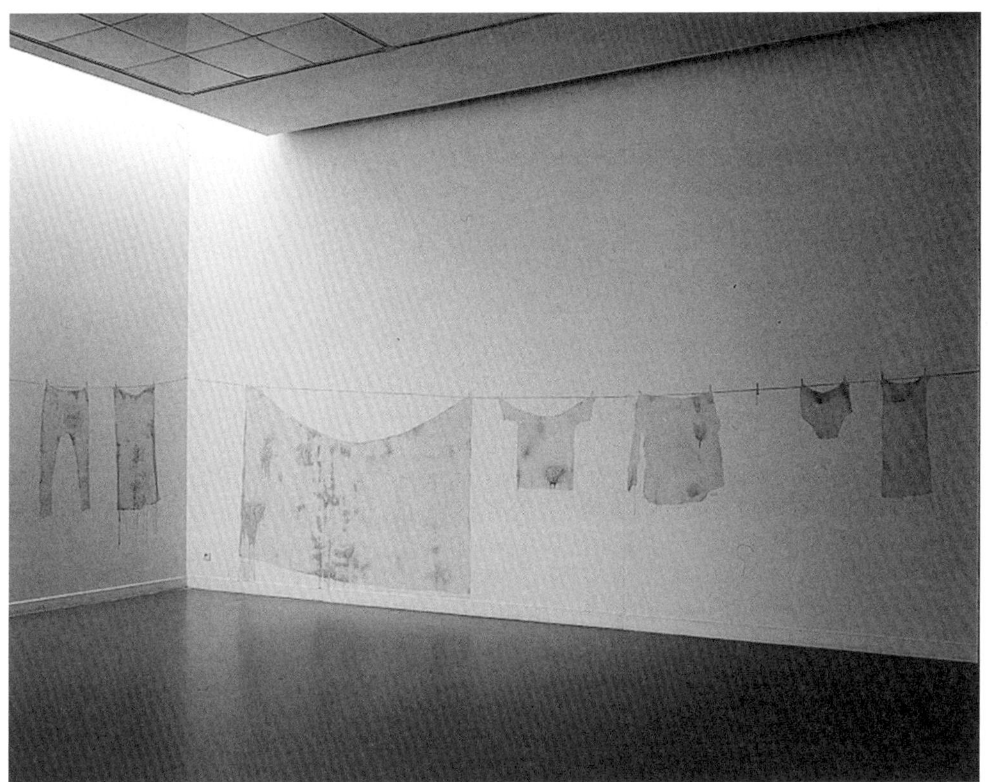

15 Job Koelewijn, *Transported Studio*, 1994. Exhibition view Festival a/d Werf, Utrecht.

Rudiment

Rudiments are building blocks: principles of STRUCTURE. Forms and motifs are building blocks in paintings and sculptures, just as bodily gesture is a building block in performances. Visual artists work with rudiments, the way a drummer practices rhythmic patterns, exploring their character and their potential. When the artist's approach of building blocks is inspired by traditions of painting or sculpture, when the artist's ambition is to forge a connection to these classical media, we are dealing with medium-specific art.[1]

Medium-specific art is driven by the focus on technique and manipulation of materials: the work of these painters or sculptors typically features a signature 'painted stroke' or 'plastic gesture'. Other artists have a different approach: they shoot ideas at their medium. They often subject their work to processes

1 Clement Greenberg, 'Modernist Painting', *Forum Lectures*, Washington D. C., Voice of America, 1960.

155

2 Umberto Eco, *The Open Work*, trans. Anna Cancogni, Cambridge (MA), Harvard University Press, 1989. Original publication: *Opera Aperta*, 1962.

3 Rosalind Krauss discusses this question in "*A Voyage on the North Sea*": *Art in the Age of the Post-Medium Condition*, London, Thames & Hudson, 2000. Her essay is dedicated to Broodthaers' *Voyage on the North Sea* (1973–1974), the 16mm colour film, which is one of the two correlates of *Bateau Tableau* (1973); the third one being an artist's book with this title (1974).

of shapeshifting and masquerade. These painters or sculptors work with the conceptual perspective, taking on board the radical shift brought about by 1960s art: art's emphasis on the here and now (the ambition to make direct connections with the everyday, through performances, land art, concept art, et cetera). This type of artistic practice exemplifies the idea of the open work.[2]

It took me a while to develop an eye for the rudiments that artists work with. Such building blocks mostly become pronounced over a long period of time. But they are never stable; artists may have to make the choice of going against them, casting familiar rudiments aside and opting for an altogether different approach. When thinking about an oeuvre and its development in time, the curator/art writer may benefit from asking basic questions: What are the rudiments of an oeuvre? How do artists work with building blocks? To what extent do they challenge themselves, by renewing familiar methods, for instance, or finding deeper grounds, or completely changing course, opening the work to opposite energies?

Is matter more important than ideas?[3] One artist, susceptible to tradition, genres and their rules, relates to the reservoir of knowledge acquired in art history. Another artist, modern and obstinate, aims to break free from these heritages. The distinction between

medium-specific art and the open work is historically important: the approaches begin to manifest
with early modernism. The proto-conceptualist artist Marcel Duchamp presaged the conflict or tension
between medium-specific art and the open work.
His oeuvre is an incubator of ideas that defy general
cultural assumptions (on painting, for example),
offering a dynamic perspective. Interestingly,
Duchamp didn't cast aside traditional techniques,
see his last work *Étant donnés (Given: 1. The
Waterfall, 2. The Illuminating Gas)* (1946–1966).

Current developments suggest that the relation
between medium-specific art and the open work is
becoming more temperate. From the work of artists,
I deduce that the two notions rather operate in tandem, as spheres of influence encircling each other, as
fields of forces triggering one another. (Of course,
cultural amnesia plays a role here too, the process
where a new generation forgets the feats of the one
before, or subjects them to creative misinterpreta-
tions.) A work by Marcel Broodthaers from 1973 is a
very relevant connection to this situation: it illustrates how rudiments can instigate a game of their
own, in order to expose, suspend, even break down
the boundaries between different media.

Broodthaers' *Bateau Tableau* (1973) exemplifies
modern art's masquerade. This presentation of
eighty colour transparencies breaks down a painting,

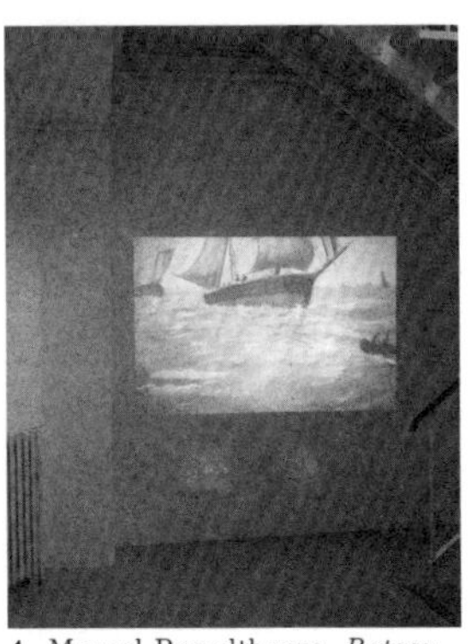

4 Marcel Broodthaers, *Bateau Tableau*, 1973.

5 Anna Hakkens, 'Inleiding', *Marcel Broodthaers: Projecties*, eds. Frank Lubbers, Anna Hakkens, Maria Gilissen, Eindhoven, Van Abbemuseum, 1994, p.25.

in an exercise of deconstruction.[4] Broodthaers had bought a simple seascape painting, probably made by a Sunday painter, in an antiques shop in Paris in a somewhat touristic area. He referred to it as *Un tableau représentant le retour d'un bateau de peche* ('A painting representing the return of a fishing boat').[5]

Bateau Tableau creates new perspectives. Material Transformation: a painting of a seascape, oil on canvas, is now a projection piece. Eighty colour slides appear in the dark, slowly ticking away time. The first shots of the piece are 'totals' of the painting with its golden frame. But soon we lose sight of the seascape as a whole, when details start to take over, having a party for themselves. Theatre: Enter Rudiments: the canvas appears in bare state (offscreen, the frame has been detached) and 'close-up'. The composition is shown: the distribution of the whites, blues, greens across the surface, as well as figurative motifs: black buoy floating on the water, the ship with its majestic sails and tiny humans on board, other ships in the distance, the longboat with three men. In between, glimpses of the painting's material support appear: nails on the backside keeping the canvas in place, raw linen shining through the coloured paints. Interzone (where media mingle): the sequence—through its alternating views, its rhythm, and accentuated details—evokes sensations of camera movement and montage: the attributes of cinema. But a slide projection is not a film nor is it a painting: this creates tension and open expectation. Here, different gazes revolve around each other: the amateur meets/scrutinizes the conceptual artist, or vice versa, while around the corner a detective appears…

Broodthaers keeps all his options open. Not choosing one medium, or one type of maker/position, over the other, keeping all close at hand, he argues for art as poetry. The work of art is a poetic act.

Artists are attached to their rudiments—the oeuvre of Marcel Broodthaers, the poet-artist, illustrates this very well, because throughout it, poetic shards, beautiful and strange in their appearance, get to say intriguing things—but they also move against them. In 2001–2002, I curated the exhibition 'Höhere Wesen befahlen: anders malen!' ('Higher beings commanded: paint differently!'). That show explored different ways of working with and thinking on painting.[6] It looked at the genre's rudiments and at possible crossovers. I included Broodthaers' *Bateau Tableau* here. I also presented a work that I mention en passant in my text on Klaas Kloosterboer: a performance where the artist, on the night of the exhibition opening, sawed a white box in half. Was his act an incantation of death? The box form is

6 'Höhere Wesen befahlen: anders malen!', Smart Project Space, Amsterdam, 9 December 2001–20 January 2002. Artists: Francis Alÿs, Tiong Ang, Ansuya Blom, Marcel Broodthaers, Jaroslaw Flicinski, Gijs Frieling, Klaas Kloosterboer, and Niamh O'Malley.

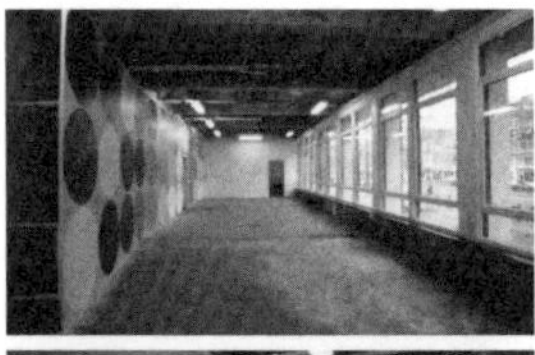
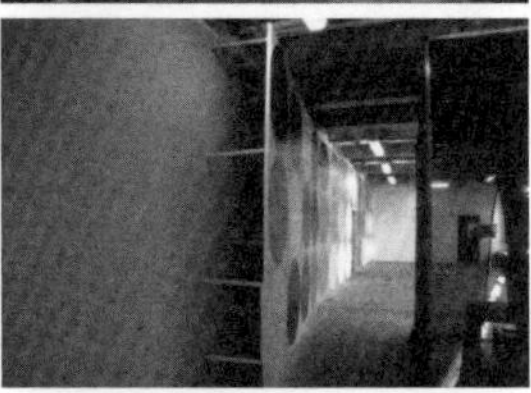
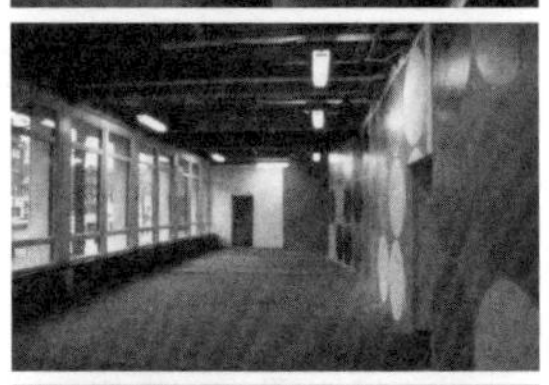
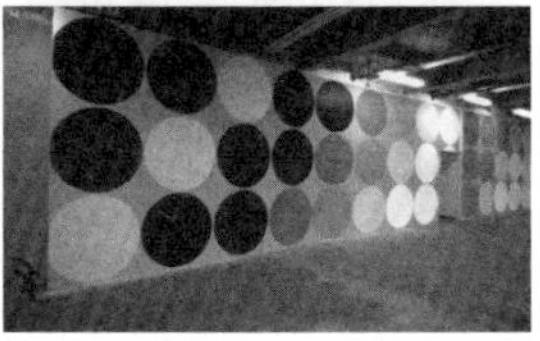

7 Jaroslaw Flicinski, *Finnish Tango*, 2001.

common to Kloosterboer's art; by handling the form this way, an animistic aspect emerged.

One more interesting work in that show was a large mural, made *in situ* by Jaroslaw Flicinski, called *Finnish Tango* (2001). The mural was in a space that looked out on the city. The artist had borrowed its circular motif from Victor Vasarely, the leader of the historical Op Art movement. By enlarging the size of the motif, and popping up the colours of his wall painting, he created a dynamic setting, an image for the urban environment's 'vita activa'. Recalling the language of Constructivism, and public art works in this style, painted in the aftermath of the Second World War, on the walls of Paris, for instance, his work was a homage to this scientific, positive approach in art. But there was also a melancholy aspect. By painting his composition on a *faux* wall—a new temporary wall, attached to the permanent wall, entered the space at a certain point, thus creating a subtly oblique effect—he articulated a sense of displacement, a feeling about his nomadic practice, being the itinerant maker of temporary murals.[7]

Some of the artists in this section began developing their work in the 1980s, the era of abstract and figurative neo styles. Growing up after conceptual art, for them it felt natural to reconnect with the historical figurations and abstractions. But many artists did not cast aside conceptual art's 'negative impetus'—manifested in the critique on conventions of genres and in the iconoclastic assault on the image-as-representation that was 'busted' and reconstructed using contemporary means (language, documentary photos, in situ work). This negative impetus appears as an undercurrent in the 1990s' practices of painting and sculpture that, inspired by notions of instability, explore form-as-potential.

René Jolink's work brings into play the rudiments of old photographic techniques, notably the slow process of bringing images to light. In his paintings, radiant forms and figures emerge in obscure backgrounds. Through their shimmering luminosity, the abstract paintings resemble mirages.

Klaas Kloosterboer is a conceptual painter who explores basic forms such as the dot. Transformation and role-playing are important in his oeuvre, where abstract paintings cross over into sculptures or theatrical sets: abstract installations with social undertones. Helmut Federle is a traditional painter who deeply relates to twentieth-century abstraction. He forged his connection to this heritage: at some point he began to paint his initials, treating the letters of his name as signs of resistance/potential, integrating them into intriguing, dramatic scenes. Pieter Laurens Mol's oeuvre reveals his interest in the secret energy of materials and the power of words.

My interview focuses on an installation symbolizing a martial energy field. The work features nine rusty iron rods suspended on tripods that are adorned with attributes referring to nine male characters. The work could be experienced as a group of street fighters and a symbol for masculine resoluteness as well as ambivalence (Mol's group has a relevant antecedent in Duchamp's *Nine Malic Molds,* which are part of his *Large Glass*).

Esther Kläs' art is inspired by *arte povera,* by minimal art, and by her journeys in impressive nature reserves. The rudiments (threads, tracks) in her drawings and sculptures approximate vegetative life reacquainting the viewer with nature. Roland Schimmel is a conceptual painter. Light is his source and subject: his works capture the intense retinal experience of after-images—our involuntary body-brain response when exposed to strong light. With their black suns and softly coloured haloes, the drawings, paintings and animations create immense energy fields. My text on Absalon investigates the artist's own inner dialogue, weighing the balance of silent contemplation versus acting out angst.

Resonating with Malevich's *Arkhitektons* and Chris Burden's performances, Absalon's works aspire to make a new beginning. André Kruysen is a traditional yet unpredictable sculptor. The dynamics of perspective is important in his works. Their form is fleeting and changeable (light sculptures made in situ) or enchanting (the polychrome masks). I discuss a recent body of work featuring a skull motif that, turned inside out, was made in response to a famous sculpture by Boccioni, the Italian Futurist.

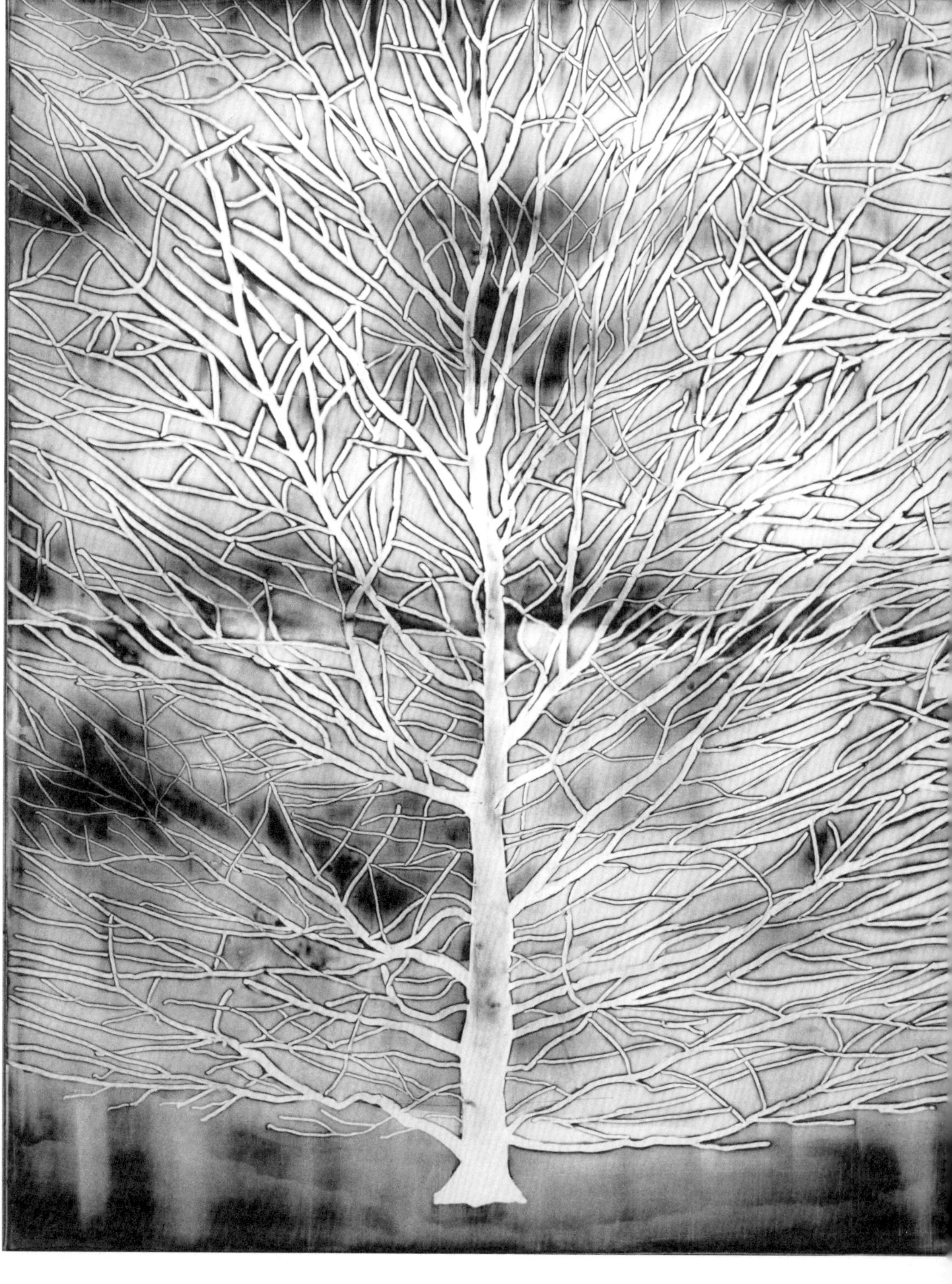

The Golden Fleece

René Jolink

René Jolink is exhibiting a new series of paintings at Vous
Êtes Ici gallery, Amsterdam. Nature glimmers in these
abstract images, as though picked out by a flash of light.
These vistas are not realistic representations but suggestions
of mental resonance, of the impressions that nature implants
in our mind: crystal-clear memory or ominous premonition.
The paintings have a remarkable sharpness and presence.
Depictions of a forest, a tree or foliage seem simultaneously to
be the vehicle for something deeper, as though probing a
thought or a feeling about life. They are reflections on what
time does to us, on the ever-changing experience of the
same, and on the companionship that images offer people.
The paintings have a mysterious mobility. There is a strong
sense of vitality; forms seem to fade into something else, as
though seeking a direct connection with the way things
were or will become. We see an image sunken in a kind of
depth, where it becomes almost invisible and devoid of
contours. But at the same time, we see an image seeping up
from that same depth, reappearing on the surface as some
brilliant sediment.

René Jolink, *ZT 180313*, 2013.
Photo: Tom Haartsen.

The painterly process that underlies the works resembles that of a photographer from the analogue era, who captures an image in a fraction of a second and later develops this slowly in the darkroom. Jolink first draws his motif on white canvas. He then covers this with a layer of uniform white paint in which he makes the initial drawing once again, by scraping and scratching the surface, thus producing a negative of the original image and the motif. Once this surface is dry, he adds a glaze of transparent colour which sinks into the negative. This too needs time to dry before the final step is made: he again applies an even layer of white paint, which he then erases (in part), resulting in a translucent film that at once reveals and hides the original drawing.

The crystalline structures exposed in the paintings stir our associative imagination. In my mind's eye, I picture a moment from the Hollywood film *Jason and the Argonauts* (1963), where a fellowship of heroes is sent on a quest by King Pelias of Thessaly, to retrieve a Golden Fleece from a far-off land. Dan Chaffey, the film director, turned this Greek myth into an adventure story for cinema, which included wonderful special effects by the famous animator Ray Harryhausen, who died in 2013. A memorable episode in the film is the one where Jason is attacked by a fearsome army of skeleton warriors. At the end, Jason arrives at the destination in Colchis (contemporary Georgia), where he seizes the ram's fleece after slaying its ferocious guardian, the monster Hydra. We see the Golden Fleece glittering in a tree. The light that shines on it makes the golden surface vibrate, igniting everything around it with its shimmering radiance.

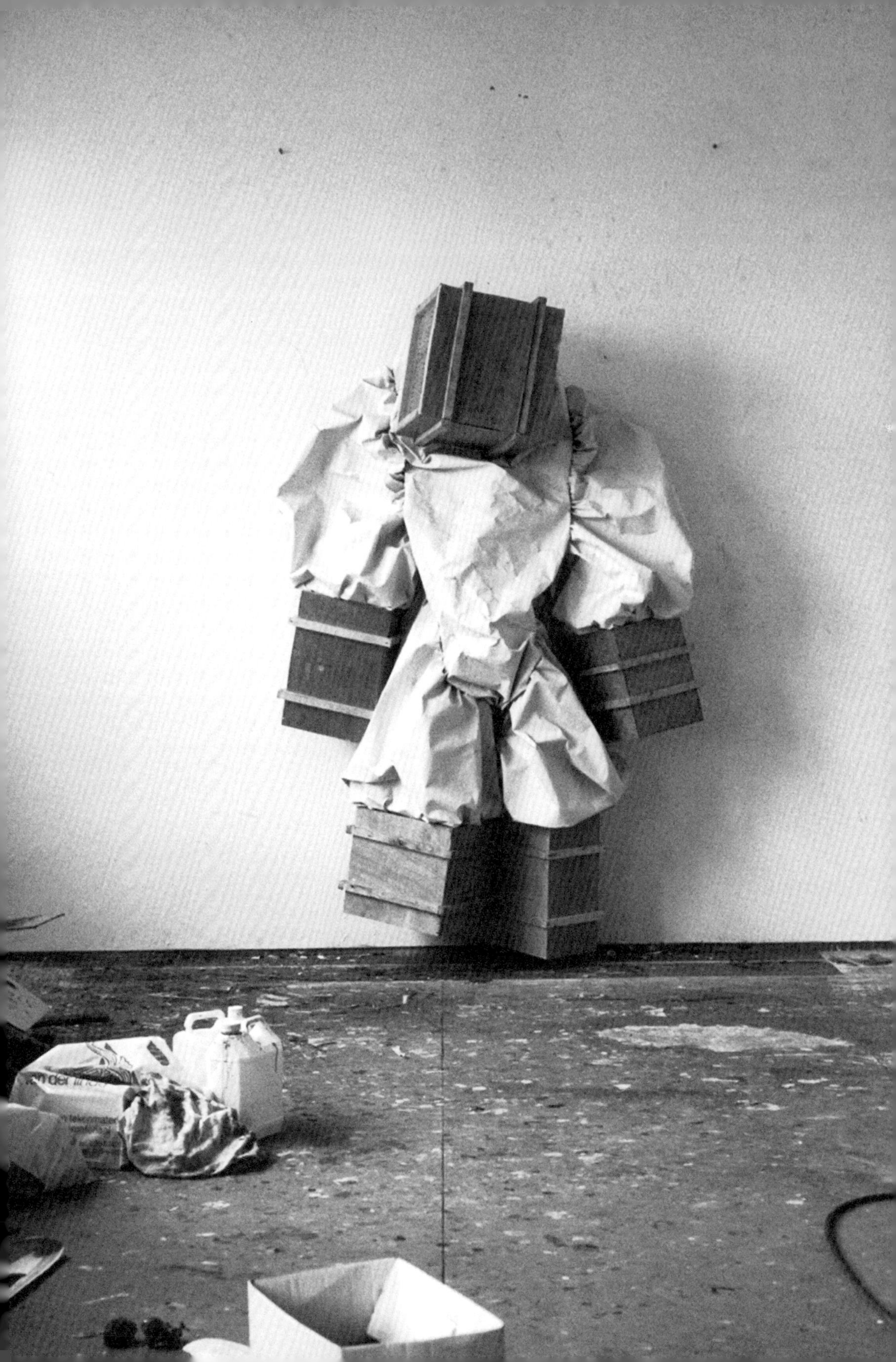

Chinaman

Klaas Kloosterboer

In my garden
Things grow in my garden
Things will grow…
—Swans, 'In My Garden'[1]

Multiple voices can be discerned in Klaas Kloosterboer's oeuvre. Someone who sees his colourful body of work for the first time might experience it as a living masquerade— comparable to the mirage conjured up in Anna Akhmatova's 'Poem without a Hero'. On New Year's Eve 1914 in her house at the river Fontanka in Saint Petersburg, the poet is visited by 'shades from the year 1913 in the guise of maskers'. Dorian, Faust, Iron Mask, Dappertutto, Glahn and Iokanaan 'hold[ing] their Dianas' are there, as are Hamlet and Salome. It is a vibrant company. But can you talk to ghosts and meet one in the flesh? Akhmatova began writing her poem in 1940 looking back on her life and thinking of the people she has lost—they must be her 'shades'! At some point she exclaims:

1 Swans, *Children of God*, album, 1987.

Klaas Kloosterboer, *02117 (Chinaman)*, 2002, wood and linnen, 250 × 180 × 90 cm.

2 Anna Akhmatova, 'Poem
without a Hero: Triptych 1940–
62, Leningrad—Tashkent—
Moscow', Part 1.

Have fun—so much fun now,
But why exactly did it turn out,
That I'm the only one alive?[2]

The image reminds me of the artist in their universe, pondering the shapes they have created. To him they are real presences, but what are they compared to life? Kloosterboer's work takes many forms. It leans towards the exuberant state—the air of elated poetry/music. His practice, which today (in 2003) spans twenty years, combines a painter's interests with existential questions. And it rests on three pillars: the primary impulse and expansive energy of Abstract Expressionism, conceptual art's use of ideas that drive the work like a machine as well as its strong interest in language, and the expectation/suspense of theatre.

His oeuvre consists of drawings and photos, singular paintings exploring various topics (several corpora), large monochromatic paintings that refer to 'sets', and the 3D shapes: 'actors' and 'props'. Painting materials are used to make mercurial objects that seem to switch between two and three dimensions. Their place would be, say, right opposite of Donald Judd's specific objects. Altogether his works create a field of tension, and a playing ground for experiments. Kloosterboer's work features elements that recall the lofty perspective of modernist painters; generally, it reflects on down-to-earth stuff. His practice can be defined with the term 'expanded painting': imagine a scaffolding where the artist, in a series of haptic procedures, forges a gamut of new connections. KK juxtaposes grand gestures—his monochromatic paintings evoke inner landscapes—with intimate stirrings. Some of his figures smack of real life, for example the *Chinaman* hanging his head: that shape was created using five wooden boxes, painting them off-white, and strapping the pieces together into one body. The figure could be moulded after a man the artist saw in the street; around him is an unmistakable air of melancholy.

In Kloosterboer's exhibits I have often felt an absence, as if something is left unsaid. It made me think of abandoned sets, a ghost town left behind by the film crew after the spaghetti western was finished. Enter Gunslinger. Stupefied, he cannot believe his eyes: all the life has gone. What is he to do? Burst out in laughter or cry? Collapse on the floor? Raise his fist in protest? Should he contemplate the emptiness?

Two forces inhabit Kloosterboer's work. Its active energy resembles that of that cheerful personage who never looks back on his deeds, as described by Walter Benjamin: 'The destructive character knows only one password: "make room"; only one activity: clearing away. His need for fresh air and open space is stronger than any hatred'.[3] The work's second force is the receptive energy, sheer open-mindedness.

Kloosterboer's basis is raw material: canvas and oil, enamel, household paint and other stuff: cardboard, wood—as well as ideas. He subjects his material to expansive or destructive processes: sewing paintings together into a 3D form; covering inventory of an art institute with an enormous monochrome painting, or crumpling a canvas into a wad that is hung from the ceiling; cutting up paintings and then stitching the rifts; perforating the canvas so that a pattern of holes emerges. Other actions result in unexpected shapes—as when he sawed through a white box, right through the middle, so the two parts fell on the floor, while still resting on their trestles. This created a slapstick spectacle: where was the beautiful maiden upon whom the magical operation was executed? As a public performance, such an act would have fitted well with an evening of vaudeville at the end of the nineteenth century. Other works resembling the tragi-comical

3 Walter Benjamin, 'The Destructive Character', *Frankfurter Zeitung*, 20 November 1931.

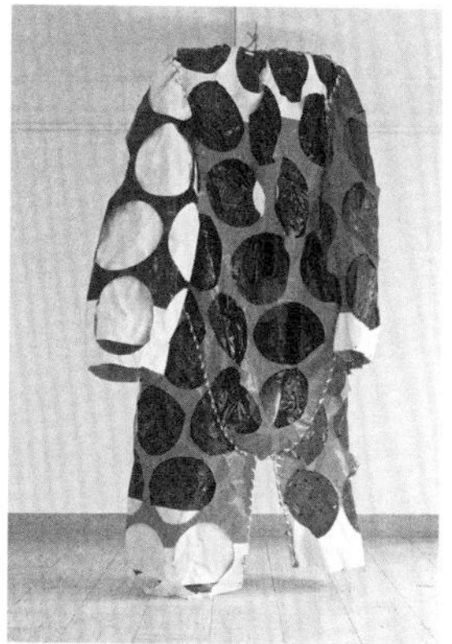

4a Klaas Kloosterboer, *00139 (Groot Pak)*, 2000, enamel on linen, 360 × 230 × 120 cm.

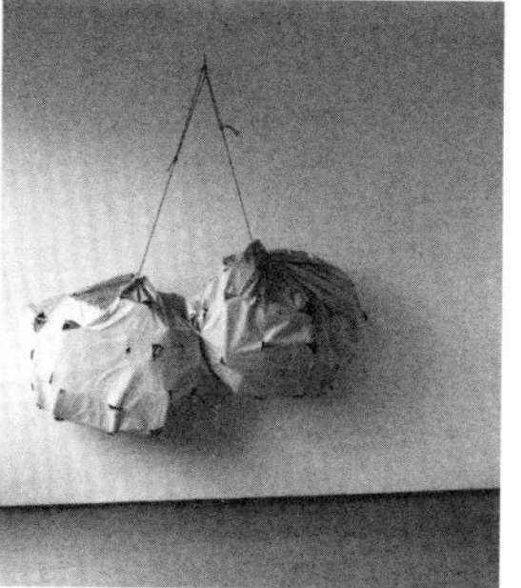

4b Klaas Kloosterboer, *99123*, 1999, enamel on linen, paperboard boxes, (2×) ø 120 cm.

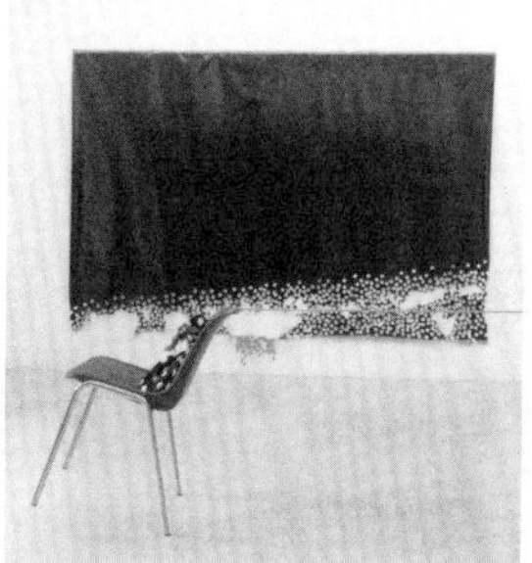

4c Klaas Kloosterboer, *95125*, 1995, enamel on linen, 217 × 320 cm.

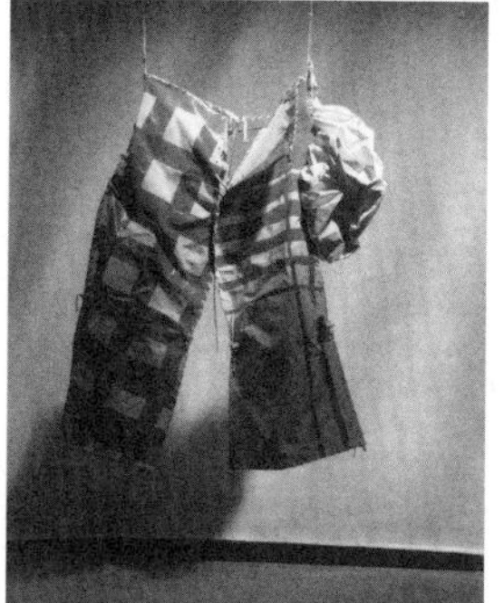

4d Klaas Kloosterboer, *03109* and *13101 (Carousel)*, 2003 and 2013.

figures from *commedia dell'arte*[4] take the shape of a blown-up suit, gloves in pairs that do not quite match, confetti bound by string. In one work, three red angular shapes linger in front of a black withered wall. The installation (set) recalls a lively formation: if you look closely, let the image sink in, you'll detect the silhouettes of a cool punk band playing in a sleazy club: underground sensation.

The receptive force manifests in the large paintings. The monochromatic works were made with a spray-paint technique. Each of them seems to express a verbal idea. The basis of a blue expansive painting is an expression—'make a point' (or, 'leave your mark')—that refers to ambition, the traditional masculine ethos. Indeed, in this oeuvre the drive to occupy space is essential. But as combative as this ambition may sound, the blue painting is surprisingly mellow. Here, a tiny but amplified blue dot becomes a grandiose, hazy blot hovering in the air. There emerges a celestial constellation, a star system not unlike a vista from the film *2001: A Space Odyssey*. A silvery grey shimmers in another large painting: psychedelic dreaminess.[5]

The artist is acting out desire, but also mobilizing counterforces. In one painting, a dramatic yellow rules. Here an enormously active power is unleashed, except for one blank pristine space untouched somewhere in the heart of the painting; here soft light is shining, as in a forest clearing. I associate this zone with vulnerability, a state of helplessness. The artist told me that, while making this work, he was thinking of Andy Warhol's *Sleep*.[6, 7] From different viewpoints, the camera is moving in on the subject: in Warhol's film, a man, unreachable and untouchable; in Kloosterboer's case, an open and virginal surface.

What issues does Klaas Kloosterboer address in his work? And how relevant are they? Angelika Stepken, director

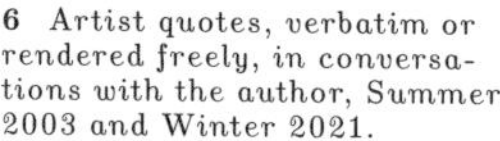

5 Klaas Kloosterboer, 95106-95121 (series), 1995, colour photo on dibond, 20 × 31 cm.

6 Artist quotes, verbatim or rendered freely, in conversations with the author, Summer 2003 and Winter 2021.

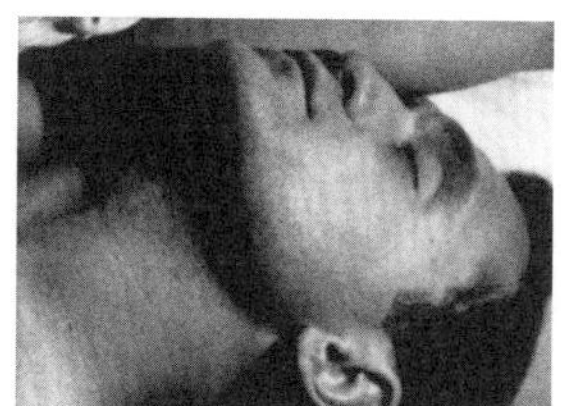

7 Andy Warhol, *Sleep*, 1964, film, 5h 21'.

of the Badischer Kunstverein, asked me this when I showed her Kloosterboer's art. 'I intuitively sense the importance of resistance—not against something, but within the oeuvre. Resistance to give up something, history maybe?'[8] I answered her questions with three considerations.

8 Angelika Stepken in email conversation with MK, summer 2002.

I

Kloosterboer intentionally engages with the traditions of art. He mentions for example Hermann Nitsch's Dionysian performances, collective rituals executed under the artist's directorship, in which painting was the co-shaper of sacrificial acts, and bloody rebirth. As well as Arnulf Rainer's Übermalungen, individual quests in which the artist spirited away his self-portrait and replaced it with obscurity. These two artists-painters had an impact on him when he was young, they made Kloosterboer grasp the potential of art.

Years later, acts of undermining become the themes in a corpus of paintings, that he made by hurling dark paint at open surfaces. The paintings are connected with a series of sculptures made of plywood and paint; they foreground the eye that chastises, the occupying gaze. *Strot* (Gorge), *Schavot* (Pillory), *Sandwichman* and *Goot* (Gutter) are contemporary Gothic Pieces.[9] The sculptures invoke the act of shaming, subjecting others, or becoming the subject of spite. As to the paintings mentioned, I see the artist in his studio, flinging clots of black or brown paint at a surface, aiming for the tender spots and smearing a canvas—as if it is a living body— with tar or shit. Who is he targeting? On one painting the word 'I' has been written. On another it says 'you'. Whilst Kloosterboer, here, mimics the gestures of Abstract Expressionism, he is creating new rudiments (for his abstract

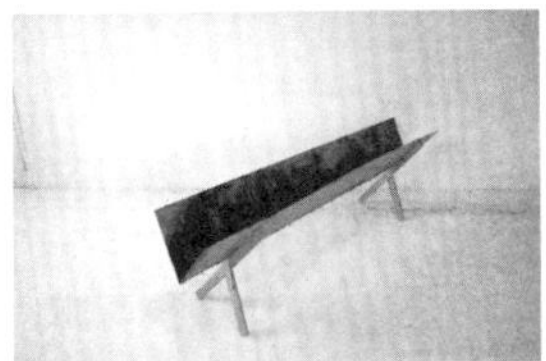

9a Klaas Kloosterboer, *03104 (Gutter)*, 2003, oil on wood, 66 × 42 × 211 cm.

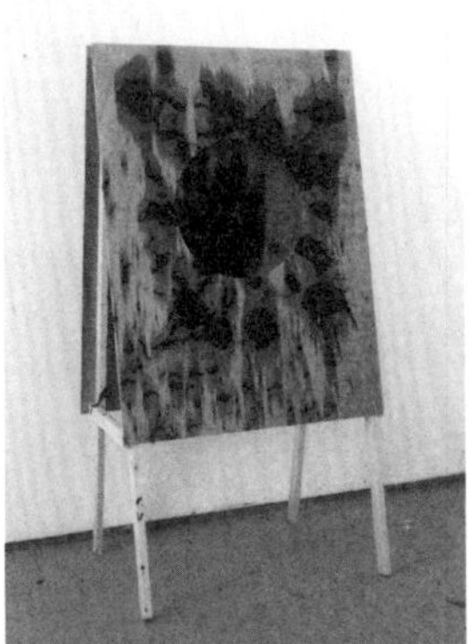

9b Klaas Kloosterboer, *03112 (Sandwichman)*, 2003, oil on wood, 170 × 90 × 60 cm.

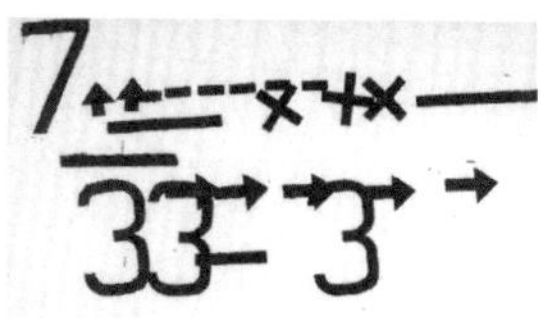

10 Jannis Kounellis, announcement card, 1960, for painting
performance and exhibition at
Galeria Tartaruga, Rome.

11 Willoughby Sharp,
'Structure and Sensibility: An
Interview with Jannis
Kounellis', *Avalanche*, 1972, nr
12, p. 21. In: G. Battcock/R.
Nickas ed., *The Art of
Performance. A Critical
Anthology*, New York, E.P.
Dutton, 1984, p. xii.

painting) to address intimacy in the social field. He meddles
with painting in a similar way as Jannis Kounellis, when the
arte povera artist was breaking down and reconfiguring the
genre:

> In 1960 I did an ongoing performance, first in my studio
> and then at the Galeria Tartaruga in Rome, in which I
> stretched unsized canvas over the walls of the room, and
> painted letters over them, which I sang.[10] The problem
> in those days was to establish a new kind of painting.[11]

But doubt is Kloosterboer's source. It gives his art a polar
quality. As if one hand doesn't know what the other is doing.
The artist mobilizes contradictions. Before him there's a sea
of possibilities, which he wants to traverse. Whereto?
Walking with St. Augustine, he says: 'I doubt, therefore I
am.' Kloosterboer steers his vessel between Scylla and
Charybdis, avant-garde and academia, experimental and traditional works. 'I cultivate my doubt. I do not want to believe
in myself: that would be the end. I want to learn and surprise
myself'.

Earnestness and fancy come together in Kloosterboer's
works. His multi-coloured *groot pak* (big suit) hangs from the
ceiling like a garb for a giant clown. The work—a mockery of
the artist who thinks himself the genius? or an incantation of
the vanished ego?—recalls David Byrne's *Big Suit*, the white
costume of the Talking Heads' frontman-singer, an oversized
dress that can be seen in the film *Stop Making Sense* (1984).
Kloosterboer's suit is gay but voices melancholy. Here a
bunch of mixed-up paintings describe a figure of fun. The

artist has said that *groot pak* was, to an extent, his response to the art discourse that prevailed in the 1990s (*Relational Aesthetics*, social practices). In that climate, painting was pushed aside. The artist raises a protest: his paintings deal with the contradictions of life; one of his main themes is—paradoxically—man in social context.

3

Through the multiplicity of his art, Kloosterboer creates a variety of 'texts'. His works invite concrete and metaphoric readings—deciphering their acts and gestures, the wordplay or expression embodied in a singular piece. His works almost discuss life, like the man in the street exchanging a few spoken words with a passer-by in a chance encounter, or the writer in the measured stanzas of a poem.

Mystery is created in autonomy, says Kloosterboer. According to him, there must be a distance, however small, between art and reality. That idea resonates with how Virginia Woolf qualified imaginative work: 'Fiction is like a spider's web, attached ever so lightly perhaps, but still attached to life at all four corners'.[12] Kloosterboer has given his exhibition in Karlsruhe a motto, *the drama of autonomy*. It reveals a concern for the fate of autonomy, the space where the artist can work without outside interference. Kloosterboer: 'Art that makes claims for autonomy, today, must highlight its own critical condition'.

12 Virginia Woolf, *A Room of One's Own*, 1929, ch. 4.

Landscape

Klaas Kloosterboer's exhibition at the Badischer Kunstverein takes its title, 'Ballast', from a video shot in a Dutch polder landscape.[13] It is part of a larger corpus of videos. Three of these videos can be described as emblematic explorations of, respectively, the creative act (and the resistance it meets), a common social situation (a meeting), and the question of experience. The scenes in *Ballast* were filmed through the rear window of a car driving on along a long and narrow road. The sequence is framed by lines of the rear window heater, and tree trunks. In the resulting grid, two spherical forms—cardboard boxes enveloped by grey rubbish bags—are in continuous movement. Tied to the car, the balls collide—giving the impression that they are trying to push each other off the road. There's an aggressive, sensual aspect here, we can see the car as a phallus. This is a picture of the artist's drive. From afar we hear him cry: 'Here I come!' Can this work be read as critique of the male ambition? So far, the road is vacant, there's no oncoming traffic.

176

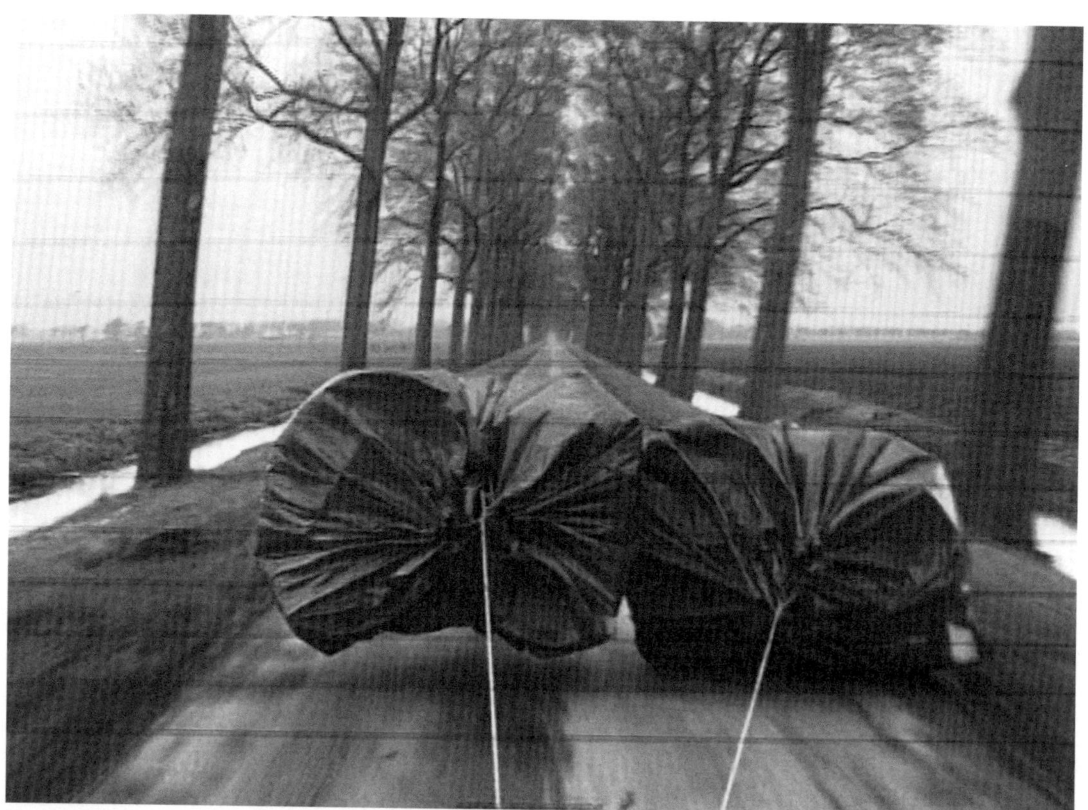

13 Klaas Kloosterboer, *01106 (Ballast)*, 2001, video loop, 2'10".

The grid in *Ballast* recalls the 'vegetal grids' of Mondrian and Malevich. The balls can be seen as jesters in a Shakespearean drama, casting icy comments. What is it that they scorn? Kloosterboer's grid frames a polder. For the Dutch, this orderly, human-made landscape is our nature. We connect it in a natural way to abstract geometry. Kloosterboer's grid is however made of trees and iron wires.

To probe the implications of his approach, I bring up the work of Günther Förg: his concern for the modernist legacy has common ground with Kloosterboer's. Characteristically, Förg's exhibitions in the 1980s were immersive installations with various media. Besides paintings, there were photos of buildings, vertical bronze reliefs on pedestals (displaying finger drawings for example), and mirrors that reflected the environment. A mono- or duotone mural was the background. Often a photo-snapshot of a woman—a lover of Förg's or a friend enlarged to the monumental scale of his photographs of architecture—would complete the set. His *Gesamtkunstwerk* recalled the modernist habitat.

In fact, Förg's surroundings addressed the gap between the modernist legacy and everyday reality: what is their place there, what is their fate? His installations conveyed a melancholic *Spurensicherung*. His photos of splendid buildings in Italy, Germany and Russia that have faded with time, illustrate loss, a feeling that we've lost touch with these modernist artefacts. In his paintings, Förg takes the modernist grid apart: his grids are clumsy, pitiful skeletons. The presence of the human figure in Förg's installations is intriguing: a woman is standing in a courtyard, for example; a woman is walking down the stairs of Casa Malaparte; a woman wearing a Chinese hat (this large photo is a close-up). In these uncanny surroundings, the only thing that was real, were the women.

Förg's environments portrayed modernism as a spectre. He is a melancholic modernist. Kloosterboer is a burlesque modernist. He takes pleasure in subverting the grand and elevated, without detaching himself from those qualities. *Ballast* is a jest, but the grid is re-grounded, as it were. The inherited visual language of modernist painting here bursts open like the bud of a gaudy flower. The video pictures the artist's output as sheer surplus. Like a Rhine bargeman who keeps some cargo apart, in order to eventually place it fore or aft on the barge—as equilibrium demands it—the artist heads right for his destination.

Kammerspiel

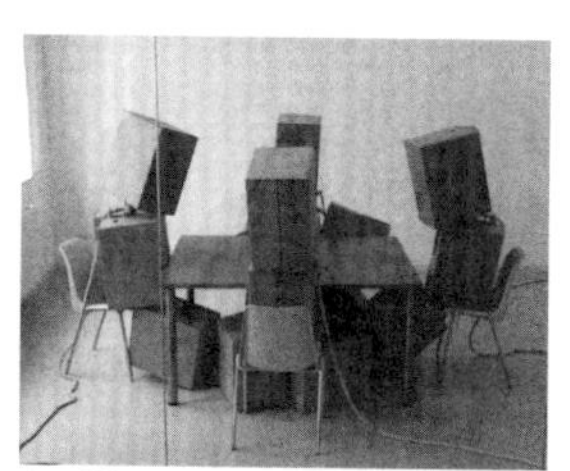

14 Klaas Kloosterboer, *02126 (Meeting)*, 2002, video loop, 1'8".

Kloosterboer's video *Meeting* presents a handful of characters seated around a table on bright green chairs.[14] The four bodies resemble dummies. They're made of cardboard boxes tied together with string. There is one box for each head, one for each torso, and one for the legs. Although their rigid limbs barely make it possible, the four characters lean forward attentively. Suddenly the deep deliberation comes to an end: in slow motion the figures are ripped from their places.

The scenes are filmed from behind glass, we look through a window onto a place that we could associate with some laboratory for human experiments. However cartoonish this video may appear; it is a serious reflection on the social domain and how it works. Individual and group behaviour (interaction with the other) are observed. A partition separated the artist from the scenes. Kloosterboer's 'heavy-handedness' reverberates in the video. The procedure ending the meeting recalls the early silent films, where a sinister protagonist creates artificial life using vile machinery. When in

Kloosterboer's video an invisible agency intervenes to end the meeting, the falling men resemble the debris and consternation that set in after the magic in those films had been unmasked.

Meeting is a critical reverie. The video voices two outlooks: one is discrete and detached; the other active and piercing. Their difference is illustrated by work of two kindred artists. The first outlook emerges in Dan Graham's work, the writer/artist who was influenced by the art, music and architecture of the 1960s. Graham's theme was the social sphere. He was interested in 'art as a social sign'. The interest is evident in his early performances, such as *Performance/Audience/Mirror* (1975), it took on a conceptual form in *Proposal for an Alternation of a Suburban House* (1978), and became concrete in later pastoral pavilions of glass and mirrors.

Graham's work can be explained as the artist's response to the social indifference in the US, something that was reflected by the late conceptual work that turned its back on society.[15] His pavilions are appealing and also accessible. They reflect the urban surroundings, human movements and interactions. Graham prefered to build his pavilions in parks. Their discrete scale invites people to enter. Graham: 'they're ideal places for children to play'. Graham's love for Friedrich's *Mönch am Meer* is an antecedent. He has often said that he wished to imitate that painting—but by incorporating the viewer's experience. Friedrich's monk is watching sublime natural scenery, but he should also sense that someone is watching over him.

The second counterpart of *Meeting* is the theme of (unfulfilled) socialization in Samuel Beckett's texts and plays. Beckett's stagings are characterized by terse treatment of form—which places them on a line with visual art. His work exposes the complexity of human rapprochement. The stasis

15 Jeff Wall, *Dan Graham's Kammerspiel*, Toronto, Art Metropole, 1991, p. 19.

16 Jan Kott, *Shakespeare Our Contemporary*, New York, Knopff, 2015, p. 18.

in which his characters often find themselves, expresses scepticism if this can be attained. Personages are buried to the neck; they can speak but not move, nor come closer to each other. The voice is their only means of communication. In *Not I*, a drama about perfect isolation, the voice is all there is: the mouth emits endless strings of words.

Four figures sit at a table, at the end, one by one falls down. That sequence has strong connotations. 'For Shakespeare,' Jan Kott writes, 'absolute power has a first and a last name, it has hands, eyes and lips. It is the relentless struggle between living persons, who sit at one table'.[16] Kloosterboer's video addresses the complexity of attachment. With paced violence, he breaks down a social gestalt. The apparent consensus of four people is easily disrupted.

Portrait

Workshop is a video of a short performance recorded in a single take (without audience). The material consists of spoken words and gestures. We see the torso of a man sitting at a table, dressed in a plain shirt. He recites an intriguing poem. He illustrates the meaning of its words with the earnest and hesitant movements of his hands; they lag behind a bit, seem out of sync, appear a bit dreamy. The language of the hands seems to look for ways to oppose the indoctrination of the words. The artist comments: 'Things get into your head. How do you get rid of them?'

> One two three
> Said decide to hesitate
>
> Four five six
> Hit replied to receive

Seven eight nine
Remarked add to subtract

Ten eleven twelve
Recited doubt to thinking

Thirteen fourteen fifteen
They all drummed together
Add and subtract
Order and select
Choose and lose
Fall and break
Multiply and die

One two three four five six

What does this poem want to express? Wittgenstein's words
spring to mind: 'Worüber man nicht sprechen kann, darüber
muß man schweigen' ('Whereof one cannot speak, thereof
one must be silent'). The poem seems to contain a lesson, an
encrypted life lesson. Earlier, the artist considered the title
'Workshop of the lost utopias'. Our wisdom and resilience
come with age. But is life not also an adventure? *Workshop*
could be seen as a Symbolist work. I have a soft spot for
Symbolist art because—unlike today's talk shows and a life-
style-culture exposing the most private emotions—such
works cherish feeling.

I want to say one more thing about the role of language
in Kloosterboer's work. I discussed the painting that came
about by verbal imperative: 'make a point'. The procedure
that led to this blue expanse recalls the conceptual practices.
La Monte Young once made a well-known work,
Composition 1960 # 10 ('To Bob Morris'), an instruction for
a performance to be executed by others. This text reads:
'Draw a straight line and follow it.' Several artists took it up:

in Denmark,1960, Piero Manzoni drew the line in a paper mill (*7200 Meter Line*) and in Düsseldorf Nam June Paik dipped his head in a bowl with ink and painted a line with his hair (*Zen for Head*, 1962).

Kloosterboer's language—spoken words or hushed instructions for acts that shape his work—comes with ambiguity. The *Workshop* poem makes me feel a subdued emotion. But the text is hard as crystal. The words connect to other sections of his oeuvre, where other 'artist rules' come into play. One such rule is: '*Na het spel, komt de hel*' ('After the game, hell stakes its claim'). This signature is Protestant, forbidding.

I want to end with a local/vernacular aspect to Kloosterboer's practice, namely the resistance of its elements and their relation to nature. For me it is hard to imagine Kloosterboer's works without the experience of the Dutch polder, the low-lying land reclaimed from the sea, where once there were brackish marshlands. The artist is familiar with the sight and smell of the earth planted with crops, naked once more after the harvest, when the fat clay masses stirred up by the plough come to the surface. The grandeur of that black earth, the vista of its sharp furrows, set against the image of budding seeds in the ground: Kloosterboer's work makes me feel life's delicacy. One figure of his epitomizes this: we are made of china.

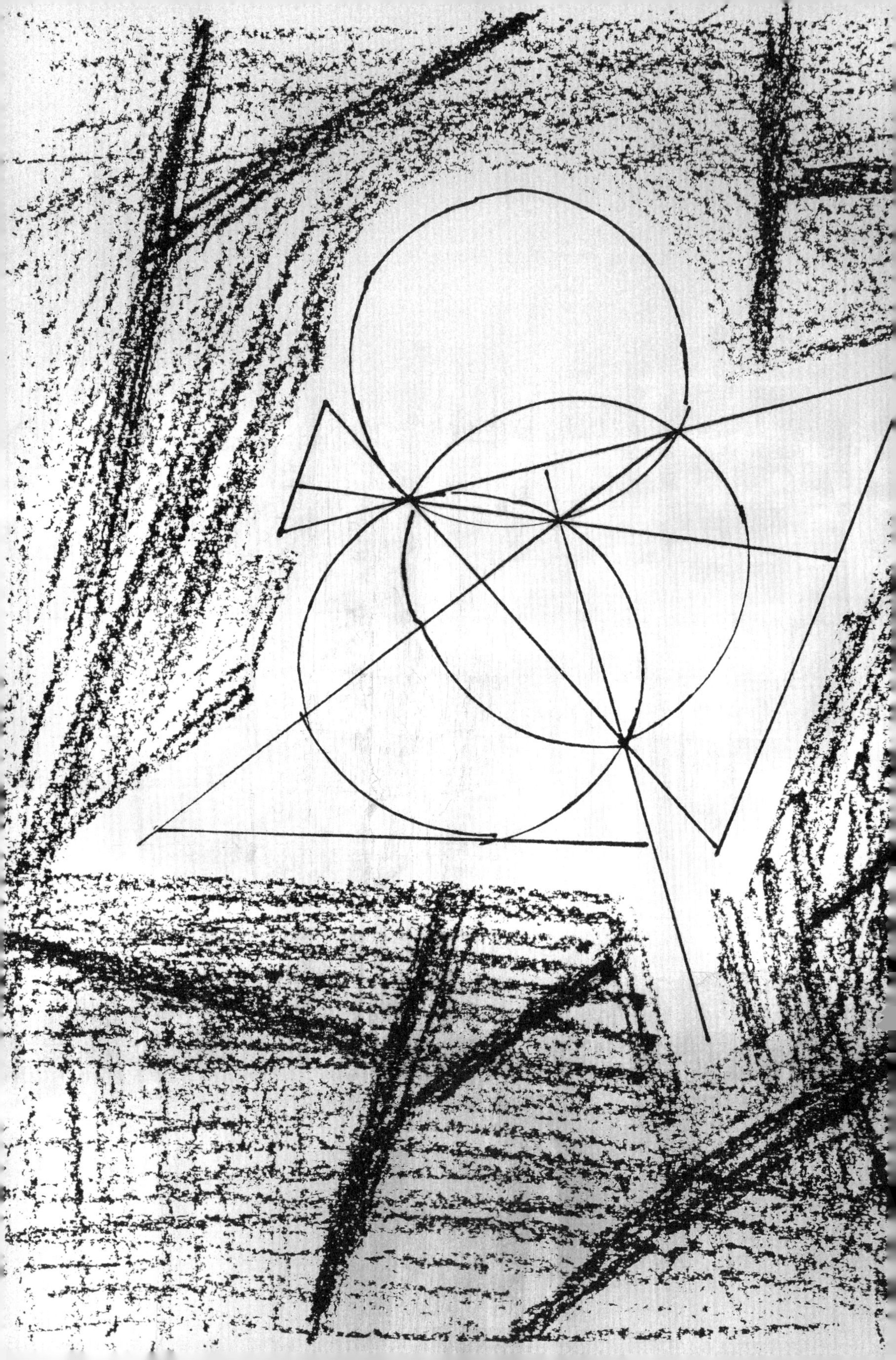

Adieu Kamchatka

Helmut Federle

Abstraction and daydreaming are related things. When I
look at a Suprematist composition, a kilim from Konya or a
Mayan ceramic cup, I am instantly carried away by the shape,
a colour or a surface, textures, intricate ornaments or elegant
figures; they transport me to a place where some inner
frequency is triggered; a thought, feeling. Agnes Martin used
the words 'abstract emotion' for her works. And there are
other examples. The first one that comes to my mind is the
opening sequence of *Kung Fu* (1972–1975) with a young
David Carradine. It starts as an old story: a solitary man
walks down the sand dunes of a desert. His gaze is serene,
he treads with grace, there's wisdom in his movements.
He seems in harmony with his surroundings.

Then the perspective shifts and the abstractions set in.
Dazzling sunshine: the camera captures after-images; its hard
specks puncture the lens and delirious colours and hues fan
out. Eerie music: metallic sounds in a far distance like a trick-
ling stream, but there's no water in these parts… And amidst
the scenes of the harsh, forbidding nature, it is as if the organism in distress musters the stillness within and creates a zone

Helmut Federle, *Untitled (NSG
II)*, 2012, screen printing on 22
carat orange double gold leaf on
aluminium honeycomb panel,
200 × 132 cm. Photo: Markus
Wörgötter © Bildrecht, Vienna
2024. Courtesy the Artist and
Galerie nächst St. Stephan
Rosemarie Schwarzwälder.

of endless sensibility for itself, a space where the mind can roam. Then suddenly there are scenes showing the most wonderful memories: the formative experiences of the boy, who under tutelage of a master becomes a Shaolin monk and a man. The sun's after-images resonate in these impressions; a bright light shining through them.

I

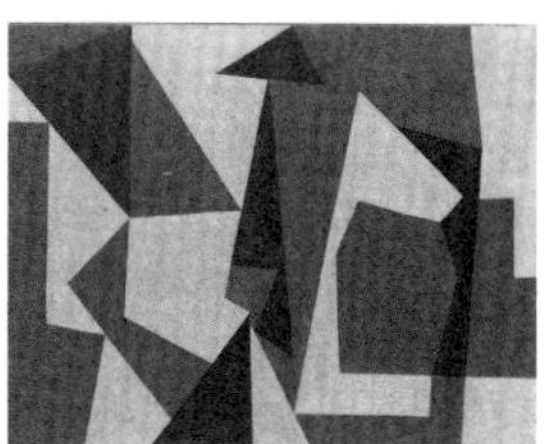

1 Helmut Federle, *Untitled (Africa)*, 1984, oil on canvas, 73 × 92 cm.

Invited to ponder Helmut Federle's current work, I happily accept. I sense a break in his art around the year 2000, new beginnings… But today I still feel the spark of so many works from the middle years (1980–2000); they speak to me, seem topical; I will have to consider them. Chronology in art is overestimated; cycles and 'the return to the same' are important.

Helmut Federle was a distinct voice in the art scene of the 1980s and 1990s. He exhibited at prominent art venues in Western Europe and the US and spoke in public fora on the importance of the intellectual and aristocratic fostering of art. His work is part of the canon of modern abstraction, has a place in the traditions of modernity and postmodernism, and it can be related to for example Donald Judd's oeuvre. Several drawing series display the advance of sequences: the calm change of a black rectangular shape on a white ground, the subtle scintillation of overlapping shapes, or the uncompromising intersections—black bars penetrating black bars.

I have always felt the pull of a feverish aspect. Colours swelter, shimmer or they dazzle us in works such as *Flower of Sadness (La Fleur du Mal)*, *Dark Night Three* and *H. Fridjonsson's New Corridor* (all works 1984).[1]

His small yet powerful paintings manifest strong undercurrents. The works are atmospheric and explore the complexity of emotion. Signs, symbols and letters—notably the F and the H (the initials of his name)—start to appear in his works, they reflect the questioning of his proper identity, but also an exploration of the meaning of signs in various cultural traditions—for instance in an archaic context of polytheism and magic, certain signs were seen as epiphanies. In the early 1980s one distinct colour appears in his works, a mercurial green-yellow that is associated with angst; Federle has called it 'a suicidal colour'. It occurs in various paintings, large semi-monochromes with geometric shapes and letters.

In hindsight I'd say that the green-yellow embodies fragility, the skin is openly exposed, an intimate reality has many dangers to endure. As I was reading about Federle again, I detected a pungent statement. In an interview with Bernhard Bürgi from 1986, Federle talks about his arrival in New York in 1979—it led to a four-year stay and confrontation with American culture (the art and the physical landscape) that was crucial for the development of his vision—and here Federle mentions wrath as the source for a particular piece:

> This first painting from that time (*Untitled*, 1980, acrylic on paper, mounted on aluminium, two parts) somehow mirrors the way I was torn at the time. There is something extremely emotional and aggressive about the composition and the application of paints, something mildly destructive.[2]

These words make me think of fierce music, underground, rock and punk (Federle once said that he sensed an attraction and connection with underground culture). But when I look at the painting that he mentions, I see a yellow opening, a door that leads to light or is it light.

187

2 'Helmut Federle talks to Bernhard Bürgi', *Abstract Painting in America and Europe*, Vienna, Galerie nächst St. Stephan Rosemarie Schwarzwälder, 1988, p. 139.

Federle's work makes new connections with a certain momentum of early modernism and the emergence of forms of geometric and vegetative abstraction (Mondrian, Malevich, Kandinsky). His work replays that momentum, but with a great unease. The signs and shapes emerging in the work are off balance, it is as though they have arrived at the wrong place at the wrong time. A painting such as *Untitled* (1990) gives this feeling. On a ground executed in a restless grimy green-yellow are two large shapes painted in dark muted tones; an O floats in space and an H—cut in half and tilted—lingers far away at the edge. This big painting has an almost uncanny atmosphere, resembling an underworld of sorts. The green-yellow colour is translucent; many layers of thin paint have been applied like in a watercolour. It is intimate and simultaneously creates an expanse, an undefined area or rather a vegetative space; reminiscent of seaweed flowing under water.

Crucial about Federle's art is that it juxtaposes contradictory phenomena. Differences and what we see as opposites interact with and permeate each other. His abstractions defy figurative painting. His shapes and signs build on the early modernist abstractions, but his spatial renditions and atmospheres speak of the Romanticist legacy (Friedrich) and of Nordic symbolism (Munch). The romantic aspect in his work has already been pointed out. Until now, as far as I know, no one has proposed: his art has *duende* (Lorca)—we can practically hear the black sounds of the artist, wrestling with death.

2

After 2000 new works crystallize. The productions are concentrated and precise. There are rather closed work clusters,

created within a limited time span, other works constitute
open groups and reflect long-term themes of the artist. The
first series (*Für die Vögel*) demonstrates a transition.[3]
Something occurs here that I understand as a new approach
to the eye's imagination (the scope of the inner eye). Perhaps
this turn was inspired by the lore of tradition (Leonardo
advised young artists to study and draw a wall, see its lines,
and discover the universe in a spider's web). In *Für die Vögel*
(2000) a shift of perspective is being staged—think also of
haiku and *tanka*, traditional Japanese poetic genres where the
viewpoint doesn't reside with the poet, but with nature. Dark
forms appear on shiny grounds, we cannot identify the forms
directly, because they keep their distance. Each painting has
a monochromatic background; gold and copper create a satin-
like lustre, delicate, robust. Its forms and textures evoke the
sensation of *frottage*, it is as if there's always more to see... At
first, I thought I saw imprints of nature: lines in a landscape,
the density of a mountain shape, the relief of steep rocks.
Today I detect façades, high towers, the page of a newspaper,
echoes of urban turbulence. And I hear a soft and forbidding
tone, as if all the noise of the world must be kept in check...

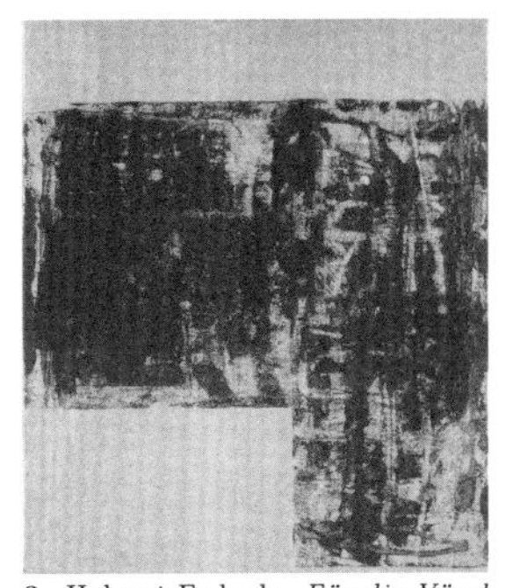

3 Helmut Federle, *Für die Vögel P.*, 2000, acrylic, synthetic resin on canvas, 60 × 50 cm. Photo: Franz Schachinger.

The search for the light, the movement to the source and
the passage it involves, is the theme in a group of works with
a luminous central section, like an organ that calls to mind
the notions of vulnerability and receptivity. Here inner and
outer world come together. *The Seven Doors of Jerusalem V*
(2010) makes me think of holy places and pilgrimages. The
title mentions the seven gates of the old City of Jerusalem,
built by Suleiman the Magnificent, which are still open today.
This composition has a series of pentagons that slide into one
another. The hovering and entangled shapes build a spiral
leading up to an opening, like a skylight; this space breathes
freedom. Here, the flat five-star-shape is being linked to the

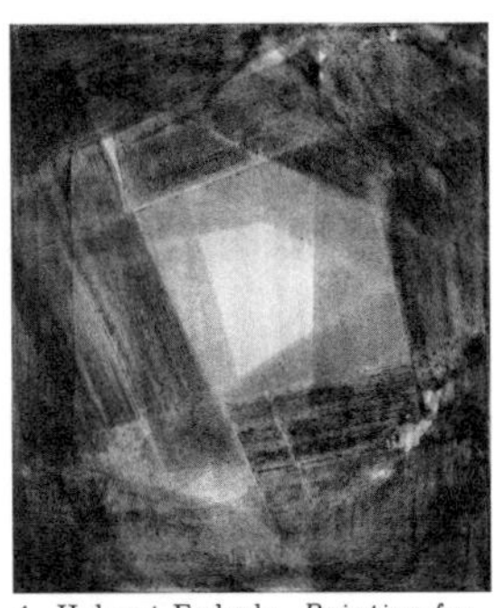

4 Helmut Federle, *Painting for Lee Harvey*, 2009, acrylic on canvas, 60 × 50 cm. Photo: Marcus Wörgötter.

5 Erich Franz, 'Inner Seeing', *Helmut Federle: The Ferner Paintings*, New York, Peter Blum, 2013, p. 32.

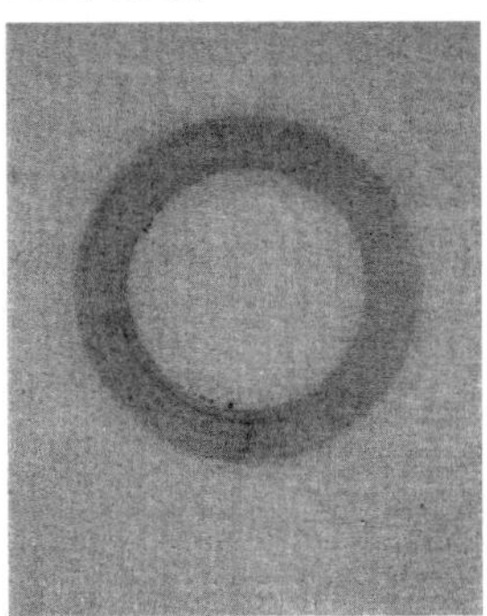

6 Helmut Federle, *Ferner E (St. Margrethen/Korea)*, 2012, vegetable oil, acrylic on canvas, 50 × 40 cm. Photo: Markus Wörgötter.

place where world religions and life philosophies meet. The form emerges again in several other works, for example in *Painting for Lee Harvey* (2009), with a similar hovering configuration of locked forms.[4] But there are difficulties here, obscure edges and disturbance on the way to the centre, like a movement in reverse. In *The Kandahar Conviction* (2009) the light is eclipsed. It triggers thoughts about the blindness of religious intolerance, and the havoc it wreaks in today's world.

The *Ferner* paintings (2012–2013) focus on the circle. These are phenomenological studies. One or more circles appear, thick or thin; the girth of their lines varies and there are curious doublings and effects (vibrations). The circular shape was not painted with a brush, but originated in a very slow process where vegetable oil is poured onto the canvas and seeps into the fabric. The surface is painted with oils and/or acrylics—creating soft encounters between the original tones of the canvas and shades of subdued colour. This corpus explores the limits of the visible. Circles appear and disappear, and we experience depth… The works open a zone of sensibility; they expand and enlarge perception. Erich Franz: 'Every perception is being questioned…'[5] The *Ferner* paintings are mirages that prompt the viewer to surrender: they unveil enchantment and restraint.[6]

Federle's late works grasp the phenomenon of space. They investigate space as a concrete presence and how this phenomenon affects us, and explore the longing for and the imagination of space as a place for spiritual refuge. That development is profound, and it comes from a strongly felt connection to exterior space (the world). His commitment to and confrontation with the world are reflected, in particular, in two branches of his works wherein the artist links himself to persons and places. The titles of singular pieces mention the names of cities or events that took place there, and of people—artists, poets and others, such as the martial artist Andy Hug. The works reflect experiences and fantasies (about persons and events).[7]

The formations or 'inner poles' are reconfigured. The longing to connect with others exists alongside solitude and a wanderer's life. These days the wanderer is a pilgrim confronting his religious doubt. We encounter desolate beauty, broken ground, in the work *God* (2000–2003). *Song for Golgotha II (Hiroshima)*, (2004–2010) reveals the ecstatic, shattered rays of a white-yellow colour—James Ensor's haloes come to mind. The experience of this work is disorienting. But we can understand it in relation to Federle's other 'bad work', for example *The Background Chronical IV (Reactionary Abstraction*, 2014) is another painting about faith and doubt, this time with respect to the art canon.

3

A series of silkscreen prints with black figures on gold-leaf surfaces point to sacred geometries. These commanding works produce an enormous tension. Their symbols, forms and configurations refer to ancient traditions—alchemy in the West, magical thinking in the East—and convey ominous feelings: presentiment and excitement. The trigram 'Heaven' from the *I Ching*, three horizontal bars layered above each other, resonates in *Untitled III* (2012–2015). *Untitled (NSG II*, 2012)—a work that deals with coded experience—features an encrypted figure like a flower shape, that is stranded in a desolate area (the work's subtitle is an abbreviation of *New Suicide Grafik*, an artist book published in 1981).[8] I associate it with a blocked heart. *Untitled* (2012) is another composition

7 The artist's paintings dedicated to the poets Mayakovsky, Baudelaire, Mishima and Pound are discussed by John Yau in: 'The King of a Rainy Country', *Helmut Federle: American Songline*, Ostfildern, Hatje Cantz, 2012, pp. 252–256.

8 Helmut Federle, *Untitled (NSG II)*, 2012, screen printing on 22 carat orange double gold leaf on aluminium honeycomb panel, 200 × 132 cm. Photo: Markus Wörgötter © Bildrecht, Vienna 2024. Courtesy the Artist and Galerie nächst St. Stephan Rosemarie Schwarzwälder.

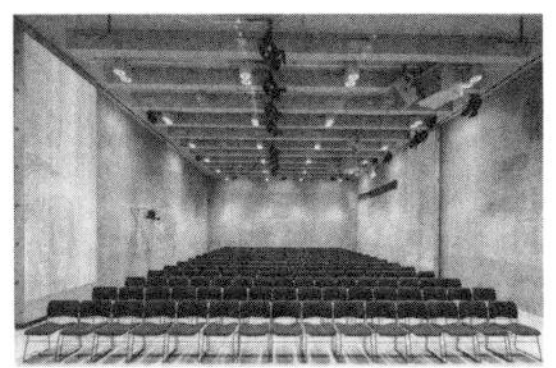

9a Helmut Federle, *The Enormous Room*, 2017, wall installation, auditorium Swiss Re Next, Zürich. Photo: François Halard.

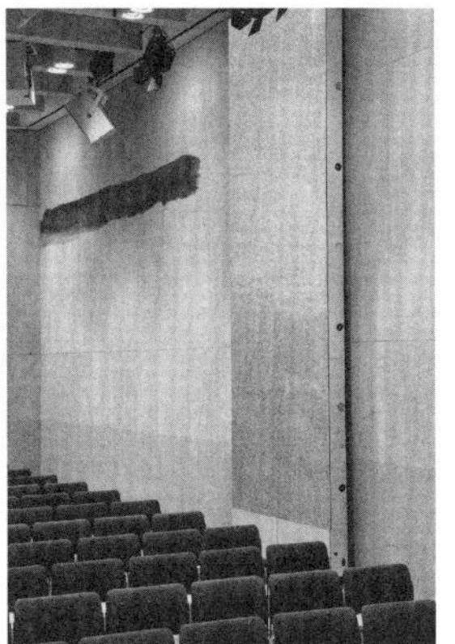

9b Helmut Federle, *The Enormous Room*, 2017, wall installation, auditorium Swiss Re Next, Zürich, detail. Photo: François Halard.

9c Helmut Federle, *The Enormous Room*, 2017, wall installation, auditorium Swiss Re Next, Zürich, detail. Photo: François Halard.

with black bars layered in a grid, the upper part is perfect, the lower part disintegrates before our eyes… Gold and Darkness, Ashes and Hope. I recognize a Romantic aspect, the need to be confronted with destiny, the urge to contemplate fate.

The Enormous Room is a highlight in his oeuvre. In 2017, Federle made this work for the auditorium of Swiss Re Next in Zürich. Realized in situ and with a team of experts, the painting with golden colours—actually fine combinations of green and yellow—covers the four walls. Called a 'walk-in' painting by the artist, we are welcome to immerse ourselves in a surround environment. The shine and golden spell establish a connection to the enchanted realities of Yves Klein and James Lee Byars. Federle's painting is inspired by Eastern calligraphy and its nature renderings. We can imagine shapes of a leaf flying in the wind, but there are many other figures and forms, such as geometric contours that frame/delineate the void. A black, horizontal bar vibrates at the left side on the wall, in a higher region: a fascinating counterpoint.[9]

The artist has created a place for daydreaming and I imagine music here. Yuan Jung-Ping is a master of the guqin; he plays this old instrument of lore. *Lament of Departure*: the first seven notes evoke a landscape and then a *parlare cantando* commences, when the musician recites a melancholic poem by Jiang Kui (who lived at the time of the Song Dynasty)—aka the Hermit of the White Stone. The last stanza goes like this:

And I didn't take your pair of scissors with me,
but if I had, I still couldn't cut
these thousand binding, silken threads
of melancholy exile.

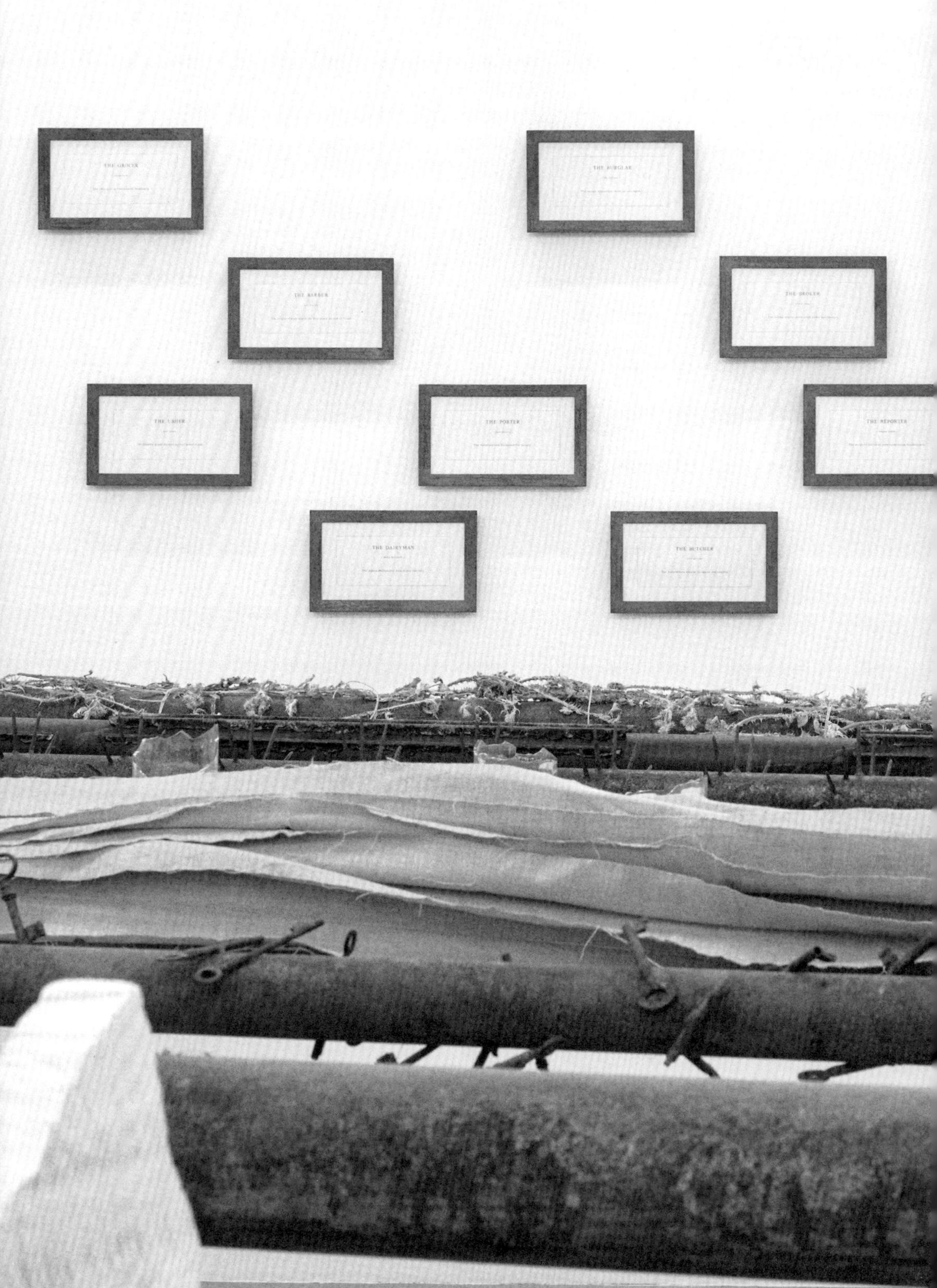

THE GROCER
THE BURGLAR
THE BARBER
THE BROKER
THE USHER
THE PORTER
THE REPORTER
THE DAIRYMAN
THE BUTCHER

Malleable Masculinity

The email conversation with Pieter Laurens Mol took place
on the eve of his show at Gallery Hidde van Seggelen in
Hamburg, which would feature his large sculpture *Angles of
Incidence (The Nine Lines)*. I first read about the work in
1989, when it was exhibited in Scotland, and it made a big
impression. The sculpture—an exponent of a large work
series that is dedicated to Mars, the planet, god of war, and
the combative disposition—could be read as a meditation on
masculinity as a dilemma.

MK

Hello Pieter!
   The Nine Lines! I still see myself standing in that room,
ICA/Amsterdam, spring 1993.
   Overwhelmed/Excited! There was a lot of light, as I
recall, quite harsh light. Could that have been the case?
Today I think, gosh, with that work, I also can imagine a very
different lighting, in which those forms emerge subtly lit from

a somewhat dark environment casting large, soft shadows over the surroundings… Are you familiar with Tanizaki's *In Praise of Shadows*?

PLM

Dear Mark,

Nice to talk to you about this again. However, in all considerations, do not forget the original title of the work. *Angles of Incidence* is a clear metaphor in the sense of 'trains of thought' or 'approaches', and that immediately gives, when you literally stand in front of the work, a whole lot of associative 'points of contact' and 'recognitions'.[1] Odd: you remember the set-up in the ICA well while I have lost that image…

I can still see the work very clearly in front of me, with Graeme Murray in Edinburgh (in 1988, the first time it was shown), at the Tampere Museum in Finland, 1992, and recently at Gallery Triangle Bleu in Stavelot. That last time, the installation—presumably this was also the case in the ICA—was on display in a large *white cube*-like space, and it was quite light there.

In the photos that Hidde sent me of the space, I do see a resemblance with Stavelot: the cool and austere architecture. I intend to place the lines at a slight angle with respect to the two end walls of the elongated space, you can then walk past it more comfortably at the front side of the whole row, a bit like the general inspecting his troops, or as you can see the F-16 fighter jets all set and lined up along the airstrip, ready to take off one-by-one on the way to a military operation.

I think harsh light, light in abundance, does not do this work any good. You should rather be able to experience it in

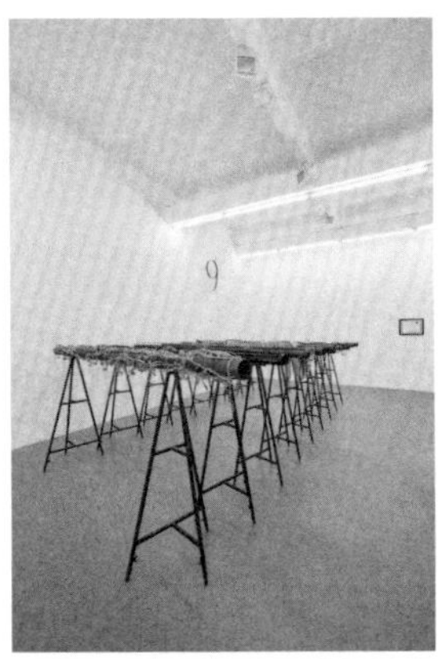

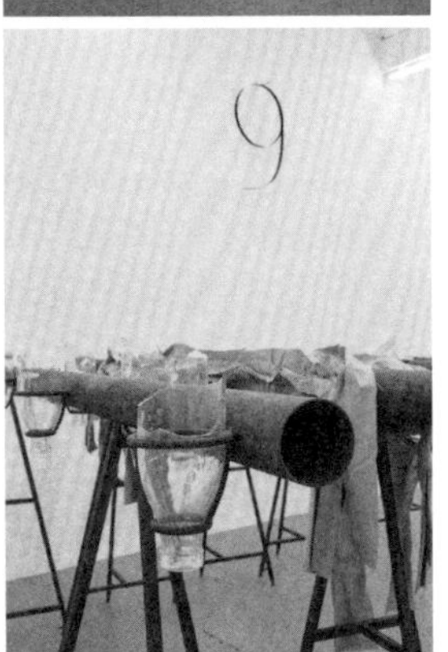

1   Pieter Laurens Mol, *Angles of Incidence (The Nine Lines)*, 1989; *Mars Ruler*, 1990, steel strip with rust patina, steel pin, 71 × 44 × 3.2 cm. Photos: Volker Renner.

an 'old' kind of light, a light with a history and not the dazzling light released by the ignition of magnesium or the young light of an exploding supernova. So no light that strikes an irreversible wound; light that blinds (representing blind rage and making blind). That kind of light belongs to polished stainless steel.

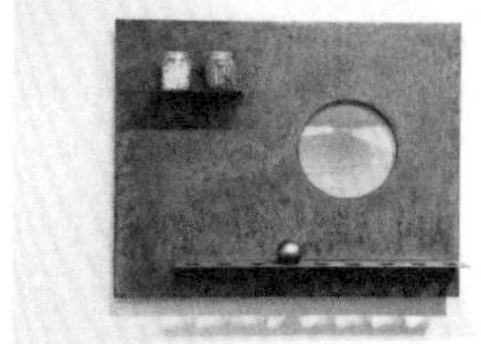

2 Pieter Laurens Mol, *The Third Martial Landscape*, 1989.

Yet, in their own way, *The Nine Lines* tell very clearly about wounds and scars and they are therefore probably no less aggressive to read than a random knife from the kitchen drawer. But if it wants to say something about the human drama, then certainly not unequivocally, with this work there is a complex story to be told about a natural and recurring cycle.

At best, we overlook a landscape and get a glimpse into our own soul, with all the signs of beauty and damage; for me, that can turn out to be just as cathartic as a walk in a flower garden, even with this rusty patina in the colour of clotted blood...

The light should therefore preferably not be too strong, but it should be able to underline all the tactility the lines contain, there is a lot to experience materially, it is a physical and sensual event as well as an entire martial field (Champ de Mars) in the close-reading of its smallest details.[2]

The work as an 'installation' can come across as an 'occupation' of space and that is interesting. It may give a somewhat oppressive feeling, but there's also open wondering. You will experience your own vulnerability ('Careful that I don't hit that protrusion!') but also the work's fragility ('Careful that I don't accidentally bend that wire!').

MK

Contemplation of the destructive power! Perhaps that is an indication of romantic discord? (And of an artist's disposition?) Inner reflection and worldly fatality…

I also sense a maker affected by simple but enchanted things: broken glass gleaming in the light, rust that still makes you feel the fire, the thrust force of a pack of rods.

But, Pieter, I want to go back a little further in time, to the genesis of the work, around 1987. Can you tell me something about the context in which *Angles of Incidence* was conceived? Was there a specific creative spark that hit you, one defining moment, an experience or encounter, for example?

PLM

Salut Mark,

Romantic: yes, I completely agree! But I don't think there was a single unique spark, it crackles on all sides in a delightful way. It was always like this with me, so it is unavoidable that this work revolves around a distinctly ambiguous event.

Perhaps you've recently seen the work *Chewed Edges/ Scratched on the Back* from 1974, since Hidde showed it at the last PAN in Amsterdam? Some, while seeing these two sheets of paper, may have thought to themselves: 'This work has to have been made by a female artist, after all boys "hit and punch" and girls "scratch and bite" when they overstep the mark!' The backstory of this work tells us something quite different. Once a young Indigenous man bit a floral pattern into a sheet of birch bark to give to his beloved wife, and an

Inuit woman chewed her husband's frozen boots smooth and soft so that he could put them on effortlessly. Here's the helping hand: 'If you scratch my back, I'll scratch yours!'

By the way, there are already quite a few drawings, all from 1975, where you find traces of what I would later call 'martial', 'iron fever' and 'sanguine surrender'. I'm talking about sheets such as *Fear and Courage, Damn (273 ×)* and *Beating 1-2-3-4 (Slaps)*.[3]

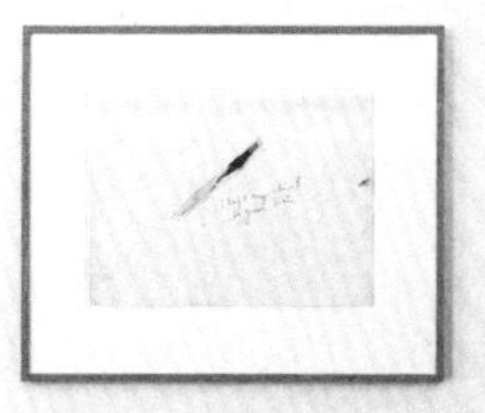

3 Pieter Laurens Mol, *I Left My Chisel in Your Brain*, 1996, pencil and rust wash on paper, 50.5 × 59.7 cm.

A growing awareness has been important to me. Subconscious things or energies that come to the fore and start to manifest, feeling part of a moment in time with all its comforts and benefits—I never experienced a war in my personal life!—but with great inconveniences and disadvantages now, after all my life completes at a time of great concerns about the earth's preservation. In the work *Ferro Diagnosis* that anxiety is stored in layers.

When I once (somewhere around 1987–1988) came across a pile of old postcards of *La Grande Guerre* in a French village at an antiquarian bookshop, I was instantly hooked. An utterly destroyed landscape printed in that beautiful heliogravure technique on the front, and the deeply human notes to loved ones written by a soldier on the card's back! Now this is a synthesis of the absurd—underlined with black lines by the 'Triumph of Death'—Bruegel already showed us his masterful premonitions.

So, there is always a wayward beauty and—while she holds the hand of Evil—she is apparently on her own journey through life. Let's see if our story is also my story and vice versa: that's a recipe for thoughts and resulting work processes.

I will tell you something else; this should not be missed in this context and basically revolves around a plant we all know. I'm talking about the thistle, similar to the artichoke.

The thistle is known as a 'weed' species, in a cultivated land-scape it is undesirable, troublesome and tough, indestructible, a true survivor. You can't do anything with it, it even thrives on the poorest soil, it can't be eaten and cows avoid it like the plague. But I admired the plant with its powerful spiky leaves and proud purple crown even before I realized what it symbolized and what the heraldic meanings could entail.

Bruegel had painted them very beautifully and later also Frans Hals, there you see a bunch of thistles in the foreground of a portrayed wedding couple, so it could stand for durability, perseverance and possibly even (marital) fidelity. In the summer of 1987, I collected a considerable number of thistles while traveling in France and had them in plain sight for a long time in the studio in Amsterdam, I felt an attraction to them and had to do something with them, and thus I gradually developed a great sympathy for this unwanted plant, this *abandonné*, this pariah.

As it happened at other times throughout the 'Ferro Fever' trajectory, the Serendipity phenomenon played a not insignificant role (as with the thistle). A piece of blue shiny strip steel jumped away and flew through the air after I cut it and, landing on the workshop floor, formed a graceful and perfect 9 (it is now literally a 'writing on the wall' as a work and called *Mars Ruler*). The magic number for *The Nine Lines*![4]

An elaborate pattern and unprecedented field of energy/ tension unfolded after my visit to Graeme Murray in Scotland, a year before the exhibition with him in Edinburgh. The thistle turned out to be the Scottish symbol (Lorraine in France carries the symbol as well) for the indomitable. Other impressions gained in the Scottish landscape, conversations (about the fascinating Scottish struggle for independence against the Vikings and the anecdote about their victory

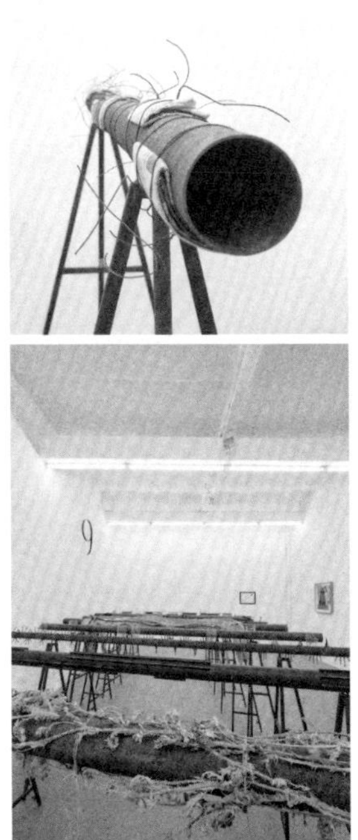

4 Pieter Laurens Mol, *Angles of Incidence (The Nine Lines)*, 1989; *Mars Ruler*, 1990, steel strip with rust patina, steel pin, 71 × 44 × 3.2 cm. Photos: Volker Renner.

thanks to the thistle) and the history of the Scottish soldier did the rest.

The drawing *HiFi Calculus* is the first note with plans for *The Nine Lines* and a thistle is depicted in the corner of one of its pages as a characteristic logo of 'high fidelity'.

And here I also have to say something about all the red chalk drawings of Western art history—why they're so invariably elegant and refined will always remain a mystery. The lovely and entertaining 'sanguine' had caught my eye earlier on and I found it very intriguing.

It reminded me of the colour choice for babies: blue for boys and pink for girls. At some point an incomprehensible switch must have been made because boys are naturally pink (Mars) and girls are blue (Venus). Very interesting psychological colour twists…

Anyway, back to the ruddy tones, horseshoes and blush of shame, the pressed red chalk stick. This starts with prehistoric cave drawings and their refined and graceful designs of animals (absolutely no primitive scratching…), via the masters of the Italian Renaissance (Leonardo) through to the Rococo (Watteau, or our Cornelis Troost). Yet red chalk is in fact nothing more than powdery iron oxide, you find it in abundance on the planet Mars, so I wondered what would happen exactly if I would treat it—in the vein of the Roman god of war—in a combative and raw way (as, for example, in my series of drawings *I Am a Wild Seismo*, 1990). Goodbye and till later, Pieter.

MK

I want to address two themes, both are complex enough, and yet I bring them up together. Destruction and

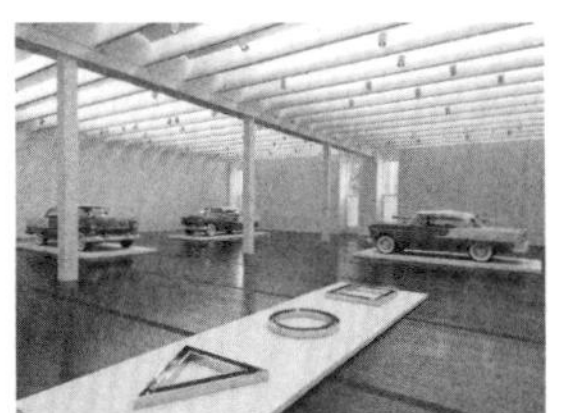

5 Walter De Maria, 'Trilogies', Menil Collection, Houston, 2011–2012.

self-destruction. I encounter these themes in your art. By the way, my current thought on *Angles of Incidence* is that it is a portrait of male vulnerability. I picture the work and think: those nine lines/figures that so wonderfully rigidly walk the line, each in its own way, make me feel empathetic… The rust makes them porous; everything lays bare…

(Self-)destruction in art, other examples. Chris Burden crawled on his knees through broken glass strewn on the sidewalk. I have always associated his performances from the 1970s with a sensation of stillness: a counterforce—to violence. Walter De Maria, in his first one-man exhibition in the US called 'Trilogies' in the Menil Collection (Houston, 2011–2012), showed a new sculpture consisting of three restored 1955 Chevrolet Bel Airs (in 2 colours: Gypsy Red and Shoreline Beige). Each of the cars was pierced with a stainless-steel rod.[5] Finally, the public action *Break Down* (2001) by Michael Landy, in which all his personal belongings were destroyed. Landy saw his happening as a critique of materialism, he wanted to question our society's equation of identity with property/possessions.

These works have, in my view, an affinity with *Angles of Incidence*. Your sculpture suggests, as it were, to take a step back and behold the male parade. Masculinity as a variable, that's what I see in other works of yours: the highflyer is trapped on a roof, the melancholic is reflecting on imminent danger and finally there is the destructive character (he is concealed, we do not literally encounter him, but we do encounter his energy). What actually drives him?

Could you tell me something about destruction and that variable masculine pole, how do they come together in the work, or do they draw circles around each other? What do they tell one another?

Dear Mark,

The order or battle formation of the nine lines as installed can be experienced as rigid, but only because it just doesn't want to be a mess, like a pack of wild dogs running in all directions in a panic. I have tried to 'hit the mark' with this work, care and control go hand in hand. It's not an unknown new arsenal of weapons, not at all. It is my Saint Sebastian![6]

In addition, it's also about conjuring space, about accuracy without being frightening. In general, this work is about control of contrasts, physically and mentally. I also had an idealistic intention with it, even though I started this work in a practical sense with a lot of uncertain factors.

Destructive aspects are thus characterized by experiences acquired as a result of raising boundaries. You have to learn the hard way: destruction and self-destruction become knowledge and self-knowledge. It is not about judging or pointing out the guilty ones, at most the aim is to mine/delve in order to try to fathom something of the human tragedy.

Men have caused a lot more misery than women, it is up to men to take a closer look at themselves and question what inspires or haunts them. But as you note: it's also incredibly complicated subject matter. That's why I've wanted to present a work where poles mingle and where their identity as 'extremes' is compromised: the work's melting form is treacherous, hot and cold in full action and reaction. It is not out to make or incite an absolute statement, it is not about a hard approach, but about the nuances.

For example, many people feel that the relationship between Mars and the choleric temperament is a solid given. From an absolute point of view, a fixed point of reference, they associate the sanguine character with gleefulness. It is

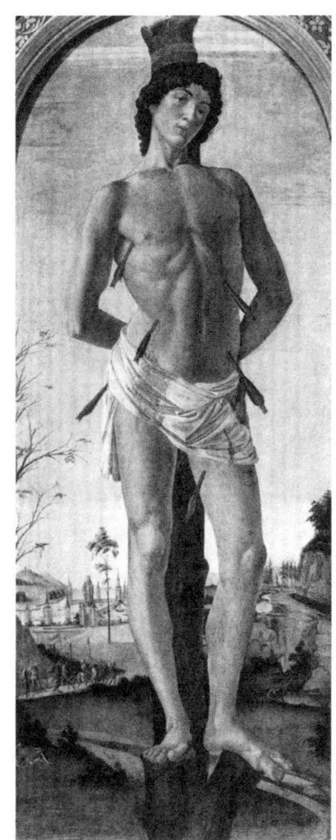

6 Sandro Botticelli, *St. Sebastian*, 1474, tempera on panel, 195 × 75 cm.

very treacherous when thought patterns get stuck! *Angles of Incidence* prefers to evoke and visualize unknown meridians! This is, of course, a quest, but not one aimed at aestheticizing violence. *The Nine Lines* are rather like tuning forks or conductor's batons, not the musical instruments themselves, but devices for adjusting norms and values. The work wants to jump over all forms of arrogance as on a hurdle track. Vain hope sometimes suggests that violence has become emancipated, but it's not that simple. That an artist may succeed in unravelling the principles of a specific type of energy is another matter, here the viewer can eat his heart out with male hormones tamed to an acceptable level.

It picks up on memory, and it invites, resignation, acceptance, and peace, comparable to the objective of (war) monuments.

So, when you compare *The Nine Lines* with the impressive examples described in your message about destruction and self-destruction, I hope my sculpture remains grand and impressive, but almost with a gentle undertone.[7]

There is hardly any noise, actually there's mostly silence, or inward contemplation. The sculpture is not expressionistic in nature, nor violent or frightening—it is not a Buchenwald doll—and indeed it has a lot to do with what you call 'masculinity as a variable'.

Perhaps what belongs to this work is an iconographic reading tied to a Christian tradition, perhaps that is the 'home' of the *Angles of Incidence,* and the motifs were basically strong personal (Catholic?) frameworks from which I've been working.

I hope that the Hamburg presentation will provide the necessary stimulation. The work deals with deep-rooted things, an energy that everyone carries within (thank God!), a 'building material of life'.

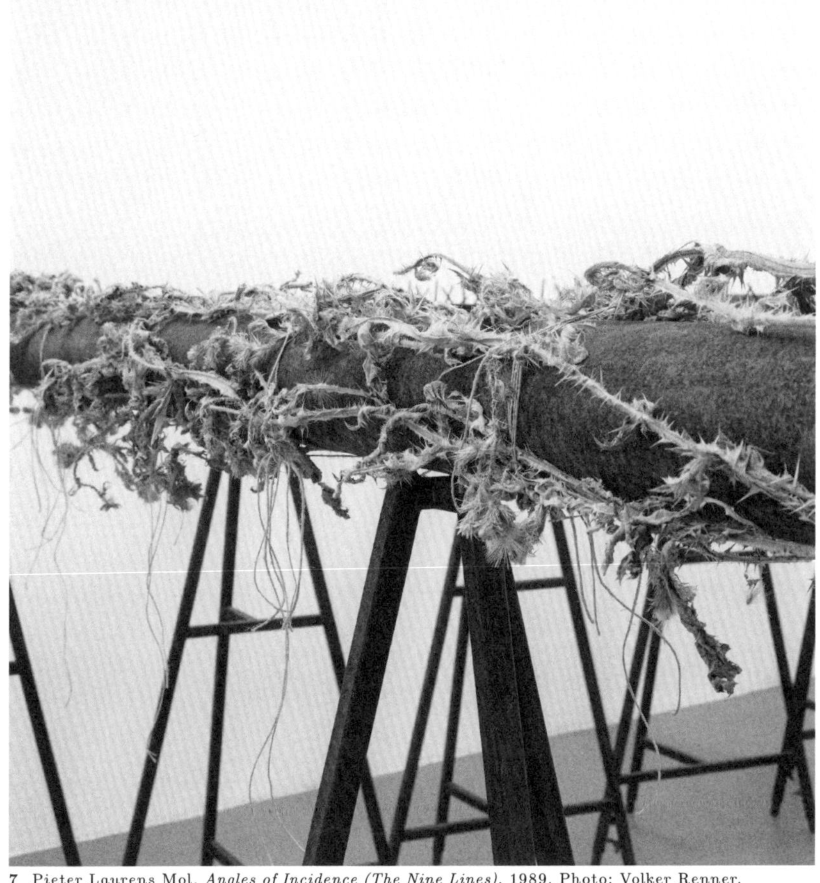

7 Pieter Laurens Mol, *Angles of Incidence (The Nine Lines)*, 1989. Photo: Volker Renner.

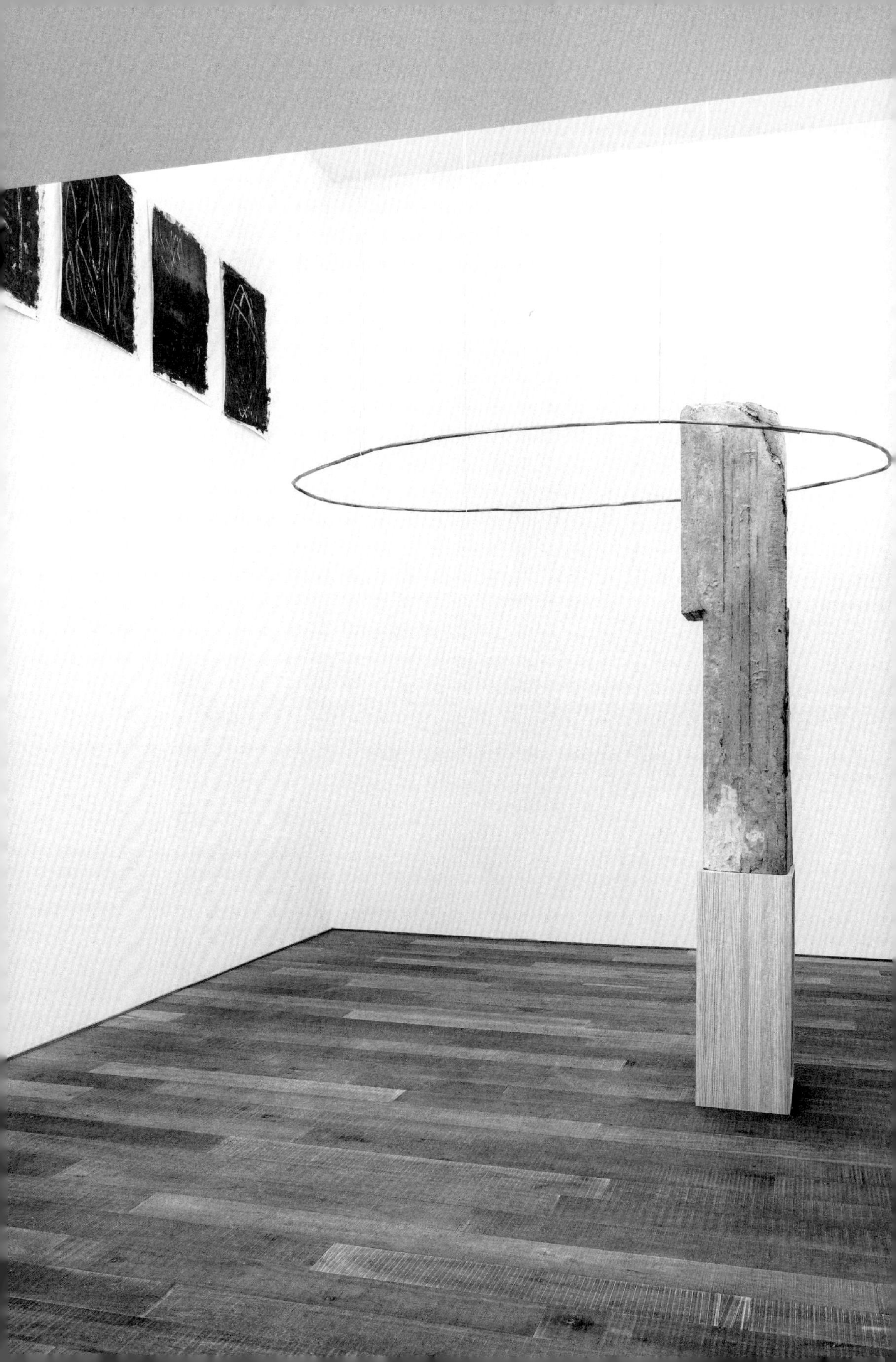

A Thousand Leaves

Esther Kläs

Esther Kläs belongs to a generation of artists who, compelled by conditions that shape today's world and how we engage with its complex issues, have taken up the old philosophical question of how matter affects us and how we, vice versa, as humans may affect matter. There is a concrete and urgent backdrop to her practice, a reality in which our natural world is in a state of precariousness; her sculptures and drawings evoke sensations of vulnerability and preciousness. In her works she uses elementary forms and malleable materials that both rekindle and challenge the memories this writer has of minimal art. EK's separate pieces are however devoid of its systemic and rather cool aspect. Instead, each of her works conveys a hunger to discover the world and it projects the idea that our bodies and souls could be brought into alignment with our surroundings.[1]

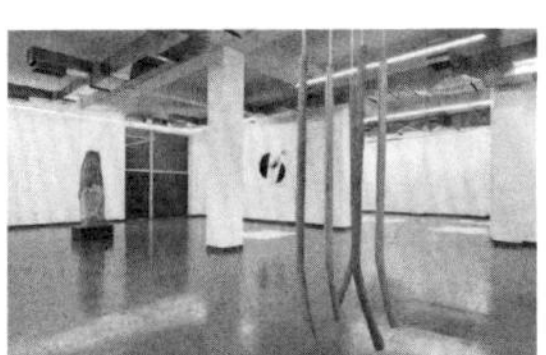

1 Esther Kläs, 'ola/wave', Proyecto AMIL, Lima, 2017, exhibition view.

207

Esther Kläs, *water*, 2013, monotype with water-based ink on paper, 121 × 439 cm; *Hi/O*, 2017, bronze, wood, rope, water-based resin and pigment, 315.5 × 286.5 × 166 cm. Photo: HV-Studio.

2

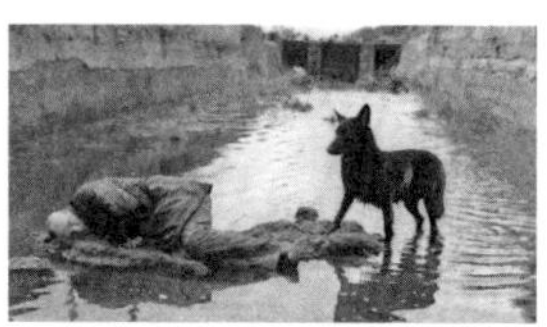

2 Andrei Tarkovsky, *Stalker*, 1979, 161'.

EK's oeuvre is primarily a body of works with a direct physical impact, but there is a philosophical impetus in the same oeuvre. EK's art is driven by an urge to explore. Her sculptures come to a space as if it were virginal territory, an unknown landscape in need of discovery. The pieces sit, lean, stand, hang, loiter or lie and bring their energy to a place. In her large drawings there is more distance, their configurations of lines could be perceived as balancing acts or graphic depictions of movements of bodies (or entities) in space. The drawings sit somewhere between a sketch and a score and are concerned with equilibrium. Sometimes a drawing seems to depict the act of cautiously finding one's way in an unfamiliar place, more by touch of hand than by the eye alone. The sum of her works produces an abstracted expansive experience, not unlike that of stepping onto ground with only few distractions, for instance, the sublime horizon of the desert, the deep black waters of the sea, the craters on the surface of the moon by night. Even that erratic area with its subterraneous spell from Tarkovsky's film *Stalker* comes to mind.[2]

3

The subject of the work could thus tentatively be defined as orientation, how we navigate the world, what our feet and arms and hands do for us, the fact that we can walk in vast open spaces, engage with stuff around us, find our way at home in a room in the dark after a fuse has blown. EK's art dwells on humankind and our relationship with our surroundings and it brings back memories of being in nature—meanwhile the city and the sensation of being around other people are not far away. Her art has a contemplative streak, as if a Chinese sage were quietly pondering the world. A separate work seems to extend the ways of our senses, as if such a work itself were an organ for feeling, hearing, touching…

4

The artist sends me some pictures of open spaces and asks me to write about the horizontal; 'active horizontal space' as she puts it. What is a horizon? What do we feel when we think about it? I ponder the subject and daydream a bit; which thoughts come up? At first, I can think of nothing pertinent. The horizontal: is that the computer on which I'm typing now? The food on my table? The eighth rank of the chess board behind which my opponent eyeballs me? For a moment it feels as if I've lost or forgotten something essential. True, I have been living in the city for a long time. 'Rows of houses, all bearing down on me. I can feel their blue hands touching me.' Then I happen upon a sentence in a book by Halldór Laxness (*Independent Folk*): 'He ate thick pieces of christmas turban cake of a cookie dish without horizon and they were so fat that he could pluck whole raisins from them, as big as human eyes'. Nonni eats the horizon in his dream.

5

Oldörp ('the old village') is the name of a mound, a human-made elevation rising a few meters above the surrounding crop fields, and above the invisible sea in the far distance.

Built from earth and clay and excrement, it dates back to the third century, maybe even further. The slope lies in the Hoogeland in Groningen. It is part of an old natural landscape above sea level, which is something of an oddity in the Low Countries (Netherlands) that are after all mostly polder lands reclaimed from waters. On this mound I grew up. I can see the line where land and sky meet. The view of this horizon is only interrupted by the occasional lonesome tree or farmhouse. As a child I must have been happy here. I used to wander in the fields and meet imaginary friends, my mother told me later. Then I was one with the world.

6

EK and MK skype. Death has crashed into my reality, and I have to share the news: Chiara Fumai (1978–2017). She was gifted. Besides art, what else did she live for? What was the horizon of her life? In 2014 she took part in a group show that I curated. Her piece 'prolonged' the lifeline of Vito Acconci's performance *Ballroom* (Florence, 1973) that had been interrupted by a lady in the crowd, who felt offended by his act. And he was only doing 'his thing': seducing an imaginary woman, with horny talk and sultry dance. Her protest made him stop the piece and give up performance art altogether. Chiara Fumai's *The Return of the Invisible Woman* (also known as '*Visites fantastiques de Vito A. au pays du fouet*') is a wake-up kiss! CF embroidered the canonical words written about VA's piece and its end, over ten sheets of paper. To this she added illustrations taken from two notorious novels in which women enact their sexual fantasies; these frivolous cut-outs float amidst the words. Vito is now in the company of Wanda (*Venus in Furs*) and O (*Histoire d'O*). His dance

continues in spirit, its strangely shy energy and erotic curiosity live on.

7

EK's sculptures make me think of *trouvailles*, driftwood
washed ashore, things that originate from an old world. Her
objects are whole and intact but shimmer with vulnerability.
They claim their place in the present, yet seem more connected to archaic pasts and pregnant lore. We often imagine
the past through spaces and places that are passed down to
us; in order to foster a living image of the past, we picture
scenes taking place within these sites, of humans interacting
with objects. A sculpture by Esther Kläs is of course not the
same as one by Franz West—a plaster *Paßstück* where an
unwritten protocol invites a viewer to interact with it in playful ways—but when contemplating her work, one encounters
a kindred lightness and the idea of possible interaction too.
A sculpture by EK does not end at its material limits; it rather
suggests the sensation of being doused in a larger energetic
field.

8

EK is interested in basics; she's quite sceptical of ideas,
believes in the immediacy of experience, says her art comes
from 'the inside', ranging from a basic desire to see something
materialize before her eyes and the need to deal with the facts
of life. EK investigates fields of forces; every work starts at
zero and is realized by following a pattern that defines the
working process. She treats form as a means to arrive at presence and vibration; the quality of her art has everything to do

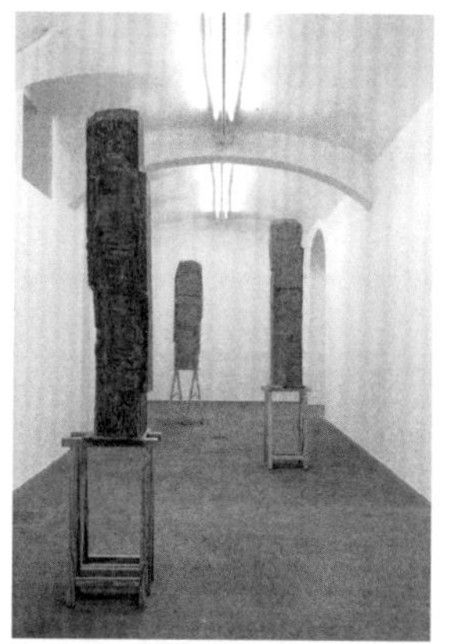

3   Esther Kläs, 'Maybe it can be different', Fondazione Giuliani, Rome, 2020, exhibition view.

with the hand that slowly feels its way over a surface, a shape, its contours and edges. In her show in Düsseldorf in 2017, three of her sculptures stood lean and tall, dignified and introverted. Made from pigmented aqua resin, the works resembled natural rocks carved in squarish shapes, and standing on their high pedestals they almost seemed to levitate. The semi-transparent sculptures produced a somewhat hallucinatory effect, like a *fata morgana*. The vertical *Gestalts* or meek monoliths revealed a different aspect from every angle, and this very instability gives the impression that the shapes could transform any moment.[3]

9

I associate E K's sculpture with that of other artists who put aside acquired knowledge for the probing activity of the senses. An artist like Giacometti made a difference by pushing the boundaries of the artistic spectrum of his time; he asked himself how he could truly depict the act of walking, its 'drama'; this way he made a new beginning. E K's art is mobile in a similar spirit; rather than projecting forceful external dynamics, I see signs of a refined inner resonance. In this art, you can sense the smallest movements.

10

What's the horizon of my words? How can I say something beyond their reach? Not long ago I spent time with a fair lady, she touched my heart and soul. Then our conversation got to a point where words failed me; now that I had reached the limits of my language, how could I express myself any further? First, I needed to recompose myself, and at that moment something magical happened. My inner tuning was reset and I was overtaken by a feeling so overwhelming that I first did not recognize it. *LIEFDE* ('love') is a book by Simon Vinkenoog. The Dutch bard wrote the diary in 1963, the year I was born. Perhaps the 1960s idealized the idea of love and its transformative power, but at least the era took to heart the question of what inner path there is for each of us, and how we can explore and realize love. Vinkenoog's book has many disarming passages on the subject. In one of them he calls on the good citizen of Amsterdam who takes the tram in the morning to go to their work: address the person sitting opposite you, make contact: 'Good morning Sir/Madam! How are you today? Beautiful day, isn't it?'

II

Another fragment from Vinkenoog's *LIEFDE*, trans. MK:

> 1 May 1964
> [Shinkichi Tajiri] tells one of the last deeds of *feu* Yves Klein: well-to-do lovers of art want to witness one of his 'experiences', 'happenings', *'évènements'*.
> He directs them (for a lot of money) to a village at the coast of Normandy, where at sunset an event will take place. At the instant when the sun touches the horizon, he (in a smoking) gives a sign to one of his assistants (also dressed in smoking), who throws a box filled with dust gold in the air and it flutters down between the setting sun and the viewers: *golddust in the sunset*, a forever unforgettable moment.

12

The child knows intuitively that (s)he can be a whole world.
There is no end to their horizon, to what a child can embrace.
Asked what it is that attracts her, EK says: 'Magic/Existence'.

13

When I ask EK which artists are dear to her, she first hesi-
tates; that is a multitude, and what first was an experience
that was alive and kicking may have become a slumbering
one. After a while she gets back to me, and I am delighted to
see her mention a lot of names that are dear to me too, among
them Alighiero e Boetti. He made work in which you find an
amazing richness in the details, as if he was enchanted by a
world of things that literally conversed with him. This gives
me the idea that the 'minimal forms' which speak up in Esther
Kläs' work, are in fact inspired by a much larger intuition
about the world. Perhaps we could call it 'anima', the notion
that spirit permeates all things.

14

Following this train of thought, I will argue that EK's art
attempts to make a new connection between minimalism and
animism. This statement finds interesting support in an
observation by the Brazilian anthropologist E. Viveiros de
Castro, when he juxtaposes the objectivist stance of modernity with the subjectifying stance of animist societies, and
describes their two respective challenges as follows:

Our problem in the West is how to connect and universalize: individual substances are given, while relations have to be made. The Amer-Indian problem is how to separate and particularize: relations are given while substances must be defined.

In the work of Esther Kläs I perceive forms that tremble, like a leaf in the wind.[4]

15

The artist writes to me: 'The search for the horizontal sculpture (not attached to the floor but hovering in space) interests me so much because sculpture in that state is independent from what we mostly know in the world, it is self-sustained energy'. I try to see the work she describes in her sentence. Possibly such a piece suspends the usual boundaries between object and subject. To connect with such a sculpture, you would have to reach out, grow a little more. An image comes to mind: that of the body of the swimmer in the water. To be one with the water is a physical and mental state that is not so easy to put into words, it defies and transcends language. I can perhaps compare this to an art experience. In Prato in 1990, I was blown away by a Mario Merz exhibit. Merz had

215

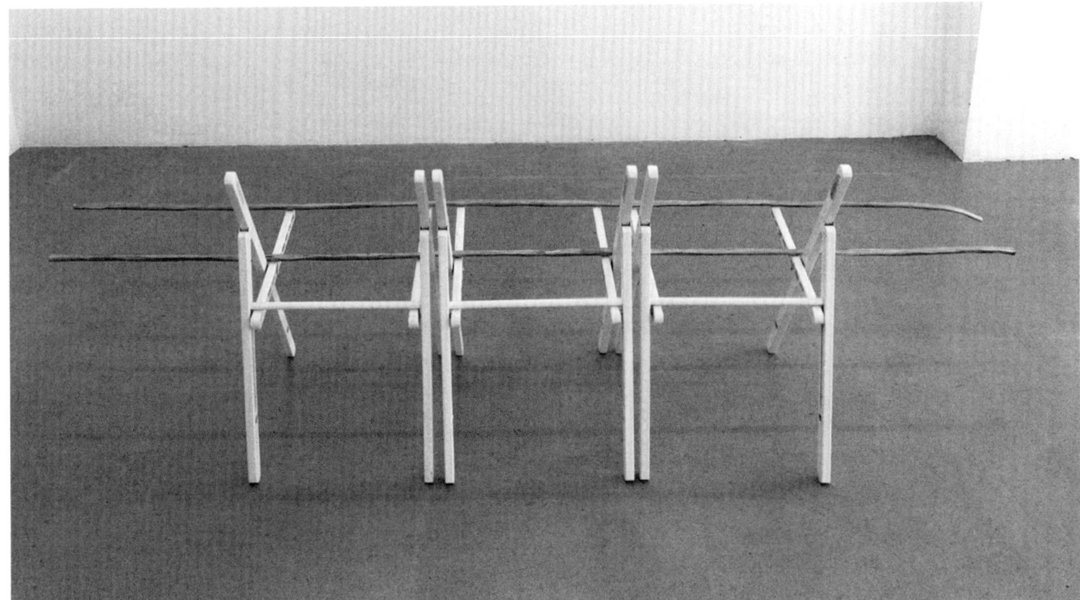

4 Esther Kläs, *3 chairs or other places*, 2018, wood, bronze, metal, 78 × 242 × 50 cm.

construed a landscape in a spiralling form, installing his glass igloos and stacks of newspapers throughout the Luigi Pecci Centre. This landscape was powerful, entering it was like walking into the heart of the maelstrom. There and then, I had an epiphany. I was in a place so energized that I could not find the words for what I saw and for what my senses told me, but what I felt was strong: I was one with this work, in a blissful state of surrender, riding the wave of pure experience. By email Esther Kläs sends me pictures, a little preview of her exhibit in Lima. I recognize these strangely natural forms: there is another rocky monolith, large drawings of black balls/spheres hang on a wall, green threads float in the air like giant stamens and a black structure with what could be steps—resembling a monument from a fable—rests on the floor. All the elements feel close-by and queer at the same time. If there is a code for deciphering this ensemble, it must be buried deep inside us; can we still turn around and find it?

In my dream I am a hippopotamus. Calmly I emerge in the exhibition, close to the floor I look around the space and something tells me—this must be a very old section of my hippo brain—that I've entered an art gallery. It is very bright here, with these white walls and all the lights. But on the ground and on the walls and in the air, I see and sense familiar shapes, forms of life nearby that beckon me. The feeling of attraction is mutual. What my eyes, my nostrils and my big muzzle now feed me unequivocally, is one line and one line only. 'Life, Come To Me, I Eat You'.

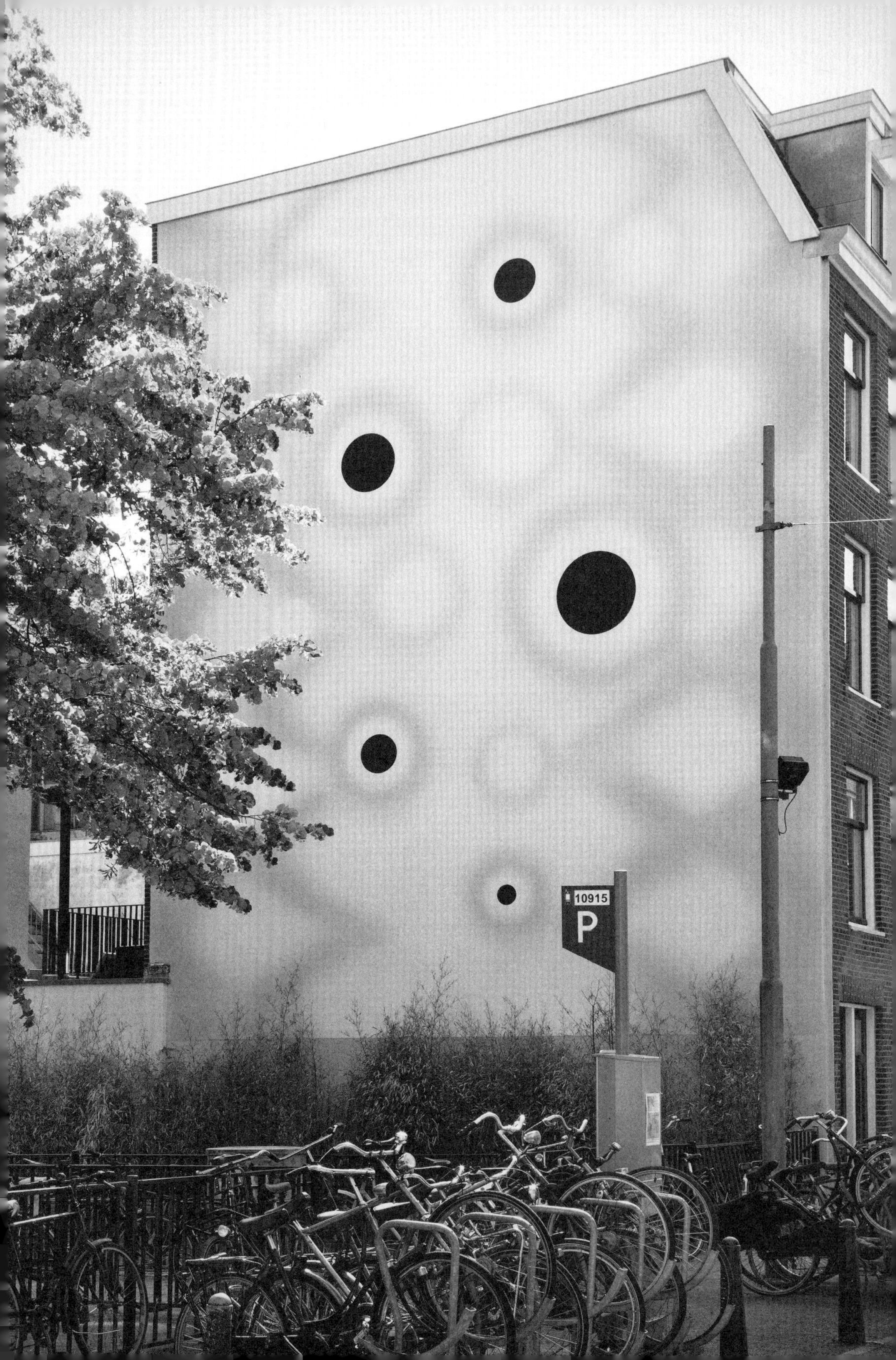
10915
P

The Burning Spear
Roland Schimmel

'Within and without are identical, are image and counter-image, but still not the integration which is knowledge.'[1]
—Hermann Broch

The abstract paintings and videos of Roland Schimmel alienate and intoxicate. Their sublime light almost instils you with fear. His work displays a reality that is so up-close that we have difficulty seeing it when it literally appears before us, as an image or sequence. Confronted with the vitality of perception, we stand speechless.

Roland Schimmel's practice is an examination of the interaction between eye and brain; his subject matter is the tension between the image and its after-image.[2] The artist has

219

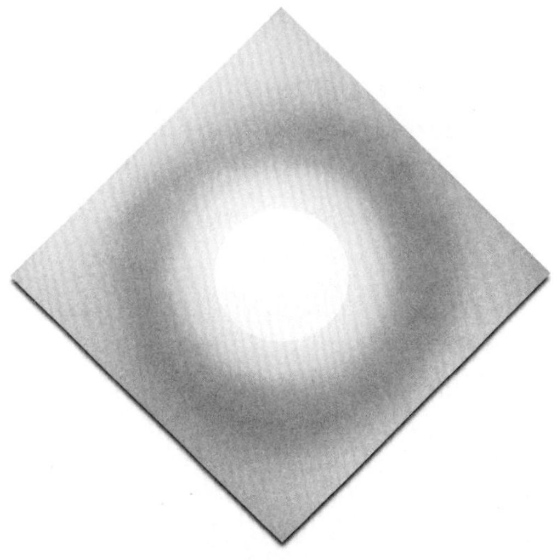

1 Hermann Broch, *The Death of Virgil*, trans. Jean Starr Untermeyer, London, Routledge, 1946, p. 36.

Roland Schimmel, *Duizend Zonnen (Thousand Suns)*, 2009, 1500 × 1000 cm, Vinkenstraat, Amsterdam.

2 Roland Schimmel, *Untitled*, 2013, acrylic on linen, 212 × 212 cm (diamond shaped canvas).

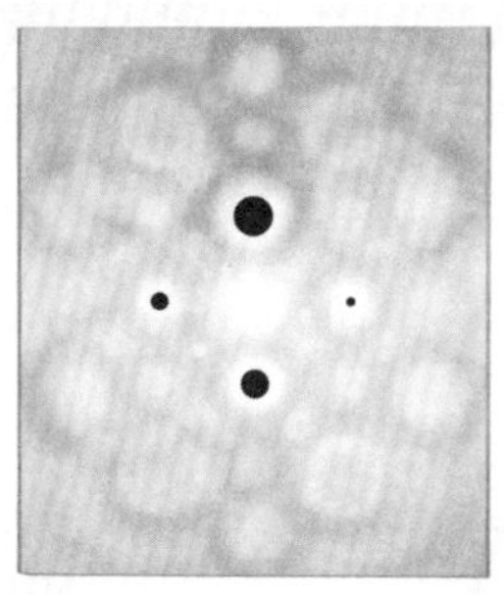

3 Roland Schimmel, *Untitled*, 2008, acrylic on linen 200 × 170 cm.

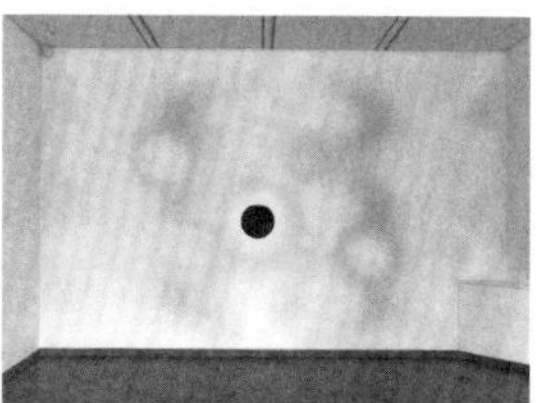

4 Roland Schimmel, *Zwarte Zon (Black Sun)*, 2009, wall painting with acrylic and projection, 350 × 500 cm, De Ketelfactory Schiedam.

always been fascinated by the question of how human organisms absorb and processes sensory stimuli.[3] And by an old philosophical question: can we really know reality, and are our senses sufficient to make us realize what is outside of us? Or do we embellish our perceptions with fabrications; do our senses add things?

His paintings on canvas, expansive murals, and digital animations—some of the videos have soundscapes of electronic music composed by David Lopato—depict the course of natural daylight and the perception of that daylight. In the course of thirty years, the artist has developed an oeuvre that shows what happens when the eye gets (over-)exposed to a light source, and the body spontaneously generates retinal after-images, in a quasi-autonomous response.

Schimmel's paintings reflect a complex visual process. Typically, they feature optical fields where soft contours of shimmering haloes reside next to hard edges of black holes. Forms and shades of painted after-images manifest themselves within the fields or structures that, thus, become ghostly configurations.

Black Sun is the title of Roland Schimmel's painting created for De Ketelfactory in Schiedam. A video projection of moving colours lights up the mural, which was produced in situ. The animation amplifies a play of light, the alternating appearance and disappearance of images and after-images. Looking at the painting is an intense event, reminiscent of an energizing nature experience. Is this an eclipse of the sun being portrayed here, or should we be looking closer to home?[4]

The artist is a traveller to an interior world and probes the limits of sensory experience. His work partly originates in a Taoist world-view, the leitmotif of which is the equilibrium between individuals and their surroundings. His paintings

and videos create optical structures/fields, in which the contours of dynamic, colourful haloes appear next to intense, all-
consuming black holes. The encounter between these contrasting forms generates a physical sensation of expansion and
contraction, comparable to the push-and-pull effect of Op Art
on our eyes.[5]

Compared to Op Art, Roland Schimmel's art is both
harder and finer.[6] The effect of after-images was already a sta-
ple in the paintings he made in the 1980s. Simple figures—
abstract dots in strong colours—painted against a monochrome background evoked retinal images of complementary
colours/shapes. The viewer would subsequently transmit the
sensations back to the works. Art brought to fruition and, in a
sense, mimicked a random physical response.

His recent works resemble membranes or skins. As if the
old paintings, with their stark contrasts, were pried open in
order to retrieve images that were already lurking within.
These compositions can be described as ethereal vistas, in
which (parts of) the painted retinal images stir our perception. Our eyes and brain attempt to grasp this composite of
vibrating colours and black holes. The viewer sees, outside of
themselves as it were, the phantasm of a retinal performance.
The ghost in the machine, unleashed.

With his interest in optical phenomena and neurophysi-
ological response mechanisms, and his urge to design artistic
correlations, Schimmel's practice can be situated in the line of
the twentieth-century avant-garde movements. It is linked to
the abstract films of artists who in the 1910s and 1920s took
inspiration from new science (Moholy-Nagy). It is also linked
to a second wave of experimental artists who, during the
1960s, continued this exploration and felt a need to incorporate elements from Eastern philosophy. See for instance the
meditative aspect of James Turrell's early light projections,

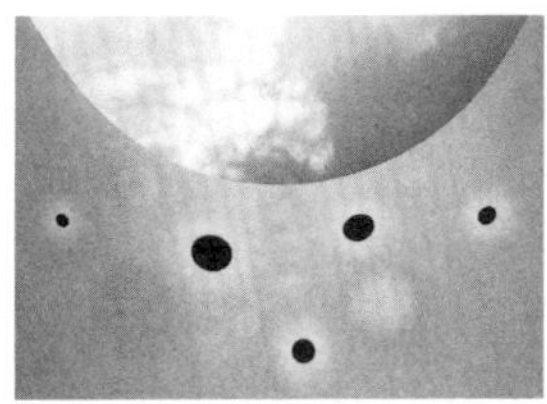

5 Roland Schimmel, *Psycho-
scope*, 1999, acrylic on wood,
aluminium structure, light
chapel, 300 × Ø120 cm, detail.

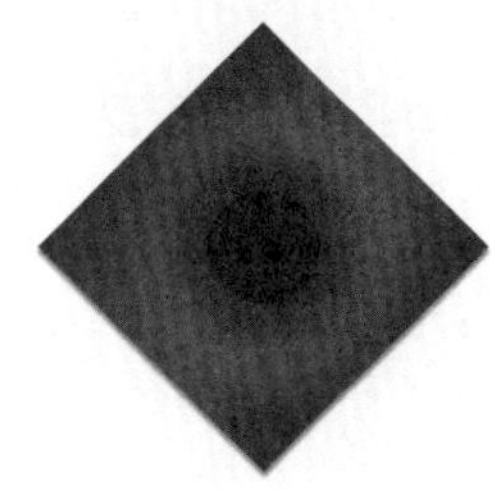

6 Roland Schimmel, *Indigo*,
2013, acrylic on linen, 212 × 212
cm (diamond shaped canvas).

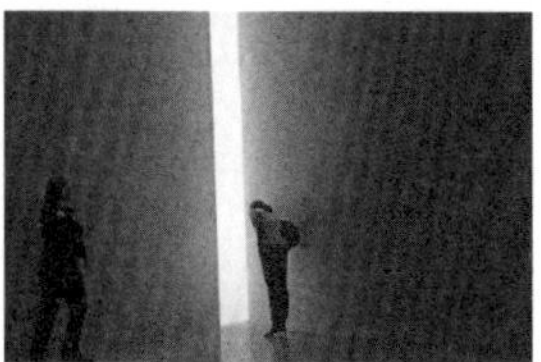

7a James Turrell, *Ronin*, 1968.

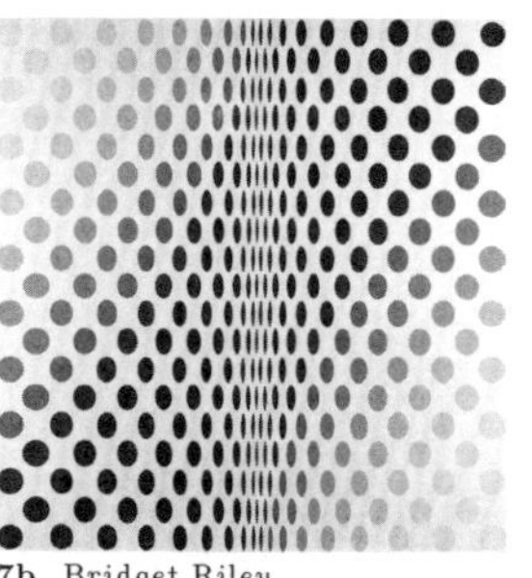

7b Bridget Riley,
Metamorphosis, 1964.

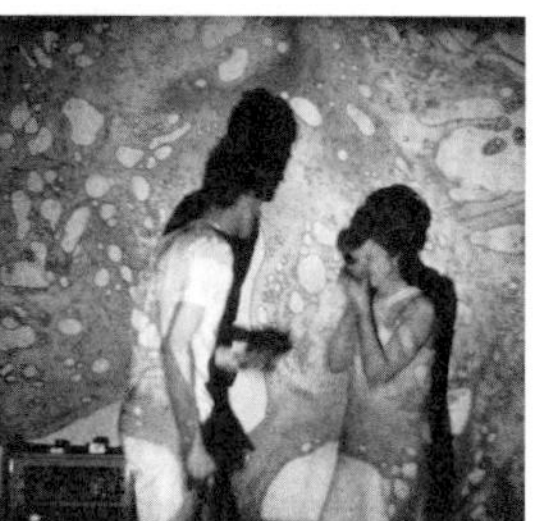

7c Boyle Family, *Son et
Lumière for Bodily Fluids and
Functions*, 1967.

the optical vertigo of Bridget Riley's paintings, and the psychedelic flow (and invitation to surrender) of The Boyle Family's projections.[7]

An idyllic image. A man is sitting under a palm tree on a Pacific island. He watches the sun set. In his studio, Roland Schimmel once told the story of his life on such an island and showed me the work that he had made at the time. The artist as a young man. I believe that the mural in De Ketelfactory returns to that period. *Black Sun* is a dramatization of a sunset. A man immerses himself in an encompassing and embracing, or, in the words of Robert Smithson, oceanic experience. The man does not know fear yet, but wants to get to know it.[8]

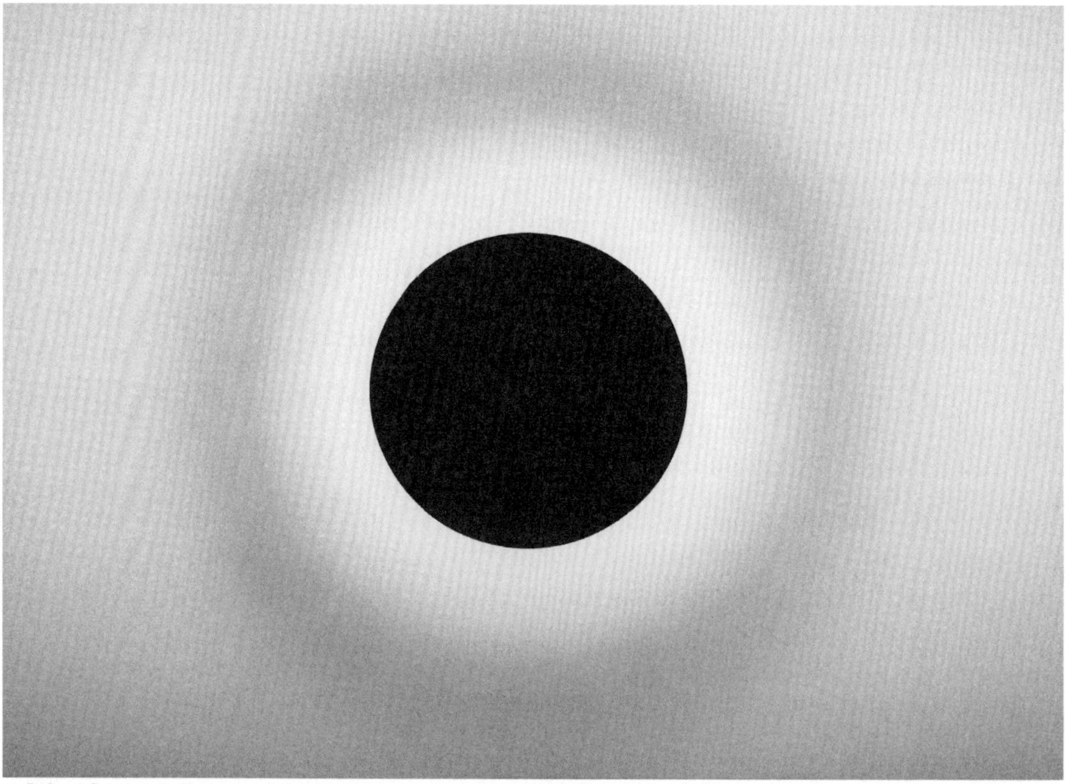

8 Roland Schimmel, *Facing the Abyss*, 2010, acrylic on canvas, 100 × 135 cm.

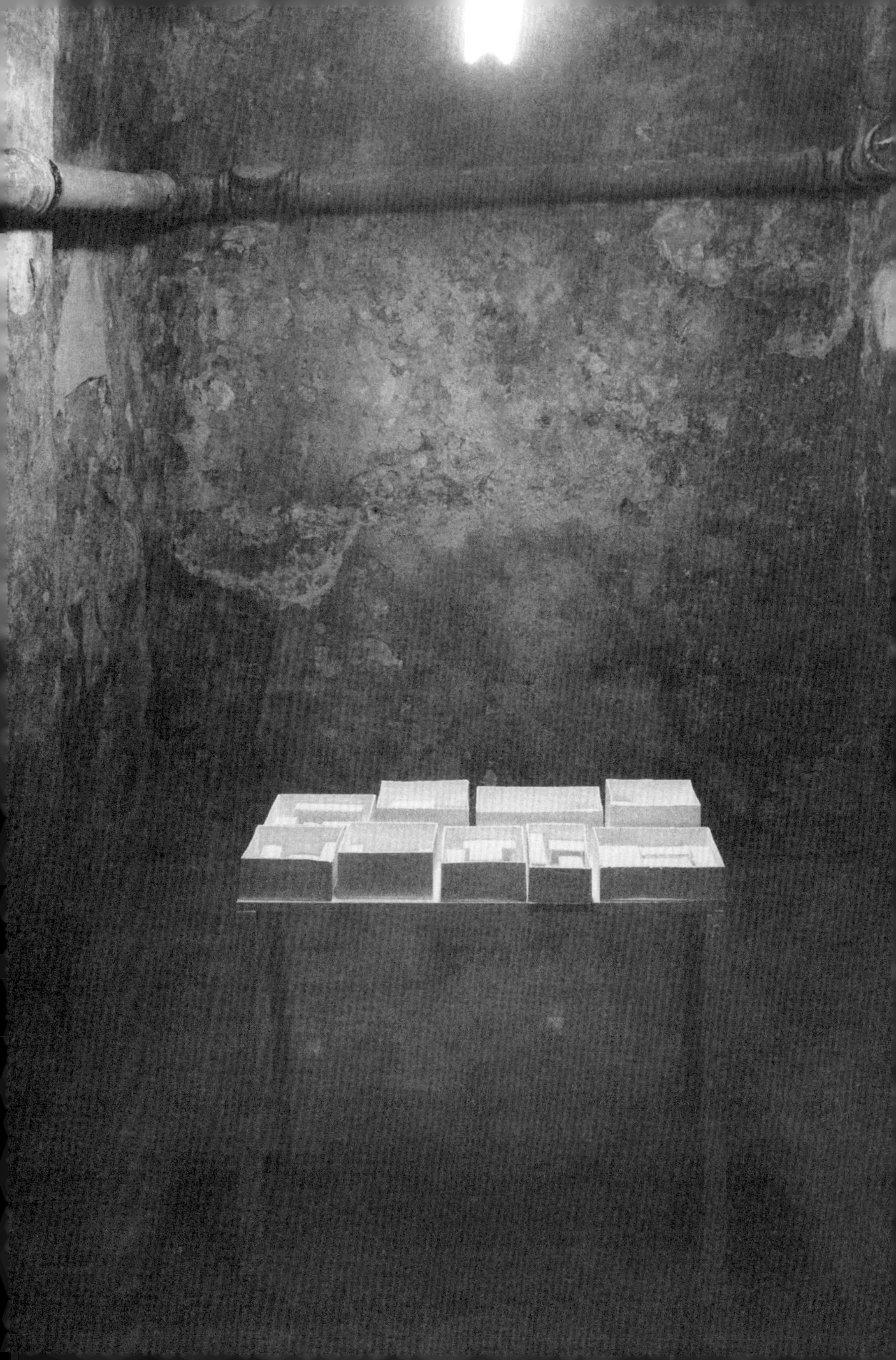

The Life Work of a Young Rebel

Absalon (Tel Aviv, 1964) died of AIDS in Paris in October 1993. In a seven-year period, starting in 1987, he had built an oeuvre that seems very mature for such a young man. Absalon anticipated that he did not have long to live. He was enormously productive before his death. Looking back, it is as though he wished to complete a life's work in those last years.

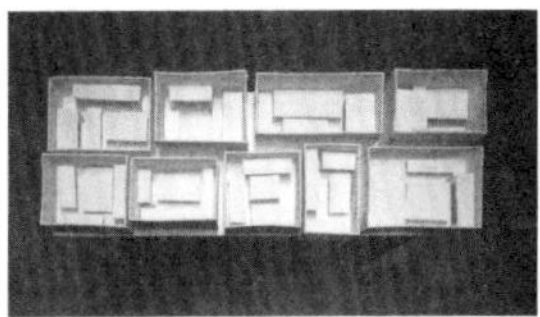

1 Absalon, *Cellules*, 1988, Nine Cells; cardboard, wood, white paint, 35 × 160 × 160 cm, top view.

Cells, proposals for residences, prototypes,[1] proposals for everyday objects: they're the terms he used for his works. Common to all these simple structures of wood, cardboard and plaster, conceived as series and generally painted white, is the controlled tranquillity they emanate. These pieces seem to mediate, in their formal reticence, between man and his surroundings.

Absalon's work was a challenge to everyday reality, which he experienced as mediocre or banal. He saw his works as proposals that were inseparable from himself as an individual. His attitude differed in this respect from the universal ambitions of Le Corbusier, Malevich or De Stijl. Absalon thought of his art as a private solution, and he distanced himself from the all-embracing concept of a future

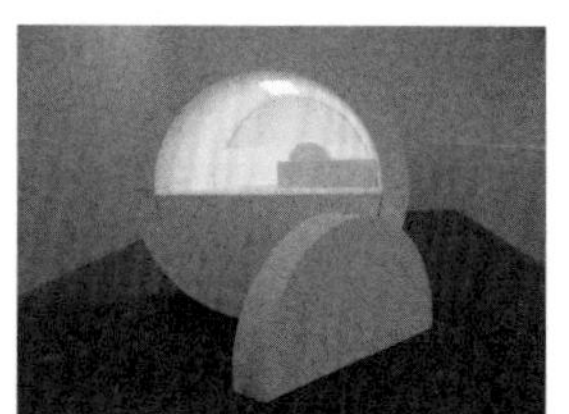

2   Absalon, *Cellule No. 2*, 1991,
isorel, acrylic paint, fluorescent
tube and Plexiglas, casing:
175 × 260 × 175 cm, door:
74 × 144 × 32 cm.

world such as that projected by the architecture and art of the
1920s and 1930s. His work was not meant as a utopia. For
him it was a concrete reality to live with and live in.

The artist's death thwarted the special plans for his exhibition at De Appel (1994). Now the exhibition took on the
character of a retrospective. Among its elements were two
existing (reconstructed) *Cellules* and several video works.
Absalon would have preferred to have made a cell that was
actually habitable, which could have been placed outside on
the roof terrace of De Appel's new premises at the
Spiegelstraat, Amsterdam, and which were meant as (semi-)
permanent works to be located in cities all over the world.

His intention with the *Cellules* was to create six permanent places to live in six cities where he would stay in rota-
tion, such as Frankfurt or Tokyo. The ground area occupied
by each cell was to be at least four square metres but no more
than nine square metres. Absalon hoped to place and anchor
the cells in their urban locations with the help of local
institutions.[2]

The importance of Absalon's work lies in the personal
project he believed in, and which he openly advocated.
People in the art world have been placing more and more
emphasis in recent years on the public manifestation of art
(where art reaches the crowds). Politicians measure the value
of art against this yardstick. The alternative basis for art that
Absalon suggests is, in contrast, the personal necessity, the
private motivation. Had Absalon's *Cellules* actually been
placed in the intended urban context, the public would have
been welcome to visit them, one person at a time, and only
when the artist himself was present. It illustrates the importance Absalon attached to individual experience.

When I visited Absalon's exhibition at De Appel,
I entered one of the cells, sat on the little stool that was there

and allowed the space to permeate my senses. Here the functions for living had been reduced to their bare essentials. There was a work area with a table, bed, small kitchen unit, and a shower/lavatory cubicle. In their simplicity, all the forms had a very powerful presence. His video work *Solution* recalled an instruction manual for the artist's celibate life and his self-chosen isolation. Absalon sits at a table, drinks a glass of whisky, eats a bar of chocolate, smokes a cigarette, plays with his genitals, picks at his nails, walks around the table and stands in a corner as though he is punishing himself. In the following scene, he undresses and lies down in a bunk.

'Subjective, in the sense of personal, and expressive, by virtue of its strongly autobiographical traits, the work—cool, white and untouchable though it may be—shows that there are no abstract worlds where art can be parted from life', writes Saskia Bos in the exhibition catalogue. (The publication, produced by De Appel, Amsterdam with Carré d'art, Nîmes, also features essays by Guy Tossato and Jean-Christophe Ammann). But Absalon's white is not at all synonymous with untouchability. In his work, white acts as an empty identity, which the user will further specify. Absalon wished to give new form to abstraction. For him, it was a source. This essence was derived from the world but he wanted to return it, through his abstract/concrete forms that do not elevate itself above reality but forge direct relations with it.

The origin of Absalon's oeuvre seems to be the urge to merge with his environment. In the video *Propositions d'habitation*, we see an actor who rises from his lying position. The back of his body is surrounded by a white form that holds him like a shell. Other postures adopted by the actor seem to be similarly inspired by a longing to become one with the surroundings. He sticks his head in a hole, encircles a

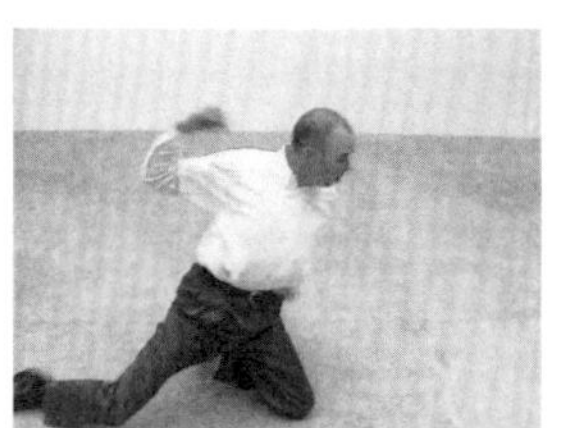

3 Absalon, *Bataille*, 1993, video, 35″ loop.

white form with his legs, et cetera. His actions, aimed as they are at the complementing of the body, somehow recall the way Franz West's *Paßstücke* can be worn by the exhibition visitor.

Absalon wanted to put up a fight with the forms in which everyday life presents itself. He chose his artist's sobriquet. The Bible, in Samuel II, recounts how Absalon the fair shepherd, one of the sons of King David of Israel, rebelled against his father, who had failed to avenge an outrage committed against Absalon's sister, by Amron, David's eldest son. The biblical Absalon let his desire for justice prevail over the bond with his father. Absalon recognized himself in this rebellious figure. The re-evaluation of his own identity corresponds with the principle of his work: the development of forms and images that function as starting points, as the origin and not the end result of a number of acts.

The spotless white of his works is therefore deceptive. His white erases the traces of the struggle by which they gained their shape. But some of his video works do depict aspects of this struggle. In *Bataille*, Absalon fights with his environment. He battles with forces that are invisible to the viewer, resisting them with movements resembling a vehement, stylized dance. That dance seems to be a conversion of enlightened rage, rage against the forces that try to curb his spirit.[3]

Absalon's work reminds me of what Mario Merz once said about the urgency of art. After serving in the resistance during the Second World War and being imprisoned for his active part in it, Merz concluded that poetry was the only imaginable counterweight to a society that, in its organizational forms, has a tendency toward evil. His igloos of stone and glass offer us a shelter. They function as a comforting thought. In a cell, however, you can regenerate in a real, physical sense. That is what Absalon had in mind with his very personal project. His work makes us encounter an optimism that arises from earnestness. Perhaps that's a good way to think of the artist, and keep the memory of his work alive.

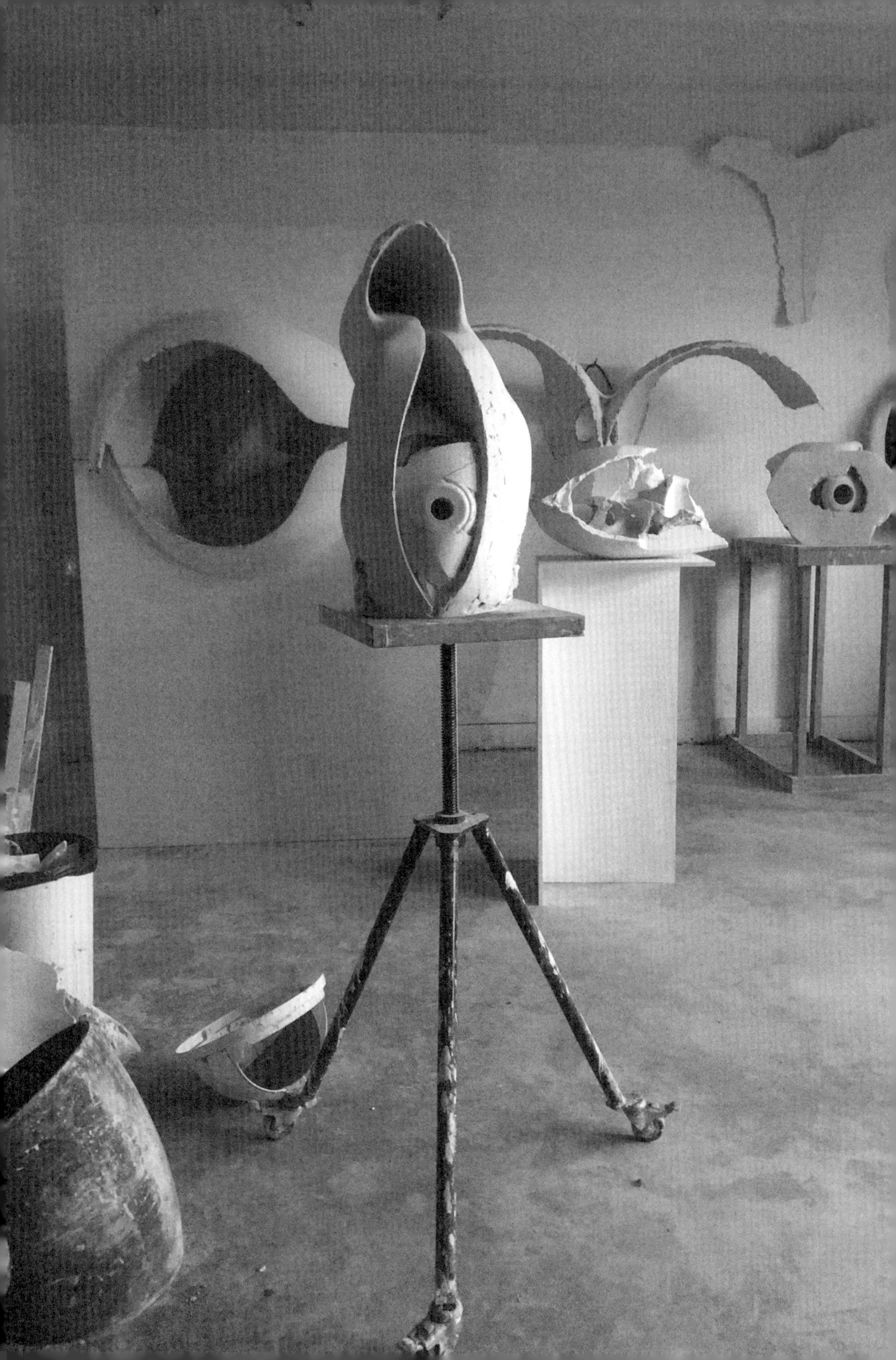

Embalmed Landscape with Soft Machine

André Kruysen

'Finite, infinite, left in peace, but on the move,
freely raucous and unabashed!'
—Einstürzende Neubauten, 'Redukt'[1]

The Dutch artist André Kruysen has created an extensive corpus of three-dimensional objects which he characterizes as a variation on a radically modernistic sculpture of the Italian futurist Boccioni. A wildly meditative energy permeates Boccioni's sculpture, where a squab figure is confined in a mass of material—like a genie in a bottle. André Kruysen utilizes comparable forces; he sees restlessness and tranquillity as polar opposites animating his work. The kinship of the two artists is a serious matter. Kruysen wrote to me in 2011 that Boccioni's paintings and especially his sculptures, such as *Testa + Casa + Luce* and *Unique Forms of Continuity in Space*, have served him as a wellspring of ideas to which he continually returns.[2]

1 Einstürzende Neubauten, *Silence Is Sexy*, album, Mute Records, Berlin, 2000. 'Endlich, unendlich, in Ruhe gelassen, aber beweglich, / frei zu lärmen, ohne Schuld!'

2 Mark Kremer, 'Ship Ahoy', *André Kruysen / Ouborg Prize 2011*, Stroom, The Hague, 2011, p. 20.

André Kruysen, studio view, 2020.

I

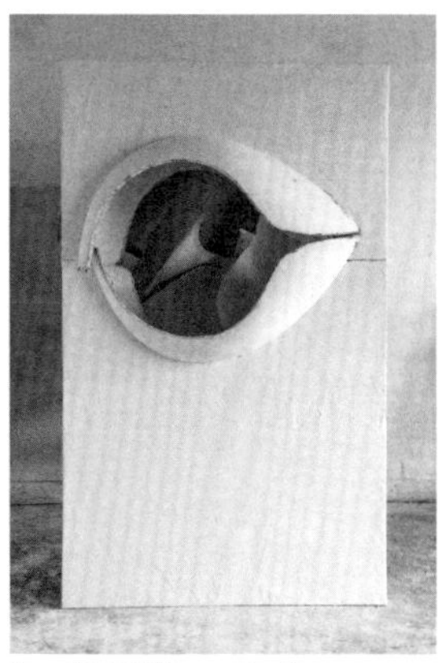

3a André Kruysen, *Inner Vision*, 2000, wood, steel, acrylic one, 250 × 125 × 120 cm.

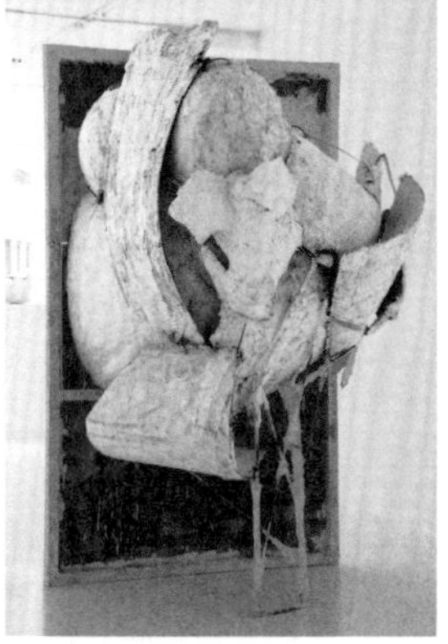

3b André Kruysen, *Inner Vision*, 2000, backside.

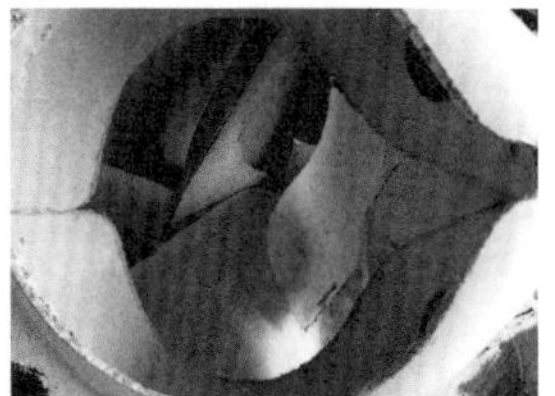

3c André Kruysen, *Inner Vision*, 2000, detail.

The studio, close to the seafront in Scheveningen, shelters a sculpture of more than human size. Titled *Inner Vision*, the upright slab of 2.5 metres in height is penetrated by a huge 'eye' with two bulging eyelids. Despite its aura of introspection, it dominates the space. Like a theatrical flat, the object projects a strong frontal effect, but it continues behind into a spherical body that juts out from the back of the slab. Shaped roughly like the drum of a cement mixer, the hollow chamber balances at the rear on spindly legs and is flanked by comb-like gills suggesting the exoskeleton of a marine creature.[3] The slab and the sphere shapes merge loosely into one another through the round eye-level opening at the front. I see this as the friendly gaze of a dolphin, or perhaps it is a porthole that invites me to peer inside.

The eyelids are clearly recognizable as castings from the front fenders of a classic Volkswagen Beetle. In the 1960s, the Beetle became a style icon of modernism as especially illustrated by the Volkswagen buses beloved by the hippies. It is as though the Volkswagen marque added an underlying skeleton to Kruysen's sculpture. It strikes me how much this differs from the Futurist tendency: the mild-mannered v w curves bear little resemblance to Marinetti's racing cars which spewed fire just like a machine gun.

The eye of Kruysen's work is a crucial part that lures us into the hollow drum, where abstract motifs engage in a round dance. Here the eye-form resonates. The suggestion of motility evokes the experience of the human eye: it is in this space that the sensory impressions are constantly collected.

Surrounding the large sculpture, a swarm of smaller objects are scattered freely around the studio space, resting on plinths, tables, or the ground. Openings in the composite forms combine to give the objects an appearance that is intense, fragile, and raw all at once. A shattered skull is overgrown with stucco and other stuff, a cabinet encloses a naturalistic eyeball, and organic matter seeps away into lifeless soils.[4] This group of objects hints at one total form, a gestalt that has been crushed or dismantled. The line-up of the large sculpture and the smaller works has the effect of a dramatic landscape: is this material for a future ruin? These lumps of substance recall the sun-scorched scenes of Max Ernst, the toxic landscapes after the catastrophe took place. I think of sci-fi mirages, a robust manifestation on the thin soil of a Tibetan plateau, or the parched bedding of the Aral Sea. It could easily be a desert scene depicted in the film *Dune* (2021). Staged sharply against that film's barren sand dunes, Kruysen's sculptural assembly would surely make a miraculous impression on the Fremen, the fierce and autonomous inhabitants of the desert planet Arrakis.

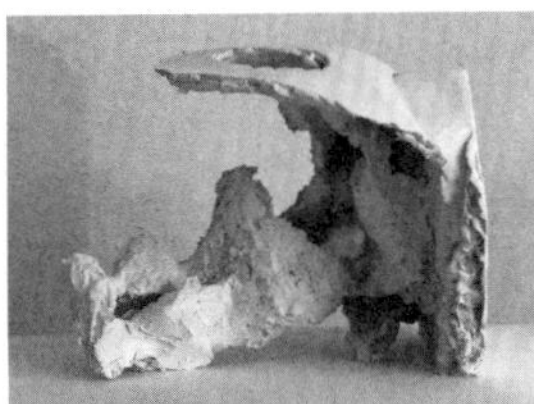

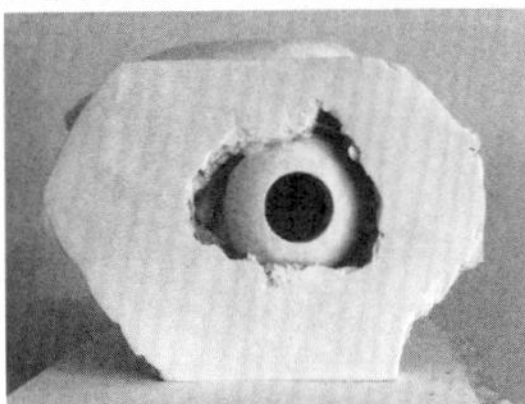

4 *Headhouselight VII*, 2019, plaster, pigments, 45 × 50 × 63 cm, destroyed.

2

André Kruysen has worked on the large sculpture for three years. *Inner Vision* (2017–2020) is his response to Umberto Boccioni's *Testa + Casa + Luce* (1911–1912, destroyed).[5] Boccioni died at age thirty-three, in 1916, leaving a significant legacy of paintings, sculptures and manifestos. Unfortunately, a man who had been entrusted with *Testa + Casa + Luce* saw little value in the sculpture and after a certain time disposed of it as waste. We know from photographs that Boccioni's *Testa + Casa + Luce* was a very impressive work: its sharp projections, grotesque distortions, realistic fragments and abrupt and brutal fusions defy us with their violence. It is striking how deeply Kruysen engages with Boccioni's work.

5 Anders Råden and Matt Smith, *Umberto Bocciono: Recreating the Lost Sculptures*, London, Estorick Collection of Modern Italian Art, 2019, p 11. Provides brief information. Important general data on Boccioni's sculptures are also provided by Uwe M. Schneede, *Umberto Boccioni*, Hatje, Stuttgart, 1994.

233

6 Michael Brenson, 'Met
Retrospective Explores Boccioni
and Futurism', *New York Times*,
16 September 1988.

One of Boccioni's Futurist sculptures that inspires him,
Unique Forms of Continuity in Space (1913), occupies the
surrounding space with one single form. 'That striding figure,' Michael Brensons wrote, 'part knight, part flame, bran-
dishing a cross on its face, seems to melt into its environment
while marching indomitably through it'.[6] This interaction
with space, with psychic energy, is fundamental to Kruysen's
oeuvre.

André Kruysen has made more works that pick up the
thread of stories spun by famous artists. For example, his
light sculpture *Before One Has a Past* (2007)[7] in the Museum
of Contemporary Art Antwerp (MuHKA) was inspired by

234

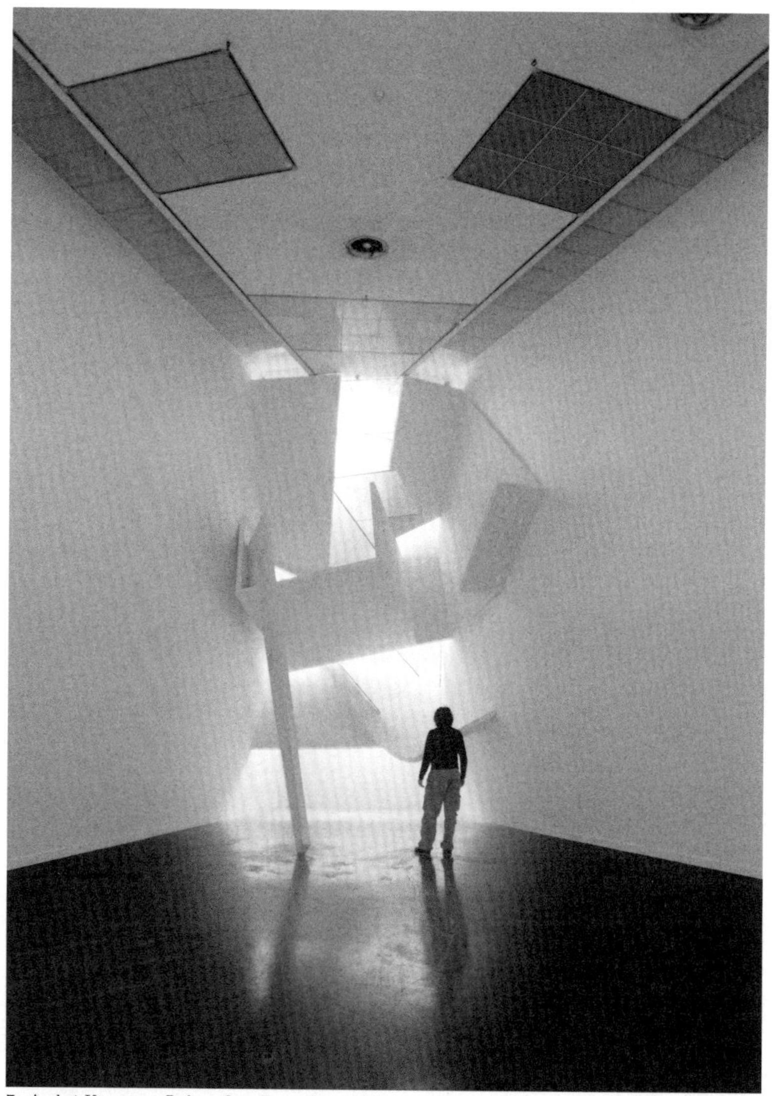

7 André Kruysen, *Before One Has a Past*, 2007, installation, wood, plaster, paint,
800 × 450 × 450 cm, MuHKA Antwerpen.

Malevich's sculptures and the 'floating motif' in his paintings, which Kruysen compressed into a fantasy about Suprematism. Kruysen's sculpture, consisting of slabs of wood and plaster boards coated with white stucco, was erected on site in the ground-floor hall behind the tall window on the street corner of Cockerillkaai and Leuvenstraat. Behind the window, the sculpture burst open as a large membrane spilling light across the floor, or as a sparkling fountain spraying its luminous rays upwards.

'Artists are nourished by dreams of the past,' Kounellis said in 1981.[8] His nonchalant statement veils the charged character of the artistic operation. Kounellis' installations make one feel electricity: a tension in which the caprices of the past and the artist's struggle with the subject matter become tangible. Shreds of the past drift around like powerless emanations: just see and smell the quenched flames and the odour of animal carcasses. Kounellis was an artist of immense vitality: *Untitled (Cavalli)*, his installation with twelve tethered horses in Rome (1969) quivered with a nervous sensitivity.[9] Kounellis found inspiration in Boccioni, who referred to his sculptures as *ambianti plastica*—that notion is an early precedent of the work of Kounellis and other *arte povera* artists, who created environments incorporating objects with the aim of immersing the spectator in a spatial experience.

Kounellis and Oiticica lauded Boccioni. Boccioni's *States of Mind* (a term from Bergson's philosophy) is a series of three paintings: *The Farewells, Those Who Go* and *Those Who Stay* (1911). The swirling compositions of line and colour in which the images open up like flowers—or alternatively remain shrouded, dark and enigmatic—are reminiscent of the activity and atmosphere of a railway station, the dynamics and melancholy. This idea returns in a work by

235

8 Paul Groot and Paul Donker Duyvis, 'Een interview met Kounellis', *Museumjournaal*, No. 6, 1981, p. 292–293.

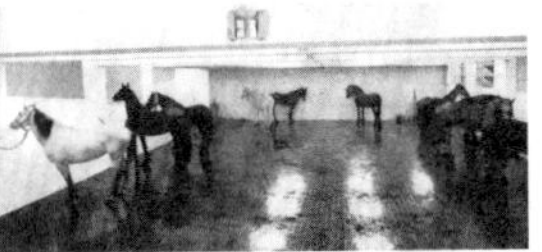

9 Jannis Kounellis, *Untitled (Horses)*, 1969, Galleria l'Attico, Rome.

Kounellis where a toy train runs in circles on curved rails surrounding a marble pillar: the perpetual motion signifies his lifetime journey. Later, Kounellis made an invitation card with a photo of himself: his mouth wide open, he swallows the horrid locomotive.

Oiticica's homage is another counterpoint. His *Topological Readymade Landscape (Homage to Boccioni)* consists of a bottle of cleaning fluid wrapped in fine metal gauze. The work is meant to shock. It speaks frankly of the confrontation that Boccioni seeks.

3

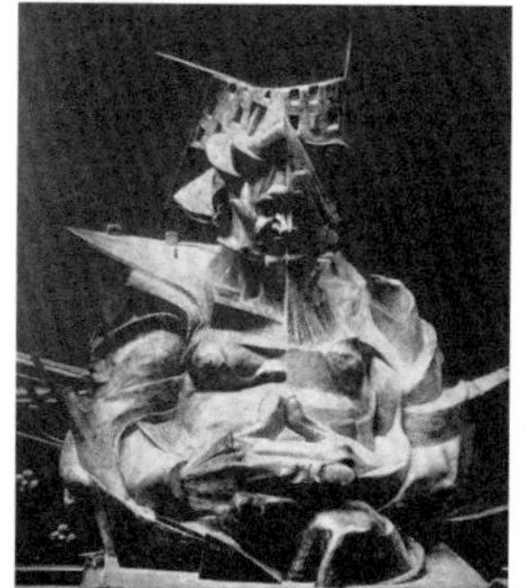

10 Umberto Boccioni, *Testa + Casa + Luce / Head + House + Light*, 1912, plaster, ca. 90 × 70 × 50 cm, destroyed.

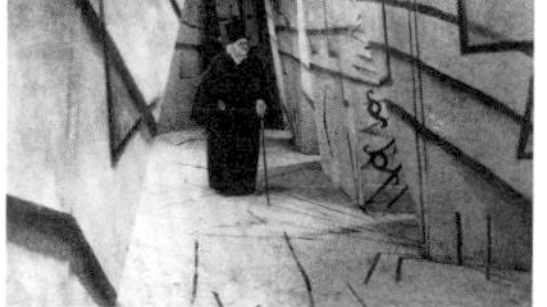

11 Robert Wiene, *The Cabinet of Dr. Caligari*, 1920, silent film, 74'.

Boccioni's *Testa + Casa + Luce* is actually a repugnant sculpture.[10] But it is intriguing and unrelenting as well. It fascinated me when I first saw a photo of it in a book. A lot happens in the work: objects and atmospheres and power lines tangle violently with another, as can happen in your mind when it is full of competing urgencies. The white plaster sculpture in which a head is entrapped in a house and light changes into material substance is a chimera. The forms are adorned with fantastic spines that protrude into the surrounding space, as though bent on bewitching it. The work rests on a tall table, reaching for your head, heart and genitals, if you were to stand too close to it. With its dense body and intricate parts, it evokes a whirlwind of impressions. Angular details and crude apertures defy exact description. I find myself thinking of Gothic sculpture, an iceberg model with a thousand crags, or a fantastic setting for an expressionistic film such as *The Cabinet of Doctor Caligari* directed by Robert Wiene.[11] The bulky head is framed by the roof of a house, while the upper body sinks into the interior below;

breasts and the powerful hands project from a torso. At intervals, the sculpture seems overgrown with spiky wreaths of light. Appendages jut out all over, with shadows incarnated as thick collars. The interplay of masses and component parts is tangible and hallucinatory.

Boccioni aimed to make a sculpture in which the 'figure', torn and dismembered as it is, embraces the surrounding space and atmosphere. Elements from outside penetrate the figure—inevitably changing it into something else—resulting in the acute tension emanated by the sculpture. Discontinuities of scale manifest themselves stealthily. A robust balcony—made of wood and steel from a real balcony—looms up behind the head. The right shoulder of the woman transforms into a horizontal piazza where two tiny figures stroll—a bit lost like figures in a De Chirico painting. Boccioni's mother sat as the model. She also appears in two later works, the painting *Materia* (1912) and the grotesque sculpture *Antigrazioso* (1912–1913). In my fantasy the entire sculpture orbits around her hands. Mother folds them on her belly. These huge hands are the hands of a maker, they almost radiate the devious force of an artist-demiurge. The fingers suggest potent erections. At the same time, I sense a great tenderness in them. These are the hands of a sculptor who caresses the face of his mother, lovingly and respectfully.

Boccioni exhibited his formidable sculpture in 1913. A photograph exists of the work on show in his solo exhibition in the Parisian gallery La Boétie. The white object stands in front of a background of floral wallpaper. The sculpture rends the surroundings to shreds. A barbarian or archaic force can be felt here. After growing up in four different Italian towns, a young Boccioni moved at age fifteen to Catania in eastern Sicily, where the Ancient Greeks once lived. In that city, a sculpture of a dwarf elephant carrying an obelisk stands on a square,[12] faced by a statue of Cervantes who was held captive by pirates from Barbary.

Boccioni's *Fusion of a Head and a Window* (1912–1913) features a countenance, like that of a grimacing pirate. We also find that barbarian or archaic element in Russia around the same time: *Victory Over the Sun*, an opera by Matyushin, Khlebnikov and Malevich in which a large, abstract, motley eye appears on stage after the sun has been captured by strong, futuristic men, is just one example. In Paris, Stravinsky's *Rite of Spring* sparked a scandal in 1913. A highly relevant instance of Futurism, in my view, is the lengthy *Ode to the Sea* (1915) by the Portuguese Fernando Pessoa published under his heteronym Álvaro de Campos. De Campos is a wildly passionate poet, bearing no resemblance to the melancholy Pessoa. In his *Ode*, Álvaro sits on the banks of the Tagus contemplating his solitary existence. A mailboat sails on the river, life on the quay gradually warms up, and the poet is sated with impressions; the entire surroundings force their way into his imagination when the poem transforms into an orchestrated delirium. The poet becomes a pirate who does gruesome things to others, but also a man who offers up his own body to the pirates and allows himself to be devoured in a voluntary game of lust—a cannibalistic ritual: 'Aguilhoo uma ânsia fria dos crimes marítimos…' ('I incite a cold passion for crimes at sea…').[13]

For his new group of sculptures, André Kruysen decided to combine two aspects of his work. On the one hand, he has long made in-situ sculptures in museums and other venues—works that silently make their way into a space and play changing light compositions onto the architecture for the time of an exhibition. The works make the viewer receptive to the dynamics of light. The basic form, the material skeleton that distributes the light, reflects the foundations of geometric

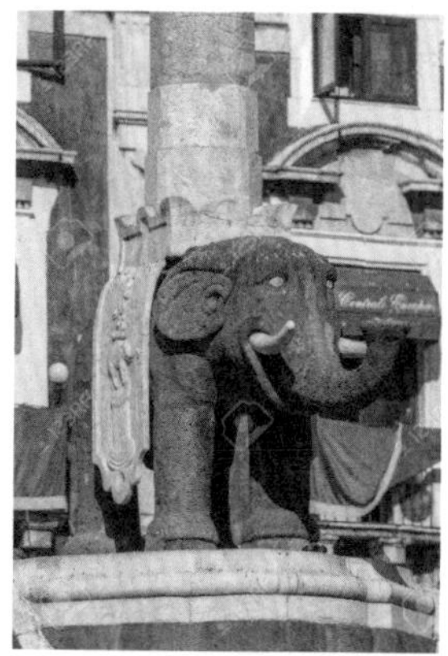

12 Giovanni Battista Vaccarini, *Elephant Fountain*, 1735–1735, Catania.

13 Fernando Pessoa, 'Ode Marítima', *Orpheu*, No. 2, Lisbon, April–June 1915.

abstraction, as in the shapes used by for example Mondrian and Malevich. Kruysen's light compositions interact with the surroundings, where they exude a meditative/introverted force. His masks, on the other hand—the multi-coloured sculptures are affixed to the wall or stand detached on a pedestal in the space—exert a strong expressive force. These compact and powerful forms produce intense plays of colour. They are incantations of psychic energy, of inner life.[14] They remind me of the restlessness of Expressionism, the modernist movement which came up in 1906 as a counterweight and companion to abstract geometrical art. Particularly in Germany, artists such as Nolde, Kirchner and Jawlenski were drawn to it. The play of light in André Kruysen's three-dimensional works is an emanation: the viewer may become absorbed in the atmosphere of absolute tranquillity. The masks expose our feelings in a different way, by creeping under the skin.

The photograph of a voodoo ceremony acted as an inspiration for the artist in the process of creating his new sculptures. We see a religious performance in which strong inner and expressive forces are elicited and spread freely. A woman is dusted with white powder. Above the image, the artist wrote in capitals:

ERLÖSUNGSVERLANGEN (longing for deliverance)
WUNSCHVORSTELLUNG (wishful thinking)
DURCHDRINGUNGSPROBLEMATIK (problems of
   penetration)[15]

I asked him if he himself had ever been present at such a ceremony. From his reply I deduce that he is very interested in animistic and shamanistic practices and respects their mystery. He briefly describes an experience—I think he was young then, in his mid-twenties?—in New York. 'Yes, once,

239

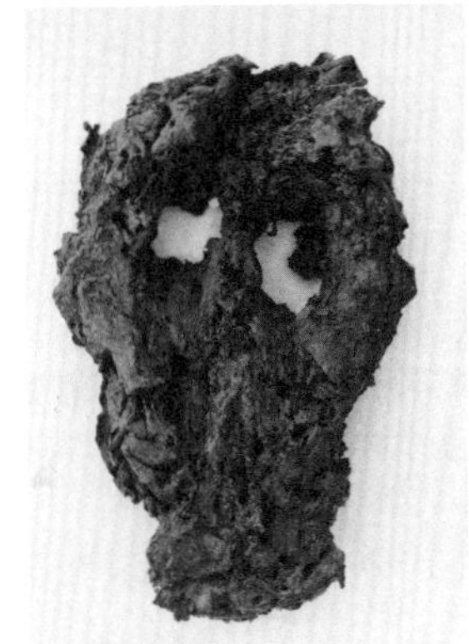

14a André Kruysen, *Demon*, 2017.

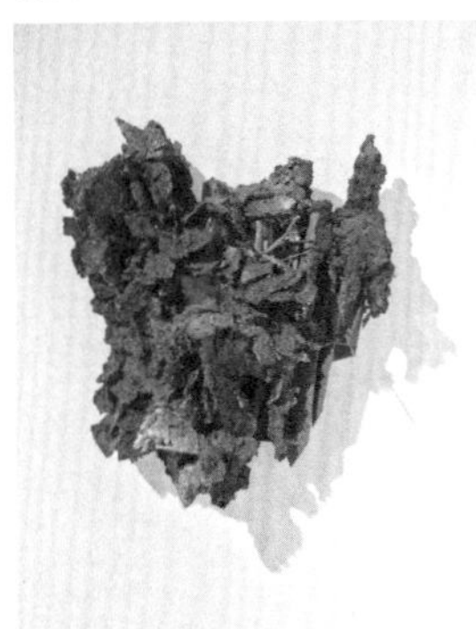

14b André Kruysen, *El Bosque*, 2016.

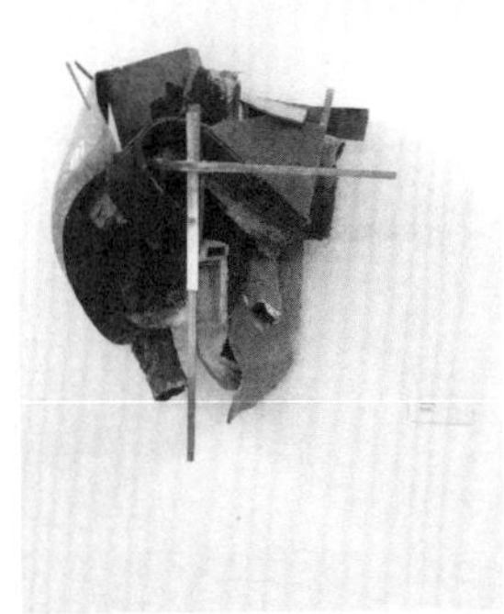

14c André Kruysen, *Melquíades*, 2019.

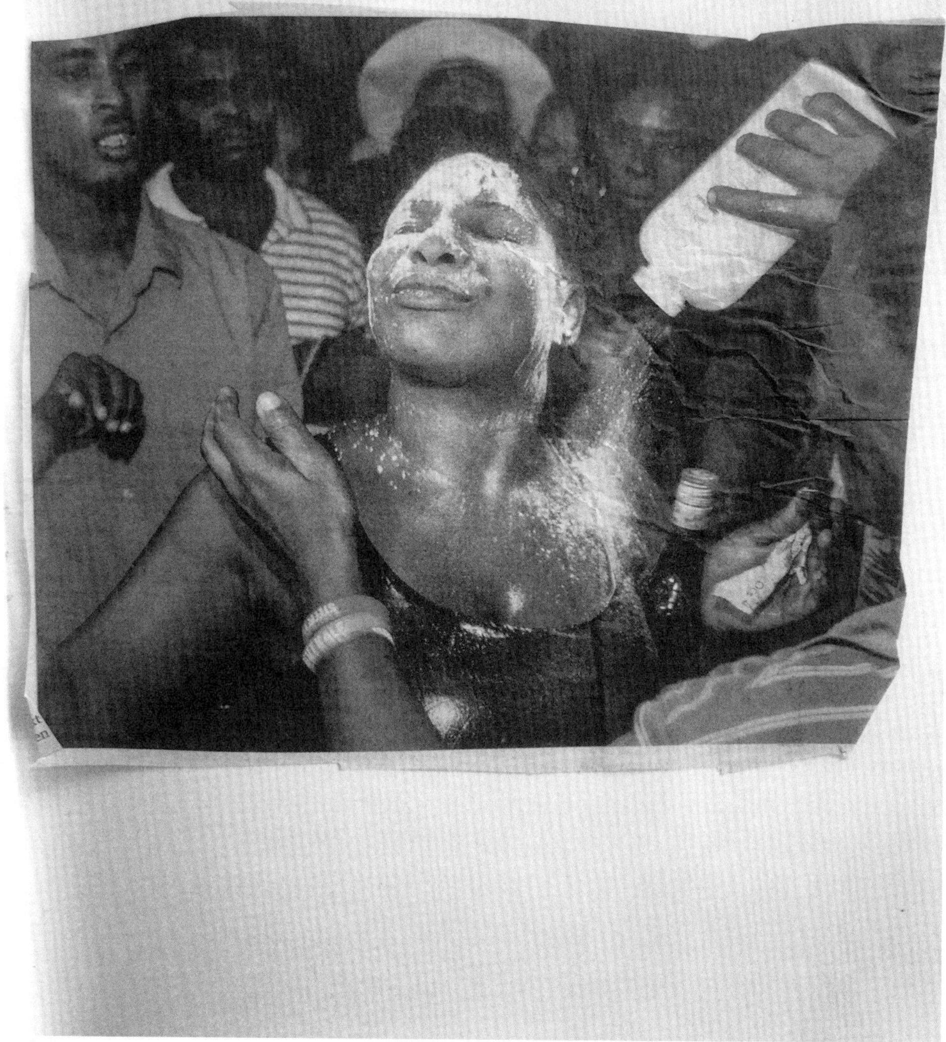

15 André Kruysen, *diary entry, 2015*.

in Central Park. It was very creepy, and I walked off after they forced me to climb down from a tree from where I was observing the whole thing. "The spirits are rising, so get away from there, get away!" they shouted!'[16]

16 Artist's statements, verbatim or freely reproduced, in email contacts with the author, April–May 2020.

4

Every artist hopes to create life. Whatever medium they may choose, from graffiti to oil on canvas, it is this force that motivates art. André Kruysen is inspired by many modern artists and architects: Picasso and Schwitters, Kahn and Le Corbusier, Malevich and Tatlin and many more. He relates his interest in voodoo to sculpture: 'I find the activation of objects in the Voodoo religion so amazing. What an intense and meaningful action! It resonates with the sculptor in myself'. This seems to be the impetus for his new sculpture group. 'I find the transitional rites for Voodoo remarkable,' Kruysen told me, 'because they have real experiences there, experiences that unconditionally link body and mind'.

André Kruysen reads Boccioni's *Testa + Casa + Luce* as a Mountain and a Buddha. The oriental world of ideas and life inspires him: the Tao in the reconciliation of extremes, where tranquillity and mutability are two sides of the coin, accompanies him in his day-to-day life. He also practises Tai Chi and Lu, a form of Kung Fu. Western phenomenology is an additional influence. According to Merleau-Ponty, 'Our body doesn't occupy space in the way of things, it is a manner of being part of the world; it inhabits space or roams around in it'. Neither of the mentalities mentioned above had a direct influence on Kruysen's decision to choose the Volkswagen parts as a mould for the works. His explanation is nonetheless philosophical: 'I looked for mechanically shaped curves as a

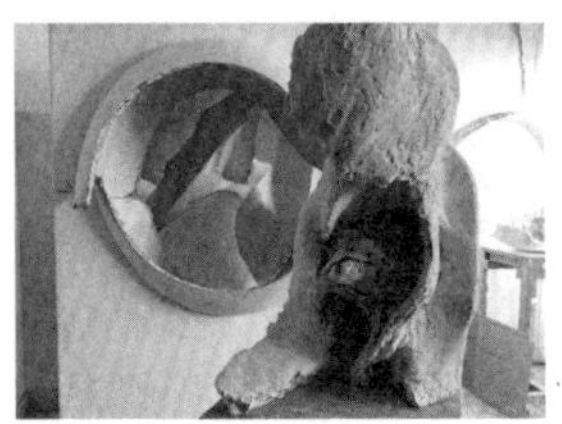

17 André Kruysen, studio view, 2020.

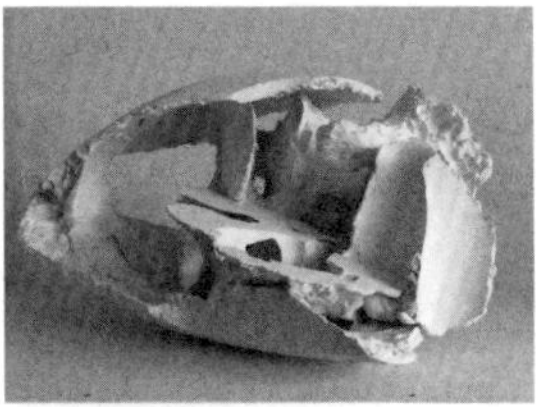

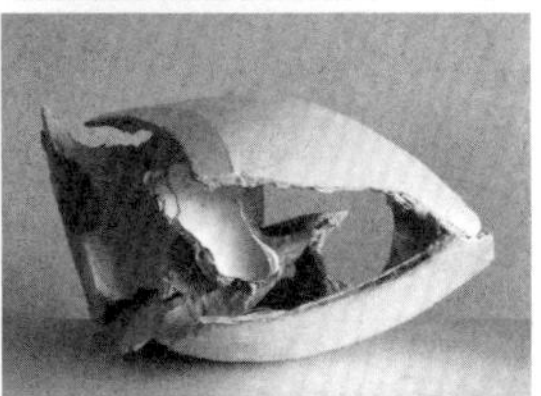

18 André Kruysen, *Headhouselight VIII*, 2019, plaster, 55 × 65 × 35 cm.

way of turning that small object (the eye) into something much greater'.[17, 18]

'I specifically wanted the artist's hand out of the way in order to keep the spectator's focus on the casting. Being there and not being there—considered as one. Or presence, the spirit of the form, if you like. Curves *pur sang*. The imperfection of the artist's hand mustn't be a distraction; the lines had to stay neutral. I ended up with the vw Beetle for its lovely arch form.' It surprises me to learn that he relates Boccioni's *Testa + Casa + Luce* to Nature (a Mountain). 'I've always found it to be such an earthy image, transcendent though it may be. It is ultimately also a portrait of Mother Earth.' My response was to ask him whether that idea was important when he made his sculpture group. In our era, after all, nature that is threatened, but there is also a growing awareness that this process of destruction has to end.

The artist describes his work as a membrane, a selective barrier that lets some things through and blocks the way of others. Every cell in the human body is encapsulated in a membrane. Kruysen's choice of that word implies a concern for equilibrium. It's striking how often I come across that word recently in conversations with artists. Tiong Ang, for example, uses it to describe a live social orchestration that he intends to realize in Bucharest; Rob Johannesma assigns the term to a series of paintings in which a dark surface opens at the edges; and Wineke Gartz qualifies her installation in the Kröller-Müller Museum as a membrane that couples inside with outside. Does this tendency imply a growing sensitivity among artists that we must stay in close touch with our surroundings? And that our individual interaction with nature and culture deserves more attention?

Taking a look at ourselves certainly plays a part in the sculptures. The eye of the main, large sculpture draws us into an intimate zone. The skin has a soft eggshell shine, and its muted shades of white suggest vulnerability. A delicate horizontal fissure runs across the front; here the overall form is split. The large sculpture wants to receive us. The smaller objects grouped around it are still hefty pieces. Each seems to be setting out on a journey, just hatched out of the egg, still entangled with the placenta—but the process that they went through seems to have suddenly stopped… The whole sculpture group reminds me of a disintegrating landscape; I already mentioned the Tibetan plateau, a drained Aral Sea and the windswept sands of a fictional planet. (Please note: Frank Herbert's book *Dune* featuring this desert planet was based on the author's actual research into the hydrology of a small American desert zone, the Oregon Dunes).

Is *Inner Vision,* and the surrounding *HeadHouseLight*-pieces, a work about today's scorched earth? This group of sculptures certainly emanates imminent destruction. It has the precarious feeling of a battlefield after the dreadful event, as pictured in the opening scenes of classic Japanese films on the feudal clashes of rival clans. Like scattered corpses in a landscape, the artist has dismantled Boccioni's sculpture and spread the parts across the space. Is this a divination of Death? Actually, Kruysen was occupied for a while with a bust of his grandfather (deceased), a larger-than-life portrait that he considered integrating into the work. But a certain point this idea began to seem too literal. By way of a detour, he turned to the Voodoo ceremony, an emotionally charged event from a distant place, in which we can nonetheless see and recognize ourselves, since it addresses a universal concept: shielding life against malevolent external forces. Seen in that light, the large eye-sculpture may be interpreted as a transformer, a machine summoning new life.

With this observation, we return once more to the theme

243

19 Mikhail Bakhtin, *Rabelais and his World*, trans. Helen Iswolsky, Bloomington, Indiana University Press, 1984, p. 332.

of the transformative power of intense bodily experiences. Mikhail Bakhtin has written about transitional folk rites such as medieval carnival, when the crowd would plunge, fully committed and unafraid of the authorities, into a collective delirium, thereby temporarily undoing the limitations of the human frame. Their eating, boozing, fornication, singing and dancing could last for days on end. One individual would merge with another, unconscious of where one ends and another begins. Bakhtin: 'In the grotesque world, the limits between objects and phenomena are drawn quite differently than in the static world of art and literature'.[19]

Kruysen defies the limitations of sculpture. His light compositions are spatial grotesques, and the multi-coloured masks are animistic objects. The new sculpture group evokes an atmosphere, a field of forces in which the mysterious interplay of life and death is the actual theme. We recognize this energy with our body: we are sensitive to its pulsations.

5

Rituals, also in the everyday sense, have always played a part in the artist's practice. Before making his light sculptures, Kruysen spends days at a place, jumping around to grasp the nature of its space. Child's play. He goes sea diving and experiences the huge difference of scale when an underwater rock just protrudes above the surface. It is a youthful adventure with persisting influence. In New York, he rides the elevator to the top of a skyscraper to see how the light in Manhattan may be cut by architecture; a sensational experience that still gives food for thought.

Jumping in Space—Diving into the Sea—Rising above the Ordinary: physical limits are sought and probed in all these activities. Outwitting Death: this plays a part in the new corpus. The artist has spent years on the battleground of his studio. His smaller sculptures resemble bones that emanate a cold glow.[20] [21] All the *HeadHouseLight* objects remain very close to Boccioni's sculpture. Its real interpretation occurs in Kruysen's large sculpture, for that is where the grotesque folds back on itself. The centre of that sculpture is stipulated movement, restrained whirlpools, serrated drunkenness. This is the length and space of an eye. And that eye observes; all around, it beholds a field of scattered hunks. But that eye is also ourselves; we long to enter this portal, to tumble through its aperture like Alice into the White Rabbit's hole. Once inside, we will observe, feel and realize: here it is silent, as silent as never before. *Inner Vision* is a complex self-portrait through which the artist gazes into his own eyes. Here, entire worlds ebb and flow, in and out.

A good work of art makes a fresh start, as we know from classic literary texts. Proust described the feeling:

> For a long time I used to go to bed early. Sometimes, when I had put out my candle, my eyes would close so quickly that I had not even time to say "I'm going to sleep". And half an hour later the thought that it was time to go to sleep would awaken me; I would try to put away the book which, I imagined, was still in my hands, and to blow out the light.

From Virgil we learn, 'My mind is intent on singing of shapes changed into new bodies'. And, according to the bard in the Finnish epic poem *Kalevala,* 'Mon esprit me transporte, mon désir s'élève dans ma pensée, je veux commencer des runos, je veux chanter' ('Mastered by desire impulsive, By a mighty inward urging, I am ready now for singing, Ready to begin the chanting').[22] The unnamed bard then asks a second singer

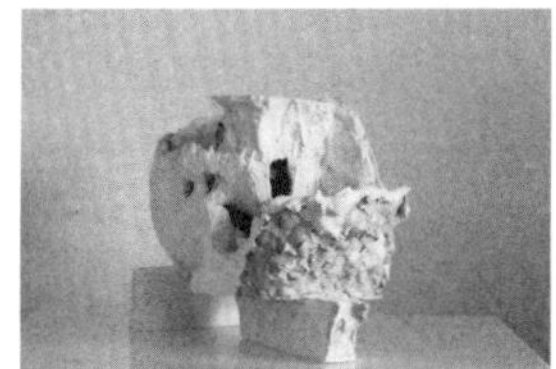

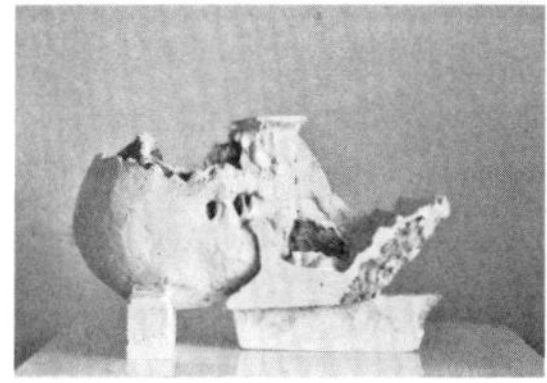

20 André Kruysen, *Headhouselight IV*, 2019, plaster, clay remains, 32 × 29 × 49 cm.

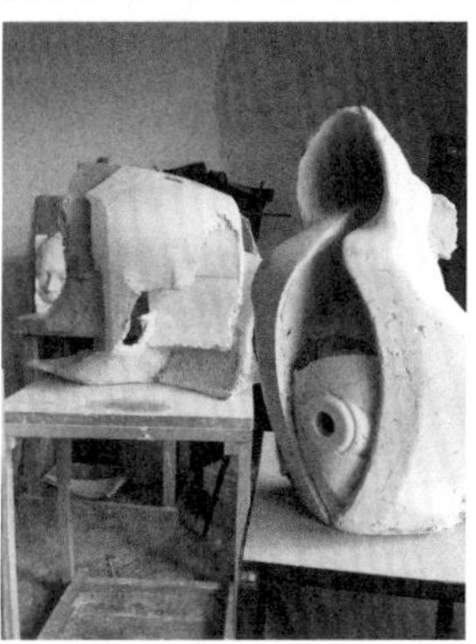

21 André Kruysen, studio view, 2020.

22 Léouzon le Duc's first-ever translation of the epic (Jules Labitte, Paris, 1845) in French begins with this description of the oral tradition, in which art lives on thanks to mutual effort. English translation: John Martin Crawford, *The Kalevala: The Epic Poem of Finland into English, Vol. 1,* Cincinnati, The Robert Clarke Company, 1898.

23 Michael Brenson, See: Paul Groot and Paul Donker Duyvis, 'Een interview met Kounellis'.

24 See: *Joseph Beuys: Zeige deine Wunde*, Schnellmann & Kluser, Munich, 1980. The publication gives press reactions (*Vol. 1*) and photographs of this environment/installation in the former shop space of an underground passage (*Vol. 2*).

25 Mike Kelley, *Playing with Dead Things*, 'The Uncanny', Municipal Museum Arnhem, 'Sonsbeek 93', Arnhem, 1993.

to take part: arm in arm, turn by turn, in speech and by song, they stoke the fire of the narrative.

The Italian artist who, for three years, clung like a monkey to André Kruysen's back, was once described as follows: Boccioni was an introspective artist who meditated about action'.[23] André Kruysen is an extroverted artist who ponders receptiveness.

In Kruysen's landscape, among the Embalmed Debris stands a Soft Machine. It reminds me of the work of Beuys and Franz West—artists who built their work on Expressionism as well. Beuys' *Zeige deine Wunde* ('Show Your Wound') was an environment that comprised biers on wheels, cupboards with *Lotta Continua* a leftist newspaper, blackboards inscribed with the call-up 'Zeige deine Wunde', and garden utensils. All the elements came in pairs, potentially fertile couples. There was no sign of colour in his landscape. The whole raised the impression of a chrysalis in which nature and culture linger in a state of rest.[24] Franz West began around 1980 with making his *Paßstücke*, clownish objects made using plaster, steel wire, papier mâché et cetera. The works were meant to be touched—visitors are free to lift the *Paßstücke* from their plinths. By way of such spontaneous interaction, West wanted to animate the sculptures, make them become alive.

André Kruysen's set-up of sculptures drifts between life and death. Mike Kelley wrote an essay on the critical condition of figurative sculpture in its attempt to imitate life while consisting of dead material.[25] Kruysen disagrees: his art is driven by animating forces. Kruysen's machine is such an animator: all these scattered pieces will still face the music! According to Kruysen, 'Boccioni made practically all his work before the First World War. As a modernist, he thought that anything old had to be gotten rid of and a totally new order had to be established. But what would he have thought after living through two world wars? What would such an experience have meant for his ideals and art?' At the heart of Kruysen's environs stands a perforated monolith with a winged eye. His sculpture group is an Allegory of Alertness for our own time.

Polyphony

I relate polyphony in art with COMPLEXITY. We
need different voices to grasp the complexity of
today's world. Music theory gives us this definition:
'polyphony (e.g., polyphonic chant) is a musical texture characterized by a simultaneous combination of
two or more tones or melodic lines (sung by different
voices).' Contemporary art sheds light on today's
complexity through works characterized by the
alignment—harmonious or discordant—of different
voices and their respective perspectives.

Current discourse often relates polyphony to
agency. By doing this, it wants to raise questions
such as: which voices can be heard in this work or
discourse? What is it they want to say? Who is
speaking and on behalf of whom? Here, polyphony
implies a firm emancipatory stake, the idea that all
voices (human *and* natural) should be allowed to

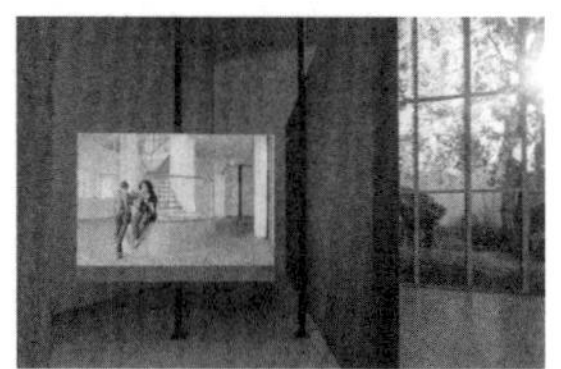

1 Wendelien van Oldenborgh, *Cinema Olanda*, 2017. Photo: Daria Scagliola.

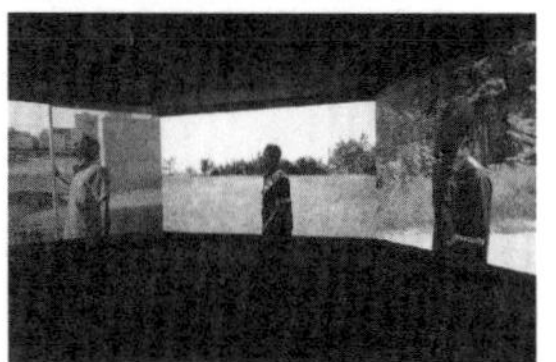

2 The Living and The Dead Ensemble, *The Wake*, 2019.

speak and equally deserve to be heard—in art *as* in society. This topical notion is important. Some exemplary works are Wendelien van Oldenborgh's *Cinema Olanda* (2017), a versatile project with a symposium and video installations on lesser-known episodes in Dutch history, in their relation to current socio-political transitions in the Netherlands.[1] The artist orchestrated a choir of voices in these iterations: persons with different backgrounds who speak their minds on colonialism and racism. The performances of The Living and The Dead Ensemble, a collective of artists, performers and poets from Haiti, France and the UK, are relevant too.[2] Their work began in 2017 in Haiti when they performed *Monsieur Toussaint*, a theatre play written by Édouard Glissant.

Its focus is the Haitian Revolution that, having begun as a fledgling slave rebellion, became a big liberation movement, led by Toussaint Louverture, against the French occupiers, under Napoleon Bonaparte. Born into slavery, Toussaint was manumitted by his owner before the French Revolution and, once free, became a French citizen. Toussaint had a prolific military and political career, but he died in a French prison (a formidable composition by Swans, the rock band, on their album *To Be Kind* (2014), called 'Bring the Sun / Toussaint L'Ouverture' is devoted to him). Set in the prison where he spent his last days, Glissant's play focuses on the recreation of Toussaint's turbulent life, through his memories of Haiti and the characters from his own past, both dead and alive, who appear before him in the cell.

The real interaction and potential exchange between different voices is an important theme. Visual art renders this type of interplay in various ways, for instance through the portrayal of conflicting forces, the dialogue with a historical artist, or the apparent take-over of the work by an external genius. This is comparable to the practice of the Portuguese poet Fernando Pessoa, who created many other writers and *heteronyms,* under whose names many different works with often conflicting and also unpopular and extreme views came out.

Mikhail Bakhtin (1895–1975) was a fervent scholar of polyphony (the orchestration of different voices), the dialogic principle (the need to express oneself and get the other's response; living interaction among individuals and their perspectives or 'worlds'), and heteroglossia ('different tongues'; co-existence of distinct varieties within one language) in the fields of language formation and literary theory. Art is a different field, but Bakhtin's ideas in particular on dialogue are so vital, that they seem relevant for art. In his study of the European novel, Bakhtin analyzes the dialogic principle. He argues

3 Mikhail Bakhtin, 'Discourse in the Novel', *The Dialogic Imagination: Four Essays*, trans. Caryl Emerson and Michael Holquist, Austin, University of Texas Press, 2021 [1981], p. 279.

4 *Ibid.*, p. 339.

5 Mikhail Bakhtin, *Problems of Dostoevsky's Poetics*, Minneapolis, University of Minnesota Press, p. 6–7.

that all novelistic utterances are based on need to dialogue. This begins at a basic level: 'The word is born in a dialogue as a living rejoinder within it; the word is shaped in dialogic interaction with an alien word that is already in the object. A word forms a concept of its own object in a dialogic way'.[3]

About our daily use of language and its formation, Bakhtin says: 'of all words uttered in everyday life, no less than half belong to someone else'.[4] Bakhtin elaborates on this in his study of dialogue in Dostoevsky's novels. In Bakhtin's view, Dostoevsky construed his dialogues in a very specific way: one character's utterances are informed/incited by what the other is thinking and what he/she will say next. This approach leads to a hugely rich literary texture, full of inner contradictions, hidden thoughts, and doubts. Characteristic for Dostoevsky's novels is their 'plurality of independent and unmerged voices and consciousnesses, a genuine polyphony of fully valid voices'.[5]

Which voices express themselves in the work; which forces are active on the surface or manifest in a more subcutaneous way; who are the artist's dialogue partners (dead and alive)? These are relevant questions for curators/art writers to consider when they engage with the work and oeuvres of artists.

We find a beautiful alignment of voices in a work by Tomo Savić-Gecan, produced for the

Venice Biennale in 2022. For his *Untitled (Croatian Pavilion)* the artist tapped various artistic disciplines and knowledge fields, in order to look at today's world, and notably at the extent to which information streams and the human body interlock. As proof of that, take a walk in the city, observe a person tending closely to his iPhone, and note how this modern citizen tailors his behaviour to information. Savić-Gecan worked with experts from various fields, connecting everything with a strand of early and radical conceptual practices in Zagreb/Croatia (1960–1980) that took computer operations on board, as well as more recent practices of expanded performance. His work was preceded by this announcement:

> Every day for the duration of the 59th edition of the Venice Biennale of Art, the lead story from a different, randomly selected global news source provides the data that feeds an artificial intelligence algorithm, which in turn prescribes the time, location, duration, movements, and thoughts of a group of five performers in the city of Venice to constitute Tomo Savić-Gecan *Untitled (Croatian Pavilion)*, 2022.[6]

I find this work by Savić-Gecan so interesting because, despite the precise definition of its structure and how all the components come together, the total

6 Tomo Savić-Gecan, *Untitled (Croation Pavilion)*, 2022.

endeavour escapes you. This is precisely what happens when you try to think about today's systemic reality, how all kinds of levels are connected by computer technology, and how it escapes our thought. In Venice, in tune with the work, a few persons would be wandering through the city for a brief moment of time…

Art as the result of group interaction, where a team of expert scientists and artists put their minds together, would differ from art born from one person's inner dialogue: this is a logical thought. In reality, though, these two positions, the collective and individual one, have much in common. Here I am reminded of Bakhtin's observation regarding language's inner resistance and its resilience: 'The word is born in a dialogue as a living rejoinder within it…' Is not the image born in a dialogue as well?

This section brings together texts on Tiong Ang, Astrid Nobel, Hugo Canoilas, Lorelinde Verhees and Rob Johannesma. The voices of other makers, with whom they are in dialogue, can be heard in their oeuvres, or they resonate in the background. My interview with Tiong Ang traces a shift, from his early individual practice and the making of reticent-introverted paintings, to his later and exuberant polyphonic practice. Ang realized many multi-media projects, on the basis of collective authorship dialogues, creating space for other makers 'to do their thing'. My interview presages his later project *The Second Hands,* an outdoors installation and durational performance produced for the Bucharest Biennial of 2022: an inquiry of the idea of revolution. The text on Astrid Nobel describes her works as surrealist dreamscapes that are often construed in dialogue with passages from literary works. The text on Hugo Canoilas addresses a polyphonic body of work, titled *Um Corridor entre M. e K..* This orchestration of a film, paintings and sculptures was inspired by a day trip to Brussels, where the artist saw René Magritte's paintings and Mike Kelley's sculptures. There are many sides to Canoilas' practice; its character evokes Pessoa's universe and his revelations. Lorelinde Verhees is an artist working in photography and drawing. Her exhibition at P/////AKT, Amsterdam, revealed her receptivity to words, Robert Crumb, and the American natural landscape. My text is an ode to her receptivity, a free response to her work, and a rather personal note. The essay on Rob Johannesma explores a recent body of paintings that, set off by a personal, dramatic event, was in fact conceived in conclave with two historical figures: a painter and a poet who, in their works, examined inner life.

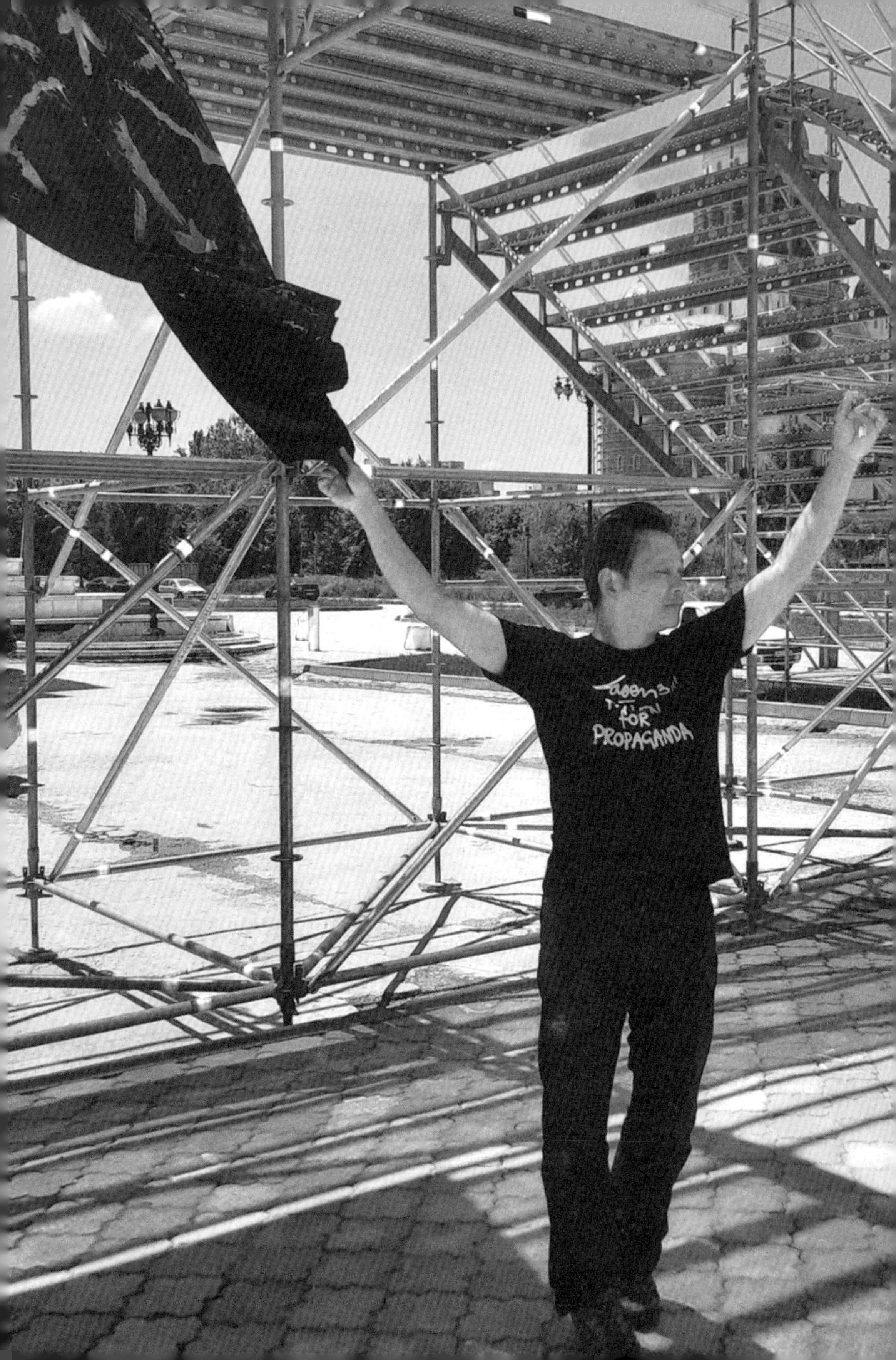

fоr
PROPAGANDA

This Revolution
Will Not Be Televised

Interview with Tiong Ang

The interview with Tiong Ang took place during the Covid-19 pandemic and the subsequent, partial lockdown of public life in large parts of the world. Because of that, the artist had to postpone his project for the Bucharest Biennial 9, a collective performance called *The Second Hands*. With this philosophical work, the artist wants draw a sort of parallel line with the events in Bucharest and Timișoara at the end of 1989, leading to the deposition of Ceaușescu and the end of the communist rule—but in today's world.

Tiong Ang is developing a work entitled *The Second Hands* for the Bucharest Biennial 2020–2021, a collective enterprise. Under the name Tiong Ang & Company, he leads a core team of ± fifteen people; for certain parts of the work, it will be expanded with a group of dancers or extras. *The Second Hands* reflects in an indirect way on the Romanian Revolution. At that time, we in the West were able to follow the important events. Special about the revolution of 1989 was how close the media and reality came together and almost merged. The Romanian State Television broadcasted live images of a dictator who appeased the masses, while gunshots,

Tiong Ang & Company, *The Second Hands*, 2022, MNAC Bucharest, 9ᵗʰ Bucharest Biennial.

clamour and chaos in the background wiped out his story.

Rebellion, revolution, and the celebration of freedom are imagined as moments of passage in Tiong Ang's work of art: that is the intention. It is not made explicit, the indicated line is fictitious, but this is palpable and emerges in descriptions of the project. Essentially, *The Second Hands* is conceived as a large film production, divided into five films under the direction of different makers. The themes of the five films are strongly interconnected: political oppression (Ola Hassanain), mass demonstration (Esther Arribas, Bart van Dam), coming of age in uncertain times (Fey Lehiane), a voyage through Europe to Romania filmed as a road trip movie (Robert Wittendorp), and finally the Congregation, a collective performance in Bucharest (Tiong Ang) as an Ode to Freedom.

Because of the Covid situation, Ang had to postpone *The Second Hands*. In March 2020, I spoke to him for the first time about his project. Just before that, he had had to stop all the film productions. That June, Ang proposes to talk further. A new momentum has emerged, with waiting as the motto, now that the opening of the work in Bucharest has been postponed for a year. Let's deepen, he suggests, our conversation by juxtaposing the Bucharest plan with another complex work: *Universality: Decorum of Thought and Desire* (Guangzhou, 2015). Ang wants to use that installation, whose set-up resembled that of *The Second Hands*—for *Universality*, eight different films were made as part of a fictional evening programme, a full night of television—as a template for his new project. I suggest to also consider a third presentation, that of a young Ang at the Havana Biennial in 1994. His participation in that biennial, at the very start of his career, was a formative experience of a 'revolutionary' manifestation in a changing art world.

Freedom

MARK KREMER   Tiong, next to film and performance, architecture is an important component in *The Second Hands*. You want to build a temporary scaffolding construction on the square behind the former People's Palace in Bucharest. A modern, streamlined structure, both a car park accommodating cars and caravans, and a contemporary motel where people stay. Your construction is based on the caravanserai—the Persian word is a contraction of 'caravan', a group of people travelling together and 'palace', a building with courtyards, i.e., a safe place, an inn. Why do you actually use that exotic concept? Caravanserais were in use in Asia along the Silk Road, in North Africa, and to a lesser degree in the Balkans—and more in the country than in the city. Originally, they belonged to a vast Islamic world. There was also one in Bucharest: Hanul lui Manuc, built in 1808 and run by the Armenian entrepreneur Emanuel Mārzaian, better known by his Turkish name Manuc Bei. Does the construction you want to realize represent your idea of freedom?

TIONG ANG   Through this old form I refer to a time prior to contemporary geopolitical thinking. Cultural exchange was a slow process, it occurred haphazardly, in relatively small doses, and by means of physical encounters. The personal stories are marked under *1001 Nights* and *History of the 20th Century*, and buried below them. The social revolutions have ended up on Wiki pages, shreds of an archive that concerns abuse of power, oppression, revolt and violence, roam on the internet. But how can one retrieve or get to the true emotions of those involved, their hopes and sufferings? The former People's Palace (now Parliament's Palace), the pinnacle of Ceaușescu's megalomania, is now the number one Bucharest

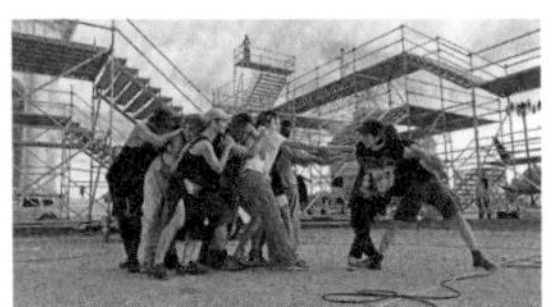

1 Tiong Ang & Company, *The Second Hands*, 2022, MNAC Bucharest, 9th Bucharest Biennial.

tourist attraction. You can get a guided tour of all those huge, unused, marble halls. At the back of the building, the Museum of Contemporary Art has been set up. At the very site of its parking area, we will build the scaffolding and put our caravans, as if we give the building and its history the finger. And then young people join in.[1]

MK   And they give it their finger as well?

TA   That's not what I'm saying… (Laughter followed by silence.)

Doing

MK   I'm curious to know more about the people in your team! In project descriptions of *The Second Hands*, you give your collaborators a prominent place, you cherish artistic friendship, and express appreciation for their expertise. You lead a team of ± fifteen 'employees'. In March you told me: 'Four of them are crucial: Esther Arribas, Robert Wittendorp, Ola Hassanain and Andrés Novo form the house of this project, the construction.' You use their knowledge of choreography (Esther), architecture (Andrés), and politics (Ola) for your work. Robert is the leader of the band that would drive two cars and two caravans to Bucharest. He is one of your artists who in older work of yours transforms into a true performer. Ingrid Sanghee Edwards, Jan Yongdeok Lim and Heekyung Ryu are others. How is the contact with your team now?

TA   I keep in touch via email, apps and phone calls. But things are shifting. Some of my people are struggling because of the pandemic. Isolated from their families abroad, they focus on their own situation. In a small group we celebrated the day of the (non-)opening of the Bucharest Biennial on the Museumplein in Amsterdam. We drank a glass of wine, on mats in the grass. Andrés was there, Esther, Ingrid and Heekyung, and me. Robert couldn't be there, he lives all the way in Drenthe, up north. He looks after the caravans that we bought; they're in a farmer's barn in Kallenkote.

MK   Robert Wittendorp is the instigator of *The Second Hands*?

TA   That's right! A work of his from 2012 still accompanies me, it's a source for my project. Before I go into this, first some context. Robert belongs to a small group of ex-students with whom I have often worked in recent years. When I started as a tutor at the MA department of the HKU, this was in 2003, I didn't want to look over the shoulders of students, and survey their attitude and work, but I wanted to stand beside to them, or in their midst. I wanted to learn from both their artistic perceptions and how they organize their lives and develop as human beings. Their motives to do so impress me. With some former students there is a natural contact that allows us to stay in touch, and which can turn the mentor-student relationship into something new.

I met Robert at the HKU Master, he was already in his thirties when he started. He himself taught new media at the Willem de Kooning Academy. He had really lived, left a heavy history behind him. And he has certain obsessions, is fascinated by Kinbaku (Japanese bondage): mystical counter-culture. In our Master period, he made a piece, a 'conversation on the road', for an exhibition at De Appel in 2012 of young curators who wanted to work with art students. For that work, called *Symphorophilia,* he had invited three scientists, a philosopher, a geopolitical economist, and a sociologist who he drove around in a car and talked to. He recorded those conversations. At that moment he was homeless, he only had his car. I have a special bond with Robert. I saw great potential in him. Not necessarily as an art professional—he didn't see a career for himself with the kind of work he wanted to do—but as a free spirit!

In Utrecht he graduated with a bondage work; a professional rope artist had completely laced him up. He was blindfolded, gagged, and almost naked, except for a loincloth, and some mottled scarves around his neck and torso. The work intertwined burlesque elements with sado-masochism. After his graduation, I asked him for a performance at Galerie Lumen Travo, as part of my exhibition *How To Act* (2013). Again, he did a very physical bondage, which I filmed. Two years later I integrated these images in *Universality* as if it were a documentary about the behaviour of animals on an evening of television! When I approached him for *The Second Hands* and told him what role I had in mind for him, he simply said: 'Okay! Let's do it!'

Universality

MK   Let's go back to 2015, to the Guangzhou Triennial in China, which also bore the name 1st Asia Biennial. How did *Universality: Decorum of Thought and Desire* come about? To do justice to this installation we have to talk about various elements: context, motif, design, title, inception.

TA   Curator Henk Slager said: 'I'd like to invite you. The Asia Biennial suits you perfectly, but what do you want to do?' By now I was experienced in China, I knew pretty well how I wanted to tackle this. So I said to Henk: 'I think I'm going to go even bigger. I want to expand. In my orientations, references, and methodologies'. I then made some drawings for a curators' meeting in China where Henk would discuss artist proposals with Chinese colleagues. I said:

I'll give you a complete television or film studio. Give me a large museum room—16 × 16 m—and I'll build sets in it. There will be projections and objects. Posters and sound. Light and darkness. Different 'illusory spaces'. And I concluded my text with: "The space seems like an abandoned TV-studio."[2]

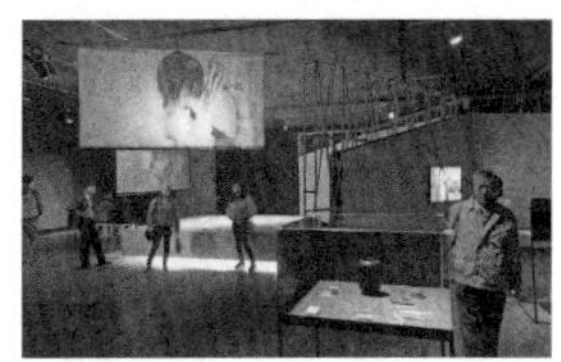

2 Tiong Ang, *Universality: Decorum of Thought and Desire*, 2015, Guangdong Museum of Art, Guangzhou, 1st Asia Biennial / 5th Guangzhou Triennial. Photo: Japo Knuutila.

MK   I remember a model in your workplace in 2015! At that time, you told me about *Universal Studios*, the film studio and theme park you visited in Hollywood, and mentioned it as a source of inspiration. You are fascinated by the idea of the studio as a place of creation, in which the atelier of the solitary artist is only one relevant model! This is most evident in your sitcom *The Making of Painted Strokes* (1995) where your own studio, very literally, turns into the workshop of a collective.

TA   I visited *Universal Studios* in Hollywood in the autumn of 2001, just after 9/11. The theme park was open, there were hardly any visitors. It was desolate, in hindsight the atmosphere resembled the lockdown this spring, 2020. In China, I used the form of the studio to play on, and address a larger art context. *Universality* was a critique, dressed up as a fantasy. Fantasy in the broad sense: an imaginary, abandoned television studio, a fictitious television night with disposable images! In China the first reaction was: that's special, to address the world or idea of 'universality' in a work of art.

I was interested in the concept of universality, which at the time was seen as something obsolete in the identity debate, as mostly a Eurocentric convention. The concept seemed to suit my purpose, namely to harass the Chinese art context that for some time has had its eye on the Western artist typology—organized around the individual, the solitary artist-genius. Today that art context has in fact adopted such a typology with star artists, galleries, auctions, collectors, a mass of new museums, biennials, you name it.

MK   You seem to use the concept of Universality as a trickster term!

TA   You know, that has a personal background. I want to use that term, since universality is important to me as a Diaspora Chinese. In Europe, I am an immigrant. In North America, they jokingly call me Fake Chinese or 'le Faux-Chinois'. When I exhibit in China, it's evident that I don't fit in… But I appeal to the idea of universality! 'Behold, I am human!' What I look like, what my background is, it doesn't matter. This is who I am! This reality is the condition of my art. This theme goes back a long time. At the Havana Biennial it was already a theme, but at that time I still had the feeling: I'm telling a universal story.[3]

MK   *Universality* was a large installation. You showed eight video tracks, each made following a different production method, as if you wanted to provide a television evening—a full programme of news, advertising, live sports, announcements, documentaries, and finally the late evening film. Each part was a different collaboration and the final installation of all the parts was designed as a television studio. There was a small section with posters, and objects in showcases. In the

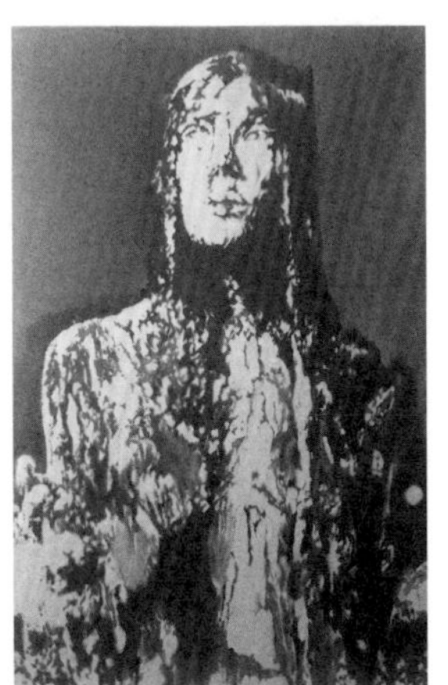

3 Tiong Ang, *Portrait of Sissy Spacek*, 2000, alkyd on linen, voile, 170 × 110 × 5 cm. After a production still from Brian de Palma's film *Carrie*, 1976.

middle there was a large sculptural stage where three performers just sat around at the opening. In your main film we
see an African man in a state of euphoria and confusion recit-
ing the Universal Declaration of Human Rights, like a historical relic.[4] Cast a light on the Asia Biennial?

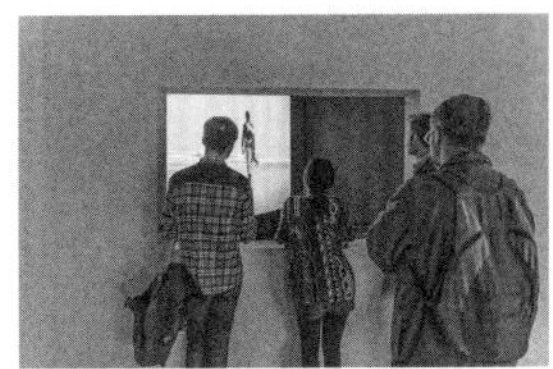

4 Tiong Ang, *Universality:
Decorum of Thought and Desire*,
2015, Guangdong Museum of
Art, Guangzhou, 1st Asia
Biennia' / 5th Guangzhou
Triennial. Photo: Japo
Knuutila.

TA   The Guangzhou Triennial was set up by the
Guangdong Museum of Art in Guangzhou, China's third
largest city, to counterbalance the hegemony of Beijing and
Shanghai as cultural centres. In China itself, the city of
Canton, Guangzhou, used to be a kind of alternative voice.

MK   Marco Polo would have loved it! (Laughs.)

TA   Certainly, in ancient times Canton was an important
place. It is relatively close to Hong Kong, southern, different
climate, different intellectual ambience, resisted the big
dynasties from Beijing plus the big traders from Shanghai,
and it is a gateway for non-Western cultures. The Guangzhou
Triennial originally intended to be such an alternative voice.
However, it takes place in the Guangdong Museum of Art.
That's a massive museum of the national apparatus, the province, and the city, thus a cumbersome institute. To give this
initiative global weight, they were looking for an alternative
name.

MK   The 2015 edition was called *Asia Time*, The 1st Asia
Biennial/5th Guangzhou Triennial. A strange artifice that
ignores important biennials in Korea and Japan!

TA   I saw the new name as a remarkable navigational error.
But I could make good use of that in my artistic orientation! I
had been active in Asia for some time now, developing a story

265

about myself through my projects. In the large installation in Guangzhou, there's also a fictional artist, a megalomaniac at work! Despite the fact that all the video tracks were made with others, I was in charge of the final direction.

MK   In almost all of *Universality*'s films, we encounter figures—human forms, but also man-made or computer-made forms—who float as it were, as if they are separated from the world, struggling to connect with their environments. It is a layer that I also sense strongly in the early Antonioni films!

TA   I wanted to make a work where the Chinese visitors—although they would probably recognize the set-up as a kind of studio—could lose themselves in the multitude of different images. In the structure and the chaos. I wanted to show different forms of production. Some forms seem to be very much studied in terms of image. They are subdued, well considered, well recorded and so on. On the other hand, the much sketchier forms suggest that you can also make something out of looseness. The feeling of losing yourself is also a sensation of freedom.

Titles

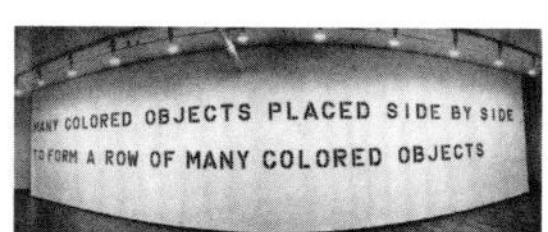

5 Lawrence Weiner, *Many Colored Objects Placed Side by Side to Form a Row of Many Colored Objects*, 1979, Castelli Gallery, New York.

MK   The title of your work for Guangzhou is *Universality: Decorum of Thought and Desire*. I considered that an allusion to the ambition of big biennials. But I could not reconcile that with your idealism. Then I was reminded of a famous work by Lawrence Weiner, the sentence that appeared on the façade of the Fridericianum in Kassel: *Many Colored Objects Placed Side by Side to Form a Row of Many Colored Objects*.[5] It was his commentary on 'Documenta 7'

266

(1982)! (The work was part of this exhibition.) A factual observation in which I sense sadness.

TA   That is right. My title has a subdued critical component.

MK   I don't know much about the Chinese language but I like to watch the films—preferably the Wuxia films, because of the beautiful wild Chinese landscapes—and they often have strange titles, *A Princess and the Warrior*, for example. Your title is Chinese-like? It seems to mix up big notions… Chinese language works with hanzi, doesn't it? Characters or pictograms, in which the visual and the conceptual come together.

TA   This was my umpteenth exhibition in China. And the titles have invariably been difficult, a one-to-one translation obviously is impossible. The visual element in Chinese is essential, but we can't say anything about it, to us it is obscure. Even more important in the Chinese context is that many key concepts have been distorted by the communist system. In 2008, I had an exhibition in Beijing with Ni Haifeng, which we wanted to call *Between the Light and the Dark*. Ni Haifeng had talked about it for three hours with his friends. When he came back, he said: 'if we translate it as it is, we'll get this: "…" But that's a Cultural Revolution slogan!' We had better avoid that!

MK   So how has *Universality* been translated?

TA   I have no idea! It got a translation. They reassured me: we have a Chinese word for it. And that means: 'what applies everywhere'. I love this game, precisely because it's

267

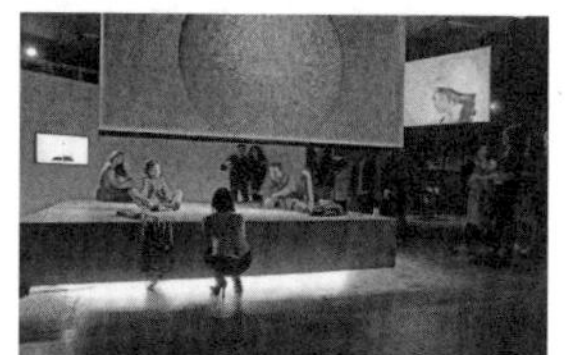

completely beyond my control. *Decorum of Thought and Desire* was even more impossible to translate.[6]

Objects

6 Tiong Ang, *Universality: Decorum of Thought and Desire*, 2015, Guangdong Museum of Art, Guangzhou, 1st Asia Biennial / 5th Guangzhou Triennial, opening performance. Photo: Japo Knuutila.

M K   What did you tell your fellow workers when you started the work process? I mean, the people you had in mind to work with you on *Universality*. How did you pitch the collaboration?

T A   Good point. I didn't give them the whole story because we our working relationship was still new. For example, Heekyung Ryu graduated in 2014 with a relational, almost immaterial work that included objects giving light. She had approached many people with an invitation: 'Please, bring your own lamp, or anything that can make light to the exhibition.' She asked if the lights—bed lights, desk lamps, torches—could be on display for the time of the show. Some were on a shelf, other ones were placed among other artists' works around the space. After the exhibition, the lights were switched off and returned, the work disappeared again. After graduation, she wanted to keep in touch. She could become my assistant in Taiwan, where I had a film production going: *House of Shyness*. That also worked out very well. So, we had that history.

M K   What was the framework for collaborative work? How did you instruct her?

T A   Nothing specific really. We had to find out. We decided to make a staged video recording.

MK   In which she has a part or acts?

TA   Well, she came to my studio. I found her way of per-
ception very significant. I wondered how I could catch that.
Her open, yet inquisitive gaze. How she interacts with the
world, how she looks at things and takes them in her hands.
How she doesn't speak. How to translate that into a work?
I told her that I would like to make a video with her, but
I didn't know what to do yet. I just set up the light, as if I
wanted to make a photo portrait. I had several lamps, and
I saw to it that the illumination was just right. This resulted
in all kinds of things, but we didn't find the essence immedi-
ately. I asked her for another session. In the week before,
I brought together a collection of things, that were very per-
sonal to me, but would not mean anything to someone else.
Very diverse things.

When she came back, I simply said: 'Look at those
objects, I'll just record you. Sometimes I want you to look
into the camera and show the things to an invisible audience.'
She looks at all those strange objects and examines them. She
turns them in her hands, like props. A plastic helmet from
Indonesia, an old colander, the hand of a mannequin, a camera stand on wheels, a letter holder from my parents. Her
movements are unrehearsed, the way she observes is pure,
but slowly her engagement with the things is being saturated
by her own projections.[7]

269

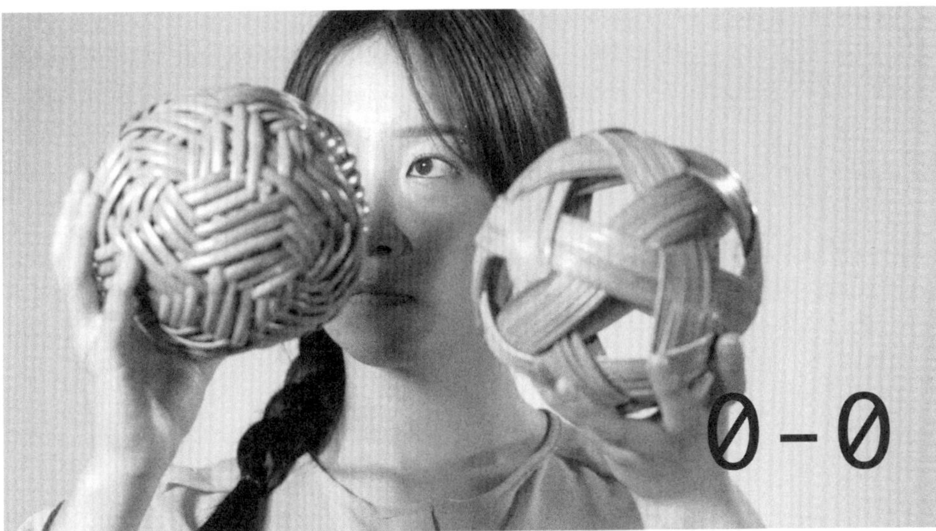

7 Tiong Ang, *Universality: Decorum of Thought and Desire*, 2015, video stills: *Ghosts (Woman and Objects)*, with Heekyung Ryu.

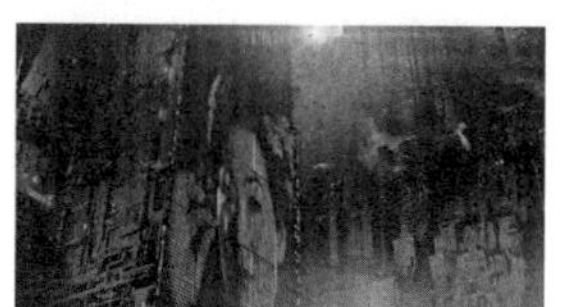

8 Ridley Scott, *Blade Runner*, 1982.

There's a particular passage in which she holds a braided Takraw ball, from the South-Asian ball sport (sepak takraw). From out of frame, I give her another ball, almost identical to the first one. She holds one in every hand. She takes time to weigh one ball against the other as if confronted by a choice. When you look closely, there's a tear of emotion when she's about to drop one of them.

MK Beautiful. You juxtapose universality with specificity! You told me that the scene you edited of this, in which the objects in the picture are also given a letter-and-number code, was inspired by the *Blade Runner* films where the monumental face of a woman lights up at night, like a futuristic hologram. Striking![8] I perceive your character as a Spirit from the Future: she looks in wonder at today's world and its objects!

TA When I finished that recording and looked at the rough cut, I knew right away that it could become very strong when I would show it as a large projection. A silent, Asian woman— Heekyung had once told me that she sometimes felt like a ghost in Western society—with things that belong to someone else's life. An ambivalent presence that defies stereotypes, unveiling unexpected emotions. And I realized I had the first building block for my installation, which inspired me to design my 'multi-dimensional' space.

Layers

MK I see these layers in your work: 1. As an artist you challenge art as power, you work with art as poles, for instance the biennial discourse, or 'art speak'. Your titles make this skirmish very clear. 2. Your work tells stories—shreds, fragments, tales falling apart—or with the story unfolding, a viewer suspects a larger back story that remains implicit; the universal story of humankind? In short, the narrative is important. 3. Every work is probing emotions, fathoming a deeper layer of feeling. For instance, the universality of the tear in your work for Guangzhou. My question concerns this last dimension. In our conversations you give a lot of information about the first two dimensions. With the third one it is different, as if you are protecting it. Once in a while it suddenly comes in the open. But you don't bring it up about it spontaneously. Is this third dimension evident to you? Or are you also groping and searching there? As if it needs to be tapped over and over again?

TA   The importance of that layer is undeniable. I even think that this layer is the key. It is my motive to work with images. And not with language.

MK   Language is interwoven in your work. But you don't say, for example: 'I work with actors who put raw emotion on stage, through their bodies and their words'.

TA   I'm talking about something under the skin, suppressed, or hidden…

MK   Feelings that need to be released?

TA   Feelings need to be released and for that to happen, a tissue needs to be created in which they can thrive. (Short silence.)

Scream

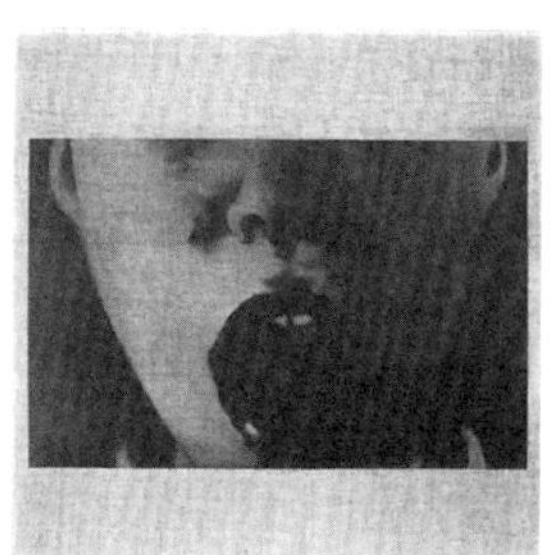

9 Tiong Ang, *Untitled (The Scream)*, 1994.

MK   Let's go even further back in time. The first biennial you participated in was in Havana as early as 1994. You were still a young artist, and had only just had your breakthrough. You showed a powerful and charged installation with paintings and veils. One painting shows a young face, depicted from the nose to the bottom of the chin, with the mouth wide open. A scream but without sound, as if something fundamental cannot be expressed.[9]

TA   The works were the result of a longer period of work. I think it goes back to 1990, when I was still at the Rijksakademie. There was this adage there: a work of art is only good when it is finished: the perfect object. This affected me; that polished aspect also occurs in my paintings from that time. I did my utmost on their execution, the choice of materials, of the veils of course, but that intensive process was a gruelling business. That, and the heavy themes of displacement, ritual blindness and the unfinished body... I was successful with the paintings, they gave me my breakthrough, got sold. But public appreciation is relative. I struggled with my work, found the paintings too decorative. Too restrained, too passive. As if I didn't manage to bridge the distance to myself.

When I arrived in Havana I quickly finished installing. I was able to compare my presentation with how many of the other artists, on site, were in the midst of a process of making things. At the 5th Biennial of Havana some 200 artists from mainly non-Western countries participated. And then I quickly thought: how stupid that I screwed my works into those crates, put so much time and money into transport! I saw that most of them didn't do what I had done. I saw the nomadic practice of art! Its verve! My encounters and intense conversations with British Black Art artists and curators Rasheed Araeen, Keith Piper, Chila Kumari Burman, Gilane Tawadros (Iniva), as well as the art critic Jean Fisher (*Third Text*) made a big impression. They spoke with heart and soul about the post-colonial discourse that was much more developed in England than in the Netherlands at that time. It gave me a lot to think about.

MK   You felt like doing things differently! Earlier you told me about the revolutionary character of that biennial, where the spirit of Che Guevara was still alive.

TA   A rather double-edged experience was the visit of a Communist Party official to the Biennial headquarters, the Centro Wifredo Lam, where I showed my work. All the young curators instantly swapped their normal clothes for military uniforms and paid their respect. Fear and Trembling, as long as the big chief was there. Once he was gone, all attention went back to art. This was what I would call decorum! (Laughter!)

Crates

TA   Still in the Netherlands I had already had a fax from Havana. The organization wrote me: 'There is a South African artist who is asking permission from all the artists who have a transport planned, whether—after the work has been removed from the crates and they've been shut again— he may use these crates in his work, for the duration of the show.' I gave permission. It was a conceptual and critical work. It addressed the problem of all those transports arriving for a huge exhibition. With finished art works that have a value, and have to be in crates, with protective material and the needed forms. The biennial was happy with the idea because they had no storage: problem solved! The idea for storage as a work came from Kendell Geers. He arrived with nothing but spoke with all the artists who had said 'yes'. He piled up all the boxes and built a kind of Tower of Babel! What attracted me to his work was the potential of the relationship, with the place, the context, the people; he also talked to me, and after I was finished, we went on reconnaissance, to see the other artists' work. The circumstances were difficult, also because of the economic crisis, but among the artists I saw a lot of solidarity.

The people I was hanging out with—the English, South Africans and Brazilians in particular—were busy in the city. They still had to produce the work, make it and negotiate for it.

MK   They connected with everyday life?

TA   Yes, and with concrete spaces such as the historical Morro Castle. I remember their work, but above all, all kinds of working activity. I can still see how a group of young people, led by the Argentinean Victor Grippo, worked on old tables for his installation. And how Sue Williamson, another South African, was talking to young people with a lot of concentration as she needed a sound installation for her spiritual lamentatio. She exhibited in that fortress, in a bunker. Her solemn work featured a black female musical voice; it almost made me cry.

MK   There is a difference between object-based art and art that seeks the relationship, in which people are the central subject.

Universal Noise

TA   Right! And I felt then, I'm going to do it differently. Make and Break was a given anyway, I was quite familiar with it. My paintings had deep grounds: intense emotions vibrate underneath that serrated surface. A year later, in 1995, I made the sitcom *The Making of Painted Strokes* in the Netherlands, with Carter Kustera. At that time everything had to be destroyed. I blew up my entire painting production!

MK   Cool! Walter Benjamin has written a fine observation, 'Der destruktive Charakter', about the pleasure of destruction and the creation of space. In *Universality* there is an animation of one of your old paintings. That futuristic representation of 'the new still life' relates to the Korean woman and her objects. Good motif for an animation! And on yet another animation, also part of *Universality*, a logo is shattered in front of your eyes. This 'leader' is a kind of ironic commentary on universality. What I get from this is an image, even an ode to Universal Noise!

TA   The communist and post-communist spirit manifests itself rather differently in contemporary China than earlier in Cuba in the 1990s, or in Romania after 1989 until today. To what extent can one translate such a revolutionary spirit into an art manifestation, or into an artwork? The question is huge! Critical confusion about ideology must be part of that![10]

275

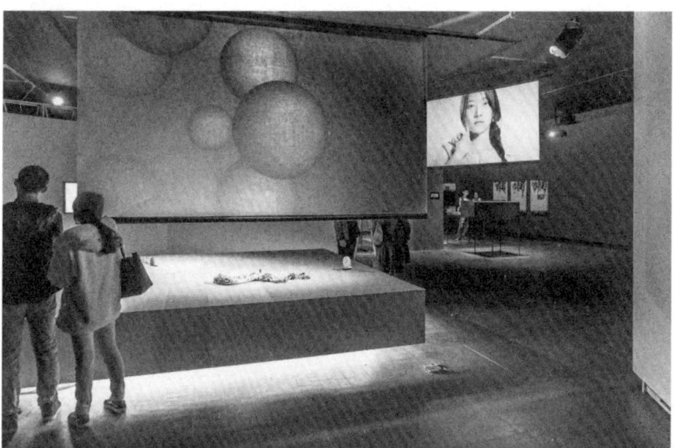

10   Tiong Ang, *Universality: Decorum of Thought and Desire*, 2015, Guangdong Museum of Art, Guangzhou, 1st Asia Biennial / 5th Guangzhou Triennial. Photo: Japo Knuutila.

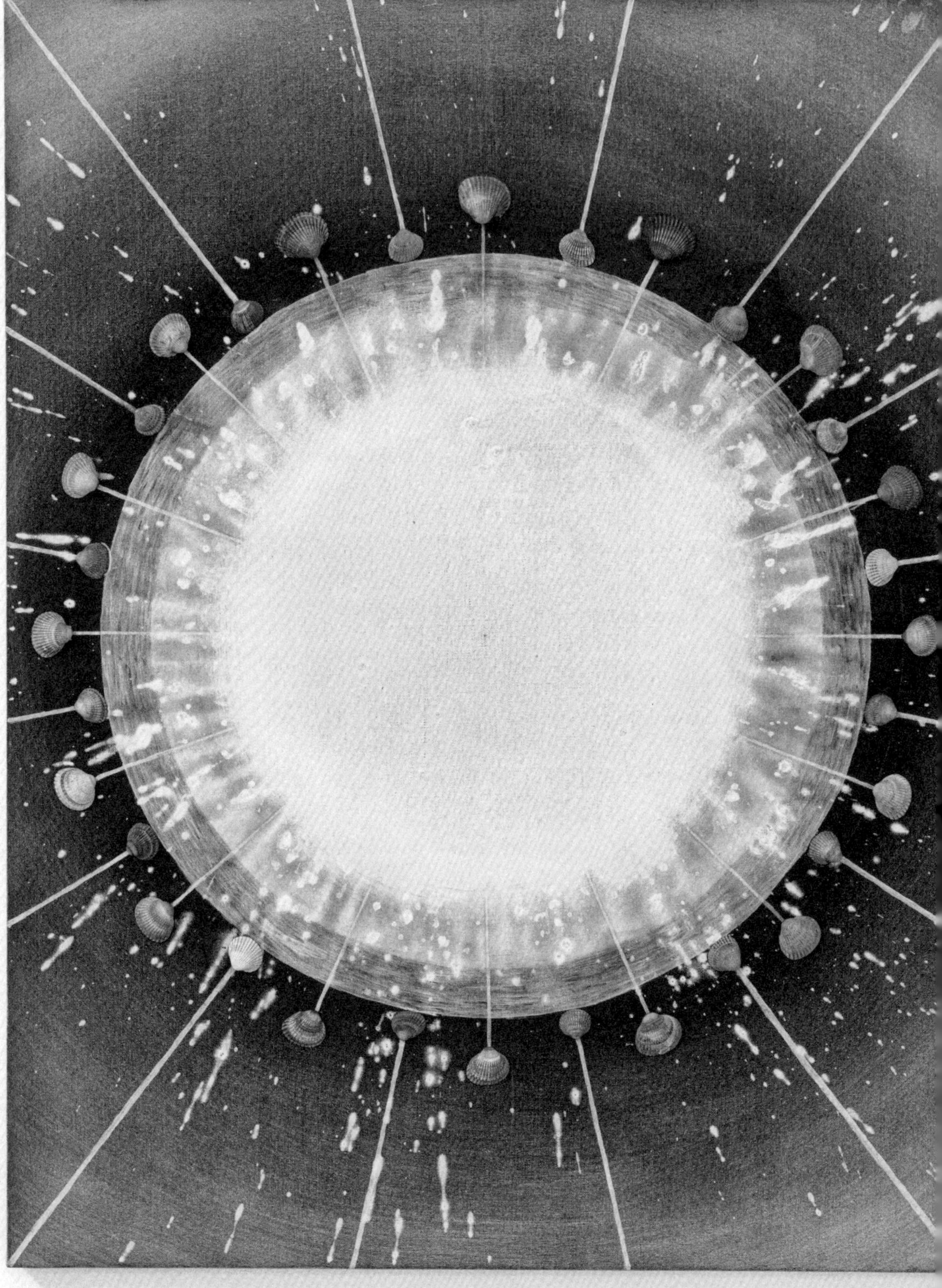

One Wee Drop

A s t r i d   N o b e l

When Astrid Nobel is busy making work, there's always also a book in the background that's asking to be read. The nineteenth century is in demand: Balzac, Kierkegaard, Melville; the twentieth century as well: Blanchot, Kafka, Slauerhoff. How does this literary aspect return in her art?

Works have been conceived through the lecture of one sentence that stuck with her, for example a small, gloomy painting from which a tear of oil protrudes, *That one wee drop* (2010).[1] This painting re-imagines a serrated, but oh so melancholy, passage from Melville's *Moby Dick*: 'From his slouched hat Ahab dropped a tear into the sea; nor did all the Pacific contain such wealth as that one wee drop.' (Chapter 132) Then there is the ominous sculpture *What requires waiting and what waiting awaits* (2011); the title refers to an observation by Maurice Blanchot on Breton's novel *Nadja*. A white piece of furniture, where parts have been cut out, takes on an abstract shape (as if memories can be stored in the apertures). You can open the two drawers that contain a photo of the sea irradiated with light; one image comes towards you; the other one recedes into the background.[2]

277

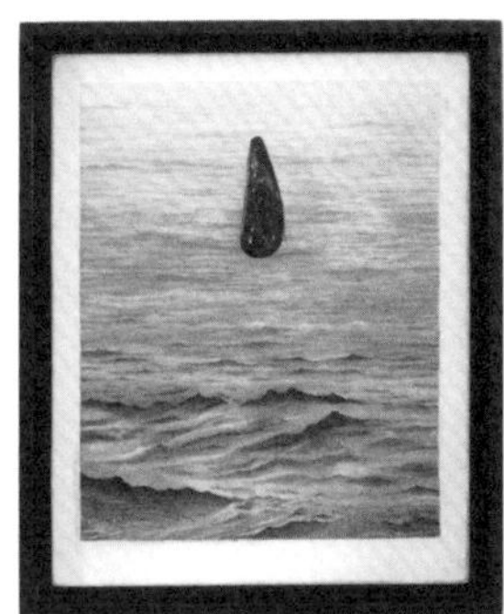

1   Astrid Nobel, *That one wee drop*, 2010, oil and gesso on wood, 52.5 × 42.5 × 4.5 cm.

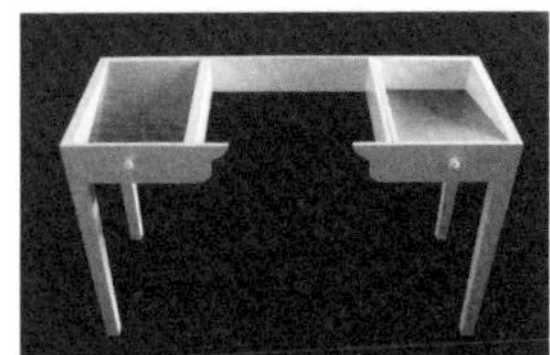

2   Astrid Nobel, *What requires waiting and what waiting awaits*, 2011, wood, prints on aluminium, 120 × 50 × 75 cm.

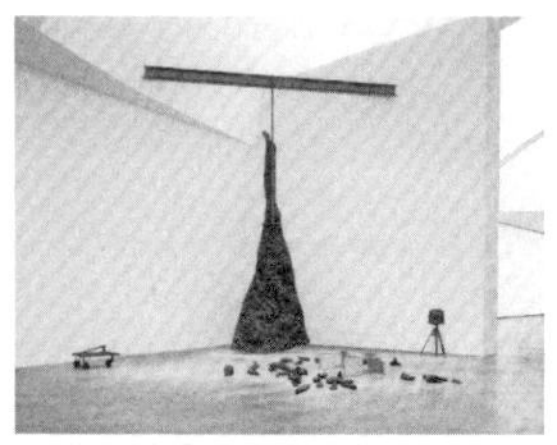

3 Joseph Beuys, *Lightning with Stag in its Glare*, 1958–85.

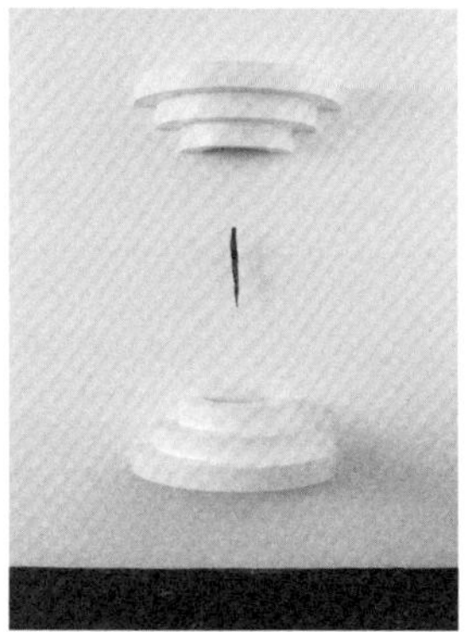

4 Astrid Nobel, *Autobiography*, 2010, wood, horse hair, 180 × 94 × 45 cm.

Nobel converts text to image. A sentence that briefly catches our attention in a story is reborn—and the circle of art thus continues. Here is a link with modern art that deliberately employs fragments to tell a story. Think of Rodin, of Bacon, of Beuys.[3] Kees Fens (the literary critic): 'The sky has come down and lies around us, in shards on the earth'. Nobel writes in her prosaic way:

> In my work, I distil fragments from their context and assemble them into a new connection. This constellation can be a compressed depiction of a time course or of something that is happening on the edge of time. A paradox, a mystery, or something else that is not easy to grasp.

In the same way she considers herself. The work *Autobiography* (2010) creates an energetic field.[4] Between two white consoles placed high and low on the wall, hovers a pierced and gnawed piece of wood hanging from a horsehair. Dread and Bliss: the wood could be experienced as a sword of Damocles, or instead as a figure moving upwards to the light. *Du bist der Liebste von allen Schlangenmenschen* ('You Are the Dearest of All Contortionists', 2008) refers to a dream about the threshold. The work consists of a white jamb, the aperture of which is filled with stacks of paper from a trade administration from the 1940s and 1950s—the fine layers work as a barrier. This is a haunting image, like an artistic compulsive exercise; at the same time the work alludes to deliverance.

A distinct tension qualifies the appearance of her works; objects and ideas presented by the artist linger in a state of physical-mental suspension. Is this a representation of the conflict between lyricism and reason, dream and reality? Her precious objects and thoughts move us, the mind is touched on the intersection of those two planes, our personal experience is built from that. (Take love: you love someone because you're moved by a body and your imagination.)

Lyricism and ratio, dream and reality: the boundaries and transitions between these areas are 'illustrated' in the oeuvre by motifs of openings such as the staircase, the door, the window, the gate, the horizon, the surf. These are places of becoming and transformation, where inside turns into outside, bottom into top, day into night. There is even a work where the viewer seems to end up 'behind the mirror': three photos—with different vistas of the interior of a house—have been placed on the backside of three old frames. The reversal creates a curious effect, as if the house is enchanted. At a certain point you find yourself caught up in it, as if you're looking from behind and through the wall on which the photos hang, into the space where you are standing and watching.

She folds dreams into art.[5] Fragments from dreams, rendered in text, are markers in an exhibition space that becomes the cradle of a self-portrait *Waanbeelden/Delusions 161201-080808* (2008). *Wait, I'm in the middle of something* (2009) consists of three parts. *Here/There* is a postcard, sent to herself by the artist from China, with urgent questions about the future and the past. *Up/Down* is a drawing where the sky at night is illuminated by stars and the sea by micro-organisms.[6] *Before/After* is an assemblage: two drawers hang on the wall; white miniature steps lead to them; inside are two prints of a dead-end staircase and a path as an invisible end.[7] This work circles around the motif of orientation; it resembles a fantastic apparatus to navigate place and time.

Formally, the works range from texts and photos to composite sculptures with the spirit of Surrealism—that movement that had an eye for the reverse side of the world of visible phenomena. The conceptualism of the 1960s and 1970s is

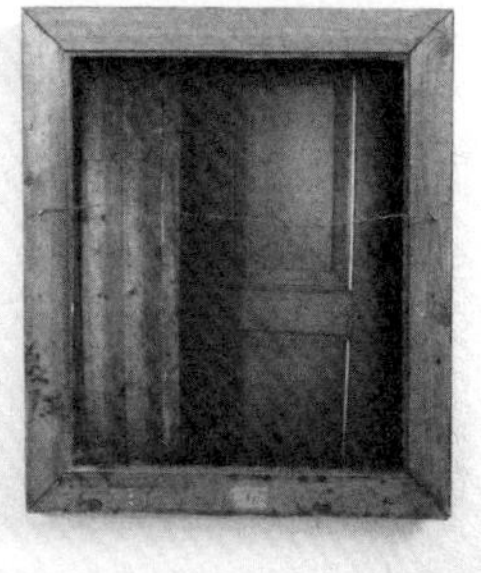

5 Astrid Nobel, *1202082123*, 2008, digital print, frame, glass, 61.5 × 73 cm.

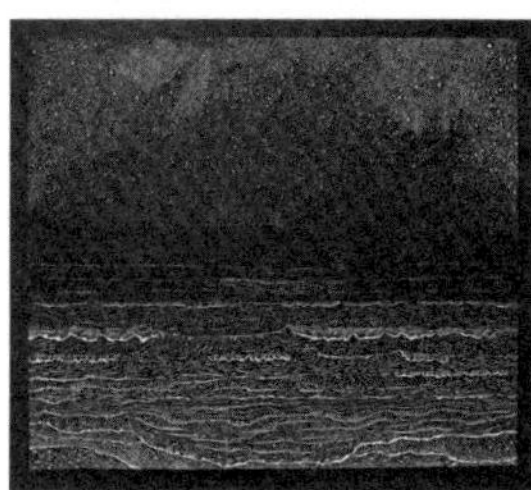

6 Astrid Nobel, *Wait, I'm in the middle of something: Above/below*, 2009, ink on paper, 74.5 × 67 cm.

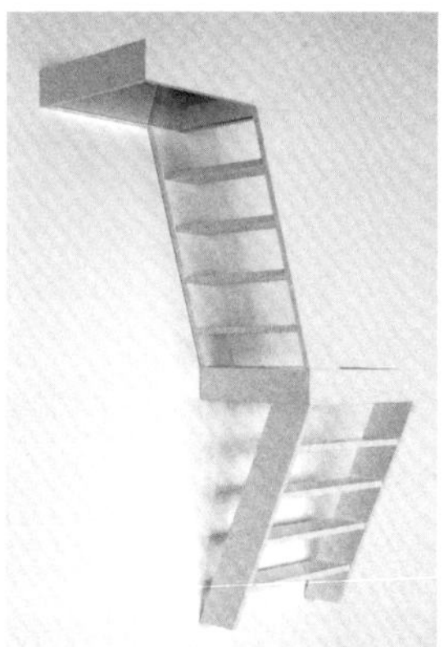

7 Astrid Nobel, *Wait, I'm in the middle of something: Above/below*, 2009, wood, digital prints, 143 × 102.5 × 39 cm.

another influence: the eruption of language in the visual domain that is typical of that art form (Craig Owens has written about this) led to an artistic freedom that today's artists benefit from.

What is special about Nobel's art, however, is how she deals with the incongruity of language and image. The border experiences she depicts are sometimes hard as nails, and at other times super-romantic. That kind of capriciousness is surprising. A work by Nobel can feel like a dream that lights up before you as you wake up but escapes as soon as thinking takes over. But it is also possible that a work confronts our thinking with its limits, setting free the dream.

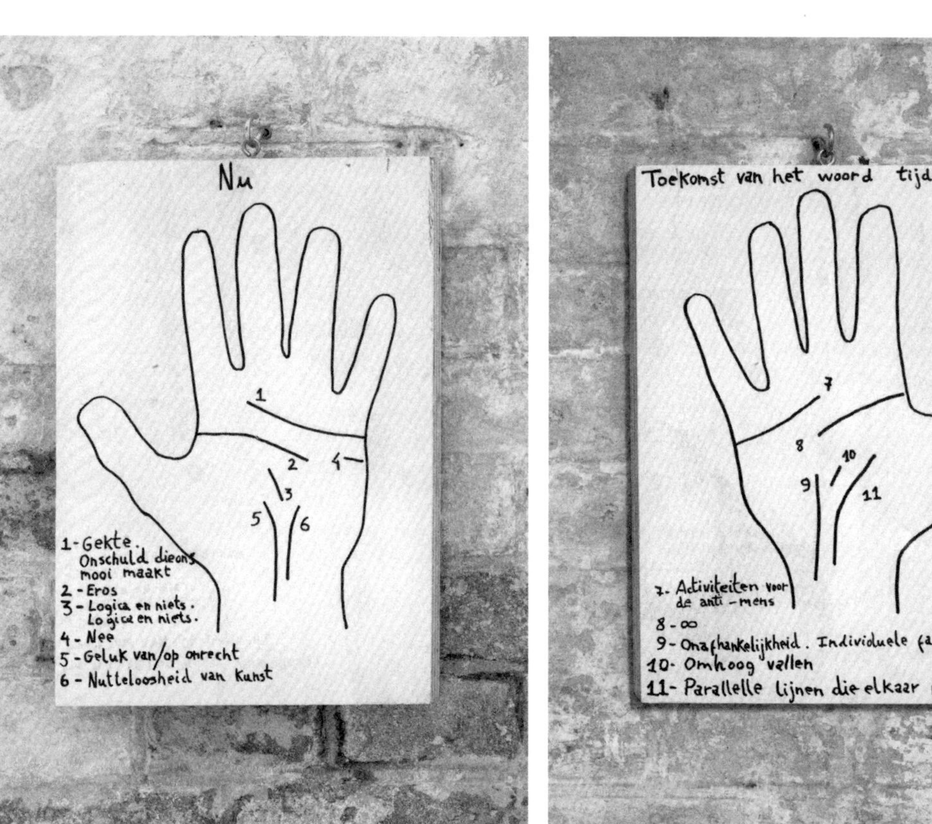

Nu

1- Gekte.
   Onschuld die ons
   mooi maakt
2 - Eros
3 - Logica en niets.
     Logica en niets.
4 - Nee
5 - Geluk van/op onrecht
6 - Nutteloosheid van kunst

Toekomst van het woord   tijd

7- Activiteiten voor
   de anti-mens
8 - ∞
9- Onafhankelijkheid. Individuele fantasie
10- Omhoog vallen
11- Parallelle lijnen die elkaar raken

It Must Be a Camel

H u g o   C a n o i l a s

Objects murmur
Paintings talk
The action painter
Is out for a walk

I

Hugo Canoilas' exhibition at Galeria Quadrado Azul in Porto is called 'Um Corridor entre M. e K.' It was originally inspired by a day trip to Brussels in the spring of 2008, when the artist saw René Magritte's paintings at the Magritte Museum[1] and Mike Kelley's sculptures at the solo presentation of the American artist at WIELS.[2] Canoilas decided he wanted to make new work that would capture his experience of the trip and the two artists. Canoilas explains his exhibition as a meditation on painting and its potential to sensitize the viewer. As its departure point, he used the idea of what a painterly action is: a happening in a parallel time-space with which an audience can only passively identify. This

283

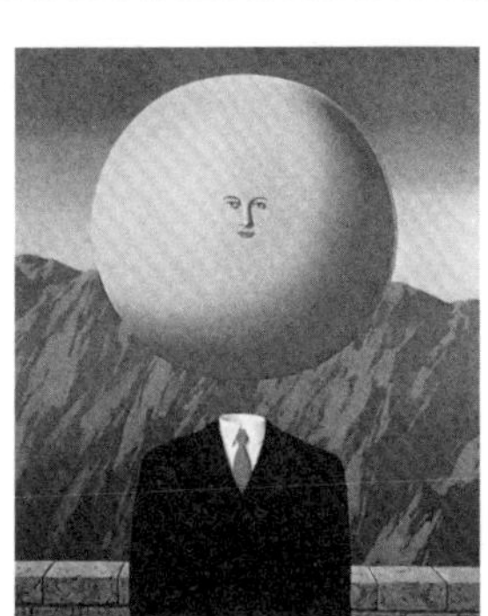

1 René Magritte, *The Art of Living*, 1967.

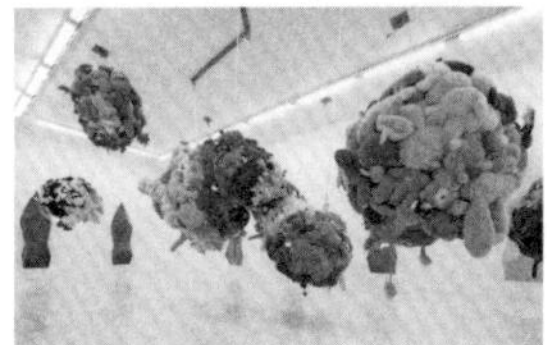

2 Mike Kelley, MOMA, New York, 2013–14, exhibition view.

happening transforms into a constellation of objects, paintings and texts creating an ensemble, that reads as a symbolic call for action.

A man is calmly making a drawing on a flour-covered floor, his two bare feet gently leave traces and a composition is born.[3] The act originally captured on super-8 film has been transferred to DVD and looped; it is now presented on a flat screen in the gallery entrance. The drawing action takes place in the dimly lit studio that has become historically familiar: the same bare place where Marcel Duchamp let dust accumulate randomly on configurations on the working place floor;

284

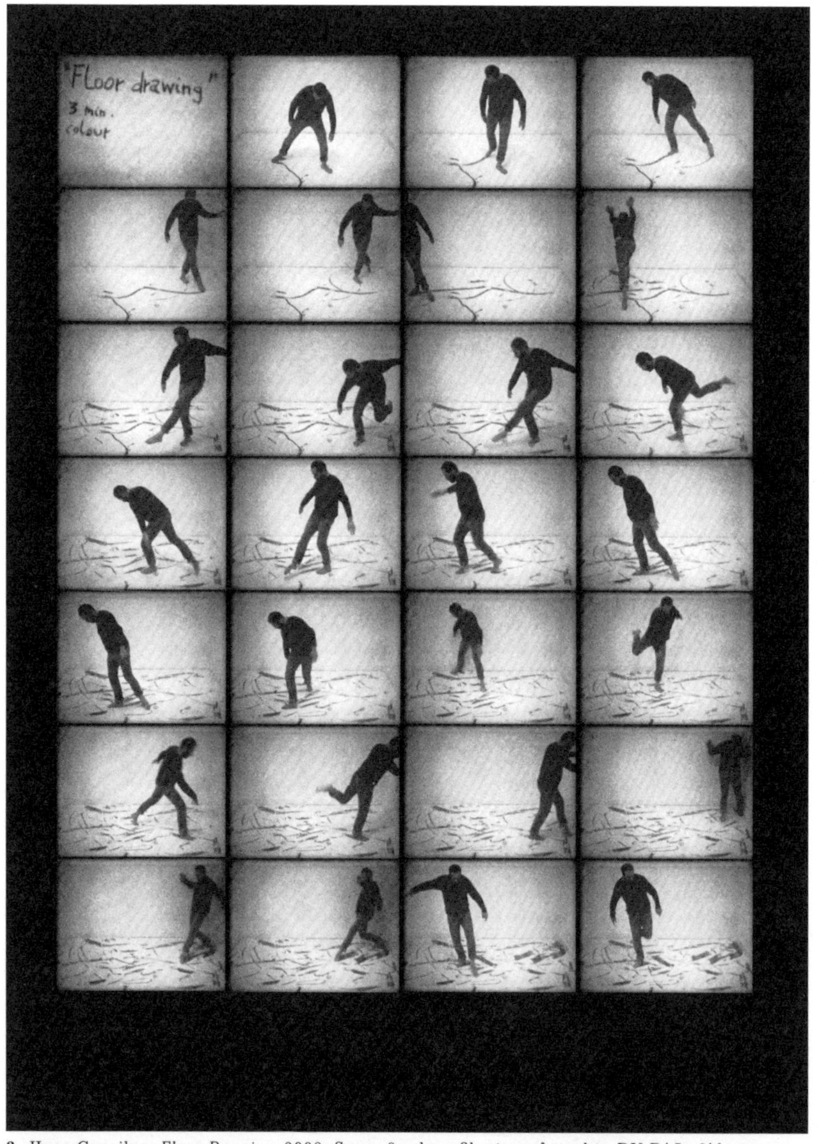

3 Hugo Canoilas, *Floor Drawing*, 2008, Super 8 colour film transferred to DV PAL, 3′ loop.

where Bruce Nauman, to study his own behaviour in the studio, movement and poses, subjected himself to repetitions,
such as playing an endless note on the violin and walking a
prescribed route. In Hugo Canoilas' film, an action is
repeated endlessly as well; again and again, the making of a
drawing, the fabrication of an artwork comes full circle.

There's something noteworthy in the images of a human
figure immersed in the artistic act: encapsulated in a barren
space the artist becomes a sort of troglodyte, a cave dweller.
The making of a floor drawing seems to become more than
only an exhibition prelude. Is it perhaps a portrait of a
twenty-first century action painter? Or is Hugo Canoilas'
film a homage, and a goodbye to that prototypical artist
whose exorcizing painterly acts once staggered the collective
imagination? Jackson Pollock, the famous action painter, lost
touch with his own art at the moment he agreed to have his
painterly process filmed. In 1950, Hans Namuth succeeded in
recording Pollock at work in his studio. The act resulted in
500 photos and two films. One year later, Namuth made a
colour film of the painter working in the open air, creating the
familiar sequence of Pollock painting from behind a glass
panel. The glass was to act as a canvas, so that the spectator
would feel as if they were in the painting as it was being
made.

The film from the 1950s is revealing as Pollock is talking
in a very down-to-earth way, about the procedures of his
painting, while some of his acts are accompanied by Morton
Feldman's eerie music. But the arrival of the camera at the
heart of Pollock's working place had dramatic effects. It
placed the painter and not his paintings at the centre of attention, turning Pollock, in the last years of his short life, into an
actor or performer who stood in the way of the painting.
Hugo Canoilas' floor drawing brings into play that naive look

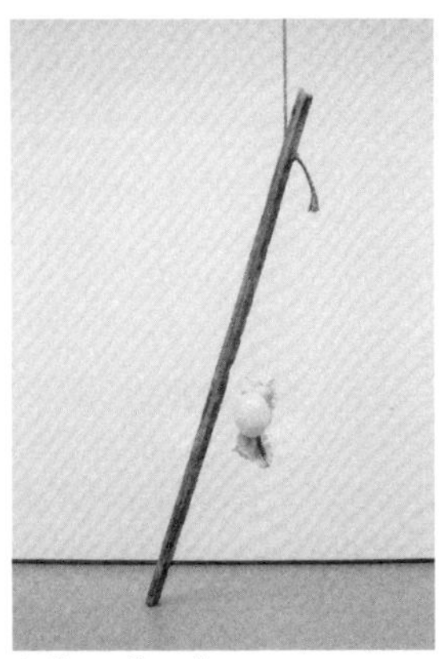

4 Hugo Canoilas, *Hermaphrodite*, 2008, found wood, ostrich eggs, whelk, rope, 170 × 40 × 30 cm.

at history that only an artist can get away with. Knowing the facts, he simply replicates them, but with fire, starring in his film as a performer who is in the way of a painting. Though the film is silent, it is as if one hears the artist speaking up, claiming that only a literal re-enactment of Abstract Expressionism's deadlock can undo the historical spell. Through calm and meditative gestures, Hugo Canoilas, post factum, is placing his charm on the idea that the intimate side of the artistic process loses its credibility once it is exposed in public.

And so it is exactly this intimate side of the process— coined by the popular view of what an artist does with notions such as heroism, mysticism and reverie—that reveals itself in Hugo Canoilas' exhibition. His work reads as an entry into the dreams or chimeras of an artist's mind, and it comprizes a variety of several natural and manufactured objects; small and larger text paintings, some of which have texts that read like call-ups; creating a verbal resonance or feedback in the gallery space. Together, these items converge into a large and fantastic 3 D constellation. Walking into this 'total picture', stepping through the fake doors that give access to different rooms, we come across:

the hermaphrodite, an animistic sculpture composed of a worn slat, two seashells and an ostrich egg; a symbol of fertility;[4]

suspended paintings, six small pictures adorned with texts: passionate requests and observations that mingle artistic and political imaginations;

polychrome, an abstract multi-coloured sculpture in the form of a large mobile that has two wooden and two Perspex sheets suspended in the air;

286

black and white and pink and orange interior, a 'hovering room' has been created in the space using black-and-white and coloured cloth, its soft walls are decorated with meditative and also dynamic abstract paintings;[5]

drawing, rope with variable thickness and length is connected and becomes a drawing in space;[6]

peinture affirmatif, a large painting is describing how it sees its own happy-go-lucky state, just going with the flow, on its back side it has attached

peinture offense, a large painting describing its wish to make the critical difference; and

convex space, two connected and suspended board-shaped mirrors have been put square on top of one another, they transform space into a spherical experience.

Retracing our steps and walking back towards the gallery entrance, we encounter the last work, entitled *hands.* Two small paintings show the lines of a left and right hand, quite possibly the artist's own accompanied by a legend explaining their meaning. The legend tells the magical story, what the lines mean for the individual, now as well as in the future. But the clues could alternatively be read as an explanation of the energy, naivety and fancifulness of the constellation at large, its present and future tense.

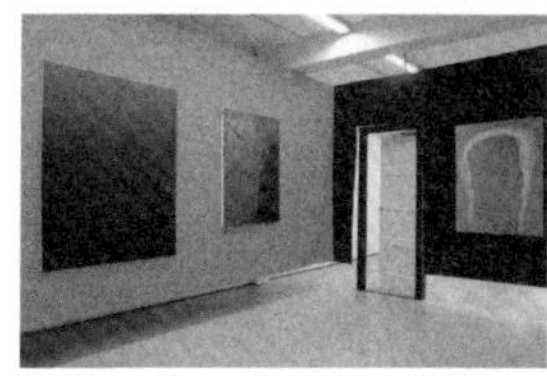

5   Hugo Canoilas, *The Middle Room,* 2008, 5 acrylic paintings mounted on suspended canvas and 2 free-standing doors, 300 × 680 × 540 cm.

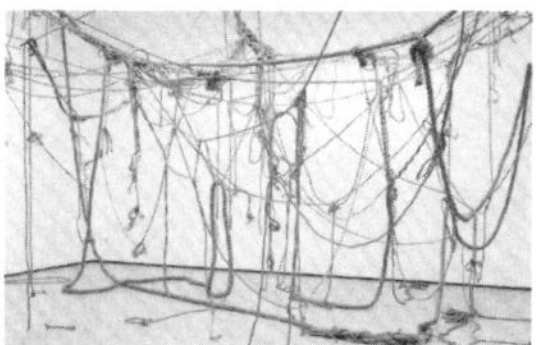

6   Hugo Canoilas, *Drawing,* 2008, rope, variable dimensions.

2

An earlier version of the work in Porto, was made for 'de kleine biennale' (klein being the Dutch word for small), an international group exhibition of works created for an audience of children ranging in age from seven to twelve (Utrecht, 2009). The framework of that exhibition brought out an essential aspect of Hugo Canoilas' art: euphoria. The young visitors in Utrecht only needed to go through a few fake doors, to become experienced. Their act resembled that of Alice who travelled down the rabbit hole to Wonderland. *A Corridor between Magritte and Mike Kelley* was an environment in seven interconnected bunkers of a nineteenth-century fortress. Doors were erected between the spaces, creating the corridor that tied the work together. Grounded matter and lofty thought came together in an environment that extended the sensorial range.

A room for the eyes had mirrors suspended in the air, reflecting the space behind an old cast-iron, spiral staircase; in a room for the nose the floor was covered with yellow spice so kids could leave traces; a room for the sense of touch had a forest of rope so children could climb trees. Explaining the work, the artist pointed out the notion of initiation or rite-of-passage, and the cleansing effect of this experience, its deep impact on mind and body. In practice, a child would open a door and just like that, a whole world and all it had to offer came within reach. This experience is referred to by the work's title, which introduces Magritte and Mike Kelley, so to speak, as the gatekeepers of Hugo Canoilas' world. Making a journey from one to the other 'giant'—as the artist once quite literally did, when on the aforementioned day trip to Brussels he first visited the house where Magritte spent most of his life and then went to see Mike Kelley's show at WIELS—means going into two artistic worlds and engaging in strong and contrasting experiences, ranging from crystalline rationality to visceral obstinacy.

Yet in fact, Magritte and Mike Kelley have much in common. In both you find a fascination with the trip as a mental experience and a recognition that there are unknown regions of the mind, that are worthwhile to visit. In both there is also a strong interest in the body as an entirely independent organism, a force of its own, primitive and intelligent. The contrast between Magritte and Mike Kelley is, in reality, more of a paradox. Their case offers a fresh perspective, and it shows how the elective affinities of two artists may outplay traditional categorization.

Another example of elective affinities, this time of two art movements, may be found in the 1960s, which are key in the formation of what we today call contemporary art. I am referring to two fields of artistic research and production that were intimately connected in the 1960s: Psychedelia and Conceptualism. The exact relation between these two fields needs to be studied further, for good and bad reasons a gap between them was created in art history; they do however come together in the work of different artists. Psychedelia and Conceptualism played with the senses and the mind. The vestiges of the complexes are still traceable. It seems to me that it is worthwhile to explore where the traces cross with each other in the 1960s and in today's art.

In the last years, the image of 1960s art and artistic configurations has been deepened through various researches and exhibitions. We realize now that Conceptualism also had romantic features; that was the thesis of the exhibition 'Romantic Conceptualism' curated by Jörg Heiser in 2007. Recent material also illuminates the social-critical aspect of Psychedelia, such as *Reflections from Damaged Life: An Exhibition on Psychedelia*, Raven Row, London, 2013, curated by Lars Bang Larsen. New insights have been gained, regarding the conjunction of the senses and the brain. Psychedelia highlights the complexity of sensory intoxication; Conceptualism entrances the mind but also confronts this with the limits of thought.

Many of the interesting works made in the 1960s connected with both Conceptualism and Psychedelia. For example, the psychedelic light projections of Gustav Metzger, The Boyle Family, and Livinus van de Bundt were based on rational, sophisticated underpinnings, and used scientific optical effects. Whereas many conceptual works, for instance those by Nam June Paik, Richard Long and Walter De Maria that explore the subject of the line, often have mystical elements. The chalk lines that Walter De Maria drew on several occasions in the desert were examples of visual clarity, and of wonder (anthropologists have compared these desert lines to shamanistic portals, in accordance with certain Native American beliefs).

3

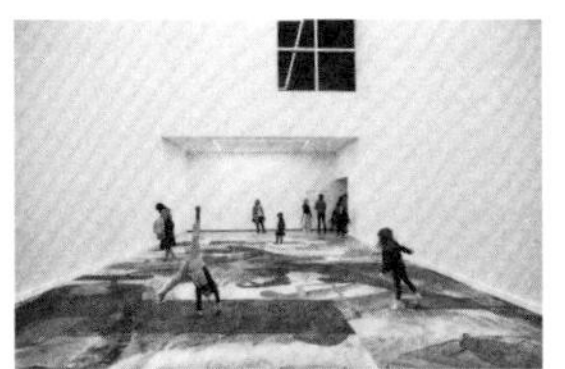

7 Hugo Canoilas, *God Is Good and the Devil Is Not Bad*, 2015, acrylic on linen, 1560 × 800 cm.

The wish for a fresh perspective on the 1960s impacts the perception of today's art. Can we look at the contradictions or paradoxes in Hugo Canoilas' work—the fact that his practice includes different kinds of painting, performance, sculpture, installation, drawing, and also collective work—to the contradictions or paradoxes found within 1960s art? Would his work then possibly have a place in the legacy of the 1960s?[7]

The artist himself has emphasized two forces that come together in his work: stomach and brain. In the context of his art, the terms refer primarily to painting and to conceptual art. The two works discussed here, *A Corridor between Magritte and Mike Kelley* and *Um Corridor entre M. e K.*, combined the material reality of objects with the virtual reality of concepts. And yet both works seemed to be built around the idea that illusion is at the core of both the world of matter and the world of ideas. Objects, paintings and texts, those items had a presence that was concrete and grounded. Yet the same objects, paintings and texts had another presence too, as if they, with all their sharp contours and abundant colours, were only projections cast from another time and space.

Hugo Canoilas is part of a young generation of Portuguese artists who investigate legacies of today's art, taking their inspiration mostly from Anglo-American and Latin American contexts. What does it mean that artists at certain moments and at certain places, came to their artistic proposals? It is interesting to observe the Portuguese process of inquiry today; the country's quite recent history was one of isolation and separation from the main centres and histories. Nowadays, these negative aspects have become positive incentives. As a parallel, one can look at the relatively isolated city, harbour and island of Vancouver, that in recent years produced many internationally active artists who've bridged the gap. Portugal's cinema and literary tradition (Pessoa!) resonates with today's art. On recent visits to Lisbon and Porto, I saw a lot of original work that seemed to be strongly informed by 1960s art.

Hugo Canoilas is inspired by the experiments of the 1960s, but also by other sources. His work refers to maestros ranging from Hélio Oiticica, via Barnett Newman, to Blinky Palermo. His artistic trajectory resembles a true odyssey: at every station sirens and other fine creatures call out for him and paint their illusions. Of course, the artist can't resist. His work *Um Corridor entre M. e K.*, to which this text is dedicated, is unusual, and it makes large and liberating visual leaps that somehow resemble camel humps; hence my reference to Frank Zappa's song from which this text borrows its title.

291

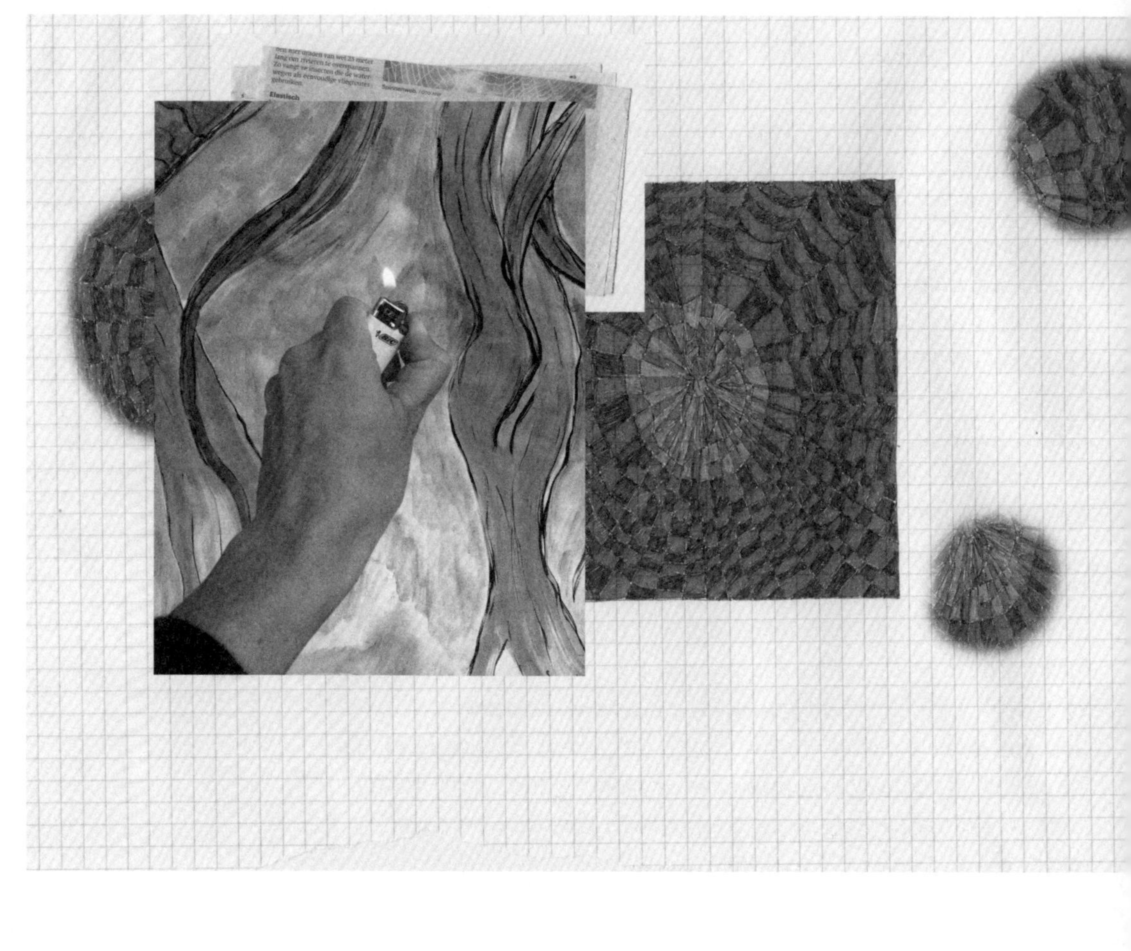

...hun draden van wel 25 meter lang om rivieren te overspannen. Zo vangt ze insecten die de waterwegen als eenvoudige vliegroutes gebruiken.
Spinnenweb. FOTO ANP
Elastisch

What the Psychic Told Me, or: Various Meditations Upon a Stone

Lorelinde Verhees

'The devil, the devil and nobody else, has mixed me up
in this business!'
—Miguel de Cervantes Saavedra, *The Ingenious
Gentleman Don Quixote of La Mancha*
(Part 2, Chapter 10)

I

In a session with my medium, suddenly, out of nowhere,
appeared a stone. She sits across from me with her eyes shut.
Two yards in between us, we are in a bright apartment in
South Amsterdam. Her deep-grey eyes are rather large. On
the floor lie many stones, minerals in all colours. She has a
fine appearance, of porcelain, a damselfly. Her skin is almost
transparent. She greets me by the door, looks at me with soft
impelling eyes, and I follow her into the work-space for our
seeing-through session. See, we are talking about an inner
eye, one that must get to work. Once she explained this to
me. She said: 'Imagine a panopticon or kaleidoscope with all

293

kinds of images in full flight, too many to name. I'm in the middle of that. Depending on your question and on what goes on in your life, one or another sequence pops up, a life in another time, another form and setting, and I am naturally led there.'

I had a personal problem that bothered me. However, this was not the reason for my visit. It's simply something that I do, every other year. I began when I was going through a deep crisis, and had to do everything I could in order to keep my fragile boat adrift. A thorny life-adventure in a country of cold and depression, one that I had to abruptly bring to an end, had saddled me with sadness and feelings of guilt. The medium gave me new courage. This lady touched me with her language, with her fiction if-you-will; she opened unexpected layers in my world and I regained hope. Sometimes I picture myself as a character spilt from the page, who tries to pick up the thread. She experiences life as an ocean of possibilities and takes me with her in this vision.

Over the years she has become dear to me. At the start of the session her voice sinks, she falls into a trance. The ritual is about to begin. She chooses her words carefully and then something happens that touches me every time, I simply feel how much she enjoys the images she perceives in her lucid descriptions of events far removed in time, of energy waves in all the colours of the rainbow. When we say our goodbyes I notice her hair, she still wears it like a blushing girl, shoulder-length with a neat parting in the middle. She appears a little greyer now, her body is slightly more brittle, but her eyes radiate.

In order to see her you make an appointment and then you must always wait for a long time until it is your turn. Half a year is no exception. But now sitting there again, I told her about an altercation with my father. I was thirteen and I said:

'I'm not going to church any longer. If you don't agree then give me your valid reasons as to why I should go'. My father was not verbal—which I was at that age—and there was no match. He retreated full of grief. I was yet to realize how deep the wound was that my rebellion had inflicted. In his world— the generation that had matured after the war, had respect for their parents—my defiance was inconceivable. The act caused a huge disruption. In my father a silent rage was ignited—a bewilderment that festered deep within him for an entire lifetime. But I had not escaped unscathed either. A rift was born between us, contact seemed impossible, but this natural desire never left.

The lady said: 'While thinking about your father, fantasize about a stone, a primordial mineral form of life that develops very slowly. From the outside you don't see what is going on within a stone. But in nature, it is in the right place.'

2

Two years later I was standing in front of a stone in an art space in Lisbon. I was allowed to address him, but couldn't manage more than 'hello, stone'—a mere two words which I was barely able to scrape from my throat without quavering. I've always been shy behind a microphone. I need a plan, the certainty of a text to be read, a song to be sung. Now my predicament was even stronger. A paralyzing force appeared to have bewitched the entire environment; as if I was nailed to the floor. Had perhaps some malicious spark flown off the stone? Magritte let stones float through the air; Beckett gave Molloy sixteen pebbles in four pockets which he takes turns sucking upon. One artist says: a stone is bald and aloof and yet you can care for it, another claims it is a dark and mysterious thing that can come knocking at your door at any given moment, perhaps in some forbidden dream in the middle of the night. None of that however sprung to mind. My encounter with the stone was arduous, very different—one would imagine—than with a human. I had been defeated, and today I believe the stone's stillness to have taken me by surprise.

'The stone doesn't judge.' This is what João Ferro Martins wrote to me about it. His stone, stuck to the surface with suction pads, is the protagonist in a series of works about sound (or the lack thereof). A curious set-up, with a philosophical undertone, visualizes the possibility of a dialogue between a form of nature and man. An absurd experiment, according to the artist, in which everything could be said. The visitor could also listen to the stone. That sensory experience goes further than what we are used to; the possibilities are expanded, the conventional perspective tipped over.

Now my thoughts turn to 'choses tuées' by gerlach en koop (De Appel, 2015). At the heart of that exhibition a closed (or fake) space had been added to De Appel's architecture—compare the sealed burial chamber in the pyramid of the Egyptian Kings. The artists created an implosion, an artwork as obstacle. This brings to mind Symbolism and her convoluted imagery.

One similar work-as-obstacle is figured in an essay by Jeff Wall from the 1980s, named 'Dan Graham's Kammerspiel', which is primarily about Dan Graham's *Alteration of a Suburban House* (1978). That artwork is like an oyster. It is a proposition to replace the façade of a normal house in a suburb with a glass wall; in the middle a mirror would be placed through the length of the house, dividing the public part from the private. The idea is illustrated and embodied by a 3D model in bright colours; a striking feature of which is a perfectly mowed fresh-green lawn.

You can imagine what you would see from the street, a hallucinatory image of—well, daily life… Wall saw this work to be the endpoint of conceptual art, he wrote that the project of common space of the 1960s—the act of sharing, open dialogue, accepting love in manifold forms, et cetera—comes to an end here. Once again, the personal aspect of life is abruptly removed from the public gaze, while the right to keep secrets is emphasized. According to Wall, conceptual art was dead-beat around 1980, and entrapped in endless self-reflection. (An aside: here, Jeff Wall painted an intriguing association with the nineteenth-century French poet Stéphane Mallarmé, whose work created a bridge between symbolism and modernism. Mallarmé's *tombeaux* poems—a forged concord of words as perfectly solitary as shining stars—are, besides reflections upon death, notably of colleague-poets such as for instance, Edgar Allan Poe—avowals of a language that regards death as the final point.)

The aforementioned artworks have in common that they create situations—impasses, obstacles—that have much to do with our lives. They offer creative solutions so that all that is stuck becomes loose and light, and things resume their beloved course. With the show by the Portuguese artist, I also get the feeling there is a musical element in play; besides an artist he is also a drummer-composer. His exhibition was called '20–20000 Hz', and that is the range of the audio frequency audible to the human ear. But the title also signifies a mysterious detail pertaining to physics, namely the particular frequency of a stone. Somewhere in the vast range of audio frequencies hides this natural frequency: a unique vibrancy that—activated by an external source— makes the stone resonate.

297

3

I cross another corner, and yes, in the distance I distinguish a familiar form. In the middle of the road lies a stone. The following poem, 'In the Middle of the Road', is by the Brazilian poet Carlos Drummond de Andrade. He wrote it in the early 1920s, when a crisp modernist wind gushed through the Brazilian written word:

> In the middle of the road there was a stone
> there was a stone in the middle of the road
> there was a stone
> in the middle of the road there was a stone.
>
> Never should I forget this event
> in the life of my fatigued retinas.
> Never should I forget that in the middle of the road
> there was a stone
> there was a stone in the middle of the road
> in the middle of the road there was a stone.

Here two approaches come together: on the one hand a registering and detached gaze; on the other hand, a stranger perspective—it seems older—one that I would characterize as animistic or even pagan; see and hear (!) the repetitive, rhythmic, invocatory aspect. The visions affect one another, and from their interaction emerges a new balance. The poet begins the first line with something that could easily happen to any of us. In the second line, something peculiar happens.

Where initially the poet narrates, the point of vantage shifts to that of the stone, who at this point seems to take the lead entirely. It has energy, there is more life in him than in the man; the latter discusses his tired eyes. Take note: this is a remarkable paradox, it is after all the poet who has constructed the role-reversal; *he is the man*, his willpower or his receptiveness allows us to feel the strength of the stone.

Drummond grew up with the classics, in the beginning of his poem we hear an echo 'Midway upon the journey of our life', with which Dante's *Divine Comedy* begins. The great Renaissance poet continues with 'I found myself within a forest dark, for the straightforward pathway had been lost'. And these lines verbalized, according to tradition, the intense life-crisis that Dante experienced at his thirty-fifth year. Did Drummond experience such a crisis? It's conceivable; when he wrote his poem, he was slightly younger than Dante—but I myself have felt old and weary at thirty. If you read the poem in Portuguese, the original language, you hear how the stone seems to change into water, into the gurgling streams of a river. This takes me back even further in time, to ancient Chinese poetry, and to the philosophy of Empedocles, according to whom the elements constantly merge into one another in order to give the world her outward appearance.

Perhaps the poem appeals to me so much because of the many walks that I, still a boy, used to make down a muddy path, one that was frequently firmed up with fresh rubble. Labourers would smash up old bricks and scatter the pieces. I only have vague memories of it, but by writing down the words, they are somehow returning. Apparently, as a boy I resolutely walked this old and ancient path, on my way to distant fields. I was going to my friends, whom I called Barney and Remmelt, which had of course been prompted by *The Flintstones* that I had seen at home on the newly acquired second-hand black-and-white television.

My mother told me much later about those trips, by which time I'd already long forgotten them. Where did my friends live? In the celestial spheres? What brought us together, what did we do? How I'd love to linger in these times again. A hundred steps upon the donkey's trail: See what I had then Seen, Feel what I then had Felt, Think what I had then Thought. This is a lot! Meanwhile, a mouse scours my stove in search of sweets. I think I'll call him Hamish.

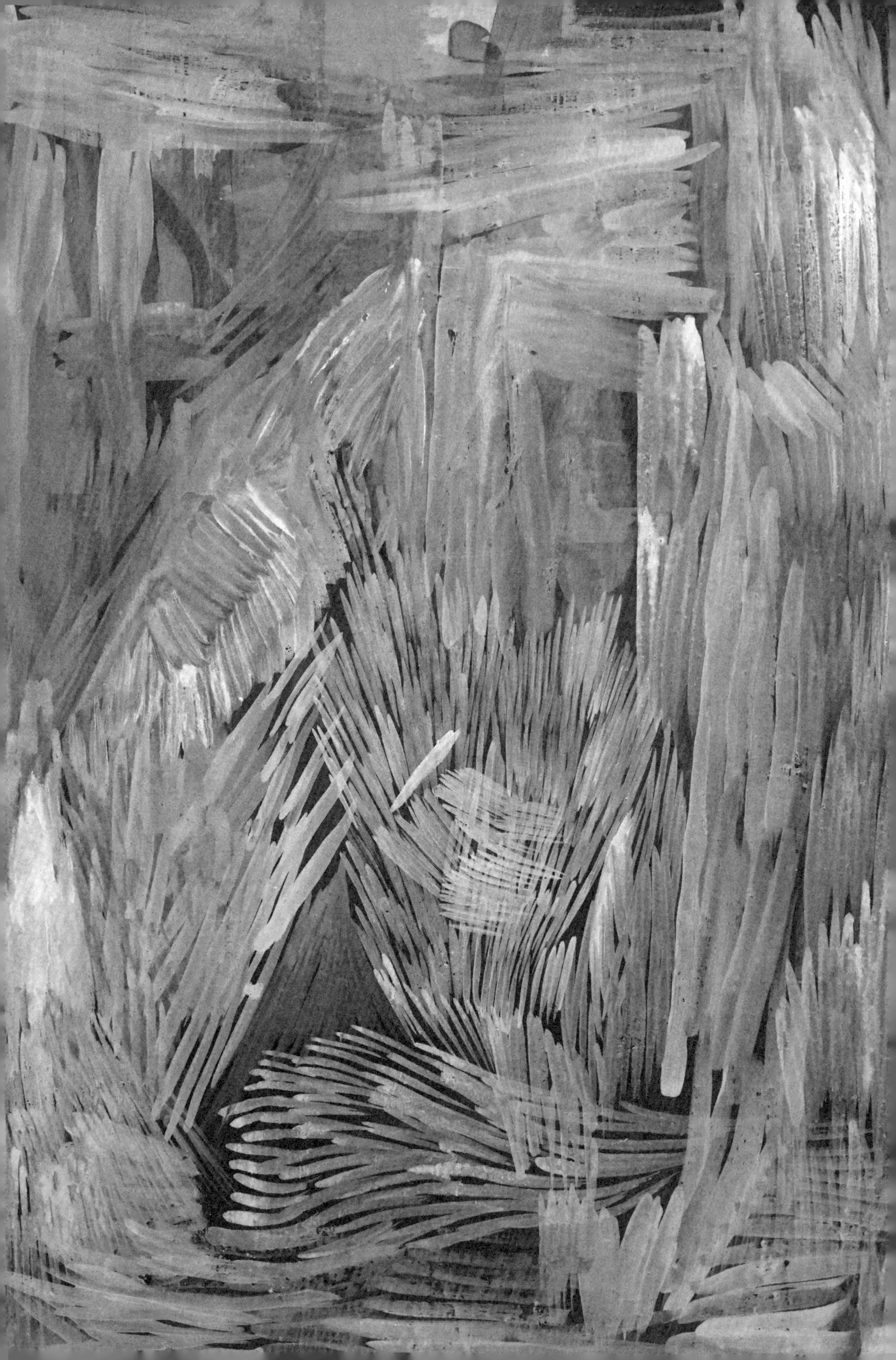

Sublime Mortification

Rob Johannesma

'"If you rely only on your eyes, your other senses
weaken." It was a Bene Gesserit axiom.'
—Frank Herbert, *Dune*[1, 2]

I

Attention is an important subject. I remember an early video
work by the artist: it was a landscape in which time morphed
like syrup and space seemed to swell or contract as if it were a
vital organ. One could feel the silent pulse of a beating heart.
In this landscape a viewer could roam endlessly and be at
ease. The work had been created with a medium that also
demanded endless patience from the maker. Two film slides
were pressed together and slowly slid across from each other,
while the surfaces that passed through the frame were being
filmed. Such a technique refers to the nineteenth century,
when many artists-scientists experimented with moving and
still images. Today Rob Johannesma recalls: 'At the time I
was frequently on the move. Finding myself in the world was
a theme'.[3]

303

1 Frank Herbert, *Dune*,
London, Golancz, 1966; originally published as *Dune* in
Analog Science Fact & Fiction,
1963–65.

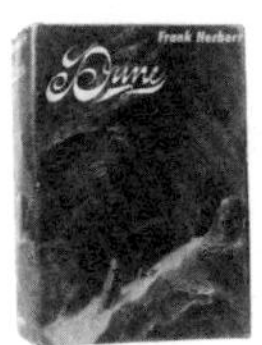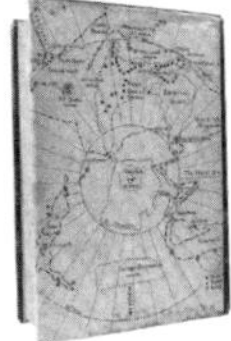

2 Frank Herbert, *Dune*, 1965,
front and backside.

3 Artist quotes rendered in
verbatim, or paraphrased, come
from emails and conversations
with the artist, April 2020.

Ten years later, it is as though a different maker is standing before me. This artist's ear is pressed against the planet: he discerns vivaciously, poised in amazement. The sacrosanct *In Dark Trees* (2009, inkjet on paper, 780 × 590 cm) is a complex poetic assemblage in which a photo from a reportage of a rocket attack in Gaza territory is interwoven with a reproduction of John the Baptist in the desert by Geertgen tot Sint Jans (1485).[4] Embedded within a cascade of newspapers, like a passe-partout—layers of superimposed images and texts, which have been partly painted over with white hues, produce a kind of calm palimpsest—the two main pictures sit loosely together. It gives the impression of an improvisation. At the same time the composition has been carefully construed. Pieces appear as over-saturated images, bleached by time, or on the contrary as obscure chunks. The effects echo a printing process, yet the images recalibrate the act of looking itself by jamming the gaze: lingering upon the violence, suffering, and decay, because 'this is really happening in the world!' The work generates a sheer biblical flood of

304

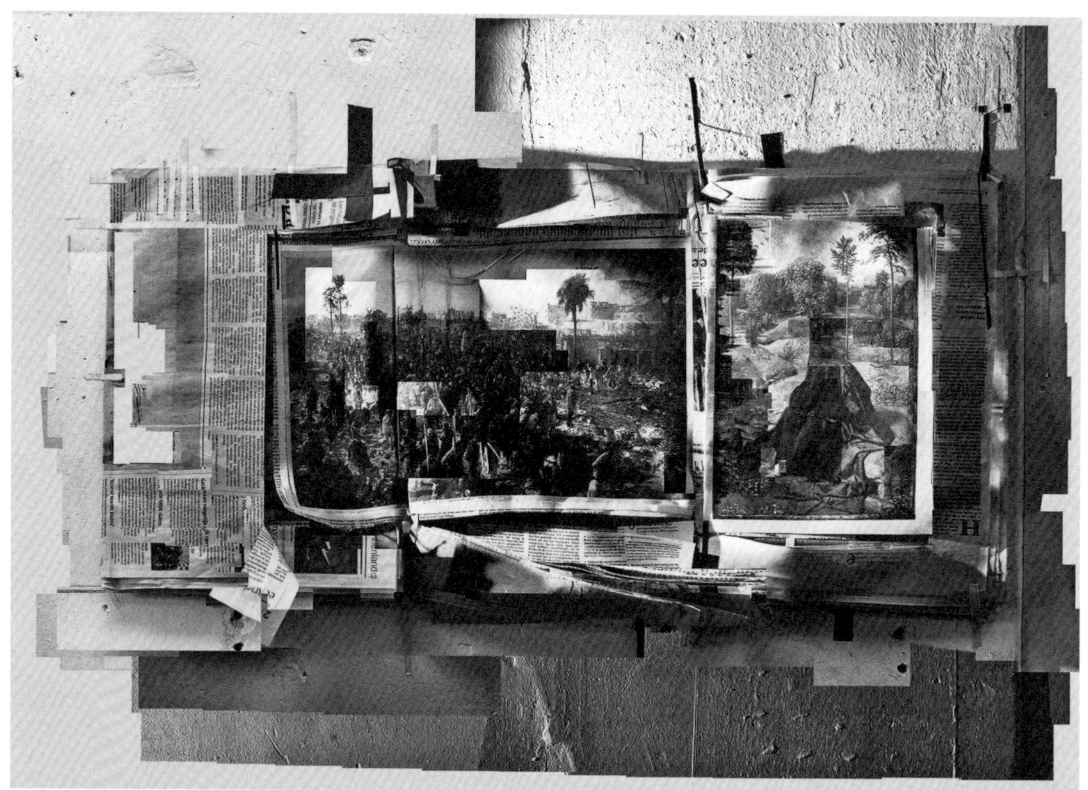

4 Rob Johannesma, *In Dark Trees*, 2009, inkjet on paper, 780 × 590 cm.

impressions; a beautiful dramaturgy of light and shadow conjures stillness and peace.

Afterwards, Rob Johannesma remained out of the public eye for a while. *In Dark Trees* was exhibited in De Vleeshal in Middelburg,[5] and in the following years he had various exhibitions at home and abroad. But personal circumstances prevented him from focusing on art full-time.

Now he is showing new work at the gallery Albada Jelgersma in Amsterdam. There is a familiar ring to these pieces; he nudges us: be quiet, look attentively, scrutinize the images. Yet, nothing is the same. The artist shows seven paintings, vertical formats, oil on canvas. I see the painted wings of the theatre. They represent a kind of in-between world. The artist uses the word 'membrane'. He qualifies the paintings as porous, connected with the inside and outside. Pondering these works, I am reminded of a fleece or of plumage.[6] The first impression is of an opaque field or a sealed space: intense, multi-layered colours draw the viewer into the depth. But the painterly touch—the final layer, often applied *ton sur ton* spontaneously and adroitly, comes to the viewer in a convoy of sparks or stripes—gives a contradictory feeling. It is the sensation that right here, live before your eyes, everything works in unison to pry open the space within a field or plane.[7]

It reminds me of a painting by Helmut Federle, *The Death of Wladimir Majakovskij* (1983). A small but powerful and dramatic work, the abstract representation of a falling and tearing colour curtain. The difference is that in the latter a profound, tragic end is being visualized.

The exhibition of RJ combines three interconnected workgroups. His paintings are shown in the first room of the gallery. It is the space of The Struggle. In the second room a series of small works are hung, in which issues of the

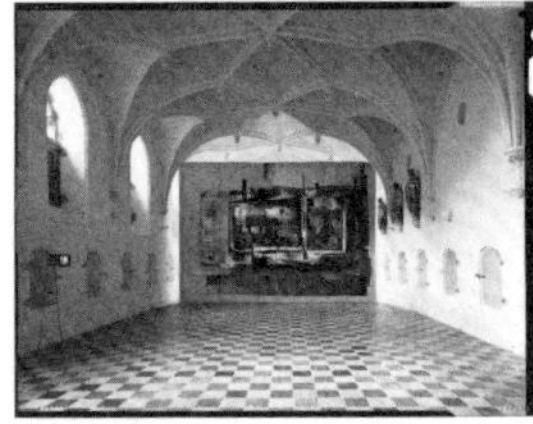

5 Rob Johannesma, *In Dark Trees*, 2009, exhibition view, De Vleeshal, Middelburg.

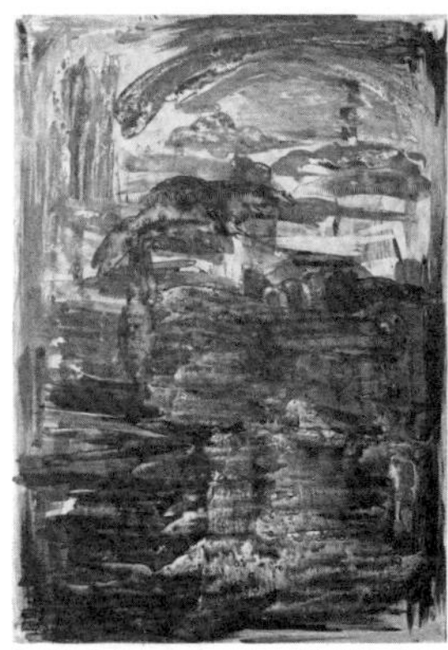

6 Rob Johannesma, *Untitled*, 2021, 175 × 120 cm, egg tempera on canvas.

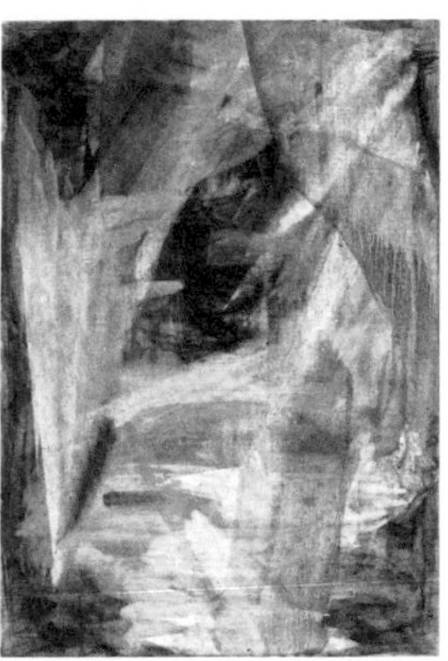

7 Rob Johannesma, *Untitled*, 2024, 60 × 40 cm, egg tempera on canvas.

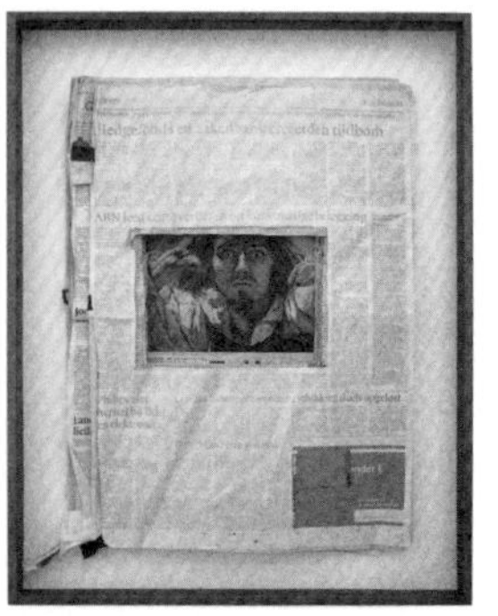

8 Rob Johannesma, *Le Désespéré* (The Desperate Man), 2015, newspapers, tapes, maple wood frame, 109 × 63 × 7 cm.

architecture periodical *Domus* form the canvas. Among these smaller works is *Glass-Blue Days,* the artist's book the show is named after. In this expansive work the artist looks back at twenty years of activity and his inspirations. He started the work in 2017.

The book contains a collection of rudiments. It features stills from video-works, props that once had a function within his productions, newspapers of which the pages have been painted over, and a plethora of reproductions—among them a lot of recordings of little details of classical artworks telling their stories through the coarse grain. All the elements have been bound within a book that opens up an entire universe. Above it hangs a recent assemblage: a collar of newspapers— layers of paper forming a backdrop—frames the reproduction of a painting, an anxious self-portrait. Here Gustave Courbet presents himself as *The Desperate Man* (1843–1845). The titular character is seen pulling hair out of his own head.[8]

RJ's paintings evade description. Mutability can only be experienced live. The suggestion of landscape plays a role. I'm taken to the deepest heart's core of the Amazonian rainforest, a haze of glowing mist. Here reigns the fleeting, and the natural: some colours resemble birds from fairy tales. In one painting a cloth of feathers, iridescent within the dark background, is featured… A trippy image: exhilaration, peril! Animal energy penetrates 'free forms'. These works depict interior life—'deep landscapes'. Paint appears as pure structure. The colours are introverted, lightly shivering, and bright. The artist lays out the structures for you, soft and subtle or conversely, administered against the grain with unruly vibrations. In my fantasy, I picture one colour to pull the strings: an iridescent blue, a fluorescent green, or a restrained lilac/mauve… It smoulders in each painting; it shimmers and twinkles: like the vicissitude of quicksilver. Weren't these

306

colours born from the peacock's tail?

The peacock's tail is a fascinating spectrum of—not only—dark and introverted colours. These colours can pop, bright as day, depending on the point of view and amount of daylight they're exposed to. They are an Alchemist's best friend. Zeno of Bruges, the alchemist-protagonist in Marguerite Yourcenar's novel, *The Abyss*, experiences something he has been searching for all his life. 'Night had fallen, but without his knowing whether it was only within himself or in the room: to him everything now was night.'[9] Before his eyes he sees a black that shudders; changing first to a pale-green, and after a while into a maidenly white; finally, the bleached white mutates into golden-red. When colour starts to act as a signifier for a dialectical ontology ('altered states'), it becomes a merciless tool for artists. Hitchcock used reds, purples, and greens for Scottie, one of the two lead personages in *Vertigo*, for cinematic orchestrations of doubt, fear, and desire.

2

The works have three sources. The first inspiration is a critical and personal experience. One morning in 2012, the artist woke up to a shocking apprehension: the light in one eye had gone out, died. He began a process of revalidation: picking up the pieces of his life, beginning anew as an artist. RJ is retentive about this confrontational episode; it shouldn't determine the perception of his art career. He does mention that in 2012 he began working in a more tactile way, touching and feeling the materials, discovering them anew. New kinds of works began to emerge. He painted in black ink a stain upon a sheet of paper, almost a visual reproduction of the

9 Marguerite Yourcenar, *The Abyss*, trans. Grace Frick in cooperation with the author, New York, Editions Gallimard, 1976, p. 354. Originally published as *L'oeuvre au noir*, Paris, Gallimard, 1968.

eye's blind spot; he let it dry after which he painted a new contour that dissolved at the edges. Was this an icon for fusion or submission? The experiments resonate in his paintings. About this he says: 'I wondered what I would see if I were to paint with my broken eye. Now I would like the viewer to see what I see'.

The second source is *The Dream of Constantine.* Piero della Francesca's fresco takes us to the night before the battle of the Milvian Bridge (Rome, 312 CE) depicted in the adjacent fresco.[10] In his dream—flown to him by an angel from heaven—the emperor sees what he must do in order to defeat his opponent. The painting is exquisite and sassy. How gracefully this man rests! Emperor Constantine I sits in his bed in a calm upright pose. If there had not been a second figure painted on the fresco that signified sleep—the third figure (the angel) representing flight, and the fourth watchfulness—one would never have guessed that this man was peacefully sleeping let alone dreaming.

RJ acknowledges an intriguing parallel: 'The past ten years were rather calm in my practice. I was given the chance to reflect, ponder on what was important in my art, what was not. But the work process was, unfortunately, also disturbed, I was very sick. Perhaps one can speak of a sleep of sorts'.

The fresco is part of *The Legend of the True Cross.* Piero was asked in 1452 to finish the cycle, a composite narrative, left incomplete by Bicci di Lorenzo. He would work on this commission until 1466. The subject matter ranges from Genesis to the Crusades; the historical events of his own time (1096–1271). It was realized in the Basilica of Saint Francis in Arezzo. RJ recalibrates his practice by visiting Piero's fresco: he appropriates his work. It is fascinating to see how he conducts his dialogue with the maestro—but perhaps this is also a struggle.

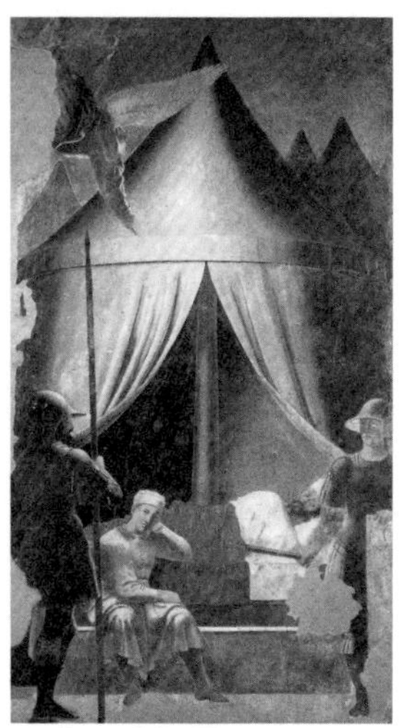
10 Piero della Francesca, *Constantine's Dream,* 1452.

Piero's art is in on the conversation in the exhibition. RJ's paintings are built of very thin layers of paint with light crevices at the surface edges, and this creates a spatial effect. The world emerges from these light spots. Similar crevices appear in the smaller paintings made on the covers of the architecture magazine. Through their paint we sense the glistening fine lines and volumes of large edifices; the objects are barely perceptible, almost too fine to see, but their material presence is grasped intuitively. The world is spiritualized space. I think of the lyricism of watercolours. Between the paint a vista opens up; the light makes its entrance and it serves as an unequivocal reminder of Piero's scenes of the open air, the natural images. Cedars stick into the sky, the horizon turns up, and, lo and behold, the sun shines delightedly. Here reigns serenity and ebullience.

The paintings have a demure character. And their verisimilitude—the material expression that RJ seems to have taken from Piero—is ambiguous. Amidst these dark, soft, and light colour surfaces I feel vitality: the will to live, but also despair to bring that vitality within reach once more, and incumbent gradations of mortification.

Gerard Manley Hopkins is the third source. The exhibition's title is taken from the poem 'The Blessed Virgin Compared to the Air We Breathe' (Stoneyhurst, 1893). At about two-thirds into this long poem—in fact this is one strung-out thought, a deep rumination on a confrontation with a major religious-artistic life problem—we run into the words 'glass-blue days':

'The glass-blue days are those / When every colour glows, / Each shape and shadow shows.'

It is as if everything is put on standby; as if the organism switches back to the *factory settings...* The poet finds in his nature observations a new balance. Up to this point he has

11 Kees Fens, 'When the Iron Is Hot: Hopkins', *Finding the Place: Selected Essays on English Literature*, Amsterdam, Rodopi, 1994, p. 156.

made much ado about the blessed virgin, Maria, describing her at length. Meanwhile you sense him grappling with God, or the image of God.

Afterwards he moves on to nature: somehow he relates better to this, for nature enables his own intimate experience of the divine. I ask RJ: 'What do you see on glass-blue days?' His response prompts me to believe that Hopkins' words offer him a form of solace. Hopkins describes an experience that permits you to gaze as far as the horizon: this is something RJ can't do anymore or only really in part. It is a shortcoming.

Gerard Manley Hopkins was a Jesuit and a man of doubt. The poet struggled with the contradiction between his inner world and the beauty he saw in nature. Kees Fens, the Dutch literary critic, has portrayed him wonderfully. This passage points towards his happiness: 'There was a little track in Stoneyhurst that always shone in the sun after it had rained. Many years after Hopkins' death one of the fraters recollected: "Why yes, a strange young man, kneeled by the gate in order to look at some humid sand".'[11]

> RJ: 'On 'blue-glass days' one can see everything: objects and colours, and the depth of colour. I think that is the effect my paintings, that you can literally stroll across the surface with your own pair of eyes; this is a tactile experience, because you pick up on minute holes in the canvas, or crevices through which deeper, lighter layers appear. Those openings represent the horizon in the distance. This is what I think 'glass-blue days' symbolizes for me: the three words are crystal-clear, yet also milky and diffused.'

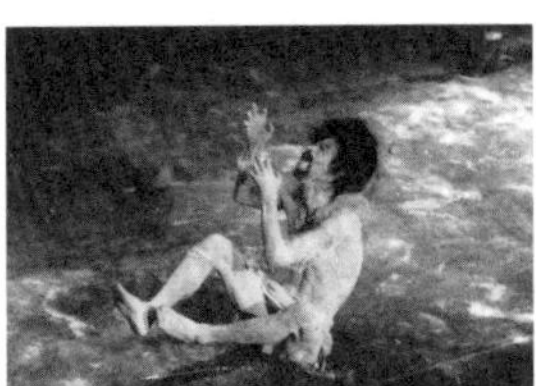

12 Hijikata Tatsumi, *Butoh (Dance of Shadows)*.

RJ's paintings evoke a singular visual process, they are avowals of vulnerability and the immanence of jeopardy. Where does his research/position resonate? Intuitively, I think of artists who have been able to make great art despite or rather thanks to certain limitations. Chuck Close, for instance, whose facial impairment meant he could not distinguish faces from each other; only later in his life did he address this in public. As countermeasure, he began to paint his friends' faces, close-up, blown-up, larger-than-life. Yayoi Kusama is another example. Kusama lives with a psychosomatic condition which changes her experience of sensorial perceptions, the impressions that the external world leaves upon us, into an exponentially amplified experience of the stimuli entering the organism at full speed, hard as hell. Her work reflects her own inner process: a visual world built around awesome powers. However, her art is also her oasis, her safe haven in which the inside/outside dichotomy loses meaning.

Other artists apply the limitations or obstacles to themselves. I think of Hijikata Tatsumi, the Japanese artist who together with Ohno Kazuo stood at the cradle of Ankoku Butoh (literally meaning 'dance of darkness').[12] I am moved by Hijikata. I feel the urgency of the dancer/choreographer; I sense his commitment. Hijikata developed his dance in the decimated and traumatized landscape of postwar Japan. He wanted to create bodily movements that could represent the pain, sadness, and trauma, and by doing so process the experience. Death was a major part of daily life at the time. Darkness is the limitation in his Butoh performance *Forbidden Colors* ('Kinjiki', 1959). This adaptation of Yukio Mishima's book of the same title from 1959, focused on the force of attraction, erotics, and display of power. Hijikata

13 Bruce Baird, *Hijikata Tatsumi and Butoh: Dancing in a Pool of Grey Grits*, New York, Palgrave Macmillan, 2012.

staged the dance for a large part in the theatre wings. Bodies loomed from the dark and retreated again. Spectators could often only hear the dancers.

Two figures, an older man (Hijikata) and a boy (Ohno Yoshito, the son of Ohno Kazuo) move together, portraying an ambiguous relationship. A dazed chicken struts on to the stage; it has switched owners, perhaps the boy was hungry and exchanged his affection for sustenance, or alternatively the boy is in prison and must perform an initiation ritual of slaughtering a chicken so as to be accepted by the prison establishment of hardened criminals. The darkness is suggestive, it magnifies the sensations of roughness and intimacy, brutality and vulnerability. There is Danger in Submission.[13]

Bruce Nauman is another artistic soul rooted at the heart of the earth. He has made work alluding to torture practices of dictatorial regimes. *Dream Passage (Cross)* is an installation from 1984. It was based on a recurring dream about a corridor where the artist encountered his own ghost. Was this an experience of death? The work hearkens to his earlier, minutely demarcated, 'performance arenas' from the late 1960s, in which the artist wandered around in his studio, for example his *Walk in Contraposto*. Later he reversed the roles: now the viewer became a performer who was invited to enter a narrow passageway, which made going back a difficult task.

Dream Passage (Cross) was a part of the exhibition 'Quartetto' (Venice, Scuola Grande San Giovanni Evangelista, 1984). A cross-shaped structure lay in the space, from its open ends spilled electric yellow and red light. In the central room of this network of corridors—an aperture, leading like a heart unto its blood vessels—stood a table and a chair. The space had been mirrored/reversed: another upside-down table hung from the ceiling with another chair, they lurked inconspicuously as if from beyond a metaphysical looking glass, spying/gazing back at you.

Danger and Threat are part of Rob Johannesma's proposition. His work is deft and intense: it articulates deep feelings. His exhibition has a dramatic quality—in spite of it being obscured. In an earlier design, he wanted to transform the entire gallery space. An Etruscan tomb was the inspiration for a space whose windows would be sealed with foil; the spectators would contemplate the paintings from a little bench, as if they were gifts for the after-life: 'Living yet dead already. Dead and yet still alive'. I think of how in order to become a shaman, one must first die underground, so that the transformation can be steered in the right direction.

We find forms of living decay in Hijikata's Butoh, for example his *Pillar of Ashes,* and of course in Bruce Nauman's art—sovereign and trippy. For Rob Johannesma, mortification is a quiet, intense occurrence. Seven paintings invite the viewer to undergo a sublime initiation. All senses are addressed, seeing is as important as listening and feeling: painting is a rite of passage. The poet found it in the sand. I experience it in dark paint.[14]

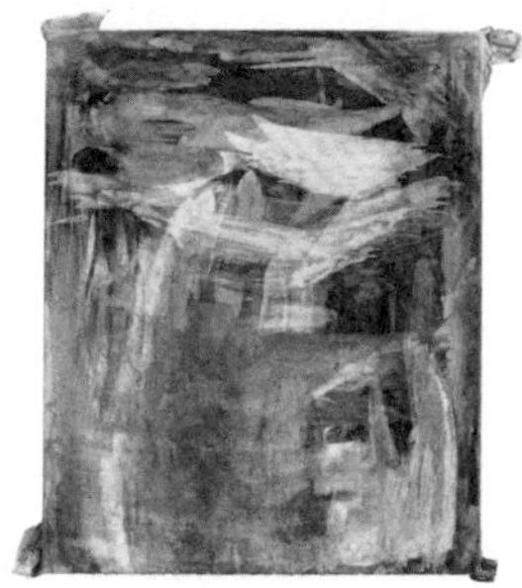

14 Rob Johannesma, *Untitled,* 2024, egg tempera on canvas, 50 × 40 cm.

Steadfastness

Steadfastness or grit is a mindset, central to which is a firm COURSE OF ACTION.[1] Steadfastness refers to the artist's drive. Art makes us feel this resolve. This connection (between maker and work) is illustrated, in a humoristic way, in an image by Giovanni Anselmo, *Entering the Work* (1971).[2] Here we see the artist running into a wide-open field, symbolizing a space for thought and wonder.

The artist's steadfastness or commitment is admirable. It affects their daily practice *and* work in the long run. Curators-writers can learn from this. I will give three examples. Two cases involve thematic exhibitions, curated by me, for which I invited artists to re-activate works from their past. The first example is of when I was a still student of exhibitions, but already working as a young art writer. Many oeuvres make us feel the artist's steadfastness. I recall my

1 *True Grit* is a 2010 Western directed by the Coen Brothers, about the determination of a fourteen-year-old farm girl called Mattie Ross, who hires a boozy and trigger-happy lawman to go after an outlaw who has murdered her father.

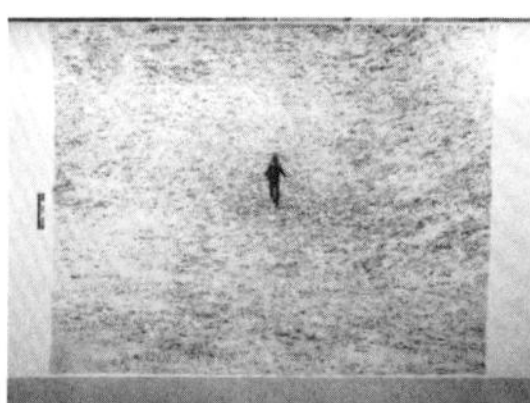

2 Giovanni Anselmo, *Entrare nell' opera* ('Entering the Work'), 1971, inkjet photograph on canvas, 350 × 510 cm.

3 Francesca Passini, 'Mario Merz', *ArtForum*, December 1990.

visit to a show by Mario Merz in summer 1990. At the Centro per l'Arte Contemporanea Luigi Pecci in Prato, Italy, an installation called *Lo spazio è curvo o diritto* ('Space is curved or straight') played the whole museum. The primary element of Merz's work was an ongoing border of stacked willow twigs, whirling their way through the spaces in vigorous movement, reminiscent of a nomadic raid. The spiral zone was a habitat for Merz's blue neon lights with numbers of the Fibonacci sequence, igloos of glass and metal, and stacked newspapers. At that time, Francesca Passini wrote: 'In Prato, an imposing spiral of bundled sticks rose up from the exterior courtyard of the museum to the upper floors, where it expanded into all the rooms, thereby suggesting an organism originating within the earth'.[3]

I remember my experience of Merz's exhibition, the feeling of being lured into a pulsating energy field. Wandering through this enchanted landscape, I observed distinct rivers, rocks, even an entire city. But what was Merz's intention? His work circumscribed, I think, both his actual experience and a dream image. A poignant aspect of Merz's background is his incarceration, during the Second World War, for his part in the Italian anti-fascist resistance movement. Once in prison, he began to draw. Having seen and experienced terrible things, he decided: 'When the war is over, I will dedicate myself to poetry'. This information offers a relevant perspective. Today I'd say that Merz, with his Gesamtkunstwerk in Prato, carved out the contours of a new humanistic habitat. His set-up was not naive: this gorgeous-menacing landscape embodied resistance. Through the integration of the spiral form (the stacked twigs) in the museum architecture, Merz revitalized a power symbol usurped by the Italian fascists, that was however already part of the life and culture of the ancient Etruscans and Romans: the *fasces*, the bound bundle of wooden rods. The artist pushed this material toward a new imaginary horizon.

My second example comes from 'To Burn Oneself With Oneself: the Romantic Damage Show' in De Appel, Amsterdam, 2008 (Joan Jonas' video-piece *Vertical Role* (1972), discussed in my essay in this section, was shown here as well).[4][5] The exhibition investigated the viability/esprit of the Romantic artist's position in today's art landscape. Harmen Brethouwer was one of the ten artists. He presented 'a suite of nine sculptures' made of fibrewood, paint and other basic materials. His 'suite' advanced a paradoxical connection between a conceptual-rational approach and a radical-Romantic attitude driven by emotions. The suite's elaborate titles—*The Cares of the Pagans: Poverty, Abundance, Lowliness, Loftiness, Presumptuousness, Self-Torment,*

4 'To Burn Oneself With Oneself: the Romantic Damage Show', De Appel centre for art, Amsterdam, 23 February–6 April 2008. Artists: Harmen Brethouwer, Günther Förg, Rodney Graham, Joan Jonas, Michael Landy, Renzo Martens, Jewyo Rhii, Christoph Schlingensief, Annika Ström, Richard T. Walker. Curator: Mark Kremer in cooperation with Ann Demeester.

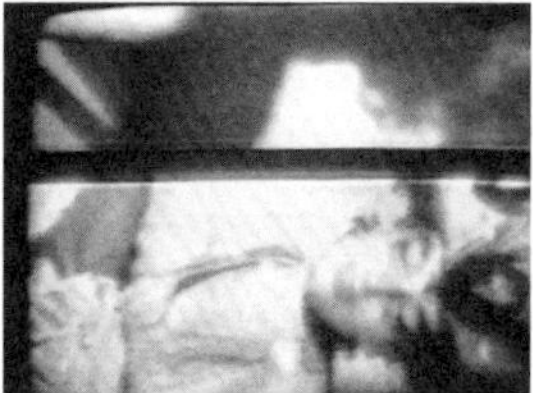

5 Joan Jonas, *Vertical Roll*, 1972, video (black and white, sound), 19'38".

6 Harmen Brethouwer in email to author, 5 January 2018.

Indecisiveness, Vacillation, Disconsolateness—refer to a discourse by the philosopher Søren Kierkegaard on the troubles of earthly life, called 'The Cares of the Pagans'.

The years attached to his sculptural corpus—1984–1989 (2008)—tell us that the artist reopened a field of enquiry, producing new and better works (he dismantled them, though, sometime after the show). Minimal art—recognizable in the basic forms—and a world of repressed emotion, notably the shame of Protestantism, came together in them. With subtle (self-)mockery, similar to the jest of Kierkegaard himself, Brethouwer's works evoked a landscape of complex emotions. Today I believe that through them the artist (re)staged a personal crisis. His suite embodied inner conflict. It was a portrayal of feeling that, curtailed, seeks freedom. Monuments for a frustrated youth? Later the artist wrote to me: 'It was my time in the desert!'[6]

Unearthing a body of ideas, looking at their current potential, making decisions, and then staying the course is the background story and motive of a particular work by János Sugár, my third example. Writer-curators can learn from this: take your own ideas seriously, follow your intuitions, present them to artists, see them through. *The Bull of Reversibility in the China Shop of Present (Exhibition-Set)* (1985–2007) was developed for and created in situ in the exhibition 'The Projection Project: Budapest Episode', Kunsthalle Budapest, 2007.[7]

The first iteration of 'The Projection Project', hosted by the MuHKA, Antwerpen, 2006–2007, occurred at a time of transition, when as a result of the digital revolution (PowerPoint), various techniques hallowed by modern art tradition fell into disuse. Slide and film projection will probably remain important media in art, but they can hardly be separated from the melancholy feeling of looking back on a past era and technology. This is a good reason, we thought, to consider the idea of projection anew from a variety of perspectives. Projection occurs in various *formats* in art practice and in thinking about visual culture. The many applications of projection are the result of a development in which sometimes very different fields of knowledge interact: physics, geometry, cartography, optics, psychology, fine arts and show business. In this period, when projection is losing its technological usefulness and corresponding disciplinary status, the concept can regain its allegoric eloquence ('alleu-agorein' = 'to say something differently'). In short, artists today are again articulating the artistic application of ideas of projection.

János Sugár's work related to the idea of 'projection as a signage system'. The systematization of projection as a linear principle started in the

7 'The Projection Project: Budapest Episode', Mücsarnok/ Kunsthalle Budapest, Budapest, HU. Artists: Marie-José Burki, Paul Van Hoeydonck, Fiona Tan, Marc De Blieck, Kaszás Tamás + June 18th Collective, Matthew Stokes, Timothée Ingen-Housz, Yeondoo Jung, Ana Torfs, Benjamin Verdonck, Bruce Nauman, Krassimir Terziev, János Sugár, Pierre Huyghe, Joost Rekveld, Cerith Wyn Evans, Klaas Kloosterboer, Rodney Graham, and Várnai Gyula. Curator: Mark Kremer in cooperation with Edwin Carels and Dieter Roelstraete. Local advisor: Edit Molnár.

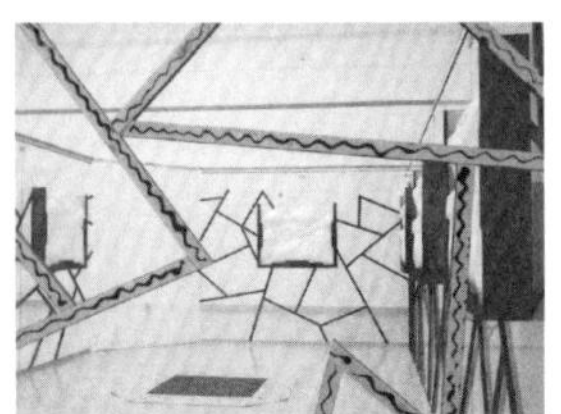

8 János Sugár, *The Bull of Reversibility in the China Shop of Present (Exhibition-Set)*, 1985–2007.

Renaissance with, for example, Dürer's drawing machines. Projection is a drawing method and a process of converting worlds into graphic systems—with all its implications upon which Western art history is based, in its notion of the painting as a window that brings the world within direct reach. In the twentieth century, beginning with the avant-gardes and non-figurative art, a resistance against this paradigm is emerging. This resistance could be felt in *The Bull of Reversibility in the China Shop of Present (Exhibition-Set)*.[8] A glass room had been built in one of the Kunsthalle's galleries. Here the visitor encountered a modernist phantom: its transparent walls showed a display of forms in a strangely familiar visual language, hovering between the abstract/spiritual and the concrete/earthly.

A grid structure with a scarcely recognizable tree motif followed the room; this held the sequence of forms, identical white reliefs resembling an abstract pillow-shape. The room was like a time machine that transported you back to an earlier era and its projection of a future art. In fact, this environment evoked that idea once before—originally it featured in János Sugár's 90' long 16 mm film *Persian Walk* (1985), where two men stroll through the streets of Budapest and, at a certain point, visit an exhibition of new art. That exhibition was restaged! In 1985, Sugár did a detailed drawing of an exhibition set and gave it to the stage designers' workshop of the Hungarian film industry. They enlarged it, put it in 3 D, using wood for the grid structure and vacuum-formed plastic copies of a plaster original for the reliefs. The reliefs' form referred to the reliefs in the kitchen of Rick Deckard, the protagonist of *Blade Runner* (1982). Sugár preferred to suggest that they reflected the structure of his own film, as 'reliefs of a forgotten explanation'. His glass room evoked the idea of an orphaned modernism. He described *The Bull of Reversibility in the China Shop of Present (Exhibition-Set)* also as the debut of his set as an artwork, like in spy stories or fairy tales where persons are woken up from innocent sleep.

I give you my last five texts. Steadfastness typifies the art, in their handling of motifs, of Harmen Brethouwer (folly/dedication), Joan Jonas (perseverance: investigations true to inner life), Jos van Merendonk (resilience: shadow-boxing with abstract art), Roee Rosen (transformation) and Lutz Driessen (grotesque imagination). Their works forge strong connections to reality. The artists take what is here, adding their fictions/fantasies and critical thoughts, transforming and returning their findings. Walking a fine line between knowing and not knowing, these findings suggest alternative viewpoints. There's no end to their narratives.

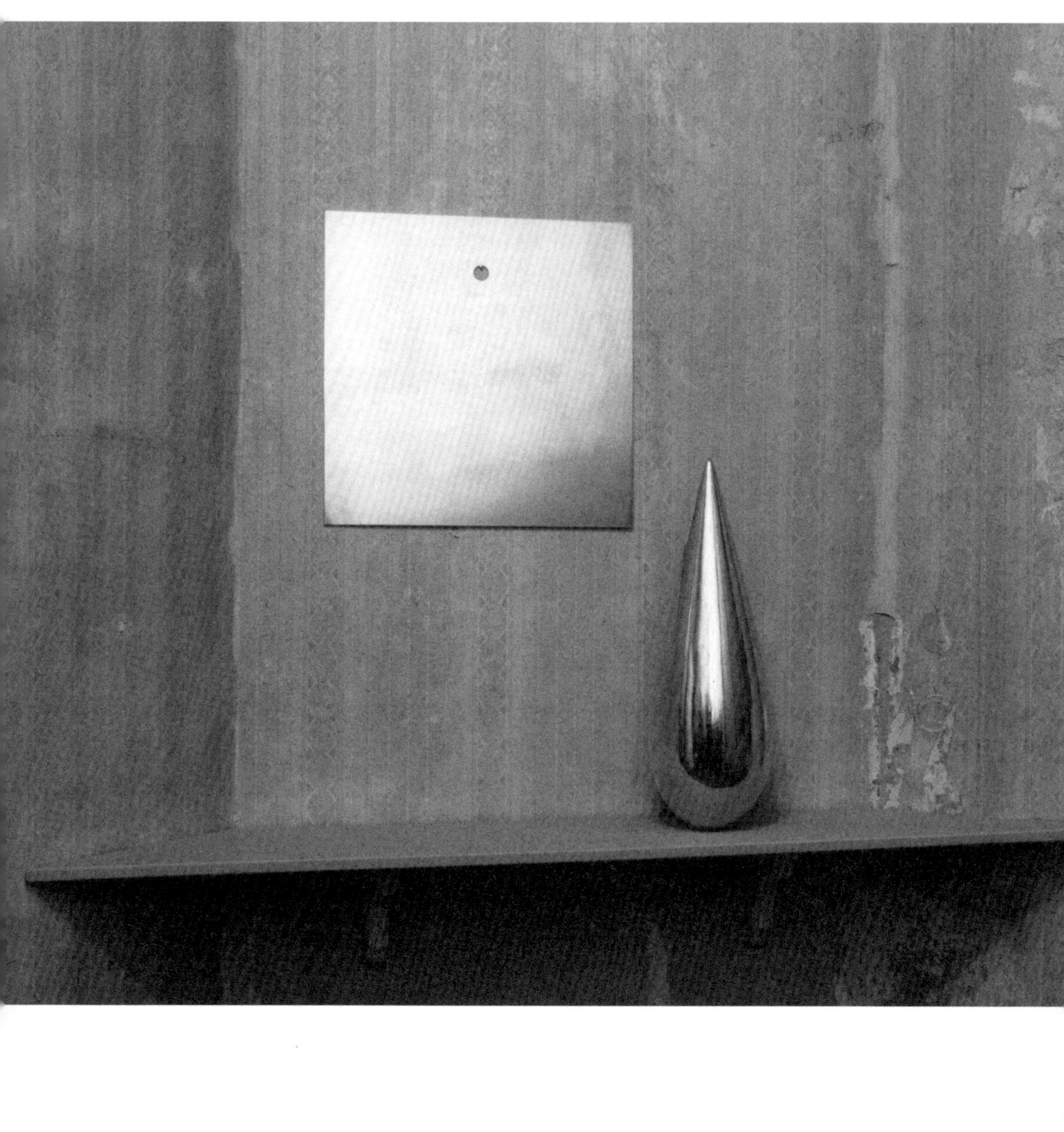

The Polder Dandy Takes a Stroll

H a r m e n   B r e t h o u w e r

In 1992, Harmen Brethouwer started a project that is still going on to this very day, a project to which he will possibly devote the rest of his life. Driven by a desire to do something that no one had ever done before, his aim was to create an oeuvre incorporating all existing art as we know it. What he had in mind was a real contest with the history of art, but not like some Picasso, who took other people's art by the horns, like a mad bull does with a toreador. Brethouwer wanted to operate in a more subtle manner, seeing himself as a medieval copyist rather who, having ended up in our time, devotes his life here to the study of human-made artefacts and art styles. In the margin of all the documents lying in front of him he wants to make notes that question our understanding of art.

What form would be best suited to an ambition to do more than just make comments, and to make the tree of art bear fruit? What would an oeuvre uniting various, completely different art styles look like? What would concrete works uniting miscellaneous, sometimes even conflicting styles, look like?

Harmen Brethouwer, *Untitled (Cone and Panel)*, 1996, bronze/ brass, stainless steel nail, height 66 cm / 50 × 50 cm.

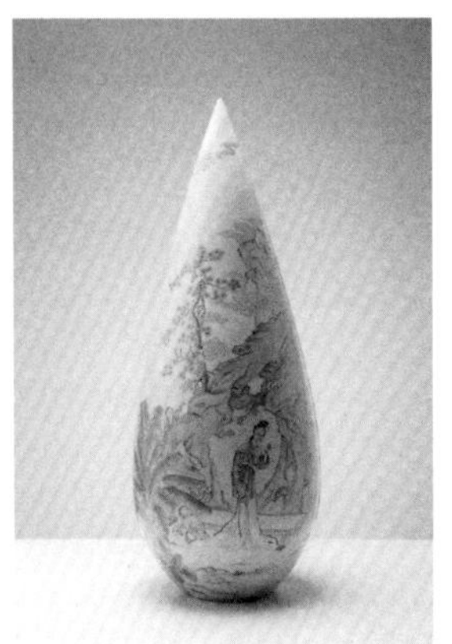

1 Harmen Brethouwer, *Looking for Dragon Droppings*, 2013, faience, height 89 cm. Edition of 3. Collaborators: Li Xiaoqian and Royal Tichelaar.

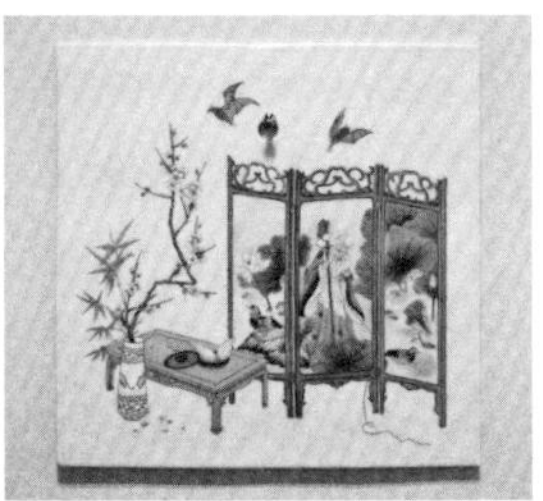

2 Harmen Brethouwer, *May Your Divorce Be Happy*, 2013, porcelain, stainless steel peg, 45 × 45 cm. Collaborator: Li Xiaoqian.

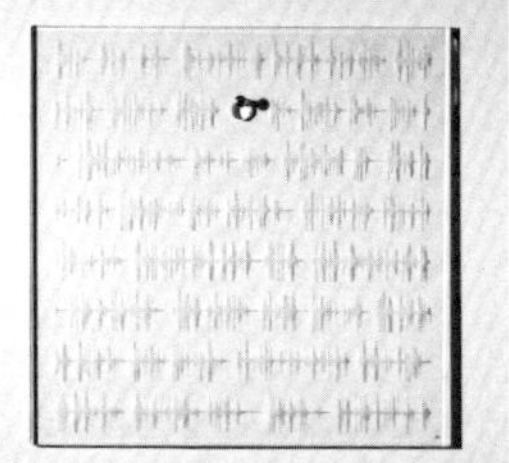

3 Harmen Brethouwer, *In Vitro Biography—Kurt Schwitters*, 2015, optical glass with internal laser marking, stainless-steel peg, 50 × 50 cm. Collaborators: Hester Eymes and Laserit.

Harmen Brethouwer decided to design a collection of objects, which were to embody his ideas. The uniqueness of these ideas would be emphasized, among other things, by special and precious materials. He quickly came to realize that he would never be able to complete this task on his own: the artist needed others. What started out as an artistic magnum opus thus assumed the dimensions of a business enterprise that needed to be secured far and wide. By the year of writing, 2007, a small but very fine oeuvre has come into existence, the result of both the artist's efforts and those of a host of other individuals, ranging from craftsmen (execution) to collectors (funding). In a closely-knit group of objects, a whole range of topics from many times and places have found a place.

What is interesting here is the appearance of these objects. For instance, *Three-Magi Paint*, dating from 2004, was developed by the artist to enable him to paint his own works and transform them into *Gifts*. The work consists of three pots of paint, in the colours gold (rich sheen), incense (cream colour) and myrrh (matt). Medieval paintings show the Three Magi offering the Holy Infant the precious gifts, which are rendered in such a way that they seem to be real. Harmen Brethouwer's paint is also for sale, and people can use the three colours for interior decoration as they see fit. A traditional, very rich textural expression, which we know from a much earlier art period, is translated here into a minimal-like form.

Works of this kind are curiosities, of course. The artist characterizes them as superfluous things, but to my mind this explanation is a dandyish statement, behind which the artist is hiding, in a certain sense. Each of his objects tells a story; in any case, they are all coded in such a way that these may be inferred from them.[1, 2, 3] And I think that Harmen

Brethouwer has a bigger plan with these stories. With his work he wants to actualize little lines from the history of art—often of more interest to artists than to historians. In that way he tells stories that would otherwise remain untold and would probably be forgotten. His stories are touching, witty, and imaginative. Also, because it often combines ideas and styles that the history of art has put at a great distance from each other, his art is a provocation directed at the keepers of the art canon.

Situating the Work

Harmen Brethouwer's work is of a hybrid nature that fits in with the art context of the 1980s. In his oeuvre you will encounter both the ascesis/control found in conceptual art and the exuberance of appropriation art. The idea behind Harmen Brethouwer's oeuvre, for the first time taking concrete shape around 1992, was at complete odds with the spirit of the time. In the art climate of the 1990s, for instance, the socially-oriented relational aesthetics art literally took to the streets. The 1980s had been quite different: it had been a fertile period, bringing forth original, plastic oeuvres. At times, artists managed to override a conceptual heritage featuring an iconoclastic commandment as well as a ban on everything fanciful and colourful (both figuratively and literally!), by striking out on a completely new course. Appropriation artists such as Mike Bidlo and Elaine Sturtevant copied master pieces from the art canon, from Picasso (Bidlo) to Johns (Sturtevant), and in the Netherlands Rob Scholte, bloodthirsty like a vampire, sucked dry the complete Western art tradition.

Certain artists, however, practised a delicate type of appropriation art, a fact that was overlooked sometimes in the

4 In 2023, of the three parts only the *Chinoiseries* still exist, *Art Deco* and *Minimal* have been integrated into the rubric *Miscellanea*, and certain other themes have become independent.

1990s. In Los Angeles there was Stephen Prina, who in his oeuvre presents and actualizes a complete tradition of abstract art. Around the same time, Rodney Graham was at work in Vancouver, whose supplements to the Romantic art tradition met with some acclaim. And in New York Sherrie Levine made her annotations to modern masters like Duchamp, Klein and Bloßfeld. Harmen Brethouwer creates a delicate type of appropriation art. In his oeuvre, he assimilates cultural forms and motifs, piling his own things on top of these, resulting in works that look like palimpsests. In order to channel his ambition, he decided to make use of two basic shapes: a cone and a panel. In his work, these travel through time. Executed in all kinds of materials, they appear as contemporary art, but at the same time they are distanced from our time, because they are deeply connected to the art and art traditions lying behind us.

The cone and the panel are executed in three styles: *Chinoiseries*, *Art Deco* and *Minimal*.[4] The three categories refer to history, decoration, and the present. Harmen Brethouwer:

> I make use of the atmospheres evoked by these styles in order to arrange the work along main lines. I started arranging it like this after the first five years, during which I did something different in each work, but this was unworkable. The chinoiseries are refined and full of detail, the emphasis is on the symbolic, on historical concepts, on the exotic (concepts that have nearly been forgotten, that do not play a role in current events); the Art Deco work is colourful/extravagant, with the decorative element leading (this is not restricted to the Art Deco style); the minimal series, however, is transparent/ sober, and presents us with the essential and the basic.

The division between the styles is a superficial one, by the way, the connections and combinations are much more important.[5]

The ideas for his oeuvre took shape during a period of roughly two years, in which he took the time to chart a new course. Oddly enough, he arrived at the opposite of what, as a young artist, he had deemed important. His first work, influenced as it was by minimal art and concept art, had an ascetic appearance. Typically, the kind of radical work that wanted to break with the history of art. Around 1990, Brethouwer did an about-face, exuberantly embracing that very same history of art. He wants to convey a characteristic artistic experience: all art that has ever been created, is on the same level. Through the very intensity with which art speaks to us, in our time, it may come to have a topical interest.

In order to be able to represent all categories of art, Harmen Brethouwer opted for two shapes, both in 2D and 3D. To tell stories with his work, he needed shapes that were empty and open enough to serve as vehicles for projections. In part, the inspiration for this idea came from the work of Allan McCollum, an American who, in the early 1990s, was well-known in the Netherlands as well. Brethouwer was particularly inspired by his endless series of dummy sculptures, entitled *Perfect Vehicles*.[6]

About his 3D work Harmen Brethouwer writes:

One of the sculpture's characteristics was to be that it could have all kinds of sizes without this changing the character of its shape or, as Robert Morris puts it: 'The size range of useless 3D things is a continuum between the monument and the ornament.'—And there are more requirements I [HB] want the sculpture to meet: autonomy, anthropomorphic/monolithic/blank—all in the

5 Quotations taken from conversations (on 11 October and 15 November 2006 in Zeist) and email correspondence (October through December 2006) with Harmen Brethouwer.

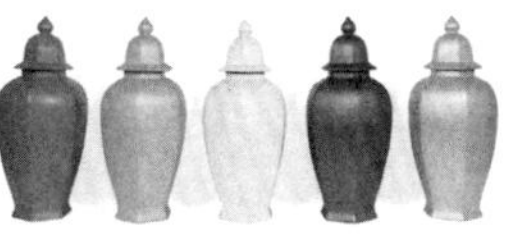

6a Allan McCollum, *5 Perfect Vehicles*, 1988.

6b Allan McCollum, *5 Plaster Surrogates*, 1982–90.

service of its model function.

And about the 2 D work he writes:

> I wanted the square (used so often, it has to be universal)
> to coincide with the object nature of the work, hence a
> panel, but as a carrier that is not autonomous enough: at
> the same time, it should be clear that we are dealing with
> a *tabula rasa* here, the panel should remain autonomous,
> irrespective of what is going to take place on it. That was
> a big problem, but the hole, which also serves as an eye
> to hang the panel on, proved to be the solution!

Sources

This artist celebrates two opposing forces, his oeuvre being
extremely meticulous and extremely capricious at the same
time. These opposites recur in the works: poised/understated
and at the same time exuberant/euphoric, so both contained
and high-spirited, and as regards contents rather explosive, in
fact. Take the Scottish ceramic cone, *Au Tartan* (1999), for

328

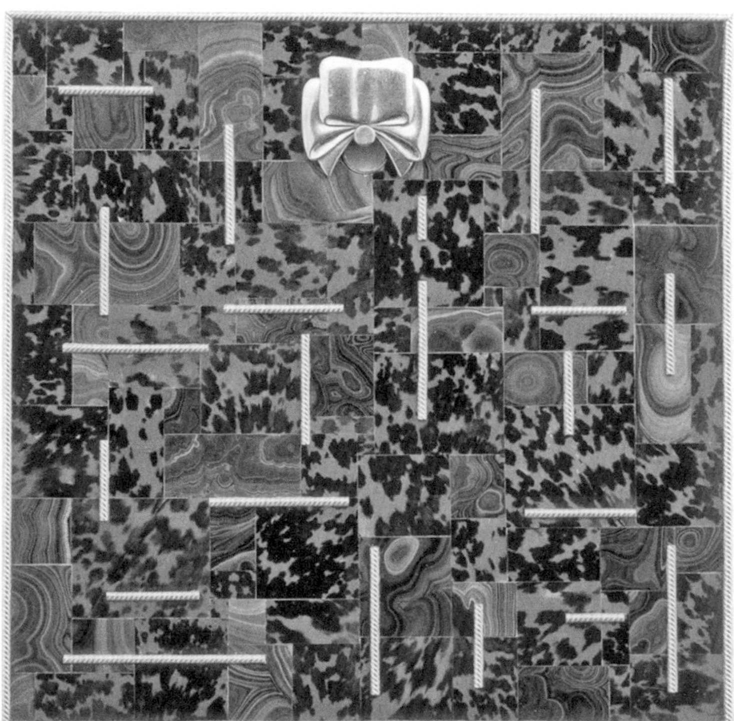

7   Harmen Brethouwer, *La Grève Perlée*, 2003, malachite, tortoise and gilded bronze on
panel, brass peg, 39 × 39 cm. Collaborator: Frans van den Oever.

instance: for the most part, it is covered in tartan motifs belonging to the important MacDonald clan from Sleat, which are hemmed in, however, by other pieces of tartan and grubby repair patches, and are dethroned as it were. Explosive combinations are also to be found in *La Grève Perlée* (2003), a panel made of tortoiseshell, malachite and gilded bronze parts.[7] This geometric composition is somewhat similar to Mondrian's *Pier and Ocean*, but it has been executed in materials and colours belonging to a decadent English gentlemen's club; the pinnacle being the gilded bow mounted above thc hole. And talking about explosivity: in *Delft Waves* (2004), a series of twelve panels, restrained temperament literally comes to the surface. These modern seascapes, variations on the typically Dutch marine genre, are computer-calculated representations of the sea, that is to say, of the height of the waves in different weather conditions, ranging from a gentle breeze to an apocalyptical storm.

This book introduces Harmen Brethouwer's oeuvre to us: the artist takes the floor himself, appearing a bit like a ringmaster in a circus who paints an alluring picture of the beautiful things the audience may expect. His collection manifests itself as a festive parade, a colourful pageant of panels and cones![8] Because the artist speaks to us about his work very eloquently, it is possible for me at this point to focus on the work's deeper structure.

One of the paradoxes in Harmen Brethouwer's work is that it accommodates the greatest impurity possible in a pure way: in fact, it brings 'good' and 'evil' together. In the obsessive manner with which it is often given its shape, this theme is mainly to be found in religion (rather than in art). Thus emerges the spirit of a religious phenomenon, well-known in the Dutch context: Protestantism (an especially big theme in Dutch literature).

329

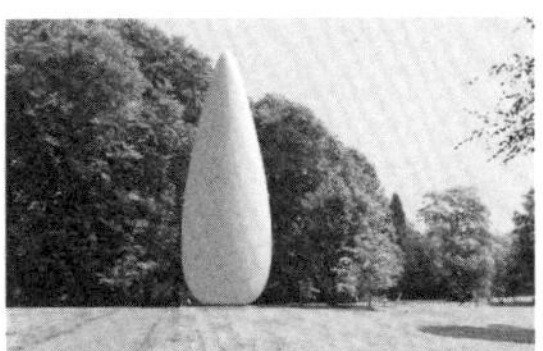

8a Harmen Brethouwer, *Landmark (Proposal for Sonsbeek)*, 2001, Lambda print on aluminium, 79 × 121 cm (framed). Collaborator: Janneke Bergmans.

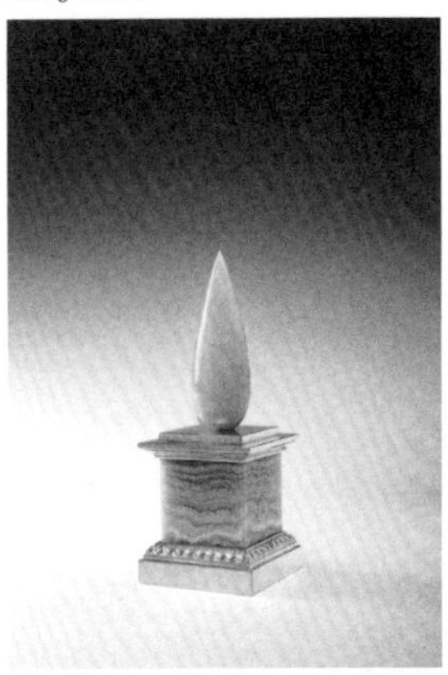

8b Harmen Brethouwer, *Bibelot (model 4:1)*, 2010, chrysoprase, chalcedony, gilded silver, height 11 cm. Collaborator: Tommaso Pestelli.

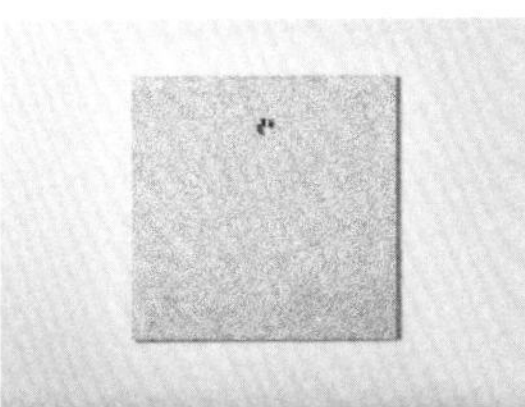

8c Harmen Brethouwer, *Broken White—piece by piece (The Lacquer Tree Series)*, 2015, Japanese lacquer and eggshell on panel, stainless steel peg, 65 × 65 cm. Collaborators: Sergej Kirilov and Marina Korotkaja.

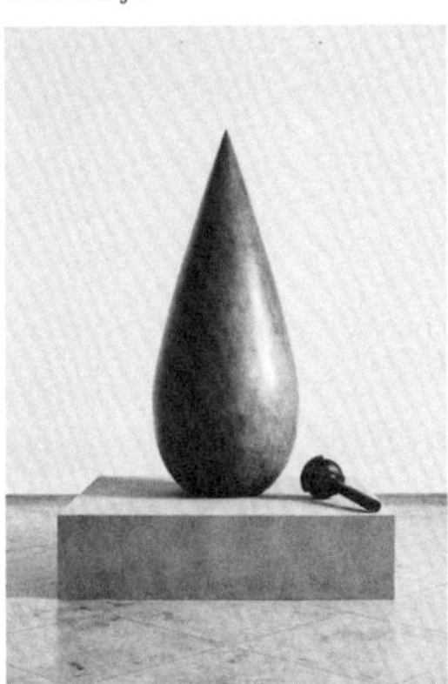

8d Harmen Brethouwer, *Bell Bronze (E)*, 2019, bronze, stainless steel, with metal and leather hammer, height 100 cm. Collaborator: Royal Eijsbouts.

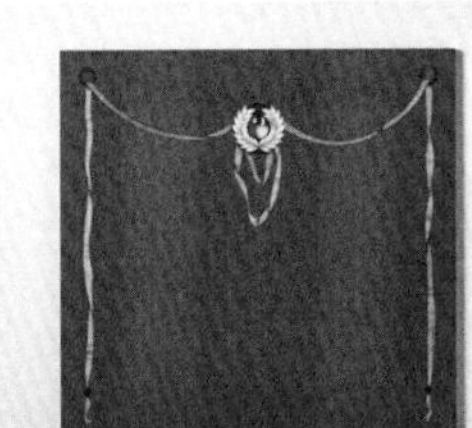

8e Harmen Brethouwer, *Historical Hommage to the Square 03*, 2015, marquetry, stainless steel peg, 50 × 50 cm. Collaborator: Sergej Kirilov.

Between 1984 and 1989 Harmen Brethouwer created sculptures which, like his recent work in fact, were vehicles for projections. The shape of these sculptures was extremely ascetic: made of MDF boards, the sculptures consisted of one or usually just two connecting elements. A work could be composed of a horizontal and a vertical board, having that typical green-grimy colour. The works had pregnant titles, for instance *Sculpture Accustomed to Content,* or *Sculpture Accustomed to Invalidity* (the artist regarded them as an answer to Carl Andre's sculptures). And there were untitled sculptures, looking like a pillory with holes or a pillory to which a notice was attached with a piece of rope, reading: 'Ada and I are not planning on having children'. These works sprang from a deep-seated feeling, the artist wanted them to be the cause of a religious strife about art.

Harmen Brethouwer: 'Shame was the secret weapon. I wanted people to be ashamed of these sculptures. I was ashamed of them myself. I wrote complete disquisitions on what I wanted with these sculptures, Kierkegaard being my main influence'. The difficulty in interpreting these works does not only arise from their unusual appeal to shame as a human reaction/emotion, but also from the fact that they were destroyed by the artist, who wanted to distance himself

330

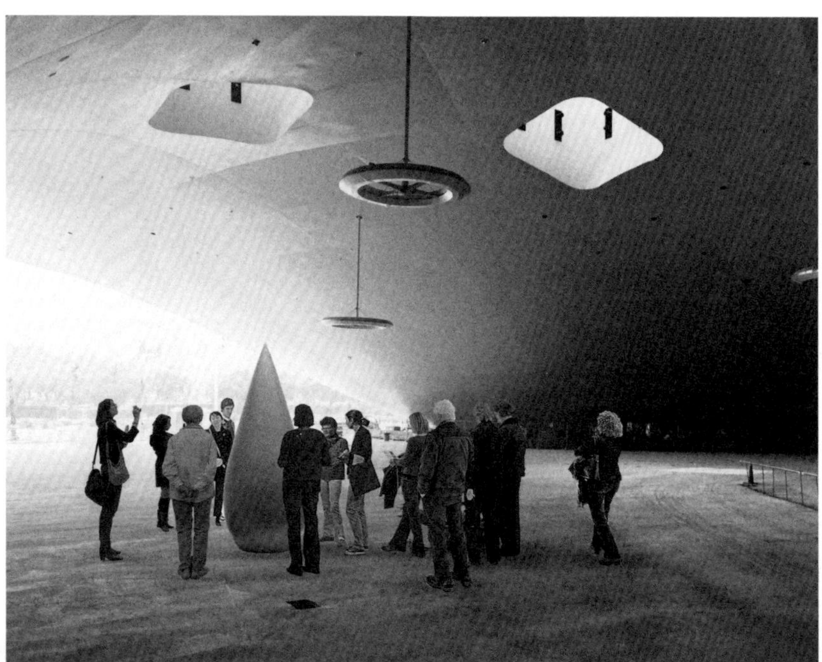

8f Harmen Brethouwer, *Project for a Large Bell Bronze,* 2015. Collaborator: Mecanoo.

radically from these sculptures. We can, however, ask questions. An interesting factor in these works is the combination of Minimal Art—that American art form celebrating space, openness, the urge for expansion—and a typical Dutch feeling, something very small: we are here but at the same time we are not…

Possibly the artist, by creating these sculptures, was able to bid farewell to an artistic trend that had gone straight to the core of his being. For it is obvious from the form he found for his work from 1992 onwards, that he has liberated himself from the, indeed peremptory, form language of Minimal Art (it is exactly this liberation that enabled him to elaborate the idea—or a model—of this art form in his own art).

We will probably have to go back even further in time to find out where Harmen Brethouwer's oeuvre springs from (or could spring from: for the artist's biography does not necessarily coincide with the work, what's more, quite often an artist wants to rise above just that…). His youth was determined by a specific experience. Until he was seventeen, he attended meetings of The Gathering of the Faithful every Sunday. This religion, which resembles the Pentecostal church and which, in fact, has also come from America to Europe, has special ceremonies or rituals. The Faithful gather in a room boasting no adornment, pulpit or organ. There is singing, though. Men sit apart from women/children. The morning service passes on the basis of Inspirations. Men who feel called upon, especially the elders seated at a special table, spontaneously make a verbal contribution. In practice this comes down to two or three people, there are quite a few moments in which Nothing is happening. In the afternoon service some of the elders engage in exegesis. On the table there are two objects: a silver plate with bread and a silver chalice with wine. That was the image presented to

Harmen Brethouwer every Sunday, until he was seventeen years old.

Art springs from art, people say and, when we look at the development of the language of art, this seems to be correct. But the deep-seated motives for creating art have their origin elsewhere. To give just one example: misery and redemption, the two states of mind pervading a complete tradition of American country music, are based on religious experiences that have a lot, if not everything, to do with the life lessons of the first European Americans in a new country, where they had to make do with the knowledge and experiences from the old world which they still carried with them.

A silver plate and a silver chalice stand on a table. Can we think of a more beautiful image of the concept of purification, the idea that by performing certain rituals one may come to terms with art as we know it?

On 3 December, 2006, the artist sent me a text, a veritable manifesto on how he sees his art in a development of art that is devoted to the idea. I have put this text in a separate section, so that the reader may decide for themselves what is more important in the genesis of Harmen Brethouwer's work: tradition or a childhood experience.

1   Fontana cuts through the membrane of representative art, allowing us a view of the quintessence of art, the realization that there is not a single quality intrinsic to art.

2   Yves Klein steps through this opening to 'the other side', leaving all qualities behind—the only thing he takes along is the sensitivity to art, that what is intrinsic to art; in its pure form this is a concept, Le Vide, it asks us to believe in art without any reservations.

3   Robert Morris couples this concept with a concrete form again, creating 'blank forms', empty sculptures that test our faith and, if that test is passed successfully, our faith in art may then be coupled with any form, in principle, anything may be art in the light of the following statement by Morris: 'Art is primarily a situation in which one assumes an attitude of reacting to some of one's awareness as art'.

4   In this space I place my project... By means of two specially designed 'Blank Forms', a sculpture and a painting, both reduced to a model, which are the perfect vehicles for embodying the most diverse definitions of art. This comes in the shape of stories about materials, techniques, styles and other details, each of them important issues, which, though not intrinsic to art, do want to make a statement on the nature of art and on the sensibility to art. I explore all kinds of definitions of art in detail, looking for the connections. You could call me a guide, steering those qualities through Fontana's hole, trying to make the public sensitive to them. To pass on this history of sensitivity to art, that's what I have in mind in my oeuvre.

An Artist's Life

In Harmen Brethouwer's oeuvre lives an artist character thirsting for grandeur and delicacy. He wants to reach beyond the horizons of thought; a comparison with an illusionist or escape artist forces itself upon us, this type of artiste training the body to reach beyond physical boundaries. Harmen Brethouwer reaches beyond mental boundaries.

Piece by piece his works make a statement on what art might be: this statement is different each time, the artist refuses to let himself be caught. In this he is similar to a modern dandy, shattering art codes with ideas that are deep and frivolous at the same time. With his works he provokes the art community and its views on taste, just as the nineteenth-century dandy challenged the bourgeoisie with behaviour and statements that still fascinate us because of their often unparalleled yet very charismatic combination of solemnity and mirth.

The historical position of the dandy in the social sparring match of his time is interesting. Being both a participant and outsider, he shot his arrows at whomever he chose, his superior irony keeping him out of the firing line whenever he himself happened to be the target. An exhibition of Harmen Brethouwer may create the same impression: this artist shoots his arrows at art, but does so in a highly ironic manner. We see a precisely calculated arrangement of objects, made of unusual materials. They have a paradoxical air: in the context of an exhibition, they quickly become showpieces, but there is an atmosphere of self-mockery surrounding them.

The work is at home everywhere and nowhere. Work and context always enter into a rather uncomfortable relationship. That is because the work takes place in fringe areas (for example as the result of the meeting between minimal and decadent); there is not a single context that fits like a glove. Sometimes the work even confusingly disappears into the context, such as for instance the chinoiseries in an exhibition at the Princessehof Museum in Leeuwarden: they were put on display amidst historical objects, as a result of which no one saw that this was contemporary art. An unintentional effect, for what artist wants to be invisible?

The artist resignedly bears with the reactions, and sometimes the lack of reactions to his art. In this he is like the figure of Pierrot, the white-faced clown, which he himself depicted on one of his cones (in white relief) in 2003. A figure cultivating an inner world, full of thoughts and emotions that remain hidden to the outside world. Perhaps his own Pierrot figure was partly inspired by a sculpture by Lucio Fontana, which has been keeping him company in his thoughts for years and years, viz. a ceramic *Arlecchino* dating from 1948, designed in such a way that it seems as if its body is under immense pressure from outside forces from all sides.[9] Not at all a romantic image of an artist's life. We know Pierrot from the paintings by Watteau. Pierrot was one of the icons of Art Deco, but it is also impossible to imagine him being absent in the art of later masters, think of Picasso's harlequins, for instance. On 4 December, 2006, Harmen Brethouwer sent me a photograph per email: Robert Morris, standing upright in one of his *blank forms* (an open box, in fact).[10] The artist like a waxwork… or like a Pierrot, ready to suffer whatever the outside world is going to throw at him and to hold up a mirror to that world by means of his white face. Something similar goes on in Morris' work. Morris made his sculptures from underlayment and painted them a very nondescript grey colour. He used these sculptures in his performances, reacting to them with his body, thus making clear this was art. For the forms themselves exuded nothing that would justify this idea, being completely blank. Morris made the following statement on this: 'Blank Form is like life, essentially empty, allowing plenty of room for disquisitions of its nature and mocking each in its turn'.

The green work Harmen Brethouwer created between 1984 and 1989 was along the same lines (he did not know Morris at the time). He wrote that his sculptures were meant to bring about a religious strife about art, with shame being the secret weapon. M D F board sculptures, blank captors of

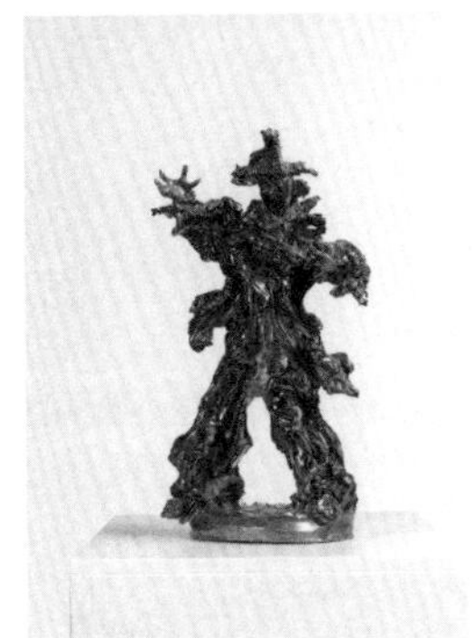

9 Lucio Fontana, *Arlecchino*, 1948.

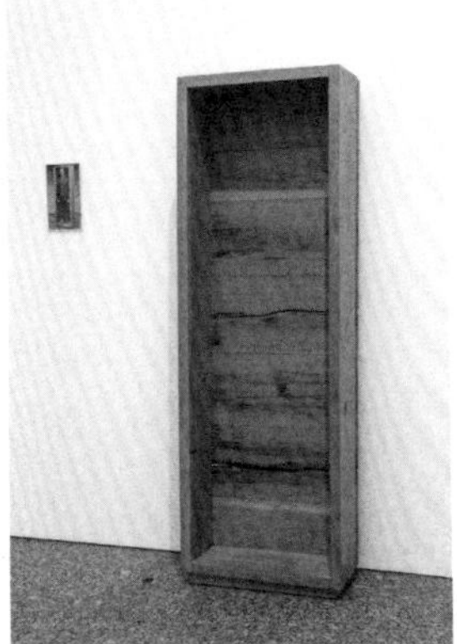

10 Robert Morris, *Box for Standing*, 1961. On the left side of the empty box, a photograph shows the artist standing inside his box.

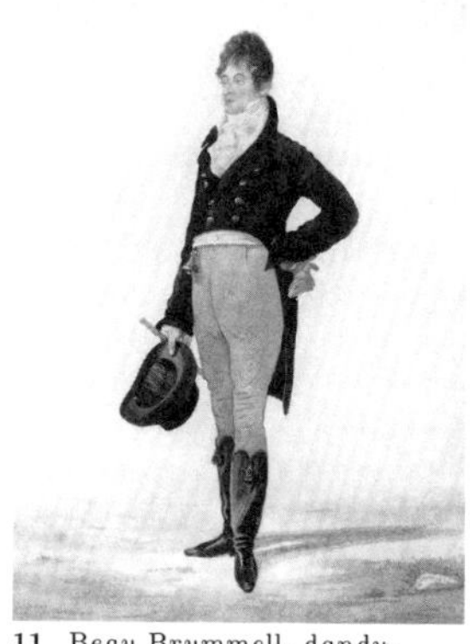

11 Beau Brummell, dandy.

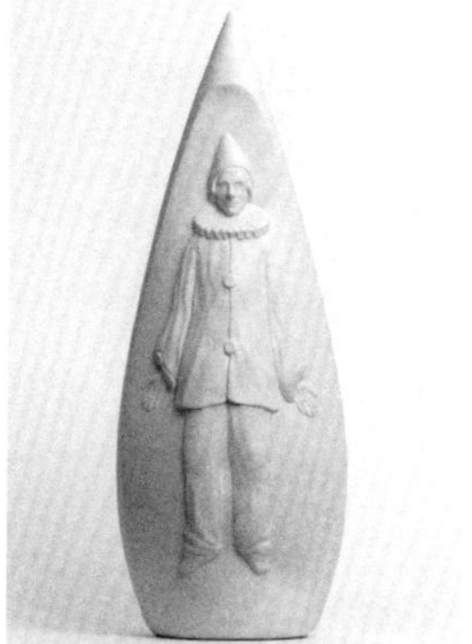

12 Harmen Brethouwer, *Le Salut*, 2003, porcelain, height 37 cm. Edition of 10. Collaborators: Sander Luske and Jan Broekstra.

projections on the one hand, on the other vehicles for expositions on life that mock themselves. It is essential in the work now, Harmen Brethouwer writes, that everything that has been added to it may also be washed away again: 'If I had the feeling that it would really stick, I would not be able to do it this way'.

So, Harmen Brethouwer considers his materials, motifs and stories indeed as blank forms at which the beholder may fire his or her projections. Purity, beauty, openness: these seem to be the qualities he advocates, which he gives shape to with his work. I call this artist a polder dandy,[11] because in his view, the history of art, into which he likes to make little excursions, is a landscape hemmed in and fenced in by humans and in need of a bit of proliferation. It is surprising to realize that this proliferation, once brought about, is in the service of a desire for purity. Embracing impurity proves to be no more than one element in an oeuvre inviting us to reflect on our own ritual interaction with art.[12]

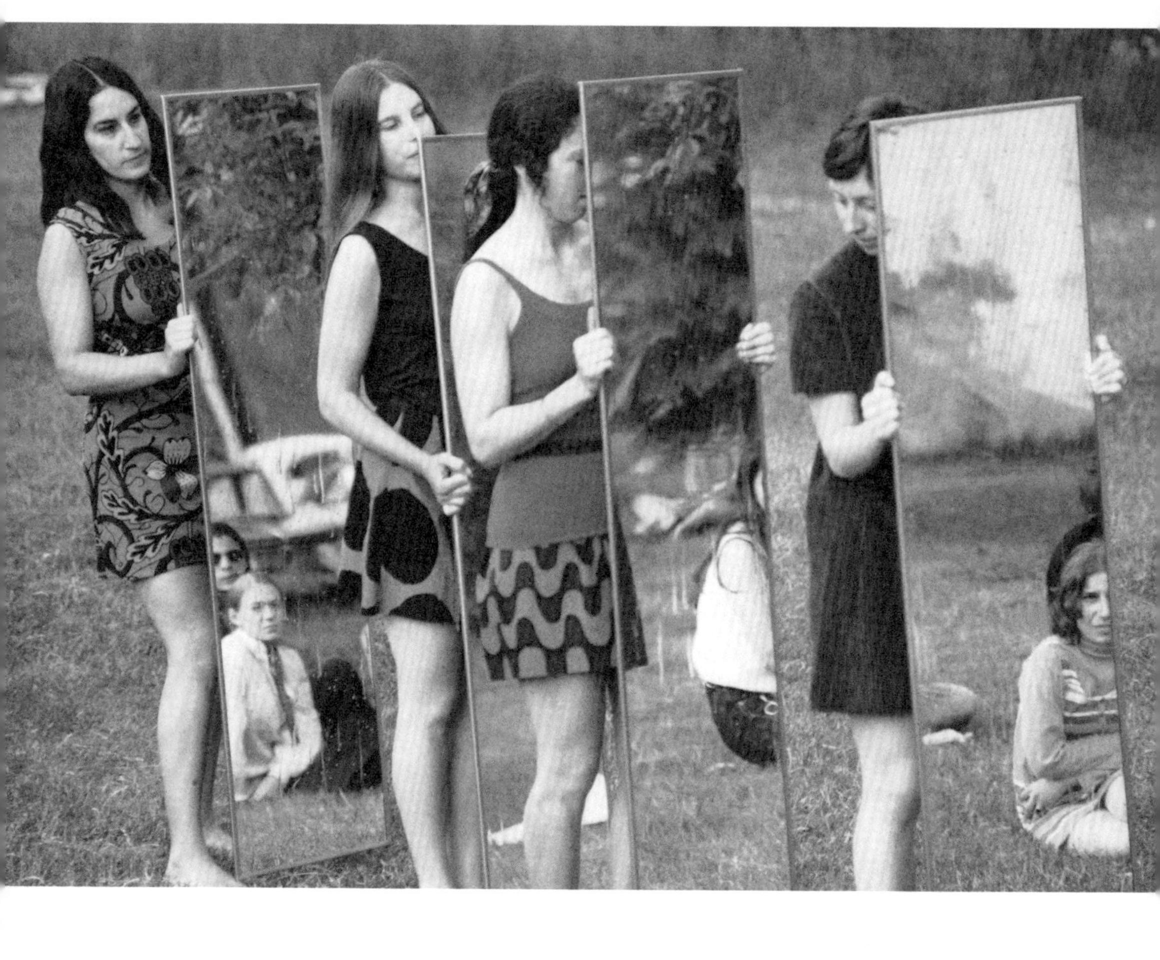

Shouting Through a Paper Cone

J o a n   J o n a s

Joan Jonas' work takes as its subject the precise rendering of inner life on all its imprecision. In her early performances, metaphors about humans and their social surroundings are concealed somewhat, but in later work the symbolism becomes overt. A particular set of props provides Jonas with company through the years. They are tools to transform such things as dreams, the will, fear, desire and longing for beauty, so that the world can be addressed in those terms. After a certain point in her career, storytelling finds a way into the work and becomes crucial. Jonas uses ancient tales as well as stories from the present to reflect her early motifs and themes and puts them into a larger context.

The development of the artist's production follows a cyclical pattern in which the early work already contains certain concerns that would crystallize over time. It is possible to distinguish several stages in the work's development and this text is built around three of them. One exemplary work of Jonas' (or a number of connected works) will be my guide at each stage. Much of her oeuvre, as it is theatrical by nature and hence cherishes the moment it is presented before an

339

Joan Jonas, *Mirror Piece I*, 1969, live performance Bard College, Annandale-on-Hudson, New York, 2016. Photo: Joan Jonas.

audience, is no longer with us in its original form. It has vanished into history. But I will step ahead light-footedly because the secondary sources that have remained speak of the presence the work once had. To begin, let's chart the ground that bore this body.

1968–1972: The Hardcore Years

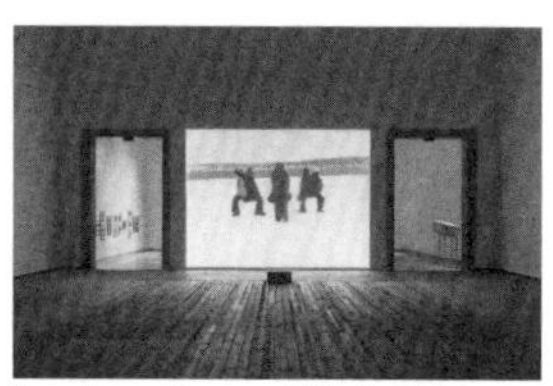

1a Joan Jonas, *Wind*, 1968, video of performance, Haus der Kunst, München, 2022, installation view. Photo: Maximilian Geuter.

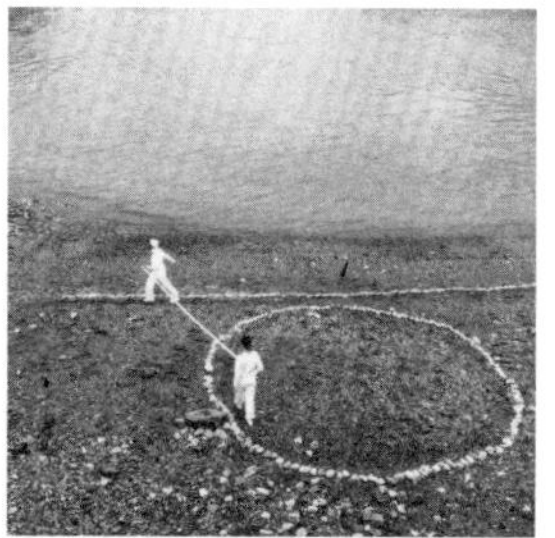

1b Joan Jonas, *Delay, Delay*, 1972, video still of performance.

Toughness is a dominant trait of Joan Jonas' early work. Outdoor pieces such as *Wind* (1968) and *Delay, Delay* (1972) are about setting the mind free in a hostile environment.[1] Indoor performances such as *Mirror Piece II* (1970), *Choreomania* (1971) and *Organic Honey's Vertical Roll* (1972) express the will to stand one's ground when besieged by exterior forces. The time when these works were made was a moment when individual freedom was the ultimate goal and it was clear what had to be contested: firstly, authority and everything to do with authorities, the very notion of something or someone above you telling you what to do; and secondly, every tendency towards conformity, as an outflow of the social pressure to adapt yourself and be good.

A brief glance at the above-mentioned pieces—to use Jonas' term for her performances—makes it clear that the work has, in current terms, superb formal qualities. Yet it also suggests that the pieces were Jonas' personal revolts, spirited by 1960s rage. They could even be read as attempts to exorcize a conservative streak.

For example, *Mirror Piece II*, choreographed for performers holding mirrors and moving around a small crowd, is a work that metaphorically represents the space that we together inhabit. What it shows is the exorcism of a defeatist view of social relations, or at least that is the view of this performance I want to propose here.[2] In form, the work is both strong and brittle. The choreography establishes a specific equilibrium that could turn about at any given moment. The performers hold mirrors in front of and between their bodies, the mirrors reflecting both themselves and the people in the audience. The fragility of the social fabric, and how it is to manoeuvre, is made tangible by the careful movement of the performers who remain in the same space as the audience throughout.

The work reveals concerted social action and its complex patterns of behaviour as it builds up in a public forum: approaching one another, seeking distance, navigating edges. The difference between real social action, with the cautiousness that would imply, and the performance suggests that a new social situation may be opening up. The (emotive) movement from inside to outside promises a great potential within reach. By way of contrast, *Performance/Audience/Mirror* (1977) by Dan Graham reverses the movement as the artist takes on the central role, describing the outward appearance of himself and his audience, and what this means in terms of physical posture and behaviour. With Jonas, we are in a moment where we can believe that people could really open up and see their fellow humans without prejudice.

Jonas' early work hints at such possibilities for change. Critical questions pertaining to social space and how to navigate in it are dealt with quite overtly. For instance, *Choreomania* alludes to our urge to control other people's steps. The piece is built around the question of who is pulling the strings and the conflict that inevitably follows. A large wall, partially clad with mirrors, is suspended from the ceiling. As it is moved by the performers, it moves them in turn.

Another work, *Organic Honey's Vertical Roll*,[3] is a performance featuring the artist herself as Organic Honey, a

2 The artist's work is extensively documented in *Joan Jonas: Scripts and Descriptions 1968—1982*, Berkeley, University Art Museum/ Eindhoven, Stedelijk Van Abbemuseum, 1983, exhibition catalogue; *Joan Jonas: Works 1968—1994*, Amsterdam, Stedelijk Museum, 1994; *Joan Jonas: Performance Video Installation 1968—2000*, Stuttgart, Galerie der Stadt Stuttgart/Berlin, Hatje Cantz Verlag, 2001, exhibition catalogue. I am greatly indebted to the third source. It contains Jonas' descriptions of her work, and Joan Simon's text 'Scenes and Variations: An Interview with Joan Jonas', pp. 25–35.

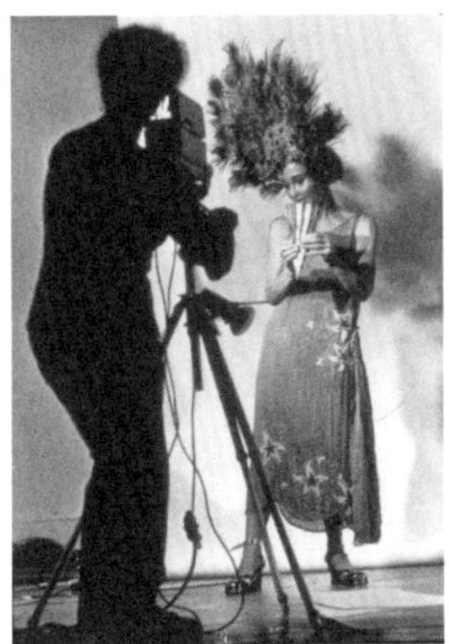

3a Joan Jonas, *Organic Honey's Vertical Roll*, 1972, performance, Musée Galliera, Paris, 1972. Camera: Babette Helligers. Photo: Beatrice Helligers.

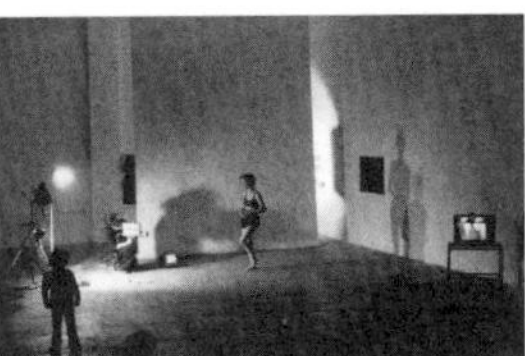

3b Joan Jonas, *Organic Honey's Vertical Roll*, 1972, performance, Galleria Toselli, Milan, 1973.

4 *Joan Jonas: Performance Video Installation 1968–2000*, p. 108.

suave lady wearing a mask in order to counter her own reflection and the projection of a self-image convenient to others. In the video that is part of this performance—or film as Jonas calls it, as it mimics the vertical movement of film through a projector—exorcizing evil becomes a very plastic thing. Scrolling images run from the top to the bottom on the monitor, an effect caused by a distorted video-signal. We see parts of a female body, pictures of the artist in different guises and postures. She appears in a fractured state, tumbling again and again, never touching base. There is something very disturbing about her movements, caught up as these are in a relentless rhythm. Stiff, metallic sounds of a spoon hitting a mirror intensify the viewing experience. Here is a work that demands full attention, the artist has put the image of woman on the anvil and she strikes hard.

'This began as anger', said Jonas later. 'I was interested in translating emotions'.[4] What comes to the fore here is a desire to make the inner-self talk, and Jonas' nakedness must be read as a metaphor for this inner region. It is what makes her work stand out alongside the bare minimalist work of the time. But Jonas' naked appearance has yet another, deeper meaning. It shows the artist as the source, and does so without the slightest reservation.

Organic Honey's Vertical Roll falls into the category of classic performance art from the 1960s and 1970s. Those works, however, also raise a question: what happens to the source over time? Jonas, with her naked body on the anvil, is one case. Chris Burden, crawling on the pavement across twenty meters of broken glass on Main Street, LA (*Through the Night Softly*, 1973), is another. And then, to mention a later, lesser-known case from my own context, the Netherlands, there is Pieter Laurens Mol, who on one occasion invited friends to come to a gig on 'Performance Day' at

De Appel in Amsterdam in 1976, with a postcard that said: 'I'd like to kiss your eyes'. All of these works feature the artist as vulnerable figure, someone who undresses in public, in the figurative and/or literal sense, revealing their naked self so as to touch others. The making of these little acts of theatre demanded the most from the artists' inner resources, as some of their authors have remarked when looking back.[5] It comes as no surprise, therefore, that Joan Jonas' work acquired other forms after this initial period in which it was stripped bare of ornamentation, and aspired to reveal what is essential in the most direct way possible.

Masks and Magic

A bejewelled and begowned woman, Organic Honey first appears in Jonas' work around 1972. She is the electronic sorceress as she likes to appear on video where her live actions are captured and transformed. This persona, who wears a mask reminiscent of the masks on the faces of Greek chorus singers, allowed Jonas to move away from her early work. What before was the movement and gesture of a naked body performing in the spotlight, now becomes a masquerade. Organic Honey is present but veiled, carrying out small actions in which props figure to reveal and hide what she has to say. They radiate a knowledge and experience that surpasses the everyday.

All the props are on a table: a big glass jar filled with water, a small shot glass, glass mirrors, a silver spoon, an old doll, a silver purse, a stone. In the performance *Organic Honey's Vertical Roll* the sorceress wears a green chiffon dress. Kneeling on the floor over a piece of paper, she slips her mask onto her head and wears it like a hat. She then

5 Chris Burden has named this as a major reason for his mid-1970s' shift to sculpture and installation. Mol, later, in 1995, 'expressed the astonishment he felt when looking back on his performances, because it seemed to him now that the potential had much more to offer than the ultimate execution, as if by its enactment the spell was broken'. See *Pieter Laurens Mol. Grand Promptness*, Breda, Artimo, 1996, p. 66.

6 Op. cit., see Note 4.

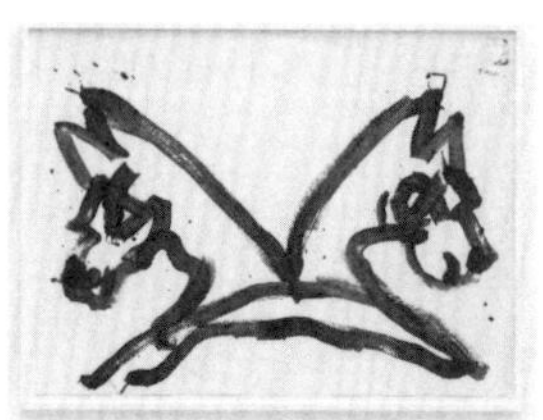

7 Joan Jonas, *Double Lunar Dogs*, 1984, performance drawing.

8 Joan Simon, 'Scents and Variations: An Interview with Joan Jonas', in *Joan Jonas. Performance Video Installation 1968—2000*, p. 27.

draws a dog's head, its top half on the bottom of the paper, its bottom half on top. All this is recorded and shown on the monitor, and, as the vertical roll bar comes down, the two halves of the drawing come together in the proper position.[6] What we see here is image-making in process, inspired by filmmaker Maya Deren's footage that was shot in Haiti of someone making a drawing in the sand again and again.[7]

Initially, Jonas was influenced by the dominant trend in the New York art scene of the 1960s: minimal art and similar experiments in music and dance. Trained as a sculptor, Jonas was drawn to Bruce Nauman's work, but it was after seeing a dance piece by choreographer Lucinda Childs in the late 1960s that Jonas knew what she wanted to do. To her, Child's dance seemed to fall between performance and sculpture. Actually, it was based on movement in architectural space and bodies covering space. The key word then was 'construction', established through repeated movement and gesture like in a Bach fugue, that did not lead to the expression of emotions but to the physical movements as such.

For a while, until about 1970, Jonas was inspired by minimal dance. But she wasn't satisfied. About the work she made when entering the New York cultural scene, she said:

> I was barely in my early performance pieces; I was in them like a piece of material, or an object that moved very stiffly, like a puppet or a figure in a medieval painting. I didn't exist as Joan Jonas, as an individual "I", only as a presence, part of the picture. I moved [...] mechanically.[8]

The quote, taken from an interview thirty years later, hints at a knot that had to be unravelled.

Minimal art has a Janus face. Striving for literalness through reduction of meaning, it focused on the form of structures and the structural relationships of objects in a space. Its nemesis was expressionism and the idea that a work could represent or be moulded out of individual emotion. Zero degree of expression: that was the goal. But once that point was reached—a radical point where art becomes a presence and a literalist type of artwork is born—other meanings do come into sight. The viewers, navigating objects in a space and projecting themselves into them, become crucial. Michael Fried argued that minimal art is theatrical as it envelops the viewer who is moving in space. Indeed, minimal art achieved something that seems to be contrary to its cool and restrained paradigm. It is the recognition that experiencing an object or structure or constellation, inevitably, evokes emotion. In its restrained visual language, minimal art brought about a refocussing on the anatomy of emotion. The knot that Jonas mentioned has to do with this. I believe that Jonas was troubled by minimal art's suppression of a symbolic potential, a claim that can be supported by a leap into the nineteenth century.

The anatomy of emotion brings us to symbolism, both as historical literature and its manifestation as visual art. Or to be more exact, it brings us to its predecessors: artists such as Odilon Redon, James Ensor, and Georges Seurat, who wanted to forge a new visual language to represent dreams and dream states, obscure emotions, and subjective perception. They were after a precise rendering of inner life, and of what happens in the realms of the mind.[9] Their art is about everything that comes before feeling. It is about states of mind and susceptibility to emotion—indeed that attitude defines a difference from the symbolists, who wallowed in feeling and its fantastic portrayal. Redon, Ensor, and Seurat were inventors of form and through it they depicted dreams, visions, hallucinations. They painted silence and stillness,

345

9 See (especially) Dario Gamboni, *Potential Images: Ambiguity and Indeterminacy in Modern Art*, London, Reaktion Books, 2002, pp. 68–85.

enchanted dances, people wearing masks. In their work, inner and outer worlds coalesce.

Form in art can delineate forms of inner life. Unhappy with what minimal art offered her in that respect, Joan Jonas created a persona to help her out. Hesitatingly, Organic Honey starts to act. The mask she wears forces her to relate to us through movement and gesture just like the actors in early cinema did, take for example Marcel Carné's *Les Enfants du Paradis* with its dreamlike, poetic narrative. The difference, of course, is that Organic Honey is a modern character. The little action she pulls off, however quiet it may seem, conveys a haunted state.

Enter the Story

10 Joan Simon, op. cit., p. 25.

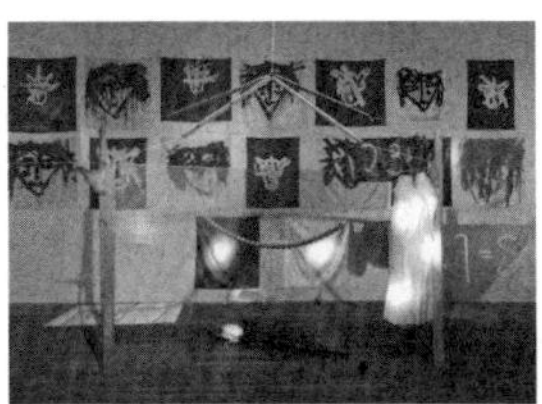

11 Joan Jonas, *The Juniper Tree*, 1976, performance set.

From 1968 onwards, Jonas realized her performances in both pastoral and urban surroundings. Grassy fields, windy beaches, city lots, gymnasiums and lofts, as well as more traditional sites offered a setting for the work.[10] Stories enter the work in the course of the 1970s and, with that, the spoken word. As a result, interiors became more suitable places to realize pieces. For example, in 1976 Jonas did a performance for children based on *The Juniper Tree*, a fairy tale written down by the Brothers Grimm. The artist recorded the text of the tale on audiotape with music and sound effects, and this became the background for her image-making, live on stage. Here, she introduced painting into the performance. Larger than life, action from the fairy tale is brought to bear on the visual realm (vivid colours enhancing the story). Red-and-white drawings are painted on red-and-white silk—'as red as blood and as white as snow'.[11]

The Juniper Tree tells the tale of a family with a wicked

stepmother who cuts up the little boy and feeds the pieces to his father. Later, the sister gathers bones and puts them under the juniper tree; a beautiful bird rises from the ground to kill the stepmother and then transforms back into the living boy. In this piece, Jonas plays three female roles: the virginal daughter, the good mother and the main character, the evil stepmother. In some parts she dances, in some she speaks, and in others she draws on the same mirror used in the early mirror works. She made different versions of the work, one of which included a ladder as a shamanistic representation of a magic tree. In the final version, a solo performance, Jonas chose to represent the story 'by going inside and allowing the demons to escape'.[12]

A similar ambition must have been the goal of the [13] solo performance *Upside Down and Backwards* (1979), out of which a video was made one year later. The piece ties together two tales, again passed on by the Brothers Grimm, to produce three stories in total. The original stories are *The Boy Who Went Out to Learn Fear*, which is told chronologically, and *The Frog Prince*, told backwards. The third story emerges as a product of the other two coming together to form a new narrative. Jonas' set consists of three painted backdrops, with props placed in front of each. The first backdrop—green and yellow—represents the prince; the second—red and yellow—is the boy, and the third—blue and yellow—the two together. Here, too, the artist projects herself into the story and becomes part of it.

What we see in these works is a wish to enter stories. On stage, the artist moves swiftly through their layers. One gets the impression that she wants to immerse herself—to go inside the fairy tales but to get out again so as to relate them to life in the present. In 1985 Jonas made *Volcano Saga*, a highlight of her oeuvre. In this performance all the layers of

347

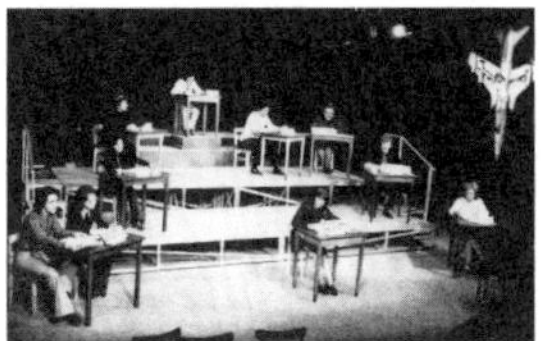

12 *Joan Jonas: Performance Video Installation 1968–2000*, p. 166.

13 Joan Jonas, *Upside Down and Backwards*, 1979, performance.

the story that were previously kept apart now melt together. The resulting video is rather surreal, with landscapes layered into bodies and the use of other special video effects. Jonas made the work at a time when the art world had lost interest in performance and video, thus we can see this work as a way to show once more that these media are apt vehicles for what art is about: projection.

Volcano Saga has a subject that we have encountered before: the transformation of a woman. Jonas herself has phrased it as follows: 'There's always a woman in my work and her role is questioned'.[14] In *Volcano Saga*, there is a woman called Gudrun, played by actress Tilda Swinton, who marries four times. In the video we hear her tell four dreams to a seer, who then interprets them. The dreams are about her marriages, the men she will wed, how they will treat her, and if their love is real. The story itself is touching; Gudrun conceives of her life and how it will unfold itself in terms of how it is connected to the lives of others. 'What is my destiny?', she asks in her dreams, and the answers speak of her fate in relation to others.

The story of *Volcano Saga* comes from the thirteenth-century Icelandic tale *Laxdaela Saga*. Jonas was struck by its straightforward character, and the way the core of the saga could relate to the fate of humans at any time. In the work, nature is a protagonist. The tale is told against the backdrop of the Icelandic landscape with its black volcanic rock and beautiful blue lagoon tempered by wind and mist. Icelanders generally believe that the nature of the landscape is so hard that it has touched the people rather than vice versa. Interestingly, the video includes shots of the typical white houses found there today in the cities and on the land. Their presence illustrates a tale Jonas tells to herself at the beginning, of an accident she had in the countryside when her car was blown off the road by the wind. The video ends with an old couple talking about how the fishing net was invented— probably by a woman, they say.

Nine years later Jonas resorts to another saga, also written down in the thirteenth century but this time originating in Ireland. *Revolted by the Thought of Known Places ... Sweeney Astray* (1994) is a performance based on an epic poem about an Irish pagan king, Sweeney, who clashes with a cleric and is cursed by him so that he morphs into a bird destined to wander the world forever.[15]

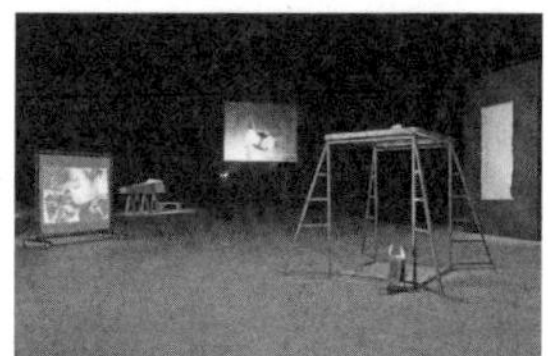

15 Joan Jonas, *Revolted by the Thought of Known Places... Sweeney Astray*, 1994, performance set.

Theatre in a Valise

In 1997 Jonas began an investigation that has continued over the years. Under the title *My New Theatre,* she develops work that follows from a rethinking of the performances and the extent to which they can live on in after-the-fact installations. The starting point may have been the solo exhibition that was held in 1994 at the Stedelijk Museum, Amsterdam. It took as its departure point the presentation of performances, both live and in the form of installations. Some earlier pieces were re-enacted and the show premiered the new work *Revolted by the Thought of Known Places ... Sweeney Astray.* This work, while conceptually strong, was a very complex production with contributions from a director, actors, a composer, and a dancer.

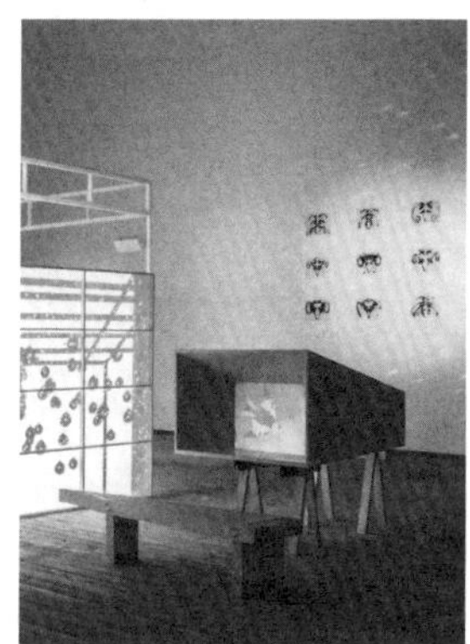

16 Joan Jonas, *My New Theater*, 1997, Haus der Kunst, München, 2022, installation view. Photo: Maximilian Geuter.

My New Theatre, seen as a collection of experiments under one generic title, can be understood as Jonas' attempt to make her working process lighter. The title refers to a portable video/cinema theatre in miniature.[16] For the presentation of the work, Jonas designed a long, narrow box (nine feet in length) that slopes from front to back and is supported by two

17 *Ibid.*, p. 135.

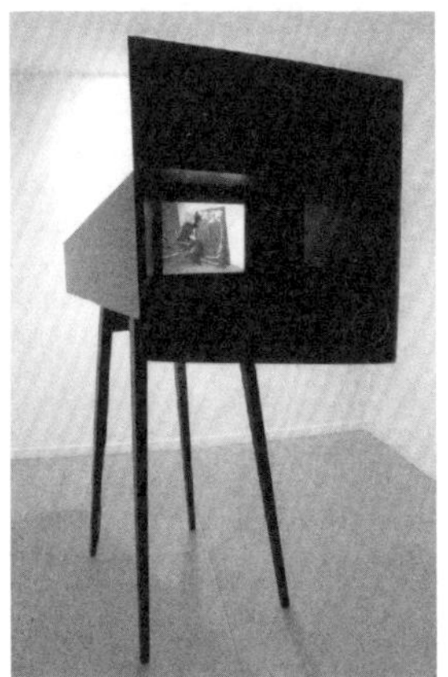

18 Joan Jonas, *My New Theater II, Big Mirror*, 1998.

sawhorses. It resembles a squared-off cone, reminiscent of the paper cones Jonas used in earlier pieces, to address the public—she sings, whispers and yells through it. The box contains a stage, placed at the larger end, as well as a wall for projections. Props related to the video are located on the stage and on the floor in front of it, alongside tiny speakers. We might call it performance-lite or installation-lite.

There is a certain strangeness in viewing the projections in the box, of which several versions were produced over the years. Pictures coming from a dollhouse come to mind, while Jonas refers to the camera obscura or, in another context, vaudeville and early cinema (pre-cinema). Those art forms were realized by wandering artistes and, in a way, Jonas' own wandering is now captured in this work. Her presence as a performer is no longer needed. The theatre box can easily be taken to other places—it does not weigh much and the props fit in a suitcase that can be opened up while the audience waits.

For *My New Theater* (1997) Jonas made a video loop that is a poetic documentary about a Cape Breton step dancer. An older man performs for the camera, in different locations such as on a board, by a waterfall, on a porch with a fiddler and a piano player, and in the local dance hall. Jonas says: 'I wanted to record the dancing of this particular man, because his simple style from an earlier age, although casual, is magical. It will disappear'.[17] The artist designed a new box for *My New Theatre II, Big Mirror* (1998),[18] and this time recorded her own dancing. She's in a bare studio, its wall appears projected at the rear end in the box. A dog jumps through a hoop—in slow motion. A nine-foot tin cone from the performance *Mirage* (1977) funnels an early American folk song with lines such as: 'Look up and down that long lonesome road'; 'You and I must go'; and 'We will all end up

350

in the country jail someday'. Jonas' signature dance step is a remarkable kind of frenzied stomping that appears as if she is gathering all the resistance in her body together in order to perform.[19] Notably, her movements are very different from those of the dog. On a chalkboard Jonas draws a waterfall and then, on a small board, she copies the same drawing as it appears in the mirror. The sound of water from the waterfall keeps her company.

Perhaps the most complex work in the series was made in 1999. *My New Theatre III, In the Shadows a Shadow* features a beautiful image of a long shadow, filmed in late afternoon, moving through a green field. It is unmistakably an image of the artist herself, who is approaching the late afternoon of her life. 'If I could remember, it would be simple things.' These are her words. The video of which these elements form a part is a kind of collage. It contains other shots taken outdoors, and shots of a performance for the video in a log studio in Cape Breton. The studio has two rocking chairs, one for an adult and one for a child, and a long low wooden couch. Stones are placed on the floor in a line.

The performance has several scenes and a lot of action. Jonas is present, wearing jeans. Another woman is also present. She is young and naked. The action begins. Jonas walks around with furniture followed by the other woman. Jonas walks to the stones, picks them up and walks to the other end of the room where she piles them up. In the next scene people enter the lodge. Some children and adults of all ages carry furniture with them. In what resembles a jam session, they slam the furniture on the floor, each participant making music in their own tempo, rhythm, and style. Next, Jonas walks on a balance beam. She draws her hand with white chalk on a black board. Again, she draws herself, but this time on her own body. Drawing black lines on her white gown, she charts

19 Joan Simon, 'Scents and Variations', p. 30.

20 *Ibid.*, p. 28.

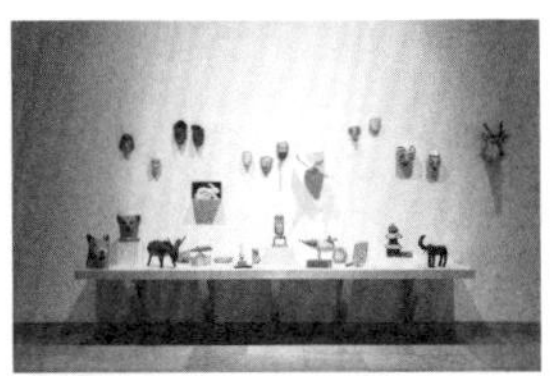

21 Joan Jonas, *installation view, Haus der Kunst, München 2022.* Photo: Maximilian Geuter.

a body. We then go outside where a dog is swimming. A woman appears at a rock, close to the water. She is naked (it is the woman we saw before). What is around her seems hostile, but the water is a safe place.

Thinking this over, I saw big-time activity—never a halt or a dull moment. Something was always being created and the energy coming out of it was reinvested, or so it seemed. But what was the purpose? Was there a purpose? It seemed like an ongoing cycle about the energy of life and about the fact that life aspires towards form, wherever it is and whatever the circumstances under which it is lived. This work recognizes that: as life proceeds, an awareness grows about the form that one's own life irrevocably takes. We should consider this seriously, but we may smile about it too.

This is as far as I will go. We have delved into an artist's world, a protagonist who underwent many changes over the years. From a dancer she became a witch and then a storyteller. The last pieces finally show Jonas as a woman—just a woman. I've argued that this body of work wants to render inner life. In answer to a question, Jonas once remarked that her work is autobiographical, not in the strict psychological sense, but in a sense that art comes from inner life.[20] Marcel Duchamp's boxes, in which he assembled miniatures of his work, come to mind when looking at Jonas' work. For Duchamp, making the work and providing it with a context was a way of staying close to himself. It allowed him to mock the idea that an artist's oeuvre is his burden as well. Joan Jonas does something similar in her new theatre. The work, in all its capriciousness, says: Life is a volatile affair. And we had better know it.[21]

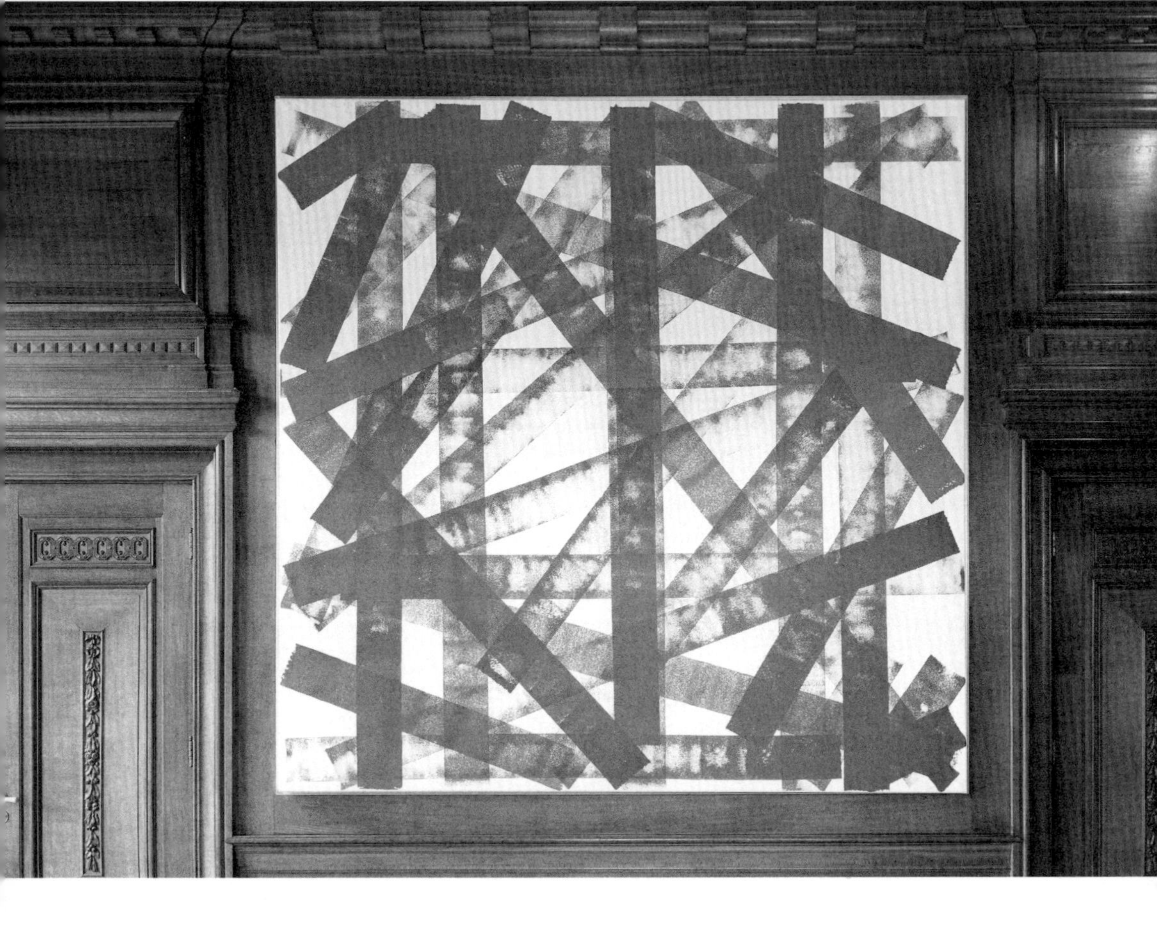

The Raving Silence

Jos van Merendonk

'—See if he is not cutting it into slips, and giving them about him to light their pipes !—' 'Tis abominable,' answered Didius; 'it should not go unnoticed' said doctor Kysarcius—[pictogram: a hand points to the right] he was of the Kysarcii of the Low Countries.'
—Laurence Sterne, *The Life and Opinions of Tristram Shandy, Gentleman*[1]

'The fields are greener in their description than in their actual greenness.'
—Fernando Pessoa, *The Book of Disquiet*[2]

Green calls the shots in Jos van Merendonk's paintings.[3] A powerful, yet introvert green throws the viewer back onto himself; the colour signifies green, but simultaneously questions the sensorial experience of green. After all, memories of the natural green world inhabit us; in our mind, there shines, as it were, an eternally green slide. But this inner ray gets in the way of the art experience, it interferes, intersects, rubs against it, drawing the viewer into consternation.

This concerns, then, a monochrome oeuvre—the pencil

355

1 Laurence Sterne, *The Life and Opinions of Tristram Shandy, Gentleman*, Henry Frowde, London, 1905, Part 4, Chapter 26, p. 287.

2 Fernando Pessoa, *The Book of Disquiet*, trans. by Richard Zenith, London, The Penguin Press, 2001, p. 30.

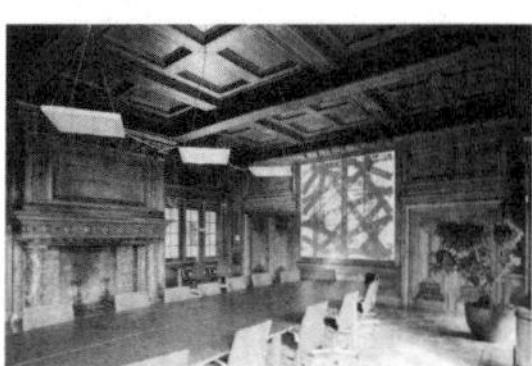

3 Jos van Merendonk, no title, 2005, pencil and acrylic on linen, 265 × 273 cm, 'Groene Kamer', Raad voor de Rechtspraak, The Hague. Photo: Riesjard Schropp.

Jos van Merendonk, no title, 2005, pencil and acrylic on linen, 265 × 273 cm. 'Groene Kamer', Raad voor de Rechtspraak, The Hague. Photo: Riesjard Schropp.

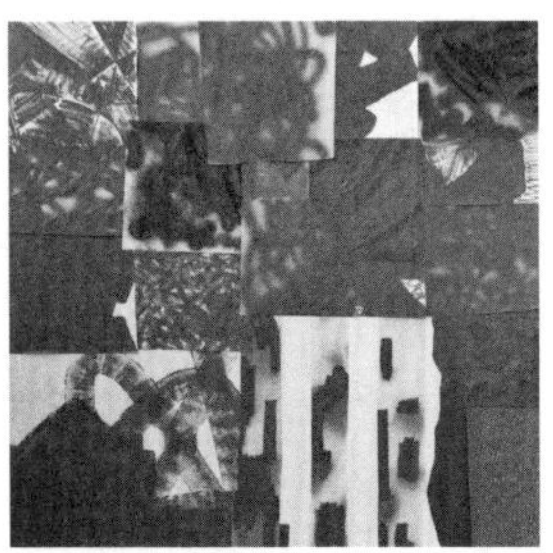

4a Jos van Merendonk, *2014-2-7*, 2014, pencil and acrylic on linen, 200 × 200 cm.

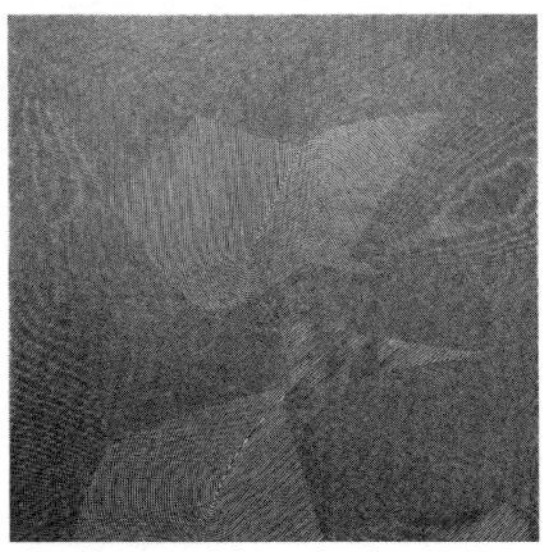

4b Jos van Merendonk, *2017-2-1*, 2017, pencil and acrylic on linen, 200 × 200 cm.

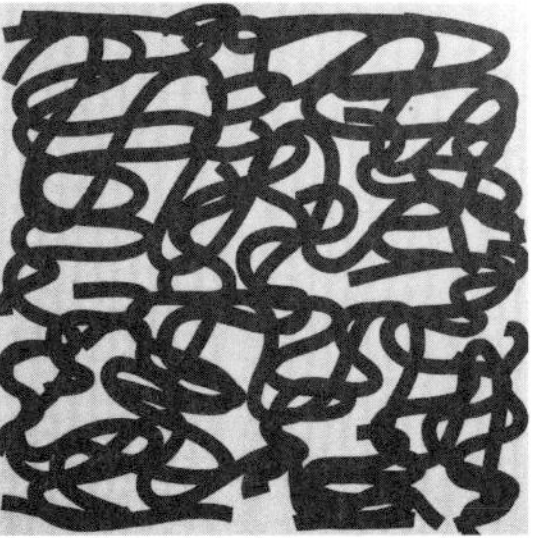

4c Jos van Merendonk, *2021-2-14*, 2021, pencil and acrylic on linen, 200 × 200 cm.

grey lines and white plains that also appear in the works do not change this as they provide the ground—with the leading role given to a colour that was considered taboo in abstract modernism. The paintings have fixed dimensions (40 × 40 cm, 60 × 60 cm, 1 × 1 m, 2 × 2 m), paint is applied on the canvas by a vast arsenal of means (brush, spray can, roller, spatula, thrown directly from the pot) in the form of graphical motifs (line, whirl, oval, knot, zigzag). The painting's surface is characterized by painting and drawing, *peinture* and *écriture*. In endless variations, it is smeared, brushed, scratched and dotted upon. Extremes/absolutes take on forms by way of velvet graffiti, fine needlework, rough sods, and also the energies/spheres that we associate with them: susceptibility, elegance, implacability.[4]

And so, the viewer arrives in an arena of a kind in which opposites are pitted against one another (such as order–frivolity, constraint–freedom, rule–desire). Inner combat, perhaps more palpable beneath the skin than directly visible, makes a return in every single painting. A single work never gives itself away, but is rather reticent and aversive, as if it doesn't wish to draw or seduce, but rather wants to fasten itself inside the head of the viewer and leave behind a mental imprint. Now let's give 'imprint' an ad-lib typification with the words that Ms. Ives and Dr. Sweet (*Penny Dreadful*) use for their hero, the undaunted Captain Nemo: swagger, love of freedom, and resilience.

Modernist Hieroglyphs

The work illustrates the complexity of a certain type of art practise that arose in the 1980s in Western Europe and the US, when artists took art history onboard again. At the time, conceptual art had reached an impasse; its iconoclasm, its need to break with history—the powers that had given momentum to this trendsetting art of the 1960s—no longer worked. Allan McCollum staged such an artistic fatigue by means of a sort of shadow cabinets in which the old medium-specific arts could dazzle the audience, *une dernière fois*; come the early 1980s, he filled walls with an endless edition of 'bedded down' gypsum paintings (*Plaster Surrogates*); a bit later followed by immense displays of empty vases (*Perfect Vehicles*).

In short, a contingency plan was devised by a new breed of artists who reclaimed the traditions of the painterly and sculptural art. Rather than shunning the conceptual heritage, more often than not these artists succeeded in interweaving it carefully into their own work. Much like other artists of his generation—such as Heimo Zobernig, Stephen Prina and Klaas Kloosterboer—Van Merendonk develops a type of hybrid painting, a variation on abstract modernism in which the concepts freely roam about. His take on modernism is inspired by a mix of identification and resistance.

Van Merendonk's paintings trace back to a minimal, almost off-hand drawing from 1983. In the drawing we make out a knot, an oval and a 'Z'; these forms make their return—magnified, fragmented or not—in all subsequent works. The drawing is an archetype, a kind of homunculus that is constantly revivified. This repetitive element aligns his work with geometric abstraction, the esteemed branch of modernist painting that, in search of a spiritual truth, continuously investigated her discoveries by way of a methodically applied course of action.

By introducing a template to which all works must comply, constructing an entire oeuvre from a single drawing, the artist does something else as well, something much larger: he subjects as it were *a posteriori* the entire tradition of modernist abstraction to a new order, and harasses it with a set of prohibitions, amputations, mutilations, so as to have his painting reflect what cannot (or no longer) be done.

This deed brings to mind the distant memory (or lack thereof) of high modernism, that by the 1980s and most certainly in the globalized twenty-first century has lost its place. Artists who still concern themselves with modernism today operate in the margins. Van Merendonk's work is crippled, his monochromes are broken, they have a certain absent-mindedness—compare his work with Günther Förg's, who traced the earth-bound vestiges of a down-and-out modernism. The grid, once a framework of concrete horizontal and vertical lines in which a spiritual message resounded, has in Van Merendonk's art become a ghostly phenomenon, something that lurks beneath the painted surface, a vague echo of 'the rule' to which a good modernist artwork once had to comply.

The template that Van Merendonk lays beneath his abstract works brings to mind the operations of conceptual art. This art paved an order of language, measurement, numbers and timescales around the world and broke with illusionism. Conceptual art shifted the focus to the here and now, to experiences of presence, of both the artwork and of ourselves, and to the observation that art lives inside our head. Van Merendonk requires a similar awareness for that which appears before our eyes. In notions like 'lacerated monochromatics' and 'ghostly grid' lives a legacy of conceptual art, that wanted to fathom the real world, to perceive what that was like, without fear of disenchantment. But Van Merendonk wants more than to merely put the modernism of say, the 1950s—Newman and Pollock—to the test. He travels back even further in time, and brings a (neo-)primitive modernism into play. He exchanges Picasso's tribal motifs for something homemade, which he then applies in his search for the primordial root of an imaginary modernism.[5] The painter's moves are ambidextrous: he embraces the tradition of modernist abstraction, but is equally attentive to her 'holy' achievements as to her 'pagan' potential. And thus he arrives at his project, an excavation of modernist hieroglyphs. A site once described by Rosalind Krauss as the place where everything swarms and proliferates beneath the calm surface of abstract modernist painting.[6]

Entropy-Quietude

I associate Van Merendonk's paintings most of all with a number of artists from after the Second World War, the era of reconstruction. This most certainly has to do with a first impression that I have carried with me for years: the earthliness of the works, the fact that they remain aloof while you nonetheless feel them in your gut. Tinguely's mechanical agility, the scorched earth of Tàpies, and Burri's fractured surfaces resonate in my experience of Van Merendonk's work. In 2015 Burri's *Grande Cretto*,[7] an impressive land art piece was completed in Gibellina Vecchia in Sicily, a village obliterated by an earthquake in 1968. The artist had covered the remains of an area where once houses stood with a thick cement layer, leaving open some of the spaces where streets used to be, so that a new sheath, intersected by various long pavements, covered the old layers.

Of course Tinguely, Tàpies and Burri[8] worked in a period shortly after the Second World War: We destruction and reconstruction are always present in their art. In Van Merendonk's work too, reality is precarious. In the event of

5 Compare Robert Storr on Guillermo Kuitca: '[T]he project in which Kuitca is now engaged seems more a matter of recovering useful fragments of other eras in order to reconstruct painting than of using painting to critique its own heritage from the vantage point of some anticipated future when all its options will have been exhausted. In short, Kuitca appears to have embarked on an archeological tour of the well documented but still partially buried monuments of modernism, curious how their recombinant elements might result in new forms.' Robert Storr, 'Digging Down', in: *Guillermo Kuitca: Plates N° 01–24*, London, Steidl Hauser & Wirth, 2008, p. 8.

6 Rosalind Krauss, *The Optical Unconscious*, Cambridge (MA), The MIT Press, 1993. Here, Krauss focuses especially on surrealism and its embrace of irrationality.

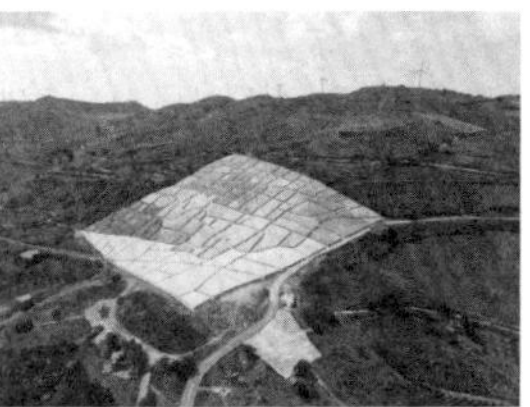

7 Alberto Burri, *Grande Cretto*, Gibellina Vecchia, 2015, concrete, 1.50 × 350 × 280 m.

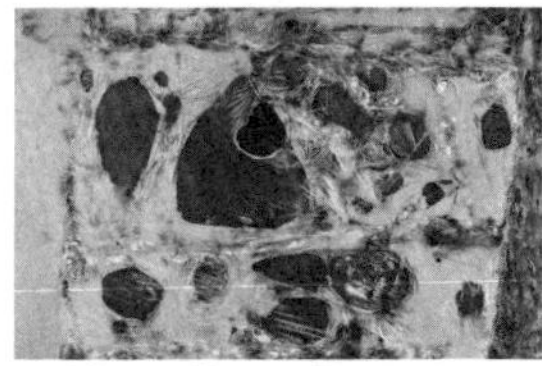

8 Alberto Burri, *Rosso plastica M 2 (Red Plastic M 2)*, 1962, burned plastic on canvas, 120 × 180 cm.

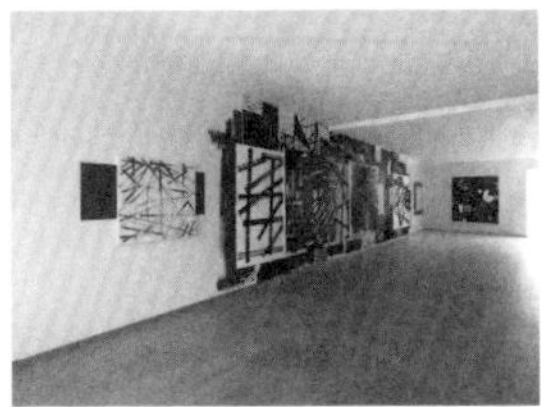

9 Jos van Merendonk, *Wall Installation*, 2016, 320 × 1500 cm, Parts Project, The Hague. Photo: Allard Bovenberg.

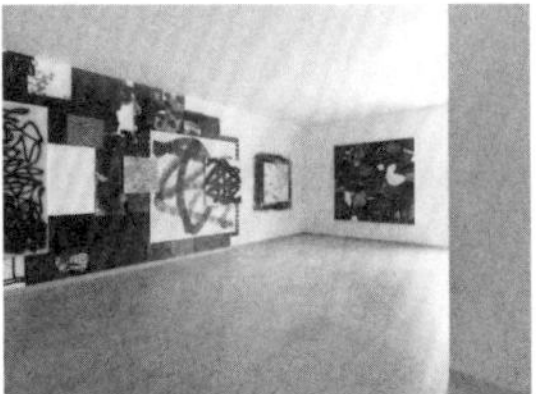

10 Jos van Merendonk, *Wall Installation*, 2016, 320 × 1500 cm, detail, Parts Project, The Hague. Photo: Allard Bovenberg.

destruction, it has the potential to be put back together. The emphasis lies in the natural course of things, Nature's Grand Scheme, and the possibility that we may no longer be part of it. He pays heed to things that are stuck in the ground, but precisely because roots *are* unpredictable and beyond our governance. In Van Merendonk's work, paint appears supple and fresh at one point, then rigid and full of languor at another, introvert and/or extravert; and the brush stroke/-cut /-line /-dent /-engraving strengthens this earthly frivolity.

Jos van Merendonk's wall-installation in Parts Project (The Hague, 6 March–1 May 2016) was a Gesamtkunstwerk—the recombining of existing works and motifs dating from a period of almost thirty years.[9, 10, 11] The work was comprised from in situ murals, existing paintings and pieces of old canvas cut from discarded works and ones that had been cast aside. The layered build-up showed, beside the *peinture* and *écriture* in their variations, a new excess; spread over the entire wall was a tableau of disorder/entropy. A cartography and calligraphy, both equally striking, crossed paths. The work seemed quite the palimpsest, in which endless layers are stacked on top of each other and the first layer gets repeatedly rewritten by the preceding layer or layers on top of it.

The installation in The Hague was earthly and stout, yet simultaneously hallucinatory and spacey, like an atonal symphony with intriguing dissonance. There was a huge

360

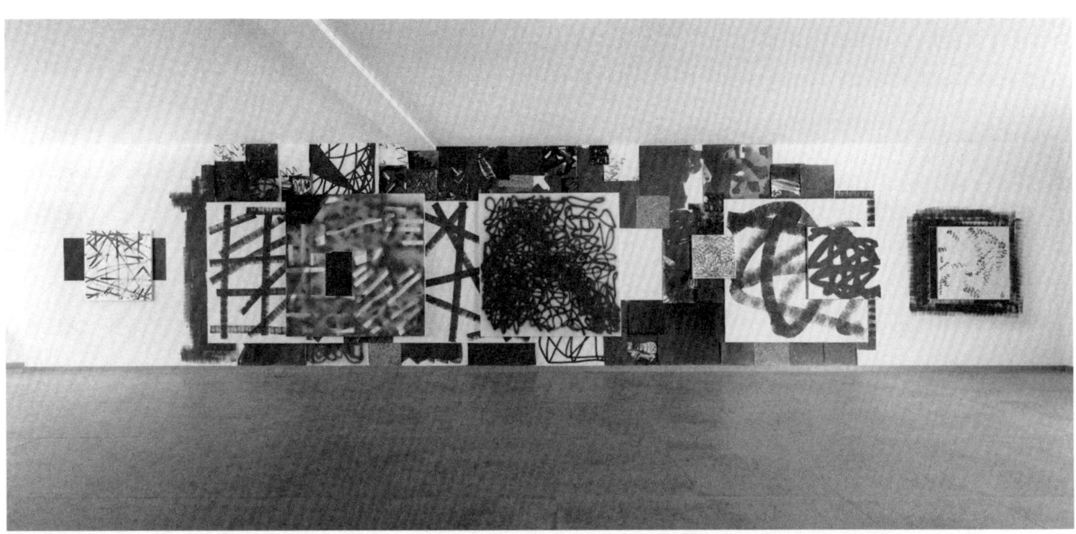

11 Jos van Merendonk, *Wall Installation*, 2016, 320 × 1500 cm, Parts Project, The Hague. Photo: Allard Bovenberg.

amount on display: throughout the length of the wall were permanent and fleeting shapes, all kinds of green fragments: rigid and fluid lines, soft contours, tight corners, broad strokes, mousey scratches, white planes and stripes, all kinds of flimsy doodles, and much swarming about. This visual delirium also had a tacit aspect, which invited the viewer to calmly travel within an inner landscape, a fantasy-in-green, an alchemical tableau.

The entropy and the quietude of this wall-installation, but also the power and inwardness of the paintings *tout court* form a veritable challenge to a writer to project his thoughts unto them. I would be pleased to write about Van Merendonk's installation in The Hague as conjoining the sediments of a Burri with the sentiments of a Federle—or rather, holding a balance between the two. But how do I get to such a notion? I'm overwhelmed by a multitude of associations, precisely because of my initially introverted impression. But can an oeuvre be so jumpy, or is it my brain's workings? It turns out that Van Merendonk feels connected with a range of painters, who we could call his 'art-family', working in many styles, in different places and at different times.

> Considering the nature of my work I could perhaps think it strange that over the past few years, in Berlin and Switzerland, I have been looking at artists like Segantini, Adolf Menzel and Hodler. But it undoubtedly has to do with a wider interest for the nineteenth century and its offshoots. Also for years I've been interested in Lucian Freud, Kossoff and Auerbach (to name a few 'English' artists). I've also spent a lot of time looking at the generation of Pollock, De Kooning et cetera, and the way in which they brought life into abstraction. But in my work one is more likely to see traces of the early Schoonhoven,

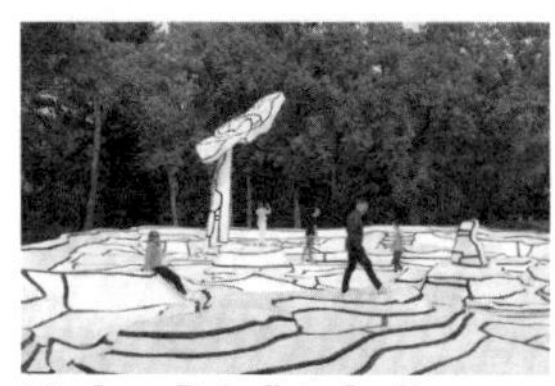

12 Jean Dubuffet, *Jardin d'émail*, 1974, concrete, glass fiber reinforced epoxy resin and polyurethane paint, ca. 8 × 20 × 30 m, Kröller-Müller Museum, Otterlo.

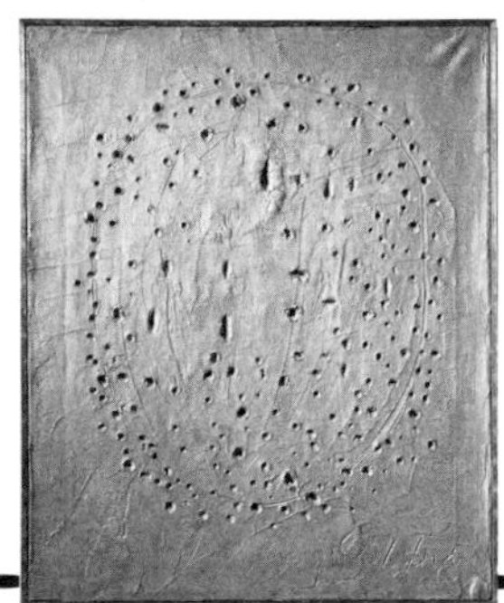

13 Lucio Fontana, *Concetto spaziale*, 1961.

14 Email from artist to author, 5 May 2016.

15 Maarten Doorman, 'De aardbeving van de romantiek: De Menon Lectures van Isaiah Berlin', *NRC Handelsblad*, 14 January 2000.

16 Isaiah Berlin, *The Roots of Romanticism*, Pimlico, Chatto & Windus, 1999.

Dubuffet, Fontana and M. Barré.[12, 13] As for contemporaries I name: Frize, Federle, Lasker, Klaus Merkel, Van den Ende and Wool.[14]

In this last sentence Helmut Federle strikes me as a remarkable name, after all, his work connects traditions of geometric abstraction, their signs and symbolism, with an provocative emotional individual spirit. My assertion is as follows: Van Merendonk's work is permeated with romantic irony. By reverting back to romanticism, he enables himself to renew modernism. His design of a (neo-)primitive modernism reminds me of the romantic endeavour; in pursuit of ideals, but aware of the prospect of failure.

Romantic Irony

Art historians do not agree on what the influence of romanticism is on modernism; much depends on how one defines the relation between historic romanticism with the Enlightenment. Cultural historian Isaiah Berlin considers romanticism to be an attack on the Enlightenment, and not as an incongruous movement/inherent counterweight.[15] According to Berlin, there is the notion in romanticism that humans are fundamentally different from one another, and that this is a very positive thing. As humans we can certainly think of things in communion, we can share each other's beliefs about life and how to arrange the world—and if we do not agree we may discuss matters with one another. But with regard to that which we feel, in our affective positioning within reality, in how feeling is the compass in our lives, there we differ substantially.[16]

362

Indeed, thinkers, poets and artists towards the end of the eighteenth century and the beginning of the nineteenth century took their own subjective feeling as a point of departure for their works. It is essential that they removed the affect from their own experience, that they placed it before them, as if to dissect it or simply see it more clearly. The example *par excellence* is of course Caspar David Friedrich and his paintings of overwhelming experiences snatched from nature, man dissolved and melted into his surroundings. Friedrich's work appeals to our imagination and has a contemporary ambiguity: his works depict total submission but are simultaneously recognizable as constructs of feeling. This ambiguity has in itself become recognizable as a romantic trope/form, as with the fragment (Rodin), the unconditional surrender (Flaubert), and the forging of a new beginning.

In contemporary art, romanticism has in my opinion assumed the position of an undercurrent exerting an abiding power of attraction. It has to do with the ambiguity with which its themes are imagined, with irony that acts as a companion to the intensity of (affective) life imagined as art. Van Merendonk: '[What interests me when I start a new work is accomplishing] a new expression, a different face, with a different emptiness'.[17] Every day a painting gets made anew—this process can simply take place in one's head, by way of preparation for the material making—a painting that needn't resemble the previous ones and yet is a repetition of the same.

This forging of a new beginning, knowing in advance that the ends are practically unattainable, but in spite of this are worth pursuing, is pre-eminently a romantic trope/form. We find a prime example in Laurence Sterne, who from 1760 to 1767 worked on his *Tristram Shandy*, a novel in eight parts in which language stars as the central force. Although three branches of science are discussed—philosophy, fortification,

17 Parts Project 01: Bob Law/ Jos van Merendonk, Den Haag, Parts Projects, 2016, n.p., brochure of the exhibition 'To the End of the World or to the Edge of the Paper', text: Judith de Bruijn.

and obstetrics—through the merry discourse of five characters, at the core of the novel stands the recounting of a story. The narrative follows trains of thought, a brushing over of all of the tempting by ways or detours that present themselves, causing the reader to get lost in a labyrinth of words. At whichever passage the reader opens this book, they will inevitably feel the story to have begun anew.

Van Merendonk's paintings are fragments of an existing drawing, cut-outs from an infinity of possibilities that is almost overwhelming, and carries silent threats. This has to do with the stealthy orchestration of his extremes/absolutes.[18] In romanticism we see a cultivation of extreme/absolute experiences. The 'I' goes berserk on fantasies about himself and the myriad of things he could experience. In art, extremes were put into focus, think of Turner who, in order to physically touch the might of a storm, let himself be tied to the mast of a ship in the middle of the sea. He wished to experience the full thrust of danger, whilst making it home alive and well. Something of that ambiguity is discernible in Jos van Merendonk's paintings.

Jörg Heiser, the writer, has made inspiring connections between conceptualism and romanticism in the exhibition

364

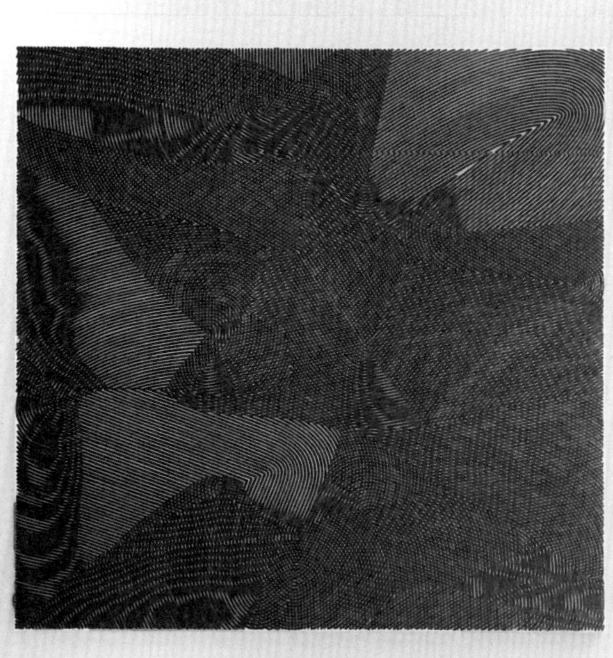

18 Jos van Merendonk, *2014-2-9*, 2014, pencil and acrylic on linen, 200 × 200 cm.

'Romantic Conceptualism', as well as in various texts.[19] In short, his thesis surmises that conceptual art also deals with a world of feeling, in works where one finds cool detachment and ambiguous irony, emotionally loaded presentations of romantic thought, that are both 'artifice' and 'reality'.

But in order to refresh our understanding of romantic irony, we must go back in time a little. Irony, of course, plays a large role in the oeuvre of philosopher/theologian Kierkegaard. He investigated the concept in his dissertation, to which he also gave an ironic form. Perhaps he felt the concept presented itself most strongly within another book that would consist solely of prefaces. By doing so, he cultivated the making of a new beginning. From the preface (sic) of this book:

> A preface is a mood. Writing a preface is like sharpening a scythe, like tuning a guitar, like talking with a child, like spitting out of the window. […] Writing a preface is like ringing someone's doorbell to trick him, like walking by a young lady's window and gazing at the paving stones; it is like swinging one's cane in the air to hit the wind, like doffing one's hat although one is greeting nobody.[20]

The contemporary artist Stephen Prina makes intriguing work according to this principle of ironic artifice. He has spent almost his adult entire life building a corpus of works in watercolour with which he redoes the complete works of Manet (a total of 556 according to the *catalogue raisonné*). What interests Prina in doing so is the time spent by the painter behind his easel, his acts of looking and contemplation in the past, and a modern-day reproduction thereof (*Exquisite Corpse: The Complete Paintings of Manet*, 1988–today). This work by Prina brings something to the fore that

19 Jörg Heiser, *Romantic Conceptualism*, Kunsthalle Nürnberg, 10 May–15 July 2007; e.g., Jörg Heiser, 'Moscow, Romantic Conceptualism, and After', *www.e-flux.com/journal/moscow-romantic-conceptualism-and-after*.

20 Nicolaus Notabene, *Prefaces, Writing Samples*, trans. by Todd W. Nichol, Princeton, Princeton University Press, 1997, p. 5–6.

is also a characteristic of Van Merendonk: being committed to going to the studio, and in dedication, practising, day in day out, producing another painting every day. His work challenges us to translate the commitment of the artist into our own commitment to viewing and, like with conceptual art, to give our attention to the here and now, to that which we see right in front of us.

Above all his work makes an appeal to ourselves, to our own fantasy, to our very subjectivity, how we deal with art, how we get on with the world, with others, and what we invest of ourselves, how we wish to squander ourselves in the process. A contemporary romantic artist who has repeatedly tempted us to lose ourselves in his film stories, Jean-Luc Godard, once said this: 'Le réel c'est les autres, la fiction c'est soi' ('the real is the others; fiction is oneself'). While watching Van Merendonk's paintings, one arrives in the middle of Godard's fine sentence.

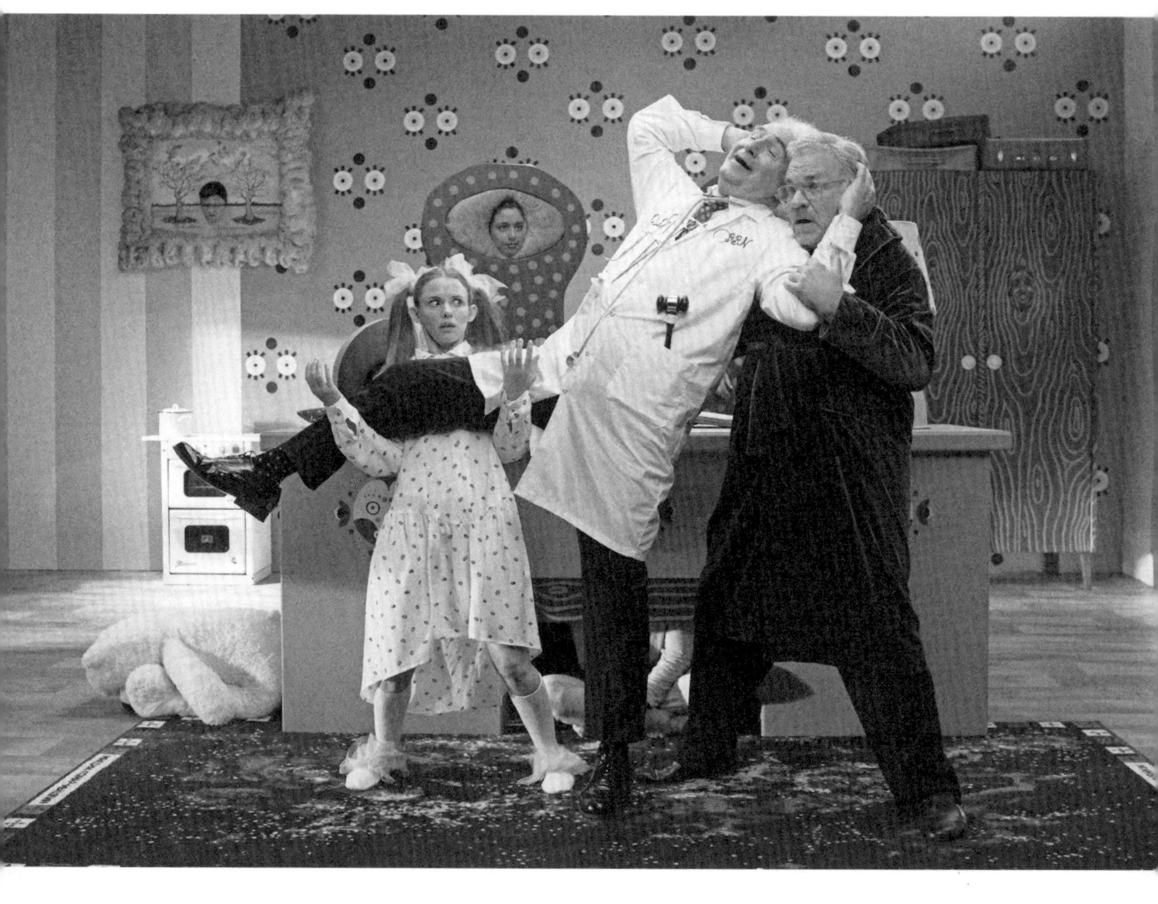

Becoming Someone Else

Interview with Roee Rosen

The interview with Roee Rosen took place half a year before his solo show 'Kafka for Kids and the Dust Channel' at the experimental art space 1646 in The Hague. At that time, the artist had just completed his feature film *Kafka for Kids*, in which he translates Kafka's stories into a television series for young children. Our conversation is mainly about that work; produced during the Covid-19 lockdown, it addresses important themes such as the fluidity of identity, trauma and transformation.

Roee Rosen, the Israeli-American painter, filmmaker and writer was born in Rehovot, 1963. He studied philosophy, comparative literature and visual arts both in Tel Aviv and New York, and is a seasoned teacher at various art academies and universities. Recently, he published his book *Desire and Dust* (2020) and the colouring book *Lucy is Sick* (2020–21). He has had many exhibitions in places in Israel and elsewhere, including 'documenta 14' and Centre Pompidou in 2018. In 2019, IMPAKT in Utrecht organized a solo exhibition about his work, entitled 'Poetry and Catharsis', with a concomitant evening programme in collaboration with Spring

Roee Rosen, *Kafka for Kids*, 2022, 4k video, 117′, still. Cinematographer: Avner Shahaf. Still photography: Goni Riskin.

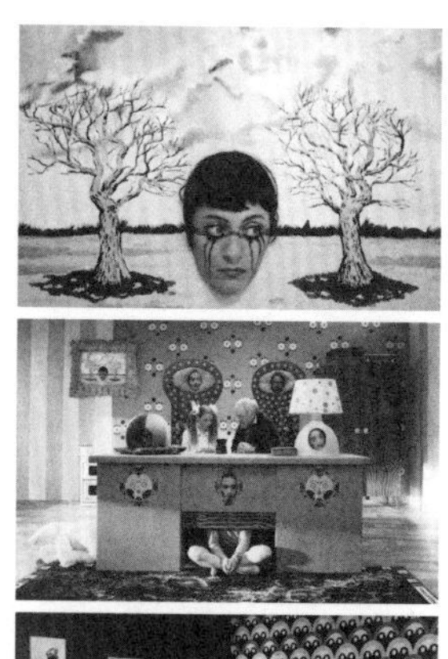

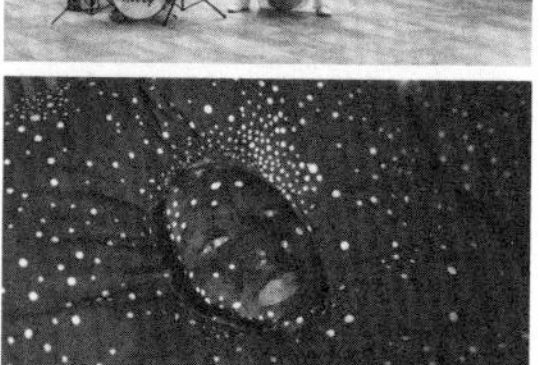

1a–d Roee Rosen, *Kafka for Kids*, 2022, 4k video, 117′, still. Cinematographer: Avner Shahaf. Still photography: Goni Riskin.

Performing Arts Festival called 'Roee Rosen, Theatre of the Awkward'.

His feature film *Kafka for Kids,* made in collaboration with editor Max Lomberg and the musician Igor Krutogolov, and based Kafka's *The Metamorphosis,* combines the genres of comedy, musical and documentary in retelling the story of Gregor Samsa through anthropomorphic furniture and props. The film is interrupted by increasingly longer commercial breaks, animations, music and shots from 'behind the screens', which ultimately develop into a purported documentation of an academic panel discussion on the troubling complexities of 'legal childhood' in the occupied Palestinian territories as defined by Israeli military law.[1]

MARK KREMER   Having just finished editing the film *Kafka for Kids,* you are now looking for ways to release it internationally. Could you tell me how you concretely worked on the film? In our pre-talk you mentioned personal illness and the Covid lockdown that intensified the working process. Could you talk about this and also explain the inception of *Kafka for Kids*?

ROEE ROSEN   Well, the idea came thirteen years ago, when I was presenting *The Confessions of Roee Rosen* in

370

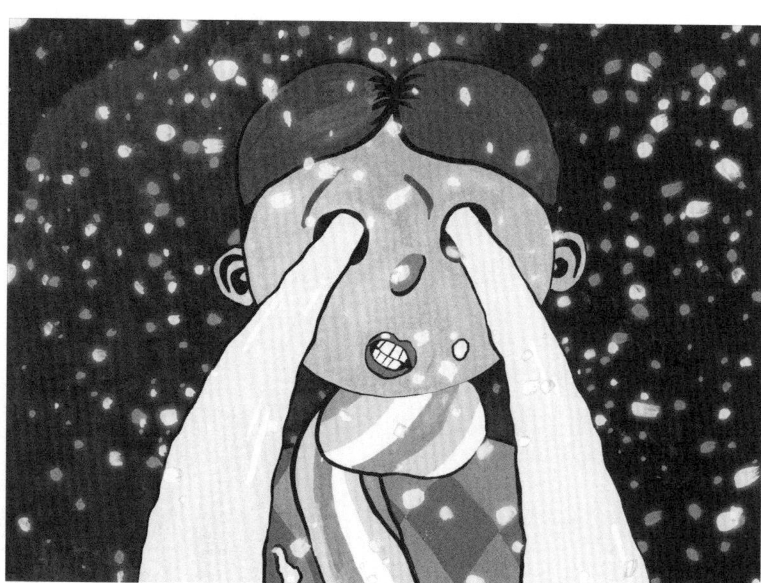

1e Roee Rosen, *Kafka for Kids,* 2022, 4k video, 117′, *Bucket Rider,* animation still.

FIDMarseille. To my astonishment, people recognized the influence of Kafka on that film, and on the plane back to Israel, I realized that author was my last remaining sacred cow. So, I thought: 'Why not do something that would be like torturing Kafka?' I try to question all my norms and values in a systematic way, in order to challenge the things that are dear to me. Kafka had to be the next.

MK   How did people recognize Kafka's influence? Could you illustrate this?

RR   The feedback in the Q&A after the screenings made that clear, and, in fact, in the film script there are some hidden quotes by Kafka. For example, Kafka has an aphorism saying, 'There is an aim but no way there; what we call a way is hesitation'. ('Zürau Aphorism 26', 1917–1918). In *The Confessions of Roee Rosen*, a labour migrant appearing as 'Roee Rosen number one' exclaims: 'There is an address but there is no street. What we call a city is only wavering'. As I began writing the script, for a long time I thought it would not work; the results were too flat. This changed when curator Hila Peleg invited me for Documenta. While discussing what I could be working on, she recalled the idea and asked me; 'What about Kafka for Kids?' She triggered the desire to go back to the project. And just as I had started writing the script, there was this incident of a twelve-year-old Palestinian girl who was detained at the gateway of a settlement with a knife under her coat, charged as a terrorist, and detained in an adult women's prison. This incident made me realize the convergence between supposedly making Kafka fit for children, and raising the question of what childhood is in different political contexts.

371

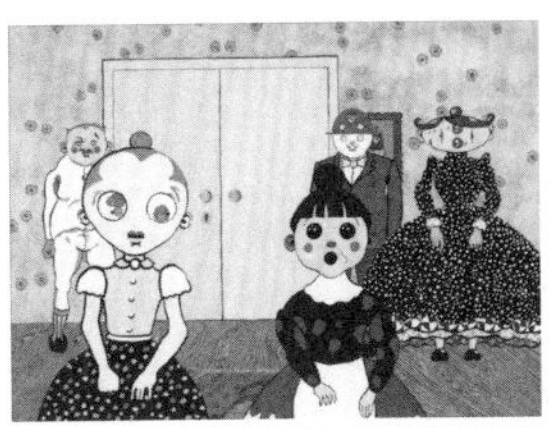

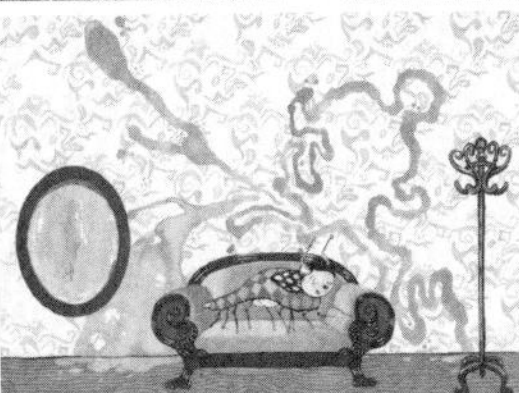

1f–g Roee Rosen, *Kafka for Kids*, 2022, 4k video, 117', *Merry Vermin*, animation still.

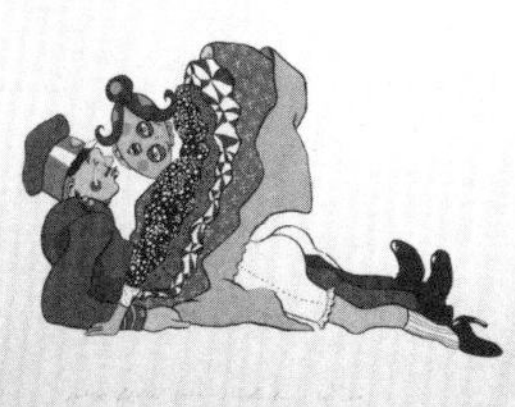

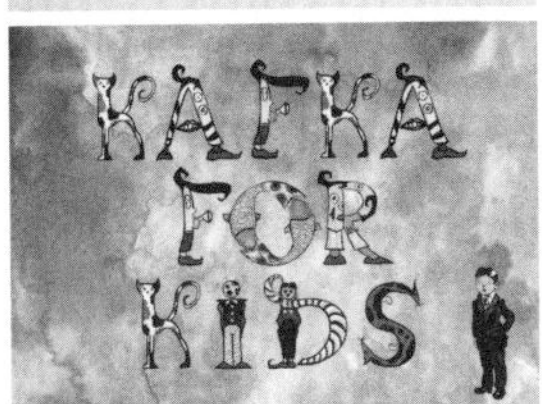

1h–j Roee Rosen, preparatory gouaches for *Kafka for Kids*, 2022, 4k video, 117'.

MK   The girl was stopped at a gate and seen as a terrorist despite her young age. She was sent to a women's prison for six months, because military Israeli law considers a Palestinian girl of twelve years to be an adult. That's a Kafkaesque ploy!

RR   Working on *Kafka for Kids* for me entailed thinking about the principles of law anew. Kafka was working as a doctor in law and naturally applied his knowledge in texts such as *In the Penal Colony* or *The Trial*. My film is imbued with thinking about legality and notions of childhood. *The Metamorphosis* deals with these subjects as well, and it is the story of a son, his sister, and his parents. Grete, Gregor Samsa's sister, is described as a child but through her older brother's viewpoint.

At one point I felt that the film itself should go through a metamorphosis, so that the child would be somehow redeemed. It resulted in a rather peculiar structure, beginning as a musical comedy adorned with animations, and shapeshifting into a fictionalized lecture—a transformation that also conceals a personal drama.

In 2018, I finished the script during a residence of a foundation called Camargo in Cassis, France, granted through the FIDMarseille film festival. Then my physical health began to deteriorate. Initially I was ignoring it, just continuing my life, teaching and travelling extensively while the pains intensified. But in April 2019, I learnt that it was multiple myeloma, a cancer of the bone marrow. At that point my physical incapacity was such that I couldn't dress myself, comb my hair, or breathe deeply; everything was painful. But I was fortunate that the diagnosis was early enough and that my treatment was good and effective. Then, I had a kind of compulsive sabbatical.

MK   You stopped working completely?

RR   Only for a short while, but I had to stay home. In the first weeks, I couldn't move my arms, I couldn't paint. But once I regained my motoric abilities, I could deal with the film's visual aspect. For about a year, I could dedicate all my time to making the artwork for *Kafka for Kids*. Designing the set, but mostly doing the paintings that are shown in the animation scenes. And then, just as I was going out of the last and most difficult stage of treatment—a self-transplant of stem cells entailing chemotherapy—I regained my powers and we scheduled a week of shooting. The Corona virus was already spreading, but it was still in China, then in Italy. Far away… About three weeks after we shot, we had to go into quarantine. I went from the personal seclusion through my illness to the collective seclusion of Covid-19.

Initially we planned to complete shooting in Berlin for the monologue 'Explaining the Law to Kwame', which had been conceived as a sovereign, separate work. This monologue, of a legal expert who lapses into ruminations and fantasies as she speaks, is delivered by the actress Hani Fürstenberg, who also plays the child listening to the adult narrator as he retells the story of *The Metamorphosis*. The legal monologue is in Hebrew, but initially I wanted to do it again, in English. Because of Covid, this didn't happen, and I'm glad for it, in retrospect. The dichotomy between the English in *Kafka for Kids* and the Hebrew in the legal exposition creates a very disorienting sensation of transformation. She turns, from this old child with one native tongue, into a legal expert—who is uncomfortably aware that she is aging— with a very different native tongue. As I was writing the script, I already knew that Hani would be the lead star. I worked with her in the past on *Hilarious* and she is a great

373

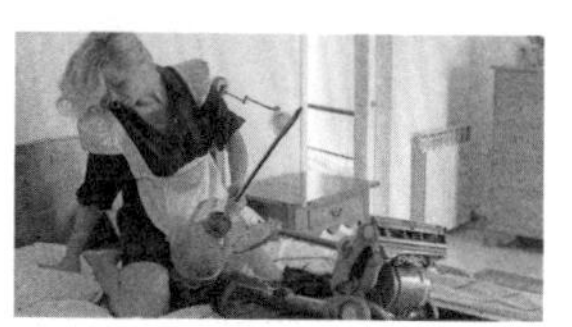

2 Roee Rosen, *The Dust Channel*, 2016, video, 23′.

actress. All the other participants had to be very musical as well, but not all of them are professional actors. In the end it turned out to be a miraculous cast.

MK   How would you define the format of *Kafka for Kids*?

RR   The work is a feature, a two-hour-long film masquerading as a TV programme with commercial breaks for food adds and trailers for future episodes. But these commercial breaks become gradually more complex and entangled, until one of them simply doesn't stop and takes over the story. That is to say: what begins as a short ad for an upcoming programme on the way the military law in the occupied territories defines the Palestinian child, becomes an entire lecture. When the lecture ends, we go back to the world of *Kafka for Kids*.

The complete story is thus told in two parallel dimensions. On one side there is the magical story-house, where an adult figure reads the story to a child in a room crowded with animated objects. Each piece of furniture is played by an actor/singer. Mr and Mrs Chair, Mrs Lamp, Mr Table, et cetera, come forth. They serve both as a Greek choir, engaged in the story, but also as a musical choir that bursts into song whenever there's a proper, or improper, opportunity. The actors/singers also dub the characters in the story. For example, Mrs Chair is also Gregor's mother and Mr Ball is his father.

The travails of Gregor Samsa, on the other hand, are told through animation. The musical accompaniment is by a toy orchestra, as if the musicians themselves are also toys. The composer, Igor Krutogolov, who also worked on the *Dust Channel* with me,[2] has a big part in the alchemy of it all. It is also important to say that the film is the core of the project,

374

but there are many satellite aspects, such as the artworks and film scenes that can become shorter videos or performances. So, the project can manifest itself as a variable exhibition.

MK   In Kafka we find many figures that seem to be part of an in-between world, such as the assistants, or the mysterious Odradek. What these figures do is no so clear, but their presence is intriguing and often they emit a benevolent energy. Did these figures inspire *Kafka for Kids*?

RR   Yes, absolutely. I don't want to talk too theoretically about Kafka, but these liminal figures, what Deleuze called 'becoming animal' and 'becoming object', are really important to me. Animism has always played a big role in my work. For me it offers a way of almost pursuing this literal state of being both, becoming a multiplicity. Being both an object and a person. Or, being a human being as well as another kind of animal. This is of course also an important aspect in *The Metamorphosis*.

Another important thing in Kafka is the liminality between a notion of being awake and the logic of dreams. Things change and glide in Kafka, in a way that doesn't make sense when you're awake, but makes perfect sense in your sleep. For example, in *The Metamorphosis*, the way that the vermin, Gregor, is described zoologically differs in different places of the story. That is typical of Kafka. There is a lack of stability, an ontological multi-layeredness, and always the underlying question of what it means 'to be'. In Kafka's texts these themes almost occur in a prosaic way. It's not presented as magic or surrealism but really as the way things are. This prosaic advance is what makes Kafka's stories very disturbing, of course, but also funny.

MK   Trauma enactment and trauma exorcism are important themes in your work. In 2019 you had a solo exhibition called 'Exorcisms' (Project Arts Centre, Dublin, curator: Livia Paldi). Earlier, Marcel Schwierin, in his essay 'Bringing Home the Horror: The Work of Roee Rosen in Germany' (2016), quotes you saying that you grew up with a father who, as a Holocaust survivor, did not talk about the Holocaust. Whereas for you, that subject permeated all your dreams. Schwierin calls this 'trans-generational trauma transmission'. How relevant are such terms/connections for your work?

RR   Of course, it's a very relevant connection, but I would avoid making it myself. Much of my work is about resistance against that connection, or at least against its rhetoric. In Israel, the rhetoric around the Holocaust is politically invested, and thus it is often instrumentalized. I could be defined as a 'second-generation' Holocaust survivor, a term that somehow suggests that the child is a witness, a victim, deserving of compensation, authority, or retribution. The place of the victim is applied to the politics of Israel. But my work has been about questioning that position and trying to destabilize it.

I believe it is clear from what I do, that this is not coming from a kind of cynical or disengaged place, but from a feeling of suffering. Notions of possession and exorcism are very much present in my work. There is always the voice or the body that are presented as contested territories. There's always more than one claimant. There's one body, or one voice, but more than one presence in that body or voice. It relates probably, on that biographical level, to the feeling of being born in the Middle East, while I see myself as a part of a European diaspora that no longer exists. I have the feeling of not belonging anywhere, of not being at home anywhere.

MK   Hence the importance you attach to the act of becoming someone else. It reads like a motto for art and life.

RR   Yes, but it's a performative logic. It's not like you really become someone else. It's the pursuit of dynamic, convulsive and ever-shifting ways of being. And it is also important to emphasize the emotive complexity here. It's about trauma, it's about exorcism, and it's also about the pleasure of changing, about playing.

MK   Roleplay?

RR   Child's play. Like a child wearing grown-up dresses. If you think of Cindy Sherman, there is real delight in her entire art of just being a kid, changing cloths before the mirror. In my own work, I avoid that kind of fun, I see myself more as a burdened artist. Yet there is child's play in my work. For example, the potential of becoming more than one. In *Confessions* there are three Roee Rosens. As *Justine Frank*, I not only become the female artist but also my own critical antagonist; a feminist critic who is angry with Roee Rosen for appropriating Justine Frank's work.[3] In *The Buried Alive*, my work allows me to become a collective. In other words, you yourself can become plural.

MK   Was there a specific point at which you began working with the real-life characters or creating the personae?

RR   I don't think there was a special starting point. It was rather part of a polemical rhetoric about 'being you' as a ploy in art. As a teenager I felt it strongly, not only in high art but also in popular culture. In the glam rock of David Bowie, his act as *The Thin White Duke* was as authentic as, let's say,

377

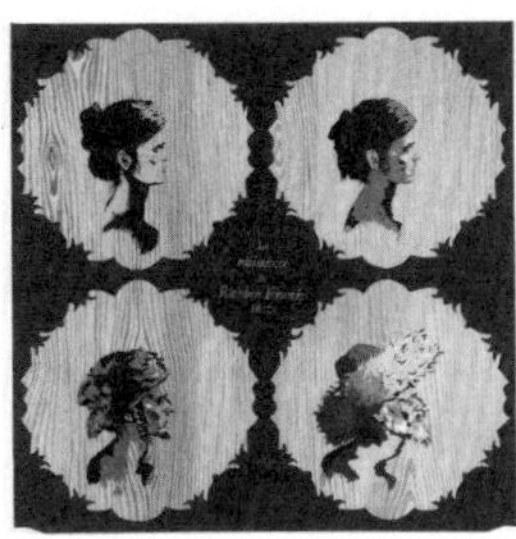

3a   Roee Rosen, *Justine Frank, The Birth of Rabbi Frank*, 1937 1997, oil on canvas, 75 × 75 cm.

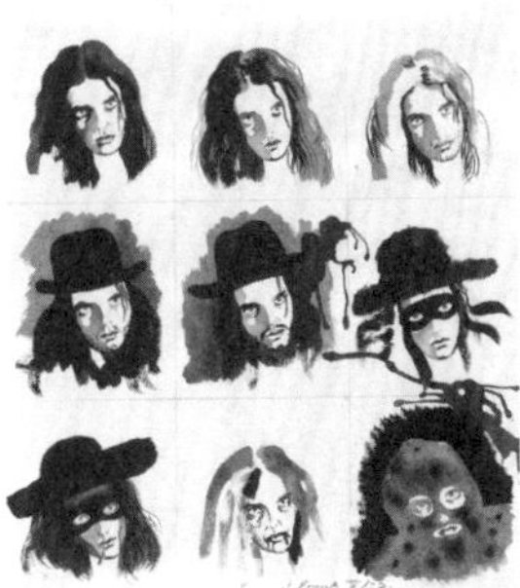

3b   Roee Rosen, *Justine Frank, From The Stained Portfolio*, 1927–1928, drawing on paper, 33 × 38 cm.

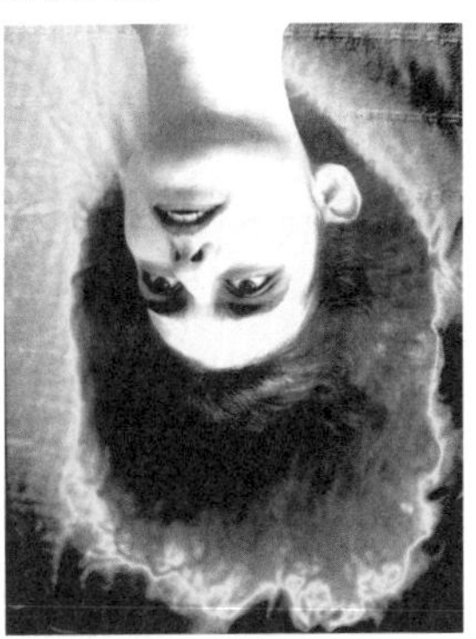

3c   Roee Rosen, *Justine Frank, Anonymous Photographer*, Paris ca. 1928, print, 20 × 27 cm.

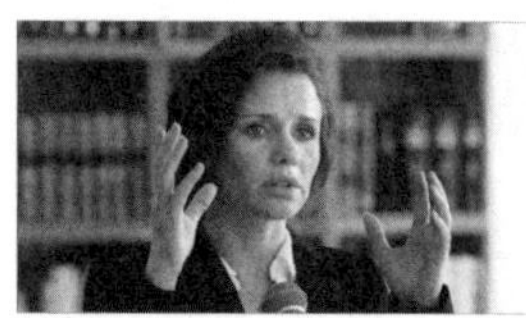

4 Roee Rosen, *Kafka for Kids*, 2022, 4k video, 117', still. Cinematographer: Avner Shahaf. Still photography: Goni Riskin.

folk music that wears the heart on the sleeve. Bob Dylan the folk singer is a good example: an iconic figure whose authenticity is based on knowingly plundering and appropriating music made by others. To me, authenticity does not stand in contradiction to a masquerade, pretending to be someone else. Fabrication and fantasy have a great potential to be authentic.

But if I were asked to point out a major turn in my work, it would be *The Blind Merchant* (1989–1991), a retelling of Shakespeare's *The Merchant of Venice* in an artist book, which I worked on for almost three years. In my parasitical text, Sherlock is blind, so whenever Sherlock is onstage, I drew drawings with my eyes firmly closed. It was a negation of the basis of draftsmanship, the relation between hand and eye. By opening my eyes and seeing that the drawings were still very much my own, I was encouraged to pursue other ways of making, in order to negate or challenge my presuppositions about what I am as an artist.[4]

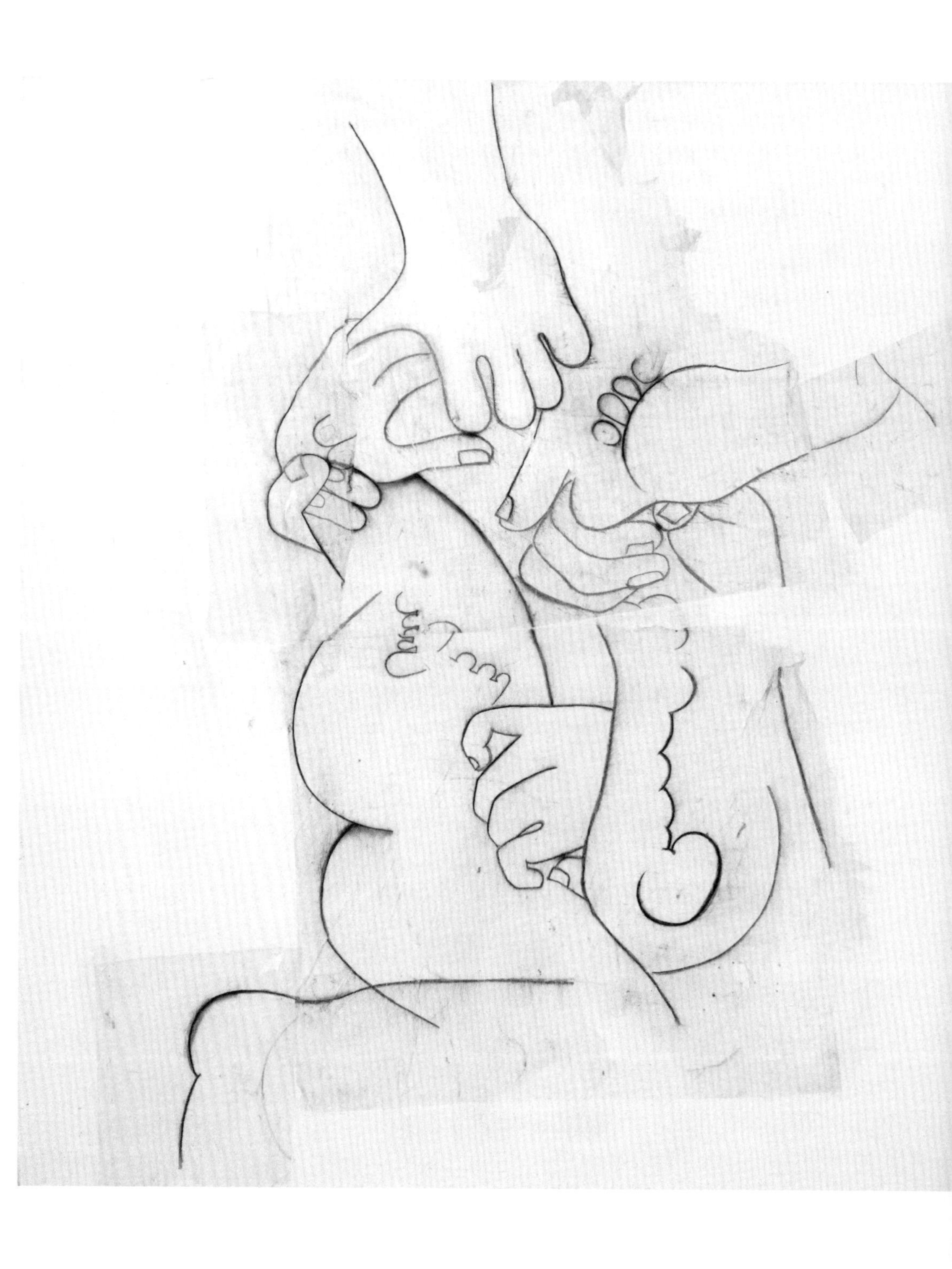

The Offering

Lutz Driessen

'I incite a cold passion for crimes at sea…'
—Álvaro de Campos (Pessoa), 'Naval Ode'[1]

In his recent paintings of the human figure, portrayed in Romanesque spaces and Mannerist postures, Lutz Driessen recalibrates Modernism with a humanist-cartoonesque touch. Visual elements refer to icons *and* cartoons: the sacred and the profane. Through their appearance, a peculiar combination of the solemn and the raucous, his works address serious topics: the vulnerability of the body, the forces that it must abide, and the relief tenderness brings to the human condition.

Is Driessen an untimely artist? His paintings prompt crucial ethical questions. Avoiding the main stream, he seeks new connections to painting traditions, even if this means that he must go underground. Fine art has been part of countercultures; the sixteenth-century artist Grünewald—admired by Driessen—continued the earnest style of late medieval Central European art in his paintings, ignoring the art of his time: Renaissance classicism. Driessen's works

381

1 Fernando Pessoa, 'Ode Marítima' (dedicated to the futurist painter Santa-Rita), first published in *Orpheu*, No. 2, Lisbon, April–June 1915, under his heteronym Álvaro de Campos. English translation: *Poems of Fernando Pessoa*, trans. & eds. Edwin Honig and Susan M. Brown, San Francisco, City Lights Books, 1998, p. 73.

Lutz Driessen, *Die Kranken (B&W (3. Hahn krähend V))*, 2023, charcoal, aero colour, gesso, paper on canvas, 160 × 140 cm.

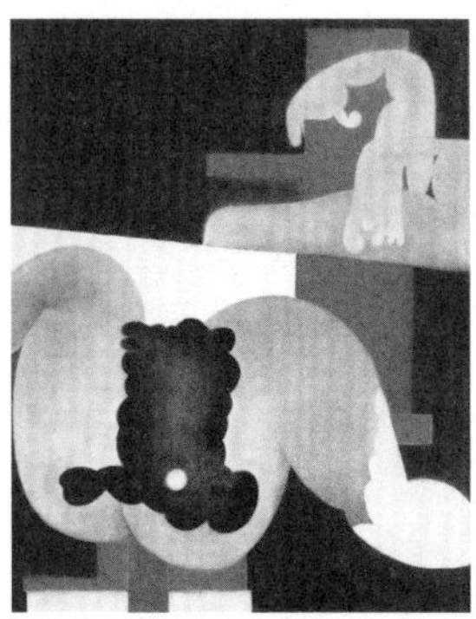

2a Lutz Driessen, *Die Kranken (Colour (I))*, 2023, charcoal, Flashe, oil on canvas, 130 × 100 cm.

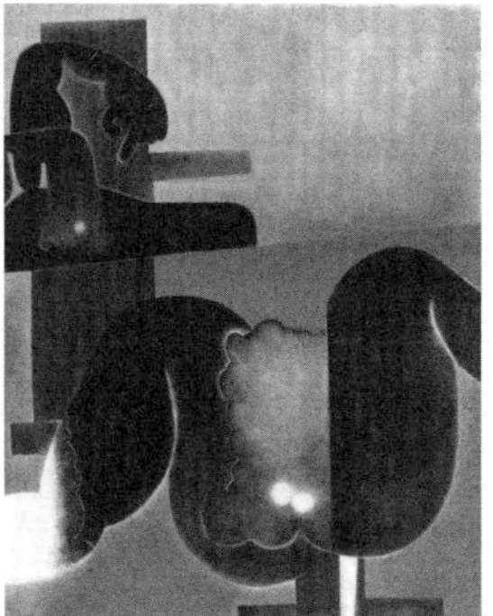

2b Lutz Driessen, *Die Kranken (Colour (II))*, 2023, Flashe, oil on canvas, 130 × 100 cm.

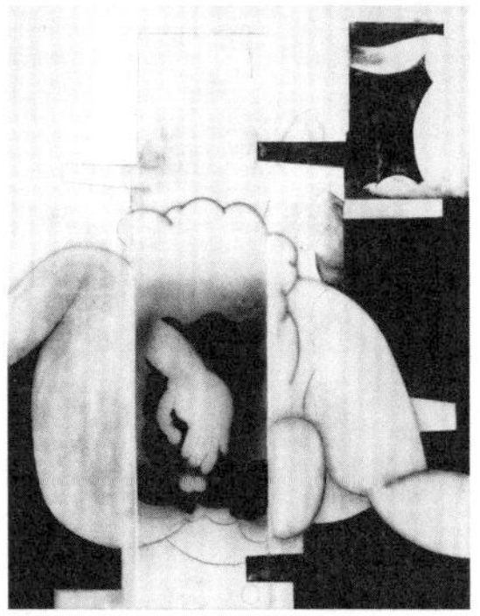

2c Lutz Driessen, *Die Kranken (B&W (X))*, 2023, charcoal, aero colour, gesso, flashe, paper on canvas, 130 × 100 cm.

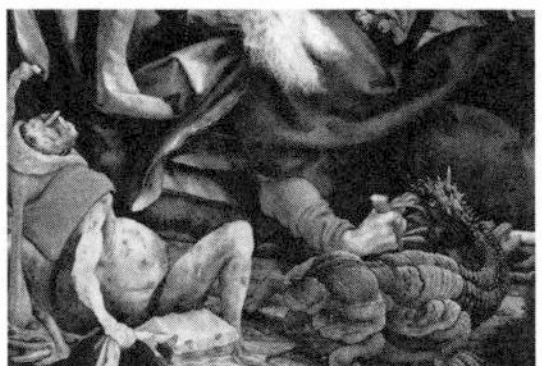

3 Matthias Grünewald, *Isenheimer Alterpiece: The Temptations of Saint Anthony*, 1512–16, detail.

portray a contorted human figure. In his 'cool', modern, abstracted body-motif, an old idea transpires: the *Pathosformel* (passionate gesture language). It is an elusive manoeuvre: the works introduce the deformed figure to us at the same time. When we see a person in pain, are we compassionate or indifferent? How do we meet the other? Do we see the original face?

Over the last few years, Lutz Driessen has created a cycle of paintings, under the overarching title *Die Kranken*.[2] The title refers to a compelling motif, portrayed by Grünewald in the third Wandelbild ('transformation image') of the *Isenheim Altarpiece*. On the (original) right wing of this altarpiece, in the left corner of *Saint Anthony Tormented by Demons*, far below, we see a figure with webbed feet and a swollen, pockmarked belly (the 'hooded man with book bag').[3] This deformed figure is thought to personify a man suffering from ergot poisoning; a condition accompanied by convulsive symptoms (also known as Saint Vitus' dance) and heavy, intense hallucinations. He (or 'she' as Driessen suggests; scholars have made the claim too; the artist prefers to see the figure as androgynous) was probably cared for by the monks in the hospital of the Isenheim Convent—where Grünewald made his rounds, studying subjects for his work.

Driessen compares Grünewald's figure to a contemporary clochard, a homeless person in our time. Why did he choose this motif? What does it signify? Driessen is outspoken. 'When I began these works, I asked myself what is sound, what is unsound, what's the difference? I wanted to explore existential questions but through the prism of art. Disease is shown in Grünewald's altarpiece as both a physical and mental condition: people struggle with all kinds of monsters; they literally crawl into their bodies or go out of themselves. And I was thinking of something else as well. In my

382

paintings, I pit 'healthy abstraction' against 'sick figuration'. This refers to a perception of art in our time—we find it in certain art circles. But nothing in the history of art prepared us for that juxtaposition! This says something about the world's perversity. It is very difficult for us to see what is sick, wrong and neurotic in our reality, and deal with it.'[4]

The cycle *Die Kranken* consists of iconic grotesques and soaring reveries. The main cluster of works has intense, saturated, starkly contrasting colours (yellow-brown-blue, red-black-yellow-white, green-indigo-black-orange-yellow-white). The other group of works is done in blacks and whites. The common motif is a contorted body, in fact a torso, indicated by two legs that are spread wide open (Peter Flötner's engraving *Der Menschliche Sonnenuhr* ('The Human Sundial', 1534) the depiction of a defecating man with both legs wide open, resonates in the motif). It is important to say that we do not see the face and the eyes of a nude figure that must be under an immense pressure. This figure beckons and confronts us. Initially, the motif is repeated in works with strong but gradual differences. During the process the artist became interested in a complete transformation. Thus, at first sight, the paintings in colour replay a deformed person's hallucinatory visions, the 'madness', in iconic images that radiate psychedelic power.

The black-and-white paintings have a different tonality: inquisitive and hands-on (their focus is external), mostly densely populated with forms and figures, yet leaving open spaces, or instead literally erasing or blocking earlier figures. Aimed at breaking up the stasis, the palimpsest technique (layered images resulting from painting/drawing *and* partially carving/erasing, scraping them away) suggests where a motif might go: its potential. Here the anxious body dissolves, at times with the help of outside forces: in one work, hands are

4 Artist quotations and information in email exchanges, phone calls, and conversations in Cologne, September 2023.

joining hands, and a new state of mind emerges! Driessen based this motif on a mural by Cocteau, of Petrus' struggle and surrender to the Roman soldiers in the Garden of Gethsemane, made in a neo-classical style. In another black-and-white work, a chair is placed in front of the legs, hiding the body (or the sex) as if it were a taboo: 'this should not be seen!' These black-and-white works are volatile, they make me think of spiritual seances to invoke a motif/form: 'that it may transform and fare well!'

Each painting has characteristic and recurring elements. The figure (contorted body, abstract legs pried wide open) appears in an open, flat space; picture planes recall Romanesque art. A looming pillar-scaffold, or its remnants, is in the background (in reference to Saint Sebastian's martyrdom; a motif explored by Driessen in earlier paintings). In between the legs hovers or sits a form/fleece resembling a membrane (the clear-cut contour resonates with cartoon figure Marge Simpson's hairdo). Suggesting the entrails/belly, or the female sex, this powerful form recurs throughout the works, in red, blue, yellow, white… Finally, the works feature discretely painted bodily extremities and holes. His hands and feet are endearing: these appendages are captured as they are about to make elegant movements: a fine dance, a graceful gesture. His holes and (sexual) organs are disarming: an anus has a mother-of-pearl shine; a fanciful penis comes in a rainbow spectrum. These bodily elements form a counterpoint: here is Happiness.

The Painter's Sources

I first saw his work seven years ago. Sensing a tension between its fine and brusque elements, I thought: 'Picasso, the neo-classical painter, meets Robert Crumb!'[5] I was reminded of the Hairy Who, 1960s Chicago. I found myself thinking about oppression as an innate element in German art, about Max Ernst's 'scorched earth' paintings and works of his first French Period, e.g. *The Blessed Virgin Chastises the Infant Jesus* (1926). Driessen is indeed interested in modern, neo-classical (and Mannerist!) forms. He is influenced by the Chicago Imagists, who opposed New York Pop Art, and by the Chicago Surrealists: these kinds of figuration fascinate him.

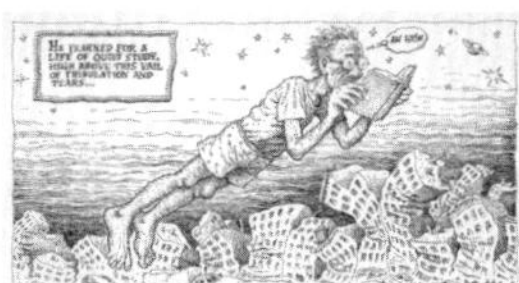
5 Robert Crumb, *He Yearned for a Life of Quiet Study.*

Driessen's oeuvre has deep grounds. When I ask him about starting points, he emails me three references. The first one concerns our society's sickness. Driessen's figures, the cut-up bodies in strange, forbidding postures, express this overall neurosis—albeit it in a rather oblique way.

The artist has sent me a text from the Bible, *Luke 8: 26–39,* 'Jesus Restores a Demon-Possessed Man'. It tells of Jesus' healing of a man from the region of the Gerasenes, across the lake from Galilee, who calls himself by the name 'Legion', for many evil spirits live in him. The demons plead with Jesus, asking him not to send them to hell, but to permit them to go into a herd of pigs. And Jesus gives them permission. The herd subsequently rushes down the steep bank into the lake and is drowned: the man is saved. Next, the bewildered community responds with disbelief. The shepherds flee to the city to tell the people what happened. When they go out to Jesus, they become afraid when they see the man, completely healthy again, sitting next to him. And they ask Jesus to leave… According to Marx, Jesus is getting rid of society's monsters here; the evil (social injustice) that the blind bourgeois society has created itself but is afraid to face: 'Perseus wore a magic cap down over his eyes and ears as a make-believe that there are no monsters. We pull the fog cap low

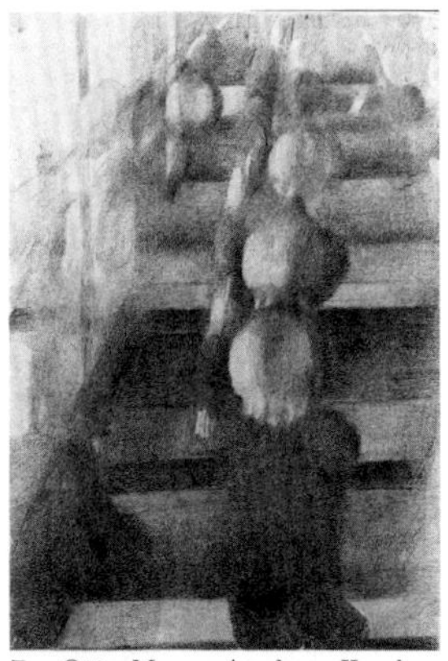

6 Karl Marx, *Das Kapital*, 'Preface to the First German Edition 1967'.

7a Otto Meyer-Amden, *Hands Up (Total Composition V)*, ca. 1920–22.

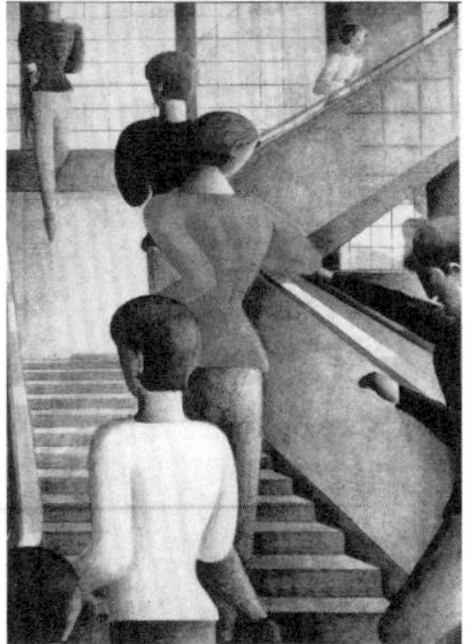

7b Oskar Schlemmer, *Bauhaustreppe*, 1932.

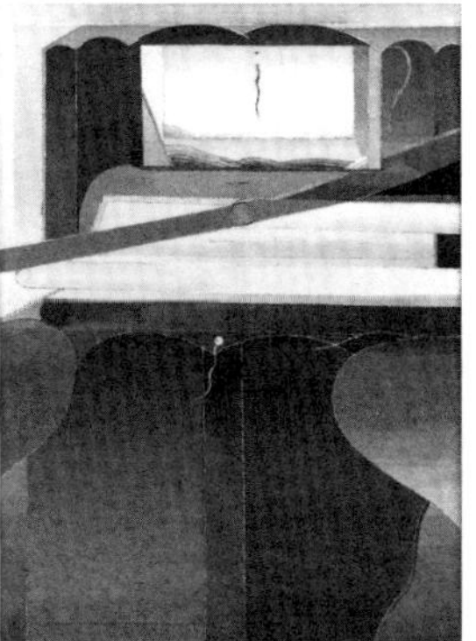

7c Miyoko Ito, *Heart of Hearts, Basking*, 1973.

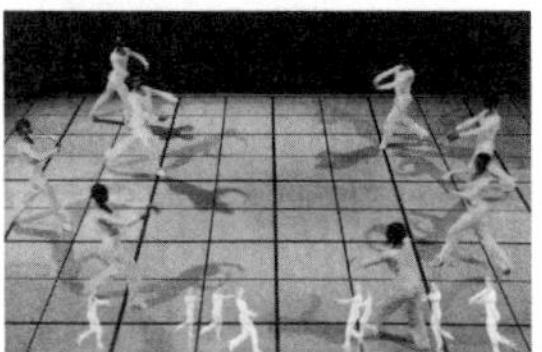

8 Lucinda Childs, *Dance*, 1979/2022.

over our eyes and ears in order to be able to deny the existence of the monsters'.[6]

Next, Driessen emails modern visual sources. Here it concerns 'the search for the figure'. He has studied many painters but is fascinated with Otto Meyer-Amden and Oskar Schlemmer (the two friends also inspired each other: 'it was Schlemmer who elaborated Meyer-Amden's search for something holy in the figure's depiction by a prototypical form') and Miyoko Ito, an extraordinary American-Japanese painter. Miyoko Ito depicts interiors, landscapes and the human body in 'allusive abstractions': mysteriously translucent settings that evoke an inner dimension.[7]

Driessen's third source is old art: 'the drama of the body'. Grünewald is very important. The *Saint Anthony Tormented by Demons* and the *Isenheimer Altarpiece* in general: an amazingly eccentric representation of 'inner life' (Sebald wrote that the *Isenheimer Altarpiece* doesn't depict 'life in itself' anywhere) and *The Martyr Sebastian*. He also mentions other 'Sebastians' for example depicted as a young man (Bronzino), or shot through with arrows and hanging from a tree (Odilon Redon), or as a beatific youth *and* a dying man, eyes aimed at the sky (Pietro Perugino; a painting from 1489–1990). Returning to Grünewald, Driessen says: 'Grünewald's hands tell me that the body wants something else than the idea'. And then —while talking—Driessen professes his love for Lucinda Childs' *Dance* (1979, music Philip Glass, stage design Sol LeWitt) and her later performances of the piece over the years, in which (an older) Childs is dancing with her (younger) projection: 'Her work conveys the timeless humanist perspective'.[8]

386

The liberation of the body is an underlying motif for
Driessen. Longing for the embrace, one of his bodies has
become a sex machine; another is burning red-hot, ready to
go up in flames. The body goes its own way. It convulses, is
violently shattered. I think it was always like that: with
Driessen, the limits/borders between inside and outside are
undefined. In his new cycle, the bodily form doubles itself
and breaks down. The fact alone that this form, at times in a
single work, seems to multiply *and* disintegrate (or dissolve)
suggests a fantastic kind of body.

Mikhail Bakhtin, the literary scholar, has made poignant
observations on the meaning of the grotesque body in
Renaissance folk culture (notably carnival), and literature, in
Rabelais and his World (written in 1936, published in Russia
1965, English translation 1984). For Bakhtin, the grotesque
imagination of the great Renaissance humanist writers, the
liberating laughter that they wanted to inspire through their
novels, represented sound resistance against the religious
authorities' narrow ideas about how people should live their
lives. And, in secret, Bakhtin must have also considered his
theme as sound resistance to the political authorities' ambition in 'his own' Soviet Russia to engineer the new human
communist/socialist soul.

The body is a source of wisdom: street wisdom
(panache) and sacred wisdom. Bakhtin writes: 'The grotesque body… is a body in the act of becoming. It is never
finished, never completed; it is continually built, created, and
builds and creates another body… the body swallows the
world and is itself swallowed by the world (let us recall the
grotesque image in the episode of Gargantua's birth on the
feast of cattle-slaughtering). [MK: Gargantua the giant is born

387

9 Mikhail Bakhtin, *Rabelais and his World*, trans. Helen Iswolsky, Bloomington, Indiana University Press, 1984, p. 317.

in a rather unusual way, making a fantastic voyage through the body of his mother, Gargamalle, and finally coming out by her left ear.] This is why the essential role belongs to those parts of the grotesque body, in which it concerns a new, second body: the bowels and the phallus.'[9]

This fruitful zone is clearly indicated in Driessen's works. The flat contour of the membrane form suggests the relevancy of Romanesque art: the artist favours its psychological perspective; 'inner life' rendered through art, over the spatial perspective invented in the Renaissance that came to dominated art discourse. Driessen's bodily form always suggests the inside: the mind. Is Driessen's grotesque body a symbol of resistance? Can we think of it that way? And if so, what is it that he opposes? I already suggested that his body is a *Pathosformel*, designed/crafted to inspire empathy. In his studio, Driessen shows me his notes: 'Veitstanz: Spastik & Tanz, gegensätzliche Kräfte, ein Körper & Der Wunsch, unbedingt abstrakt und bedingungslos zu werden. Die Unterwerfung? Der 2^e Körper? Porno?' ('Vitus Dance: Spasm & Dance, opposing forces, one body & The desire to become absolutely abstract and unconditional. Submission? The 2nd body? Porn?') The power of his imagination is vast. The artist wants to paint the unpaintable/unspeakable!

388

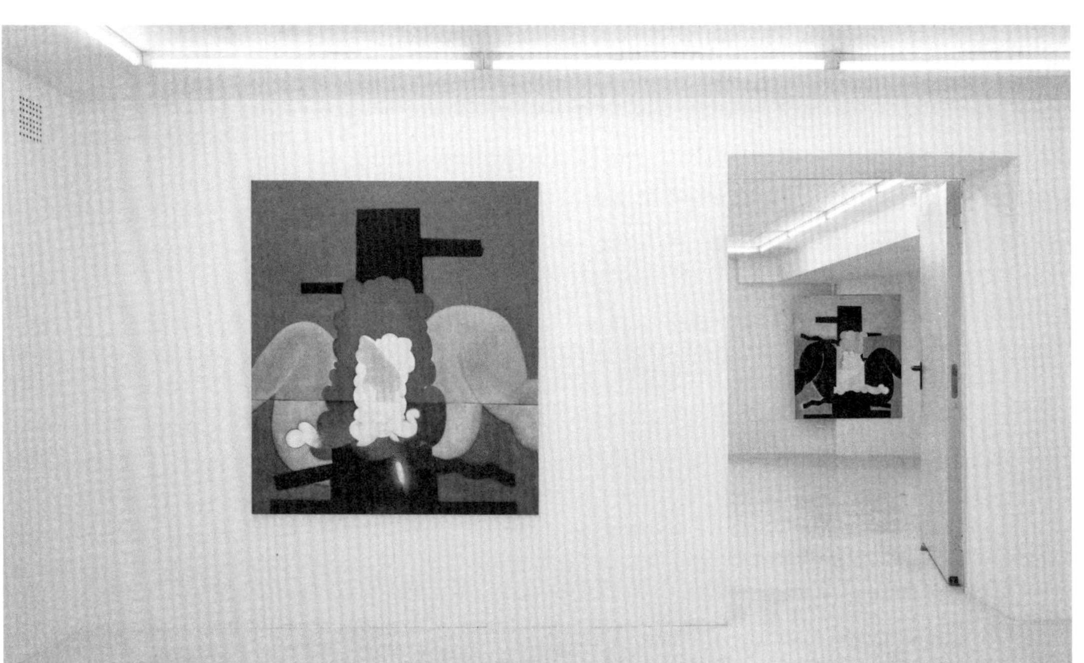

10 Lutz Driessen, 'dying', JUBG, Cologne, 2023, installation view; left: *Die Kranken (Colour (IV))*, 2023, charcoal, flashe, oil, chalk on canvas, 140 × 120 cm; right: *Die Kranken (Colour (VII))*, 2023, flashe, oil on canvas, 140 × 120 cm.

Cartoonesque Exaltation

'Dying' is the name that Driessen has given his solo exhibition at the J U B G Contemporary Art Gallery in Cologne.[10] 'That title refers to my visual language, the fact that an earlier motif, the martyrdom of Saint Sebastian, elaborated in my *Sebastian* paintings, has come full circle. Here it peters out. It is only daily practice.' With that explanation, Driessen downplays his title a bit. It gives me food for thought! Interestingly, Driessen collected his *Sebastians* in an earlier show titled 'Living' (Gallery Khoshbakht, Cologne, 2022).[11] The paintings embody hallucinatory visions as well: shards of bodies are scattered across the space, like debris in the Milky Way, or meat in a blender. These works are aggressive: their glaring, high-pitched colours slap you in the face. I am struck by Driessen's representation of space. In the 'Sebastians', the space is torn apart, cut up in sections: centrifugal forces have free play (whereas in *Die Kranken,* on the contrary, space thickens and the sections coalesce: here, centripetal forces reign). 'Living' is an interesting title: I think it referred to Sebastian's agony/exaltation, the fact that he—I imagine— was so much alive at the moment of his death. The paintings reveal and evoke this ecstasy.

Returning to his cycle, *Die Kranken,* dedicated to the sick person: in its bodily form and glowing colours I detect exotic landscapes: the desert; a seascape (the black pillar/ scaffold-form recalls the funnel on a steamship).[12] Fernando Pessoa, the Portuguese poet, wrote a lengthy ode to the sea. I mention it because it contains an archaic (pagan, barbarian) element that makes itself felt in Driessen's paintings too. As a highly relevant instance of Futurism, Pessoa's 'Naval Ode' (1915) was written at a specific moment in (art) history. We also find this archaic element in Boccioni's sculpture *Fusion*

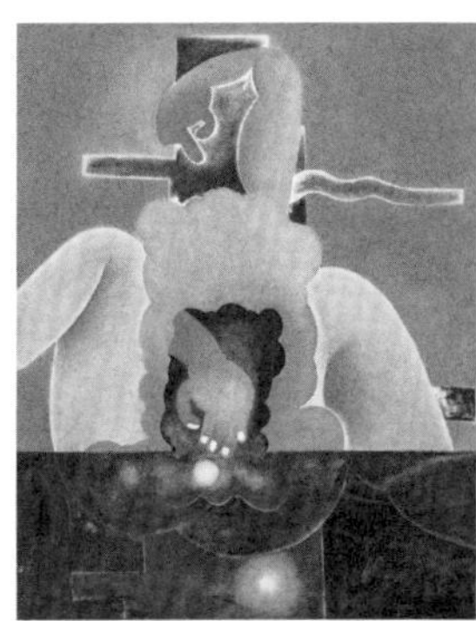

11 Lutz Driessen, *Untitled (Sebastian 1489/90),* 2022, charcoal, chalk, flashe, oil on canvas, 130 × 100 cm.

13 Fernando Pessoa, 'Naval Ode', *Poems of Fernando Pessoa*, trans. & eds. Edwin Honig and Susan M. Brown, San Francisco, City Lights Books, 1998, p. 67.

of a Head and a Window (1912–1913) that features a countenance, like that of a grimacing pirate. In Russia, in 1913, Matyushin, Khlebnikov and Malevich's opera *Victory Over the Sun* premiered: a large, abstract, motley eye appears on stage, after the sun has been captured by strong, futurist men. In Paris, Stravinsky's *Rite of Spring* unleashed a scandal.

Two years later, Pessoa published his 'Naval Ode' under the heteronym Álvaro de Campos. De Campos is a wildly passionate poet. In his poem, Álvaro sits daydreaming on the banks of the Tagus, reflecting upon his solitude. A mail boat sails on the river, life on the quay gradually warms up, and the poet is sated with impressions; the entire surroundings force their way into his imagination when the poem transforms into an orchestrated delirium. The poet becomes a pirate who does gruesome things to others, but also a man who offers up his own body to the pirates and allows himself to be eaten in a voluntary game of lust, a cannibalistic ritual/orgy:

> Oh barbarians of the ancient sea!
> Tear me apart and maim me!
> Going from east to west of my body,
> Scratch bloody trails through my flesh![13]

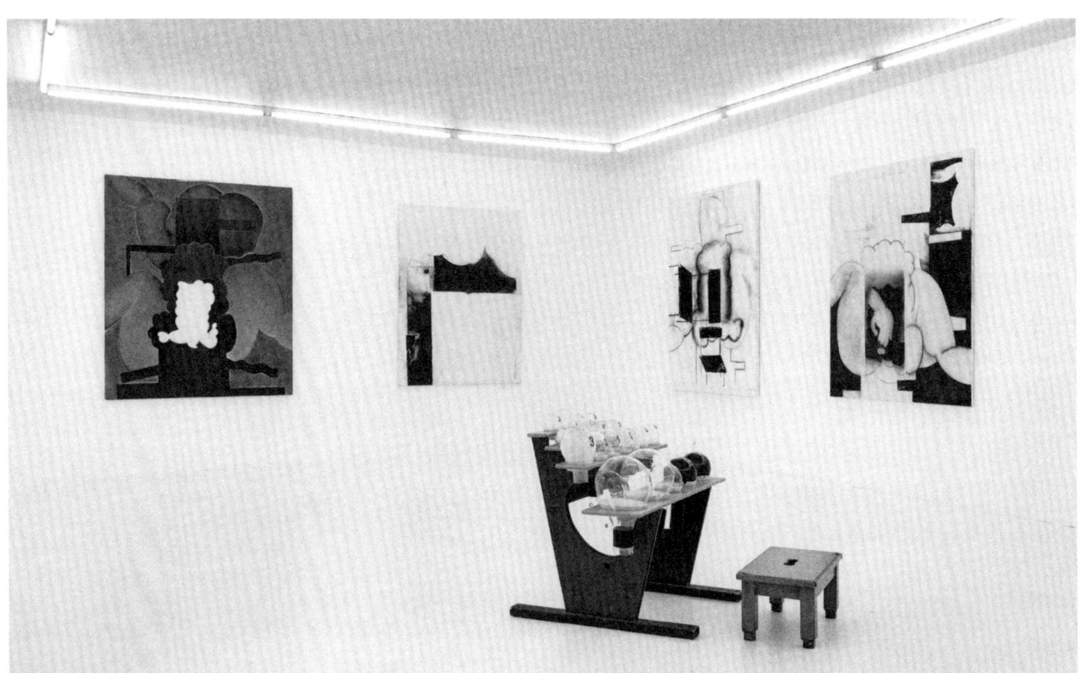

12 Lutz Driessen, 'dying', JUBG, Cologne, 2023, installation view, from left to right: *Die Kranken (Colour (V))*, 2023, charcoal, flashe, oil on linen, 140 × 120 cm; *Die Kranken (B&W (XI))*, 2023, charcoal, aero color, gesso, flashe, paper, oil on canvas, 130 × 100 cm; *Die Kranken (B&W (VIII))*, 2023, charcoal, aero color, gesso, flashe, paper on canvas, 140 × 100 cm; *Die Kranken (B&W (X))*, 2023, charcoal, aero color, gesso, flashe, paper on canvas, 130 × 100 cm. Partch Instrument: Mazda Marimba.

The poet's offering is unconditional.[14] The artist has portrayed the sick figure in the same vein. We could associate
this body with his. In his paintings, Driessen depicts the
human condition. His bodies are absolutely free and lonely.
A big idea… Driessen also professes his love for cartoons.
They are a source of joy. The cartoonish image of the puff
of air elates him, as the form lingers for a moment, after Road
Runner has crashed into the abyss.[15] On Friday morning
8 September, when we walk to his studio, Driessen notices a
drawing in the street. Lutz points to a shutter painted by
Epoc. 'This is one of his last graffiti to be seen in Cologne.
It makes me happy,' says Lutz, 'but they won't be around
much longer'. A kick scooter is spread over the entire surface;
in the space between handlebar, deck and wheels, there is a
face. It belongs to a hooded figure.

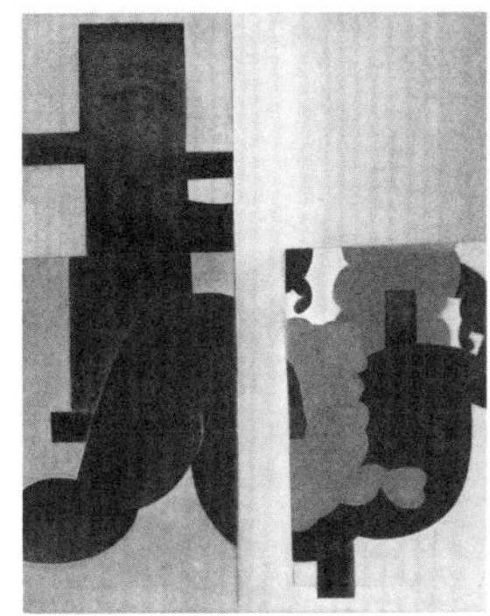

14 Lutz Driessen, *Die Kranken
(Colour (VI))*, 2023, charcoal,
flashe, oil on linen, 130 × 100
cm.

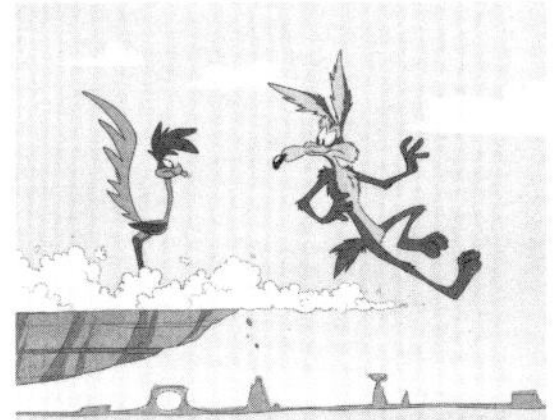

15 Warner Bros. Studios, *Road
Runner / Wile E. Coyote*, 1949,
still.

I do not think my biography is very important; in fact,
I prefer it when the identity of a writer/curator is surrounded
with a bit of mystery. And yet I cherish my own roots, and
the journey through art that I've made thus far.

I was born on a 'terp' (dwelling mound) called Oldörp
('The Old Village') in the countryside of the Dutch province
of Groningen, close to the North Sea. The milieu in which
I grew up was secluded, but there were also modern forces at
play. My father was a farmhand (the term *landbouwmede-
werker*, 'agrarian co-worker', had just come into use, reflecting the emancipatory politics of the PvdA, the social-
democratic party ruling the Netherlands in the 1970s). My
father had his own private world, spending time in his
self-built aviary, tending after his goldfinches. Whereas my
mother was more in touch with the outside world, interested
in what was going on out there; she worked part-time in the
households of kind and interesting people.

Through her I met one person who played a big role in
my formation. Frans Leenders, who came to live at my terp
for a short while with his young wife, was a young intellectual

with a critical view of his medical profession, notably its financial connection to big pharmaceutical companies. He showed me the way to a life dedicated to independent thinking. Also important to me was my meeting with Guus Leideritz, a self-taught artist who had Ad Dekkers as his first mentor. He approached me at the end of a simultaneous chess exhibition in which we took part. He encouraged me to live a life in which artistic/creative endeavours are always at the forefront of one's mind.

At school, I began listening to music, discovered literature, got fascinated with film. Art lingered somewhat in the background (despite my friendship with Guus Leideritz). Then, after a period studying History and Philosophy, I chose to change my focus to Art History and Archaeology, first at the University of Groningen (1982–1984) and later the University of Amsterdam (1984–1988). The choice was deliberate: compared to music, literature, film, I felt that art was the real challenge. I felt attracted to thinking about visual objects from new perspectives. I enjoyed putting language to work in service of investigating how a work of art is put together, and how it operates upon and affects the viewer.

After a while, not satisfied with my art studies alone, I branched out through excursions into film history and film semiotics, theatre history, comparative literature. But what do these fields of the humanities have in common? They study material objects as reflections of inner life: the intellectual process, people's thoughts and feelings, life lessons. During my studies I intuited that art objects intrinsically possess an irrational/affective dimension that defies exact description yet beckons the writer to convey it. Of course, the nature of that dimension somewhat contradicts the very workings of language. After all, in language a rational force operates that seeks to control things (Foucault), but images often speak louder than words!

During my studies I entered the contemporary art field, when I got offered a job working with a platform for experimental video, film and sound: Time Based Arts in Amsterdam. Around that time, I came in contact with living, contemporary artists for the first time. I remember heated discussions with Berend Strik, the artist, about the end of *Blow Up*, the film by Michelangelo Antonioni—through direct dialogue with my contemporaries I was finding my way to the source. Suddenly it became clear that I longed to live in contact, and in dialogue, with artists. Then I got many opportunities to do just that, when I took part in the *École du* Magasin of the Centre National d'Art Contemporain, Grenoble, France, 1990–1991.

The *École* was my initiation into the international art life. This training course for future art mediators had begun to operate in 1986. The *École* had the ambition to become the European counterpart of the Whitney Programme. Its focus was similarly to bridge the gap between academia and the practice of artists, as well as the institutions supporting their work. Here, my six curatorial fellows and I would be standing next to artists such as Matt Mullican, Lili Dujourie, and Gino de Dominicis, in the basilica-shaped Magasin, on the concrete floor of the grand hall, or on the parquet of a gallery space, when their work was just about to be installed, and, in fact, after the job had been completed. We cherished the opportunity to talk with them about their work and learned from their perspectives.

I published my first texts on art around 1987–1988. In 1993, sometime after finishing the *École* in Grenoble, and having returned to the Netherlands, I was asked to be a curator for Festival a/d Werf in Utrecht. Here I worked with many artists from the Netherlands and abroad, helping them develop new projects, for four editions of the festival (1994–1997). In 1993, I began teaching, first at various art academies (guest teaching) and then at the new curatorial training programme of De Appel, Amsterdam. From 1998–2000, I was active in Northern Europe, first as a curator for NIFCA, Nordic Institute for Contemporary Art, based in Helsinki (1998–1999), then as a freelance curator back in Amsterdam again. At a later moment, I developed various thematic exhibitions wherein the participating artists were involved alongside me as co-authors of the exhibitions.

Today (2025) I work as a researcher/writer. I still play chess (at the Laurierboom-Gambiet chess club in Amsterdam) and I am the singer of an underground band featuring guitarist André van Bergen.

—Mark Kremer

The introduction 'The Birth of Writing out of Art Curating' and each of the five introductions to the parts 'Trace', Gesture', 'Rudiment', Polyphony' and 'Steadfastness' were written especially for this book. All other texts included here have been revised, and sometimes thoroughly rewritten. Provenance of the texts and translation credits:

PART I
—'A Fucked-Up Mirror of Dominant Image-Making: Interview with Mike Kelley', *Art Press*, 1993, No. 183, pp. E5–E8.
—'Communitas: Rirkrit Tiravanija' is based on 'Rirkrit Tiravanija. Generositeit als kunst', *Kunstbeeld*, 2004–2005, Nos. 12–1, pp. 6–11. Translation: Mark Kremer.
—'Bodies Soar By: Wineke Gartz', catalogue *Wineke Gartz*, Breda, Club Solo, 2022, pp. 1–5. Translation: Lenne Priem.
—'The Dream of the Avant-Gardist', catalogue *Jan van de Pavert*, Amsterdam, Galerie Paul Andriesse, 2007, pp. 8–17. Translation: Beth O'Brien.
—'A Cheerful Nihilist Drinks Orange Juice and Eats a Brownie: Aernout Mik', was published as 'Ein heiterer Nihilist trinkt Orangensaft und isst dazu ein Brownie: Über

Aernout Mik', *Artist Kunstmagazin*, 1996, No. 2, pp. 26–29. Republished in the exhibition catalogue *ID: An International Survey on the Notion of Identity in Contemporary Art*, Eindhoven, Van Abbemuseum, 1996, pp. 63–65. Translation: Donald Gardner.

PART 2

—'Show Me Your Beautiful Madness! Christiaan Bastiaans' was written for this book. It is based on the essay 'Tegenwicht en bezwering. Christiaan Bastiaans', *Metropolis M*, No. 5 2020, 88–95.
—'Trust and Terror: Interview with Alicia Framis' and the accompanying artist text were first published in the catalogue *Alicia Framis: Wax & Jardins—Loneliness in the City*, Amsterdam, Artimo, 1999, pp. 67–69.
—'In Search of Ghost Notes: Jeff Wall' is based on 'Wonde plekken. Over enkele werken van Jeff Wall', *De Witte Raaf*, 1995, No. 53, pp. 18–19. Translation: Mark Kremer.
—'Real Phantasmagoria: Almagul Menlibayeva' is published here for the first time.
—'Hard Acts and Soft Gestures: Job Koelewijn', catalogue *Onder Anderen/Amongst Others: Biennale di Venezia 1995*, Ghent, Museum van Hedendaagse Kunst, 1995, pp. 68–75. Republished in *Kunst & Museumjournaal*, 1995, Vol. 6, No. 3/4, pp. 70–76. Translation: *translate* (buro Ghent).

PART 3

— 'The Golden Fleece: René Jolink' appeared in a flyer for the artist's exhibition 'Verzonken Beelden' (Sunken Pictures), Amsterdam, Vous Êtes Ici / KLERKX International Art Management, 2014. Translation: Vic Joseph.
—'Chinaman: Klaas Kloosterboer' is based on 'Polder Spirit' in the catalogue *Klaas Kloosterboer: Shivering Emotions +*

Feverish Feelings, Karslruhe, Badischer Kunstverein, 2003, pp. 138–158. Translation: Vic Joseph.
—'Adieu Kamchatka: Helmut Federle' appeared as 'Adieu Kamchatka: Helmut Federle—das späte Werk', *fair Magazin für Kunst & Architektur*, 2018, No. 1, pp. 38–43.
—'Malleable Masculinity: Interview with Pieter Laurens Mol' is a press text commissioned by Gallery Hidde van Seggelen for the artist's exhibition 'Angles of Incidence (The Nine Lines)' at Sfeir Semler Gallery, Hamburg, 2019, hosting gallerist: Hidde van Seggelen. Translation: Mark Kremer.
—'A Thousand Leaves: Esther Kläs' originally appeared under the title 'Life, I Eat You: On Esther Kläs' in the artist's publication *Esther Kläs, HORIZONTE*, Brussels, Galerie Xavier Hufkens, 2018.
—'The Burning Spear: Roland Schimmel' appeared as 'The world within and the world without...' in the catalogue *Roland Schimmel*, Schiedam, De Ketelfactory, 2009. Translation: Mark Speer.
—'The Life Work of a Young Rebel: Absalon' appeared as 'The life work of a young rebel: Absalon in De Appel', *Archis*, No. 5, 1994, 13–14. Translation: Vic Joseph.
—'Embalmed Landscape with Soft Machine: André Kruysen' was published on the artist's website in 2020. Translation: Vic Joseph.

PART 4
—'This Revolution Will Not Be Televised: Interview with Tiong Ang' appeared as 'Universal Noise: A Conversation between Mark Kremer and Tiong Ang' in *MahkuScript*, 9 December 2020 and in *Journal of Fine Art Research*, No. 4(1): 15. The text with images was published at the artist's website in 2020.
—'One Wee Drop: Astrid Nobel' was published on the

artist's website in 2012. Translation: Mark Kremer.
—'It Must Be a Camel: Hugo Canoilas' appeared in the catalogue *Hugo Canoilas: Um Corridor Entre (M & K)*, Porto, Galeria Quadro Azul, 2011, pp. 44–49.
—'What the Psychic Told Me, or: Various meditations upon a stone. Lorelinde Verhees' appeared in *2017 Thinging— Essays*, P/////AKT, Amsterdam, 2017, pp. 16–20. Translation: Daniel Vorthuys. This text was written in assignment of P/////AKT Amsterdam. Inspiration: the exhibition 'Daisy Chain' by Lorelinde Verhees and meetings with the artist. Her exhibit did not feature any stones, but it did have seven Magritte-esque mirages, in which thoughts were expressed out loud. The visitor could wonder around—much like Don Quixote did—between objects and written words.
—'Sublime Mortification: Rob Johannesma' was published on the artist's website in 2020. Translation: Daniel Vorthuys.

PART 5
—'The Polder Dandy Takes a Stroll: Harmen Brethouwer' appeared in the catalogue *Harmen Brethouwer: On Superfluous Things*, The Hague, De Zwaluw Publishers, 2008, pp. 7–14. Translation: Vic Joseph.
—'Shouting Through a Paper Cone: Joan Jonas' appeared as 'Get Rid of the Knots', *Afterall*, 2004, No. 9, pp. 10–19.
—'The Raving Silence: Jos van Merendonk' appeared in the catalogue *Jos van Merendonk. ASSEMBLAGE*, Hamburg, Hidde van Seggelen, 2018, pp. 7–12. Translation: Daniel Vorthuys.
—'Becoming Someone Else: Interview with Roee Rosen' appeared as 'Iemand anders worden. gesprek met Roee Rosen', *Metropolis M*, 2021, No. 4, pp. 37–45.
—'The Offering: Lutz Driessen' was published at the website of the JUBG contemporary art space in Cologne in 2023.

Author: Mark Kremer
Copy editing: Jean Tee
Project editor: Simone Wegman
Proofreading: Vivi van Leersum
Index: Elke Stevens
Image editing: Simon Pillaud
Design: Sam de Groot
Typefaces: Eldorado (William Addison Dwiggins, 1953),
    Computer Modern (Donald Knuth, 1984),
    SKI DATA (Tariq Heijboer, 2014)
Lithography: Gaëlle van den Dool, Wilco Art Books
Paper: Munken Print White, 100 g/m² 1.5 (inside),
    Munken Lynx Rough, 300 g/m² (cover)
Printing and binding: Wilco Art Books, Amersfoort
Publisher: Valiz, Amsterdam, 2025, www.valiz.nl
    Astrid Vorstermans

This publication has been printed on FSC-certified paper by an FSC-certified printer. The FSC, Forest Stewardship Council promotes environmentally appropriate, socially beneficial, and economically viable management of the world's forests. www.fsc.org

Distribution
NL/LU: Centraal Boekhuis, www.cb.nl
BE: EPO, www.epo.be
Europe/Asia: Idea Books, www.ideabooks.nl
GB/IE: Central Books, www.centralbooks.com
USA/Canada/Latin America: D.A.P., www.artbook.com
Australia: Perimeter Books, www.perimeterbooks.com
Individual orders: www.valiz.nl; info@valiz.nl

Amsterdam, 2025
ISBN 978-94-93246-36-2
Printed and bound in the EU

This book was generously supported by

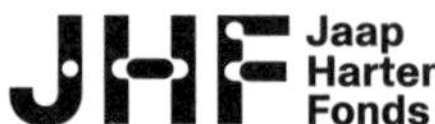 Jaap Harten Fonds

De Gijselaar-Hintzenfonds

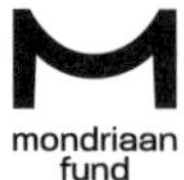 mondriaan fund

Acknowledgements
The Mondriaan Fund in Amsterdam granted Mark Kremer a writing contribution to complete this volume.

The author and publisher would like to thank Ernst van Alphen for his constructive feedback on the concept of this book. Mark Kremer also thanks all his friends for their continuous support.

Graphic Design
Sam de Groot designs in close collaboration with artists, publishers and art institutions. Alongside this, he frequently writes, publishes and performs self-initiated projects. He has taught typography at the graphic design department of the Gerrit Rietveld Academie since 2011.
www.samdegroot.nl

Publisher
Valiz is an independent international publisher and addresses contemporary developments in art, design, architecture and urban affairs. Our books offer critical reflection and interdisciplinary inspiration in a broad-based and imaginative way, often establishing a connection between cultural disciplines and socio-economic questions.
www.valiz.nl

The vis-à-vis series provides a platform to stimulating and relevant subjects
in recent and emerging visual arts, architecture and design. The authors
relate to history and art history, to other authors, to recent topics and to
the reader. Most are academic researchers. What binds them is a visual
way of thinking, an undaunted treatment of the subject matter and a skilful,
creative style of writing.

2015
Sophie Berrebi, *The Shape of Evidence: Contemporary Art and the
Document*, ISBN 978-90-78088-98-1
Janneke Wesseling, *De volmaakte beschouwer: De ervaring van het kunst-
werk en receptie-esthetica*, ISBN 978-94-92095-09-1 (e-book)

2016
Janneke Wesseling, *Of Sponge, Stone and the Intertwinement with the Here
and Now: A Methodology of Artistic Research*, ISBN 78-94-92095-21-3

2017
Janneke Wesseling, *The Perfect Spectator: The Experience of the Art Work
and Reception Aesthetics*, ISBN 978-90-80818-50-7
Wouter Davidts, *Triple Bond: Essays on Art, Architecture, and Museums*,
ISBN 978-90-78088-49-3
Sandra Kisters, *The Lure of the Biographical: On the (Self-)Representation
of Artists*, ISBN 978-94-92095-25-1

Christa-Maria Lerm Hayes (ed.), *Brian O'Doherty/Patrick Ireland: Word, Image and Institutional Critique*, ISBN 978-94-92095-24-4

2018
John Macarthur, Susan Holden, Ashley Paine, Wouter Davidts, *Pavilion Propositions: Nine Points on an Architectural Phenomenon*, ISBN 978-94-92095-50-3
Jeroen Lutters, *The Trade of the Teacher: Visual Thinking with Mieke Bal*, ISBN 978-94-92095-56-5
Ernst van Alphen, *Failed Images: Photography and its Counter-Practices*, ISBN 978-94-92095-45-9
Paul Kempers, *'Het gaat om heel eenvoudige dingen': Jean Leering en de kunst*, ISBN 978-94-92095-07-7
Eva Wittocx, Ann Demeester, Melanie Bühler, *The Transhistorical Museum: Mapping the Field*, ISBN 978-94-92095-52-7

2019
Nathalie Zonnenberg, *Conceptual Art in a Curatorial Perspective: Between Dematerialization and Documentation*, ISBN 978-90-78088-76-9
Wouter Davidts, Susan Holden, Ashley Paine (eds.), *Trading between Architecture and Art: Strategies and Practices of Exchange*, ISBN 978-94-92095-67-1
Jeroen Lutters, *In the Shadow of the Art Work: Art-Based Learning in Practice*, ISBN 978-94-92095-66-4

2020
Jeroen Lutters, *Creative Theories of (Just About) Everything: A Journey into Origins and Imaginations*, ISBN 978-94-92095-74-9
Ashley Paine, Susan Holden, John Macarthur (eds.), *Valuing Architecture: Heritage and the Economics of Culture*, ISBN 978-94-92095-93-0

2021
Florian Göttke, *Burning Images: A History of Effigy Protests*, ISBN 978-94-92095-96-1

2023
Ernst van Alphen, *Seven Logics of Sculpture: Encountering Objects Through the Senses*, ISBN 978-94-93246-15-7